Fundamentals of Database Management Systems

Fundamentals of Database Management Systems

Third Edition

Mark L. Gillenson
Fogelman College of Business and Economics
University of Memphis

VP, Content	Kristen Ford
PUBLISHER	Lise Johnson
EDITOR	Jennifer Manias
EDITORIAL ASSISTANT	Campbell McDonald
SENIOR MANAGING EDITOR	Judy Howarth
PRODUCTION EDITOR	Umamaheswari Gnanamani
MARKETING COORDINATOR	Jessica Spettoli
COVER PHOTO CREDIT	© Blackboard/Shutterstock

This book was set in 10/12 STIX Two Text by Straive™.

Founded in 1807, John Wiley & Sons, Inc. has been a valued source of knowledge and understanding for more than 200 years, helping people around the world meet their needs and fulfill their aspirations. Our company is built on a foundation of principles that include responsibility to the communities we serve and where we live and work. In 2008, we launched a Corporate Citizenship Initiative, a global effort to address the environmental, social, economic, and ethical challenges we face in our business. Among the issues we are addressing are carbon impact, paper specifications and procurement, ethical conduct within our business and among our vendors, and community and charitable support. For more information, please visit our website: www.wiley.com/go/citizenship.

Evaluation copies are provided to qualified academics and professionals for review purposes only, for use in their courses during the next academic year. These copies are licensed and may not be sold or transferred to a third party. Upon completion of the review period, please return the evaluation copy to Wiley. Return instructions and a free of charge return mailing label are available at www.wiley.com/go/returnlabel. If you have chosen to adopt this textbook for use in your course, please accept this book as your complimentary desk copy. Outside of the United States, please contact your local sales representative.

ISBN: 978-1-119-90746-6 (Print)
ISBN: 978-1-119-90743-5 (EVAL)

Library of Congress Cataloging-in-Publication Data

Names: Gillenson, Mark L., author.
Title: Fundamentals of database management systems / Mark L. Gillenson.
Description: Third edition. | Hoboken, NJ : Wiley, [2023] | Includes index.
Identifiers: LCCN 2023013761 (print) | LCCN 2023013762 (ebook) | ISBN
    9781119907466 (paperback) | ISBN 9781119907411 (adobe pdf) | ISBN
    9781119907428 (epub)
Subjects: LCSH: Database management.
Classification: LCC QA76.9.D3 G5225 2023 (print) | LCC QA76.9.D3 (ebook)
    | DDC 005.75/65—dc23/eng/20230404
LC record available at https://lccn.loc.gov/2023013761
LC ebook record available at https://lccn.loc.gov/2023013762

The inside back cover will contain printing identification and country of origin if omitted from this page. In addition, if the ISBN on the back cover differs from the ISBN on this page, the one on the back cover is correct.

SKY10075680_052124

For Leslie and

For Rochelle and Caroline

BRIEF CONTENTS

CONTENTS

3 The Database Management System Concept 36

4 Relational Data Retrieval: SQL 59

8   Physical Database Design   185

9   Object-Oriented Database Management   229

10   Data Administration, Database Administration, and Data Dictionaries   248

11 Database Control Issues: Security, Backup and Recovery, Concurrency   268

12 The Data Warehouse   289

13 NoSQL Database Management   319

14   Blockchain   341

15   Database in the Cloud   352

Purpose of this Book

A course in database management has become well established as a required course in both undergraduate and graduate management information systems degree programs. This is as it should be, considering the central position of the database field in the information systems environment. Indeed, a solid understanding of the fundamentals of database management is crucial for success in the information systems field. An IS professional should be able to talk to the users in a business setting, ask the right questions about the nature of their entities, their attributes, and the relationships among them, and quickly decide whether their existing data and database designs are properly structured or not. An IS professional should be able to design new databases with confidence that they will serve their owners and users well. An IS professional should be able to guide a company in the best use of the various database-related technologies.

Over the years, at the same time that database management has increased in importance, it has also increased tremendously in breadth. In addition to such fundamental topics as data modeling, relational database concepts, logical and physical database design, and SQL, a basic set of database topics today includes object-oriented databases, data administration, data security, data warehousing, NoSQL database, and data in the cloud, among others. The dilemma faced by database instructors and by database books is to cover as much of this material as is reasonably possible so that students will come away with a solid background in the fundamentals without being overwhelmed by the tremendous breadth and depth of the field. Exposure to too much material in too short a time at the expense of developing a sound foundation is of no value to anyone. We believe that a one-semester course in database management should provide a firm grounding in the fundamentals of databases and provide a solid survey of the major database subfields, while deliberately not being encyclopedic in its coverage. With these goals in mind, this book:

- Is designed to be a carefully and clearly written, friendly, narrative introduction to the subject of database management *that can reasonably be completed in a one-semester course.*
- Provides a clear exposition of the fundamentals of database management while at the same time presenting a broad survey of all of the major topics of the field. It is an applied book of important basic concepts and practical material that can be used immediately in business.
- Makes extensive use of examples. Four major examples are used throughout the text where appropriate, plus two minicases that are included among the chapter exercises at the end of every chapter. Having multiple examples solidifies the material and helps the student not miss the point because of the peculiarities of a particular example.
- Starts with the basics of data and file structures and then builds up in a progressive, step-by-step way through the distinguishing characteristics of database.

- A "movable chapter" on data retrieval with SQL that can be covered early in the book, where it appears as Chapter 4, *or* later in the book after the chapters on database design. This is introduced in response to a large reviewer survey that indicated a roughly 50–50 split between instructors who like to introduce data retrieval with SQL early in their courses to engage their students in hands-on exercises as soon as possible to pique their interest and instructors who feel that data retrieval with SQL should come after database design.
- Internet-accessible databases that match the four main examples running through the book's chapters for hands-on student practice in data retrieval with SQL, plus additional hands-on material.

New in the Third Edition

It is important to reflect advances in the database management systems environment in this book as the world of information systems continues to progress. Furthermore, we want to continue adding materials for the benefit of the students who use this book. Thus we have made the following additions to the third edition.

- A new chapter on NoSQL database management including key-value database, document database, column-family database, and graph database.
- A new chapter on blockchain. While not strictly speaking database management, blockchain does present a new methodology for handling data.
- A new chapter on data in "the cloud" with all of its associated advantages and disadvantages, and comparisons with distributed database.
- A new chapter on the use of data including data analytics, artificial intelligence, enterprise resource planning, customer relationship management, and supply chain management.

Organization of This Book

The book effectively divides into two halves. After the introduction in Chapter 1, Chapter 2 lays the foundation of data modeling. Chapter 3 describes the fundamental concepts of databases and contrasts them with ordinary files. Importantly, this is done separately from and prior to the discussion of relational databases. Chapter 4 is the "movable chapter" on data retrieval with SQL that can be covered as Chapter 4 or can be covered after the chapters on database design. Chapters 5 and 6 explain the major concepts of relational databases. This is done separately from and prior to the discussion of logical database design in Chapter 7 and physical database design (yes, a whole chapter on this subject) in Chapter 8. Separating out general database concepts from relational database concepts and from relational database design serves to bring the student along gradually and deliberately with the goal of a solid understanding at the end.

Then, in the second half of the book, each chapter describes one or more of the major database subfields and new approaches to data management. These latter chapters are generally independent and for the most part can be approached in any order. They include Chapter 9 on object-oriented database, Chapter 10 on data administration, database administration, and data dictionaries, Chapter 11 on security, backup and recovery, and concurrency, Chapter 12 on the data warehouse, Chapter 13 on NoSQL database, Chapter 14 on blockchain, Chapter 15 on data in the cloud, and Chapter 16 on the uses of data.

Supplements (www.wiley.com/go/gillenson/databasemanagement3e.)

The Web site includes several resources designed to aid the learning process:

- PowerPoint slides for each chapter that instructors can use as is or tailor as they wish and that students can use both to take notes on in the classroom and to help in studying at home.
- Narration of the PowerPoint slides *by the author*.
- Interactive Quizzes for each chapter that students can take on their own to test their knowledge.
- For instructors: The Instructors' Manual, *written by the author*. Each chapter includes a guide to presenting the chapter, discussion stimulation points, and answers to every question, exercise, and minicase at the end of each chapter.
- For instructors: The Test Bank, *written by the author*. Questions are organized by chapter and are designed to test the level of understanding of the chapter's concepts, as well as such basic knowledge as the definitions of key terms presented in the chapter. A computerized Respondus test bank is also available.

Finally, I would like to thank the crew at John Wiley & Sons for their continuous support and professionalism, in particular Jennifer Manias and Judy Howarth, my editors for this edition of the book.

Mark L. Gillenson

Memphis, TN
December 2022

Dr. Mark L. Gillenson has been practicing, researching, teaching, writing, and, most importantly, thinking, about data and database management for over 50 years, split between working for the IBM Corporation and being a professor in the academic world. While working for IBM he designed databases for IBM's corporate headquarters, consulted on database issues for some of IBM's largest customers, taught database management at the prestigious IBM Systems Research Institute in New York, and conducted database seminars throughout the United States and on four continents. In one such seminar, he taught introduction to database to an IBM development group that went on to develop IBM's first relational database management system products, SQL/DS.

Dr. Gillenson conducted some of the earliest studies on data and database administration and has written extensively about that subject as well as about database design. He is an associate editor of the *Journal of Database Management*, with which he has been associated since its inception. This is the third edition of his third book on database management, all published by John Wiley & Sons, Inc. Dr. Gillenson is currently University Research Professor in the Fogelman College of Business and Economics of The University of Memphis. He is also the Director of the UofM's Systems Testing Excellence Program (STEP). His degrees are from Rensselaer Polytechnic Institute and The Ohio State University.

Oh, and speaking of interesting kinds of data, as a graduate student Dr. Gillenson invented the world's first computerized facial compositor and codeveloped an early computer graphics system that, among other things, was used to produce some of the special effects in the first Star Wars movie.

CHAPTER 1

Data: The New Corporate Resource

The development of database management systems, as well as the development of modern computers, came about as a result of society's recognition of the crucial importance of storing, managing, and retrieving its rapidly expanding volumes of business data. To understand how far we have come in this regard, it is important to know where we began and how the concept of managing data has developed. This chapter begins with the historical background of the storage and uses of data and then continues with a discussion of the importance of data to the modern corporation.

OBJECTIVES

Explain why humankind's interest in data dates back to ancient times.

Describe how data needs have historically driven many information technology developments.

Describe the evolution of data storage media during the last century.

Relate the idea of data as a corporate resource that can be used to gain a competitive advantage to the development of the database management systems environment.

Introduction

What a fascinating world we live in today! Technological advances are all around us in virtually every aspect of our daily lives. From cellular telephones to satellite television to advanced aircraft to modern medicine to computers—especially computers—high tech is with us wherever we look. Businesses of every description and size rely on computers and the information systems they support to a degree that would have been unimaginable just a few short years ago. Businesses routinely use automated manufacturing and inventory-control techniques, automated financial transaction procedures, and high-tech marketing tools. As consumers, we take for granted being able to call our banks, insurance companies, and department stores to instantly get up-to-the-minute information on our accounts. And everyone, businesses and consumers alike, has come to rely on the Internet for instant worldwide communications. Beneath the surface, the foundation for all of this activity is data: the stored facts that we need to manage all of our human endeavors.

This book is about **data**. It's about how to think about data in a highly organized and deliberate way. It's about how to store data efficiently and how to retrieve it effectively. It's about ways of managing data so that the exact data that we need will be there when we need it. It's about the concept of assembling data into a highly organized collection called a "**database**" and about the sophisticated software known as a "**database management system**" that controls the database and oversees the **database environment**. It's about the various approaches people have taken to database management and about the roles people have assumed in the database environment. We will see many real-world examples of data usage throughout this book.

Computers came into existence because we needed help in processing and using the massive amounts of data we have been accumulating. Is the converse true? Could data exist without computers? The answer to this question is a resounding "yes." In fact, data has existed for thousands of years in some very interesting, if by today's standards crude, forms. Furthermore, some very key points in the history of the development of computing devices were driven, not by any inspiration about computing for computing's sake, but by a real need to efficiently handle a pesky data management problem. Let's begin by tracing some of these historical milestones in the evolution of data and data management.

The History of Data

The Origins of Data

What is data? To start, what is a single piece of data? A single piece of data is a single fact about something we are interested in. Think about the world around you, about your environment. In any environment, there are things that are important to you and there are facts about those things that are worth remembering. A "thing" can be an obvious object like an automobile or a piece of furniture. But the concept of an object is broad enough to include a person, an organization like a company, or an event that took place such as a particular meeting. A fact can be any characteristic of an object. In a university environment, it may be the fact that student Gloria Thomas has completed 96 credits; or it may be the fact that Professor Howard Gold graduated from Ohio State University; or it may be the fact that English 349 is being held in Room 830 of Alumni Hall. In a commercial environment, it may be the fact that employee John Baker's employee number is 137; or it may be the fact that one of a company's suppliers, the Superior Products Co., is located in Chicago; or it may be the fact that the refrigerator with serial number 958304 was manufactured on November 5, 2004.

Actually, people have been interested in data for at least the past 12,000 years. While today we often associate the concept of data with the computer, historically there have been many more primitive methods of data storage and handling.

In the ancient Middle East, shepherds kept track of their flocks with pebbles, Figure 1.1. As each sheep left its pen to graze, the shepherd placed one pebble in a

FIGURE 1.1 Shepherd using pebbles to keep track of sheep

small sack. When all of the sheep had left, the shepherd had a record of how many sheep were out grazing. When the sheep returned, the shepherd discarded one pebble for each animal, and if there were more pebbles than sheep, he knew that some of his sheep still hadn't returned or were missing. This is, indeed, a primitive but legitimate example of data storage and retrieval. What is important to realize about this example is that the count of the number of sheep going out and coming back in was all that the shepherd cared about in his "business environment" and that his primitive data storage and retrieval system satisfied his needs.

Excavations in the Zagros region of Iran, dated to 8500 B.C., have unearthed clay **tokens** or counters that we think were used for record keeping in primitive forms of accounting. Such tokens have been found at sites from present-day Turkey to Pakistan and as far afield as the present-day Khartoum in Sudan, dating as long ago as 7000 B.C. By 3000 B.C., in the present-day city of Susa in Iran, the use of such tokens had reached a greater level of sophistication. Tokens with special markings on them, Figure 1.2, were sealed in hollow clay vessels that accompanied commercial goods in transit. These primitive bills of lading certified the contents of the shipments. The tokens represented the quantity of goods being shipped and, obviously, could not be

FIGURE 1.2 Ancient clay tokens used to record goods in transit

tampered with without the clay vessel being broken open. Inscriptions on the outside of the vessels and the seals of the parties involved provided a further record. The external inscriptions included such words or concepts as "deposited," "transferred," and "removed."

At about the same time that the Susa culture existed, people in the city-state of Uruk in Sumeria kept records in clay texts. With pictographs, numerals, and ideographs, they described land sales and business transactions involving bread, beer, sheep, cattle, and clothing. Other Neolithic means of record keeping included storing tallies as cuts and notches in wooden sticks and as knots in rope. The former continued in use in England as late as the medieval period; South American Indians used the latter.

Data Through the Ages

As in Susa and Uruk, much of the very early interest in data can be traced to the rise of cities. Simple subsistence hunting, gathering, and, later, farming had only limited use for the concept of data. But when people live in cities they tend to specialize in the goods and services they produce. They become dependent on one another, **bartering** and using money to trade these goods and services for mutual survival. This trade encouraged **record keeping**—the recording of data—to track how much someone has produced and what it can be bartered or sold for.

As time went on, more and different kinds of data and records were kept. These included calendars, census data, surveys, land ownership records, marriage records, records of church contributions, and family trees, Figure 1.3. Increasingly sophisticated merchants had to keep track of inventories, shipments, and wage payments in addition to production data. Also, as farming went beyond the subsistence level and progressed to the feudal manor stage, there was a need to keep data on the amount of produce to consume, to barter with, and to keep as seed for the following year.

The Crusades took place from the late eleventh to the late thirteenth centuries. One side effect of the Crusades was a broader view of the world on the part of the Europeans, with an accompanying increase in interest in trade. A common method of trade in that era was the establishment of temporary partnerships among merchants, ship

FIGURE 1.3 New types of data
with the advance of civilization

captains, and owners to facilitate commercial voyages. This increased level of commercial sophistication brought with it another round of increasingly complex record keeping, specifically, *double-entry bookkeeping.*

Double-entry bookkeeping originated in the trading centers of fourteenth-century Italy. The earliest known example, from a merchant in Genoa, dates to the year 1340. Its use gradually spread, but it was not until 1494, in Venice (about 25 years after Venice's first movable type printing press came into use), that a Franciscan monk named Luca Pacioli published his "Summa de Arithmetica, Geometrica, Proportioni et Proportionalita," a work important in spreading the use of double-entry bookkeeping. Of course, as a separate issue, the increasing use of paper and the printing press furthered the advance of record keeping as well.

As the dominance of the Italian merchants declined, other countries became more active in trade and thus in data and record keeping. Furthermore, as the use of temporary trading partnerships declined and more stable long-term mercantile organizations were established, other types of data became necessary. For example, annual as opposed to venture-by-venture statements of profit and loss were needed. In 1673, the "Code of Commerce" in France required every businessman to draw up a **balance sheet** every two years. Thus the data had to be periodically accumulated for reporting purposes.

Early Data Problems Spawn Calculating Devices

It was also in the seventeenth century that data began to prompt people to take an interest in devices that could "automatically" *process their data*, if only in a rudimentary way. Blaise Pascal produced one of the earliest and best known such devices in France in the 1640s, reputedly to help his father track the data associated with his job as a tax collector, Figure 1.4. This was a small box containing interlocking gears that was capable of doing addition and subtraction. In fact, it was the forerunner of today's mechanical automobile odometers.

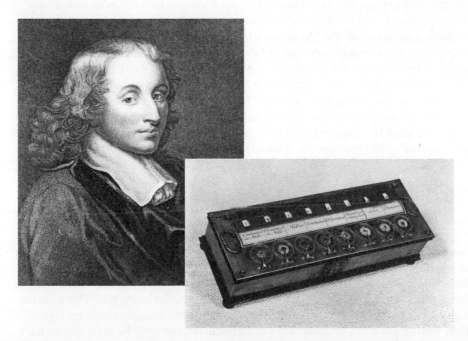

FIGURE 1.4 Blaise Pascal and his adding machine

Courtesy of IBM Archives

FIGURE 1.5 The Jacquard loom recorded patterns in punched cards

Courtesy of IBM Archives

In 1805, Joseph Marie Jacquard of France invented a device that automatically reproduced patterns used in textile weaving. The heart of the device was a series of cards with holes punched in them; the holes allowed strands of material to be interwoven in a sequence that produced the desired pattern, Figure 1.5. While Jacquard's loom wasn't a calculating device as such, his method of storing fabric patterns, a form of graphic data, as holes in **punched cards** was a very clever means of **data storage** that would have great importance for computing devices to follow. Charles Babbage, a nineteenth-century English mathematician and inventor, picked up Jacquard's concept of storing data in punched cards. Beginning in 1833, Babbage began to think about an invention that he called the "Analytical Engine." Although he never completed it (the state of the art of machinery was not developed enough), included in its design were many of the principles of modern computers. The Analytical Engine was to consist of a "store" for holding data items and a "mill" for operating upon them. Babbage was very impressed by Jacquard's work with punched cards. In fact, the Analytical Engine was to be able to store calculation instructions in punched cards. These would be fed into the machine together with punched cards containing data, would operate on that data, and would produce the desired result.

Swamped with Data

In the late 1800s, an enormous (for that time) data storage and retrieval problem and greatly improved machining technology ushered in the era of modern **information processing**. The 1880 U.S. **Census** took about seven years to compile by hand. With a rapidly expanding population fueled by massive immigration, it was estimated that with the same manual techniques, the compilation of the 1890 census would not be completed until after the 1900 census data had begun to be collected. The solution to processing census data was provided by a government engineer named Herman Hollerith. Basing his work on Jacquard's punched-card concept, he arranged to have

FIGURE 1.6 Herman Hollerith and his tabulator/sorter, circa 1890.

Bell, C. M. / Wikimedia Commons / Public domain; Courtesy of IBM Archives.

the census data stored in punched cards. He built devices to punch the holes into cards and devices to sort the cards, Figure 1.6. Wire brushes touching the cards completed circuits when they came across the holes and advanced counters. The equipment came to be classified as "electromechanical," "electro" because it was powered by electricity and "mechanical" because the electricity powered mechanical counters that tabulated the data. By using Hollerith's **electromechanical equipment**, the total population count of the 1890 census was completed a month after all the data was in. The complete set of tabulations, including data on questions that had never before even been practical to ask, took two years to complete. In 1896, Hollerith formed the Tabulating Machine Company to produce and commercially market his devices. That company, combined with several others, eventually formed what is today the International Business Machines Corporation (IBM).

Toward the turn of the century, immigrants kept coming and the U.S. population kept expanding. The Census Bureau, while using Hollerith's equipment, continued experimenting on its own to produce even more advanced data-tabulating machinery. One of its engineers, James Powers, developed devices to automatically feed cards into the equipment and automatically print results. In 1911, he formed the Powers Tabulating Machine Company, which eventually formed the basis for the UNIVAC division of the Sperry Corporation, which eventually became the Unisys Corporation.

From the days of Hollerith and Powers through the 1940s, commercial data processing was performed on a variety of electromechanical punched-card-based devices. They included calculators, punches, sorters, collators, and printers. The data was stored in punched cards, while the processing instructions were implemented as collections of wires plugged into specially designed boards that in turn were inserted into slots in the electromechanical devices. Indeed, electromechanical equipment overlapped with **electronic computers**, which were introduced commercially in the mid-1950s.

In fact, the introduction of electronic computers in the mid-1950s coincided with a tremendous boom in economic development that raised the level of data storage and retrieval requirements another notch. This was a time of rapid commercial growth in the post–World War II United States as well as the rebuilding of Europe and the Far East. From this time onward, the furious pace of new data storage and retrieval requirements with more and more commercial functions and procedures were automated and the technological advances in computing devices has been one big blur. From this point on, it would be virtually impossible to tie advances in computing devices to specific, landmark data storage and retrieval needs. And there is no need to try to do so.

Modern Data Storage Media

Paralleling the growth of equipment to process data was the development of new media on which to store the data. The earliest form of modern data storage was **punched paper tape**, which was introduced in the 1870s and 1880s in conjunction with early teletype equipment. Of course we've already seen that Hollerith in the 1890s and Powers in the early 1900s used punched cards as a storage medium. In fact, punched cards were the only data storage medium used in the increasingly sophisticated electromechanical accounting machines of the 1920s, 1930s, and 1940s.They were still used extensively in the early computers of the 1950s and 1960s and could even be found well into the 1970s in smaller information systems installations, to a progressively reduced degree.

Your Turn

1.1 The Development of Data

The need to organize and store data has arisen many times and in many ways throughout history. In addition to the data-focused events presented in this chapter, what other historical events can you think of that have made people think about organizing and storing data? As a hint, you might think about the exploration and conquest of new lands, wars, changes in type of governments such as the introduction of democracy, and the implications of new inventions such as trains, printing presses, and electricity.

Question:

Develop a timeline showing several historical events that influenced the need to organize and store data. Include a few noted in this chapter as well as a few that you can think of independently.

The middle to late 1930s saw the beginning of the era of erasable magnetic storage media, with Bell Laboratories experimenting with magnetic tape for sound storage. By the late 1940s, there was early work on the use of magnetic tape for recording data. By 1950, several companies, including RCA and Raytheon, were developing the **magnetic tape** concept for commercial use. Both UNIVAC and Raytheon offered commercially available magnetic tape units in 1952, followed by IBM in 1953, Figure 1.7. During the mid-1950s and into the mid-1960s, magnetic tape gradually became the dominant data-storage medium in computers. Magnetic tape technology has been continually improved since then and is still in limited use today, particularly for archived data.

The original concept that eventually grew into the **magnetic disk** actually began to be developed at MIT in the late 1930s and early 1940s. By the early 1950s, several companies including UNIVAC, IBM, and Control Data had developed prototypes of **magnetic "drums"** that were the forerunners of magnetic disk technology. In 1953, IBM began work on its 305 RAMAC (Random Access Memory Accounting Machine)

FIGURE 1.7 Early magnetic tape drive, circa 1953
Courtesy of IBM Archives

fixed disk storage device. By 1954, there was a multi-platter version, which became commercially available in 1956, Figure 1.8.

During the mid-1960s, a massive conversion from tape to magnetic disk as the pre-eminent data storage medium began and disk storage is still the data storage medium of choice today. After the early fixed disks, the disk storage environment became geared toward the removable disk-pack philosophy, with a dozen or more packs being juggled on and off a single drive as a common ratio. But, with the increasingly tighter environmental controls that fixed disks permitted, more data per square inch (or square

FIGURE 1.8 IBM RAMAC disk storage device, circa 1956
Courtesy of IBM Archives

centimeter) could be stored on fixed disk devices. Eventually, the **disk drives** on mainframes and servers, as well as the fixed disks or "hard drives" of PCs, all became non-removable, sealed units. But the removable disk concept stayed with us a while in the form of PC diskettes, the Iomega Corp.'s Zip Disks, and external hard drives that can be easily moved from one computer to another simply by plugging them into a USB port. These have been joined by the laser-based, optical technology **compact disk** (CD), introduced as a data storage medium in 1985. Originally, data could be recorded on these CDs only at the factory and once created, they were non-erasable. Later, data could be recorded on them, erased, and re-recorded in a standard PC. Eventually, solid-state technology became so miniaturized and inexpensive that a popular option for removable media developed as the **flash drive**. Finally, as solid-state technology continues on the path of being more compact and cheaper, rotating disk technology is gradually being replaced by "solid-state disks" (SSDs).

Data in Today's Information Systems Environment

Using Data for Competitive Advantage

Today's computers are technological marvels. Their speeds, compactness, ease of use, price as related to capability, and, yes, their data storage capacities are truly amazing. And yet, our fundamental interest in computers is the same as that of the ancient Middle Eastern shepherds in their pebbles and sacks: they are the vehicles we need to store and utilize the data that is important to us in our environment.

Indeed, data has become indispensable in every kind of modern business and government organization. Data, the applications that process the data, and the computers on which the applications run are fundamental to every aspect of every kind of endeavor. When speaking of **corporate resources**, people used to list such items as capital, plant and equipment, inventory, personnel, and patents. Today, any such list of corporate resources must include the corporation's data. It has even been suggested that data is the most important corporate resource because it describes all of the others.

Data can provide a crucial **competitive advantage** for a company. We routinely speak of data and the information derived from it as competitive weapons in hotly contested industries. For example, FedEx had a significant competitive advantage when it first provided access to its package tracking data on its Web site. Then, once one company in an industry develops a new application that takes advantage of its data, the other companies in the industry are forced to match it to remain competitive. This cycle continually moves the use of data to ever-higher levels, making it an ever more important corporate resource than before. Examples of this abound. Banks give their customers online access to their accounts. Package shipping companies provide up-to-the-minute information on the whereabouts of a package. Retailers send manufacturers product sales data that the manufacturers use to adjust inventories and production cycles. Manufacturers automatically send their parts suppliers inventory data and expect the suppliers to use the data to keep a steady stream of parts flowing.

Your Turn

1.2 Data as a Competitive Weapon

Think about a company with which you or your family regularly does business. This might be a supermarket, a department store, or a pharmacy, as examples. What kind of data do you think they collect about their suppliers, their inventory, their sales, and their customers? What kind of data do you think they should collect and how do you think they might be able to use it to gain a competitive advantage?

Question:

Choose one of the companies that you or your family does business with and develop a plan for the kinds of data it might collect and the ways in which it might use the data to gain a business advantage over its competitors.

Problems in Storing and Accessing Data

But being able to store and provide efficient access to a company's data while also maintaining its accuracy so that it can be used to competitive advantage is anything but simple. In fact, several factors make it a major challenge. First and foremost, the volume or amount of data that companies have is massive and growing all the time. At the time of this writing, Walmart estimates that its data warehouse (a type of database we will explore later) alone contains 30 petabytes (30 quadrillion bytes) of data and is constantly growing. The number of people who want access to the data is also growing: at one time, only a select group of a company's own employees were concerned with retrieving its data, but this has changed. Now, not only do vastly more of a company's employees demand access to the company's data but also so do the company's customers and trading partners. All major banks today give their depositors Internet access to their accounts. Increasingly, tightly linked "supply chains" require that companies provide other companies, such as their suppliers and customers, with access to their data. The combination of huge volumes of data and large numbers of people demanding access to it has created a major performance challenge. How do you sift through so much data for so many people and give them the data that they want in an acceptably small amount of time? How much patience would you have with an insurance company that kept you on the phone for five or ten minutes while it retrieved claim data about which you had a question? Of course, the tremendous advances in computer hardware, including data storage hardware, have helped—indeed, it would have been impossible to have gone as far as we have in information systems without them. But as the hardware continues to improve, the volumes of data and the number of people who want access to it also increase, making it a continuing struggle to provide them with acceptable response times.

Other factors that enter into data storage and retrieval include data security, data privacy, and backup and recovery. Data security involves a company protecting its data from theft, malicious destruction, deliberate attempts to make phony changes to the data (e.g. someone trying to increase his own bank account balance), and even accidental damage by the company's own employees. Data privacy implies assuring that even employees who normally have access to the company's data (much less outsiders) are given access only to the specific data they need in their work. Put another way, sensitive data such as employee salary data and personal customer data should be accessible only by employees whose job functions require it. Backup and recovery means the ability to reconstruct data if it is lost or corrupted, say in a hardware failure. The extreme case of backup and recovery is known as disaster recovery when an information system is destroyed by fire, a hurricane, or other calamity. Today, data in "the cloud" has changed the way that we think about some of these issues. We will explore this later in this book.

Another whole dimension involves maintaining the accuracy of a company's data. Historically, and in many cases even today, the same data is stored several, sometimes many, times within a company's information system. Why does this happen? For several reasons. Many companies are simply not organized to share data among multiple applications. Every time a new application is written, new data files are created to store its data. As recently as the early 1990s, I spoke to a database administration manager (more on this type of position later) in the securities industry who told me that one of the reasons he was hired was to reduce duplicate data appearing in as many as 60–70 files! Eventually, the advent of Enterprise Resource Planning (ERP) systems, which we will discuss later in this book, helped alleviate this problem.

Furthermore, depending on how database files are designed, data can even be duplicated within a single file. We will explore this issue much more in this book, but for now, suffice it to say that duplicate data, either in multiple files or in a single file, can cause major data accuracy problems.

Data as a Corporate Resource

Every corporate resource must be carefully managed so that the company can keep track of it, protect it, and distribute it to those people and purposes in the company that need it. Furthermore, public companies have a responsibility to their shareholders to competently manage the company's assets. Can you imagine a company's money just sort of out there somewhere without being carefully managed? In fact, the chief financial officer with a staff of accountants and financial professionals is responsible for the money, with outside accounting firms providing independent audits of it. Typically vice presidents of personnel and their staffs are responsible for the administrative functions necessary to manage employee affairs. Production managers at various levels are responsible for parts inventories, and so on. Data is no exception.

But data may just be the most difficult corporate resource to manage. In data, we have a resource of tremendous volume, billions, trillions, and more individual pieces of data, each piece of which is different from the next. And it has the characteristic that much of it is in a state of change at any one time. It's not as if we're talking about managing a company's employees. Even the largest companies have only a few hundred thousand of them, and they don't change all that frequently. Or the money a company has: sure, there is a lot of it, but it's all the same in the sense that a dollar that goes to payroll is the same kind of dollar that goes to paying a supplier for raw materials.

As far back as the early to mid-1960s, barely ten years after the introduction of commercially viable electronic computers, some forward-looking companies began to realize that storing each application's data separately, in simple files, was becoming problematic and would not work in the long run, for just the reasons that we've talked about: the increasing volumes of data (even way back then), the increasing demand for data access, the need for data security, privacy, backup, and recovery, and the desire to share data and cut down on data redundancy. Several things were becoming clear. The task was going to require both a new kind of software to help manage the data and progressively faster hardware to keep up with the increasing volumes of data and data access demands. And data-management specialists would have to be developed, educated, and made responsible for managing the data as a corporate resource.

Out of this need was born a new kind of software, the database management system (DBMS), and a new category of personnel, with titles like database administrator and data management specialist. And yes, hardware has progressively gotten faster and cheaper for the performance it provides. The integration of these advances adds up to much more than the simple sum of their parts. They add up to the database environment.

The Database Environment

Back in the early 1960s, the emphasis in what was then called data processing was on programming. Data was little more than a necessary afterthought in the application development process and in running the data-processing installation. There was a good reason for this. By today's standards, the rudimentary computers of the time had very small main memories and very simplistic operating systems. Even relatively basic application programs had to be shoehorned into main memory using low-level programming techniques and a lot of cleverness. But then, as we progressed further into the 1960s and beyond, two things happened simultaneously that made this picture change forever. One was that main memories became progressively larger and cheaper and operating systems became much more powerful. Plus, computers progressively became faster and cheaper on a price/performance basis. All these changes had the effect of permitting the use of higher-level programming languages that were easier for a larger number of personnel to use, allowing at least some of the emphasis to shift elsewhere. Well, nature hates a vacuum, and at the same time that all of this was happening, companies started becoming aware of the value of thinking of data as a corporate resource and using it as a competitive weapon.

The result was the development of database management systems (DBMS) software and the creation of the "database environment." Supported by ever-improved hardware and specialized database personnel, the database environment is designed largely to correct all the problems of the non-database environment. It encourages data sharing and the control of data redundancy with important improvements in data accuracy. It permits storage of vast volumes of data with acceptable access and response times for database queries. And it provides the tools to control data security, data privacy, and backup and recovery.

This book is a straightforward introduction to the fundamentals of database in the current information systems environment. It is designed to teach you the important concepts of the database approach and also to teach you specific skills, such as how to design relational databases, how to improve database performance, and how to retrieve data from relational databases using the SQL language. In addition, as you proceed through the book you will explore such topics as entity-relationship diagrams, object-oriented database, database administration, distributed database, data warehousing, NoSQL, database management, blockchain, data in the cloud, and data-focused applications.

We start with the basics of database and take a step-by-step approach to exploring all the various components of the database environment. Each chapter progressively adds more to an understanding of both the technical and managerial aspects of the field. Database is a very powerful concept. Overall it provides ingenious solutions to a set of very difficult problems. As a result, it tends to be a multifaceted and complex subject that can appear difficult when one attempts to swallow it in one gulp. But database is approachable and understandable if we proceed carefully, cautiously, and progressively step by step. And this is an understanding that no one involved in information systems can afford to be without.

Summary

Recognition of the commercial importance of data, of storing it, and of retrieving it can be traced back to ancient times. As trade routes lengthened and cities grew larger, data became increasingly important. Eventually, the importance of data led to the development of electromechanical calculating devices and then to modern electronic computers, complete with magnetic and optical disk-based data storage media.

While the use of data has given many companies a competitive advantage in their industries, the storage and retrieval of today's vast amounts of data holds many challenges. These include speedy retrieval of data when many people try to access the data at the same time, maintaining the accuracy of the data, the issue of data security, and the ability to recover the data if it is lost.

The recognition that data is a critical corporate resource and that managing data is a complex task has led to the development and continuing refinement of specialized software known as database management systems, the subject of this book.

Key Terms

Balance sheet	Data	Double-entry	Magnetic disk
Barter	Database	bookkeeping	Magnetic drum
Calculating devices	Database environment	Electromechanical	Magnetic tape
Census	Database management	equipment	Punched cards
Compact disk	system	Electronic computer	Punched paper tape
Competitive advantage	Data storage	Flash drive	Record keeping
Corporate resource	Disk drive	Information processing	Token

Questions

1. What did the Middle Eastern shepherds' pebbles and sacks, Pascal's calculating device, and Hollerith's punched-card devices all have in common?

2. What did the growth of cities have to do with the need for data?

3. What did the growth of trade have to do with the need for data?

4. What did Jacquard's textile weaving device have to do with the development of data?

5. Choose what you believe to be the:
   a. One most important
   b. Two most important
   c. Three most important landmark events in the history of data. Defend your choices.

6. Do you think that computing devices would have been developed even if specific data needs had not come along? Why or why not?

7. What did the need for data among ancient Middle Eastern shepherds have in common with the need for data of modern corporations?

8. List several problems in storing and accessing data in today's large corporations. Which do you think is the most important? Why?

9. How important an issue do you think data accuracy is? Explain.

10. How important a corporate resource is data compared to other corporate resources? Explain.

11. What factors led to the development of database management systems?

Exercises

1. Draw a timeline showing the landmark events in the history of data from ancient times to the present day. Do not include the development of computing devices in this timeline.

2. Draw a timeline for the last four hundred years comparing landmark events in the history of data to landmark events in the development of computing devices.

3. Draw a timeline for the last two hundred years comparing the development of computing devices to the development of data storage media.

4. Invent a fictitious company in *one* of the following industries and list several ways in which the company can use data to gain a competitive advantage.

   a. Banking
   b. Insurance
   c. Manufacturing
   d. Airlines

5. Invent a fictitious company in *one* of the following industries and describe the relationship between data as a corporate resource and the company's other corporate resources.

   a. Banking
   b. Insurance
   c. Manufacturing
   d. Airline

Minicases

1. Worldwide, vacation cruises on increasingly larger ships have been steadily growing in popularity. People like the all-inclusive price for food, room, and entertainment, the variety of shipboard activities, and the ability to unpack just once and still visit several different places. The first of the two minicases used throughout this book is the story of Happy Cruise Lines. Happy Cruise Lines has several ships and operates (begins its cruises) from a number of ports. It has a variety of vacation cruise itineraries, each involving several ports of call. The company wants to keep track of both its past and future cruises and of the passengers who sailed on the former and are booked on the latter. Actually, you can think of a cruise line as simply a somewhat specialized instance of any passenger transportation company, including airlines, trains, and buses. Beyond that, a cruise line is, after all, a business and like any other business of any kind it must be concerned about its finances, employees, equipment, and so forth.

   a. Using this introductory description of (and hints about) Happy Cruise Lines, make a list of the things in Happy Cruise Lines' business environment about which you think the company would want to maintain data. Do some of all of these qualify as "corporate resources"? Explain.

   b. Develop some ideas about how the data you identified in part a above can be used by Happy Cruise Lines to gain a competitive advantage over other cruise lines.

2. Sports are universally enjoyed around the globe. Whether the sport is a team or individual sport, whether a person is a participant or a spectator, and whether the sport is played at the amateur or professional level, one way or another this kind of activity can be enjoyed by people of all ages and interests. Furthermore, professional sports today are a big business involving very large sums of money. And so, the second of the two minicases to be used throughout this book is the story of the professional Super Baseball League. Like any sports league, the Super Baseball League wants to maintain information about its teams, coaches, players, and equipment, among other things. If you are not particularly familiar with baseball or simply prefer another sport, bear in mind that most of the issues that will come up in this minicase easily translate to any team sport at the amateur, college, or professional levels. After all, all team sports have teams, coaches, players, fans, equipment, and so forth. When specialized equipment or other baseball-specific items come up, we will explain them.

   a. Using this introductory description of (and hints about) the Super Baseball League, list the things in the Super Baseball League's business environment about which you think the league would want to maintain data. Do some or all of these qualify as "corporate resources," where the term is broadened to include the resources of a sports league? Explain.

   b. Develop some ideas about how the data that you identified in part a above can be used by the Super Baseball League to gain a competitive advantage over other sports leagues for the fans' interest and entertainment dollars (Euros, pesos, yen, etc.).

Data Modeling

Before reaching database management, there is an important preliminary to cover. In order ultimately to design databases to support an organization, we must have a clear understanding of how the organization is structured and how it functions. We have to understand its components, what they do, and how they relate to each other. The bottom line is that we have to devise a way of recording, of diagramming, the business environment. This is the essence of **data modeling**.

OBJECTIVES

Explain the concept and practical use of data modeling.
Recognize which relationships in the business environment are unary, binary, and ternary relationships.
Describe one-to-one, one-to-many, and many-to-many unary, binary, and ternary relationships.
Recognize and describe intersection data.
Model data in business environments by drawing entity-relationship diagrams that involve unary, binary, and ternary relationships.

Introduction

The diagramming technique we will use is called the **entity-relationship** or **E-R model**. It is well named, as it diagrams entities (together with their attributes) and the relationships among them. Actually, there are many variations of E-R diagrams and drawing them is as much an art as a science. We will use the E-R diagramming technique provided by Microsoft Visio with the "crow's foot" variation.

To begin, an **entity** is an object or event in our environment that we want to keep track of. A person is an entity. So is a building, a piece of inventory sitting on a shelf, a finished product ready for sale, and a sales meeting (an event). An **attribute** is a

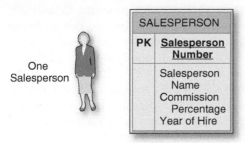

FIGURE 2.1 An E-R model entity and its attributes

property or characteristic of an entity. Examples of attributes include an employee's employee number, the weight of an automobile, a company's address, or the date of a sales meeting. Figure 2.1, with its rectangular shape, represents a type of entity. The name of the entity type (SALESPERSON) is set in caps at the top of the box. The entity type's attributes are shown below it. The attribute label PK and the boldface type denote the one or more attributes that constitute the entity type's unique identifier. Visio uses the abbreviation PK to stand for "primary key," which is a concept we define later in this book. For now, just consider these attributes as the entity type's **unique identifier**.

Entities in the real world never really stand alone. They are typically associated with one another. Parents are associated with their children, automobile parts are associated with the finished automobile in which they are installed, firefighters are associated with the fire engines to which they are assigned, and so forth. Recognizing and recording the associations among entities provides a far richer description of an environment than recording the entities alone. In order to deal intelligently and usefully with the associations or **relationships** among entities, we have to recognize that there are several different kinds of relationships and several different aspects of describing them. The most basic way of categorizing a relationship is by the number of entity types involved.

Binary Relationships

What Is a Binary Relationship?

The simplest kind of relationship is known as a **binary relationship**. A binary relationship is a relationship between two entity types. Figure 2.2 shows a small E-R diagram with a binary relationship between two entity types, salespersons and products.

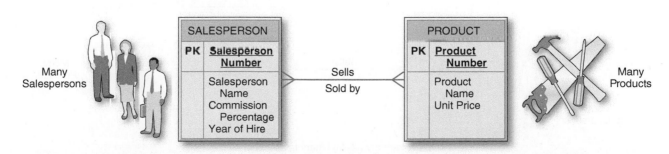

FIGURE 2.2 A binary relationship

The E-R diagram in Figure 2.2 tells us that a salesperson "sells" products. Conversely, products are "sold by" salespersons. That's good information, but we can do better than that at the price of a very small increase in effort. Just knowing that a salesperson sells products leaves open several obvious and important questions. Is a particular salesperson allowed to sell only one kind of product, or two, or three, or all of the available products? Can a particular product be sold by only a single salesperson or by all salespersons? Might we want to keep track of a new salesperson who has just joined the company but has not yet been assigned to sell any products (assuming that there is indeed a restriction on which salespersons can sell which products)?

Cardinality

One-to-One Binary Relationship Figure 2.3 shows three binary relationships of different **cardinalities**, representing the *maximum* number of entities that can be involved in a particular relationship. Figure 2.3a shows a one-to-one (1–1) **binary relationship**, which means that a single occurrence of one entity type can be associated with a single occurrence of the other entity type and vice versa. A particular

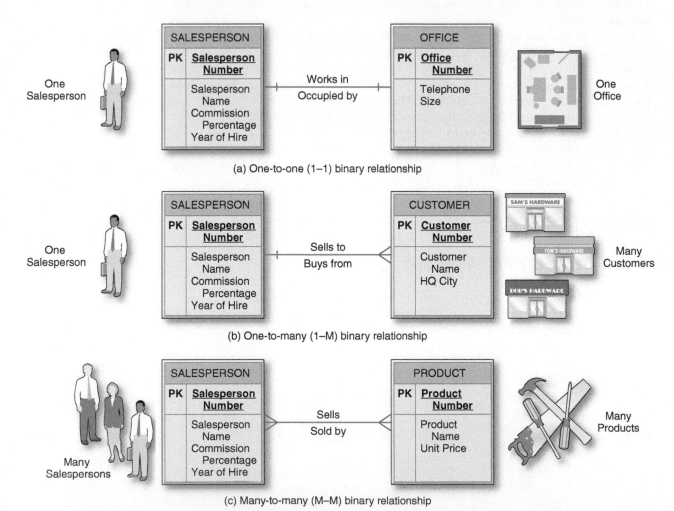

(a) One-to-one (1–1) binary relationship

(b) One-to-many (1–M) binary relationship

(c) Many-to-many (M–M) binary relationship

FIGURE 2.3 Binary relationships with cardinalities

salesperson is assigned to one office. Conversely, a particular office (in this case they are all private offices!) has just one salesperson assigned to it. Note the "bar" or "one" symbol on either end of the relationship in the diagram indicating the maximum one cardinality. The way to read these diagrams is to start at one entity, read the relationship on the connecting line, pick up the cardinality *on the other side of the line near the second entity*, and then finally reach the other entity. Thus, Figure 2.3a, reading from left to right, says, "A salesperson works in one (really at most one, since it is a maximum) office." The bar or one symbol involved in this statement is the one just to the left of the office entity box. Conversely, reading from right to left, "An office is occupied by one salesperson."

One-to-Many Binary Relationship   Associations can also be multiple in nature. Figure 2.3b shows a **one-to-many (1–M) binary relationship** between salespersons and customers. The "crow's foot" device attached to the customer entity box represents the multiple association. Reading from left to right, the diagram indicates that a salesperson sells to many customers. (Note that "many," as the maximum number of occurrences that can be involved, means a number that can be 1, 2, 3, . . ., n. It also means that the number is not restricted to being *exactly* one, which would require the "one" or "bar" symbol instead of the crow's foot.) Reading from right to left, Figure 2.3b says that a customer buys from only one salesperson. This is reasonable, indicating that in this company each salesperson has an exclusive territory and thus each customer can be sold to by only one salesperson from the company.

Many-to-Many Binary Relationship   Figure 2.3c shows a **many-to-many (M–M) binary relationship** among salespersons and products. A salesperson is authorized to sell many products; a product can be sold by many salespersons. By the way, in some circumstances, in either the 1–M or M–M case, "many" can be either an exact number or have a known maximum value. For example, a company rule may set a limit of a maximum of ten customers in a sales territory. Then the "many" in the 1–M relationship of Figure 2.3b can never be more than ten (a salesperson can have many customers but not more than ten). Sometimes people include this exact number or maximum next to or even instead of the crow's foot in the E-R diagram.

Modality

Figure 2.4 shows the addition of the **modality**, the *minimum* number of entity occurrences that can be involved in a relationship. In our particular salesperson environment, every salesperson must be assigned to an office. On the other hand, a given office might be empty or it might be in use by exactly one salesperson. This situation is recorded in Figure 2.4a, where the "inner" symbol, which can be a zero or a one, represents the modality—the minimum—and the "outer" symbol, which can be a one or a crow's foot, represents the cardinality—the maximum. Reading Figure 2.4a from left to right tells us that a salesperson works in a minimum of one and a maximum of one office, which is another way of saying *exactly one* office. Reading from right to left, an office may be occupied by or assigned to a minimum of no salespersons (i.e. the office is empty) or a maximum of one salesperson.

   Similarly, Figure 2.4b indicates that a salesperson may have no customers or many customers. How could a salesperson have no customers? (What are we paying her for?!?) Actually, this allows for the case in which we have just hired a new salesperson and have not as yet assigned her a territory or any customers. On the other hand, a

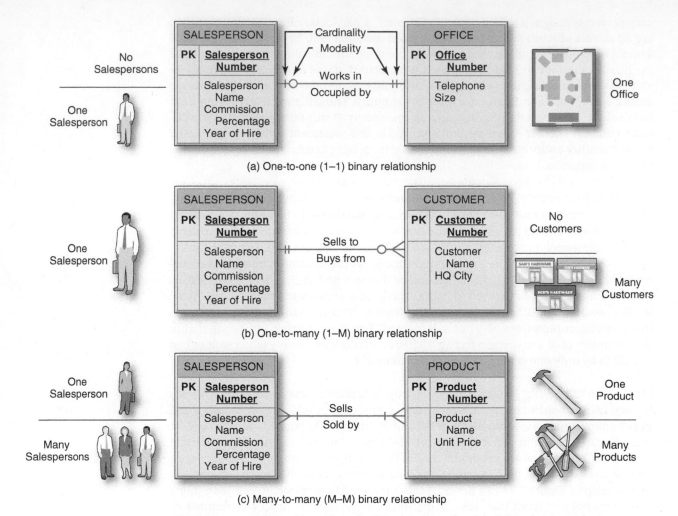

FIGURE 2.4 Binary relationships with cardinalities (maximums) and modalities (minimums)

customer is always assigned to exactly one salesperson. We never want customers to be without a salesperson—how would they buy anything from us when they need to? We never want to be in a position of losing sales! If a salesperson leaves the company, the company's procedures require that another salesperson or, temporarily, a sales manager be immediately assigned the departing salesperson's customers. Figure 2.4c says that each salesperson is authorized to sell at least one or many of our products and each product can be sold by at least one or many of our salespersons. This includes the extreme, but not surprising, case in which each salesperson is authorized to sell all the products and each product can be sold by all the salespersons.

More About Many-to-Many Relationships

Intersection Data   Generally, we think of attributes as facts about entities. Each salesperson has a salesperson number, a name, a commission percentage, and a year of hire. At the entity occurrence level, for example, one of the salespersons has salesperson number 528, the name Jane Adams, a commission percentage of 15%, and the year of hire of 2003. In an E-R diagram, these attributes are written or drawn together with the entity, as in Figure 2.1 and the succeeding figures. This certainly appears to be very natural and obvious. Are there ever any circumstances in which an attribute can describe something other than an entity?

Consider the many-to-many relationship between salespersons and products in Figure 2.4c. As usual, salespersons are described by their salesperson number, name, commission percentage, and year of hire. Products are described by their product number, name, and unit price. But, what if there is a requirement to keep track of the number of units (call it "quantity") *of a particular product that a particular salesperson has sold*? Can we add the quantity attribute to the product entity box? No, because for a particular product, while there is a single product number, product name, and unit price, there would be lots of "quantities," one for each salesperson selling the product. Can we add the quantity attribute to the salesperson entity box? No, because for a particular salesperson, while there is a single salesperson number, salesperson name, commission percentage, and year of hire, there will be lots of "quantities," one for each product that the salesperson sells. It makes no sense to try to put the quantity attribute in either the salesperson entity box or the product entity box. While each salesperson has a single salesperson number, name, commission percentage, and year of hire, each salesperson has many "quantities," one for each product he sells. Similarly, while each product has a single product number, product name, and unit price, each product has many "quantities," one for each salesperson who sells that product. But an entity box in an E-R diagram is designed to list the attributes that simply and directly describe the entity, with no complications involving other entities. Putting quantity in either the salesperson entity box or the product entity box just will not work.

The quantity attribute doesn't describe either the salesperson alone or the product alone. It describes the combination of a particular salesperson and a particular product. In general, we can say that it describes the combination of a particular occurrence of one entity type and a particular occurrence of the other entity type. Let's say that since salesperson number 137 joined the company, she has sold 170 units of product number 24 013. The quantity 170 doesn't make sense as a description or characteristic of salesperson number 137 alone. She has sold many different kinds of products. To which one does the quantity 170 refer? Similarly, the quantity 170 doesn't make sense as a description or characteristic of product number 24 013 alone. It has been sold by many different salespersons.

In fact, the quantity 170 falls at the *intersection* of salesperson number 137 and product number 24013. It describes the combination of or the association between that particular salesperson and that particular product and it is known as **intersection data**. Figure 2.5 shows the many-to-many relationship between salespersons and products with the intersection data, quantity, represented in a separate box attached to the relationship line. That is the natural place to draw it. Pictorially, it looks as if it is at the intersection between the two entities, but there is more to it than that. The intersection data *describes the relationship between the two entities*. We know that an occurrence of the Sells relationship specifies that salesperson 137 has sold some of product 24013. The quantity 170 is an attribute of this occurrence of that relationship, further describing this occurrence of the relationship. Not only do we know that salesperson 137 sold some of product 24013 but we know *how many units* of that product that salesperson sold.

Associative Entity   Since we know that entities can have attributes and now we see that many-to-many relationships can have attributes, too, does that mean that entities and many-to-many relationships can in some sense be treated in the same way within E-R diagrams? Indeed they can! Figure 2.6 shows the many-to-many relationship Sells

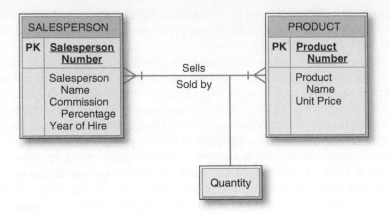

FIGURE 2.5 Many-to-many binary relationship with intersection data

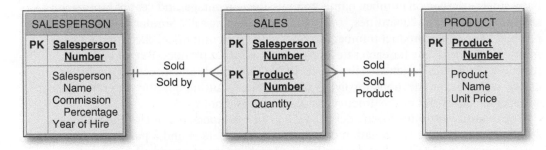

FIGURE 2.6 Associative entity with intersection data

converted into the **associative entity** SALES. An occurrence of the SALES associative entity does exactly what the many-to-many relationship did: it indicates a relationship between a salesperson and a product, specifically the fact that a particular salesperson has been involved in selling a particular product, and includes any intersection data that describes this relationship. Note very, very carefully the *reversal* of the cardinalities and modalities when the many-to-many relationship is converted to an associative entity. SALES is now a kind of entity in its own right. Again, a single occurrence of the new SALES entity type records the fact that a particular salesperson has been involved in selling a particular product. A single occurrence of SALES relates to a single occurrence of SALESPERSON and to a single occurrence of PRODUCT, which is why the diagram indicates that a sales occurrence involves exactly one salesperson and exactly one product. On the other hand, since a salesperson sells many products, the diagram shows that a salesperson will tie into many sales occurrences. Similarly, since a product is sold by many salespersons, the diagram shows that a product will tie into many sales occurrences.

If the many-to-many relationship E-R diagram style of Figure 2.5 is equivalent to the associative entity style of Figure 2.6, which one should you use? This is an instance in which this type of diagramming is an art with a lot of leeway for personal taste. However, you should be aware that over time the preference has shifted toward the associative entity style of Figure 2.6, and that is what we will use from here on in this book.

The Unique Identifier in Many-to-Many Relationships   Since, as we have just seen, a many-to-many relationship can appear to be a kind of an entity, complete with attributes, it also follows that it should have a unique identifier, like other entities. (If this seems a little strange or even unnecessary here, it will become essential later in the book when we actually design databases based on these E-R diagrams.) In its most basic form, the unique identifier of the many-to-many relationship or the associative entity is the combination of the unique identifiers of the two entities in the many-to-many relationship. So, the unique identifier of the many-to-many relationship of Figure 2.5 or, as shown in Figure 2.6, of the associative entity, is the combination of the Salesperson Number and Product Number attributes.

Sometimes, an additional attribute or attributes must be added to this combination to produce uniqueness. This often involves a time element. As currently constructed, the E-R diagram in Figure 2.6 indicates the quantity of a particular product sold by a particular salesperson *since the salesperson joined the company*. Thus, there can be only one occurrence of SALES combining a particular salesperson with a particular product. But if, for example, we wanted to keep track of the sales on an annual basis, we would have to include a year attribute and the unique identifier would be Salesperson Number, Product Number, and Year. Clearly, if we want to know how many units of each product were sold by each salesperson each year, the combination of Salesperson Number and Product Number would not be unique because for a particular salesperson and a particular product, the combination of those two values would be the same each year! Year must be added to produce uniqueness, not to mention to make it clear in which year a particular value of the Quantity attribute applies to a particular salesperson-product combination.

The third and last possibility occurs when the nature of the associative entity is such that it has its own unique identifier. For example, a company might specify a unique serial number for each sales record. Another example would be the many-to-many relationship between motorists and police officers who give traffic tickets for moving violations. (Hopefully it's not *too* many for each motorist!) The unique identifier could be the combination of police officer number and motorist driver's license number plus perhaps date and time. But, typically, each traffic ticket has a unique serial number and this would serve as the unique identifier.

Your Turn

2.1 Modeling Your World—Part 1
Whether it's a business environment or a personal environment, the entities, attributes, and relationships around us can be modeled with E-R diagrams.

Question:

How many binary relationships can you think of in your school environment? The entities might be students, professors, courses, sections, buildings, departments, textbooks, and so forth. Make a list of the binary relationships between pairs of these entities and diagram them with E-R diagrams. Do any of the many-to-many binary relationships have intersection data? Explain.

Unary Relationships

Unary relationships associate occurrences of an entity type with other occurrences of the *same* entity type. Take the entity person, for example. One person may be married to another person and vice versa. One person may be the parent of other people; conversely, a person may have another person as one of their parents.

One-to-One Unary Relationship

Figure 2.7a shows the **one-to-one unary relationship** called Back-Up involving the salesperson entity. The salespersons are organized in pairs as backup to each other when one is away from work. Following one of the links, say the one that extends from the right side of the salesperson entity box, we can say that salesperson number 137 backs up salesperson number 186. Then, going in the other direction, salesperson number 186 backs up salesperson 137. Notice that in each direction the modality of one rather than zero forbids the situation of a salesperson not having a backup.

One-to-Many Unary Relationship

Some of the salespersons are also sales managers, managing other salespersons. A sales manager can manage several other salespersons. Further, there can be several levels of sales managers, i.e. several low-level sales managers can be managed by a higher-level sales manager. Each salesperson (or sales manager) is managed by exactly one sales manager. This situation describes a **one-to-many unary relationship**. Consider Figure 2.7b and follow the downward branch out of its salesperson entity box. It says that a salesperson manages zero to many other salespersons, meaning that a salesperson may not be a sales manager (the zero modality case) or may be a sales manager with several subordinate salespersons (the many cardinality case). Following the branch that extends from the right side of the salesperson entity box, the diagram says that a salesperson is managed by exactly one other salesperson (who must, of course, be a sales manager).

Many-to-Many Unary Relationship

Unary relationships also come in the many-to-many variety. One classic example of a **many-to-many unary relationship** is known as the "bill of materials" problem. Consider a complex mechanical object like an automobile, an airplane, or a large factory machine tool. Any such object is made of basic parts like nuts and bolts that are used to make other components or sub-assemblies of the object. Small sub-assemblies and basic parts go together to make bigger sub-assemblies, and so on until ultimately they form the entire object. Each basic part and each sub-assembly can be thought of as a "part" of the object. Then, the parts are in a many-to-many unary relationship to each other. Any one particular part can be made up of several other parts while at the same time itself being a component of several other parts.

In Figure 2.7c, think of the products sold in hardware and home improvement stores. Basic items like hammers and wrenches can be combined and sold as sets. Larger tool sets can be composed of smaller sets plus additional single tools. All of these, single tools and sets of all sizes can be classified as products. Thus, as shown in Figure 2.7c, a product can be part of no other products or part of several other products. Going in

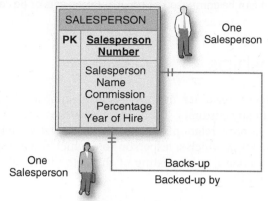

(a) One-to-one (1–1) unary relationship

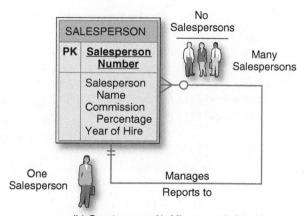

(b) One-to-many (1–M) unary relationship

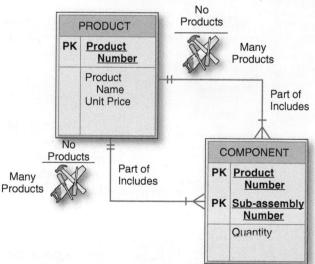

(c) Many-to-many (M–M) unary relationship

FIGURE 2.7 Unary relationships

the reverse direction, a product can be composed of no other products or be composed of several other products.

Ternary Relationships

A **ternary relationship** involves three different entity types. Assume for the moment that any salesperson can sell to any customer. Then, Figure 2.8 shows the most general, many-to-many-to-many ternary relationship among salespersons, customers, and products. It means that we know which salesperson sold which product to which customer. Each sale has intersection data consisting of the date of the sale and the number of units of the product sold.

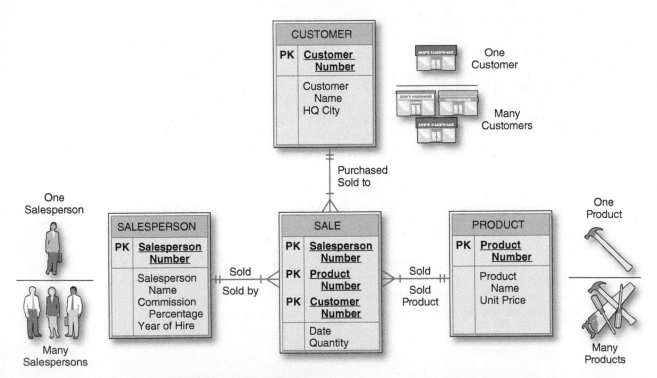

FIGURE 2.8 Ternary relationship

Example: The General Hardware Company

Figure 2.9 is the E-R diagram for the General Hardware Company, parts of which we have been using throughout this chapter. General Hardware is a wholesaler and distributor of various manufacturers' tools and other hardware products. Its customers are hardware and home improvement stores, which in turn sell the products at retail to individual consumers. Again, as a middleman it buys its goods from the manufacturers and then sells them to the retail stores. How exactly does General Hardware operate? Now that we know something about E-R diagrams, let's see if we can figure it out from Figure 2.9!

Begin with the SALESPERSON entity box in the middle on the left. SALESPERSON has four attributes with one of them, Salesperson Number, serving as the unique identifier of the salespersons. Looking upward from SALESPERSON, a salesperson works in exactly one office (indicated by the double ones or bars encountered on the way to the OFFICE entity). OFFICE has three attributes; Office Number is the unique identifier. Looking back downward from the OFFICE entity box, an office has either no salespersons working in it (the zero modality symbol) or one salesperson (the one or bar cardinality symbol). Starting again at the SALESPERSON entity box and moving to the right, a salesperson has no customers or many customers. (Remember that the customers are hardware or home improvement stores.) The CUSTOMER entity has three attributes; Customer Number is the unique identifier. In the reverse direction, a customer must have exactly one General Hardware salesperson.

Below the CUSTOMER entity is the CUSTOMER EMPLOYEE entity. According to the figure, a customer must have at least one but can have many employees. An employee works for exactly one customer. This is actually a special situation. General Hardware only has an interest in maintaining data about the people who are its customers' employees as long as their employer remains a customer of General Hardware. If a particular hardware store or home improvement chain stops buying goods from General Hardware, then General Hardware no longer cares about that store's or chain's employees. Furthermore, while General Hardware assumes that each of its customers assigns their employees unique employee numbers, those numbers *can be assumed to be unique only within that customer store or chain*. Thus, the unique identifier for a customer employee must be the combination of the Customer Number and the Employee Number attributes. In this situation, CUSTOMER EMPLOYEE is called a dependent or weak entity.

Returning to the SALESPERSON entity box and looking downward, there is a one-to-many relationship between salespersons and sales. But, below that, there is also a one-to-many relationship from products to sales. Also note that the unique identifier of SALES is the combination of Salesperson Number and Product Number. This is the signal that there is a many-to-many relationship between salespersons and products! A salesperson is authorized to sell at least one and generally many products. A product is sold by at least one and generally many salespersons. The PRODUCT entity has three attributes, with Product Number being the unique identifier. The attribute Quantity is intersection data in the many-to-many relationship and so becomes an attribute in the associative entity SALES that links salespersons with the products they have sold in a many-to-many relationship.

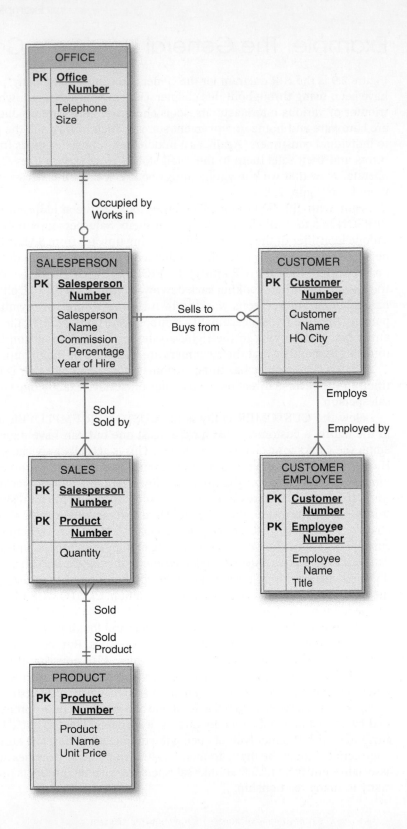

FIGURE 2.9 The General Hardware Company
E-R diagram

Example: Good Reading Book Stores

Figure 2.10 shows the E-R diagram for Good Reading Bookstores. Good Reading is a chain of bookstores that wants to keep track of the books that it sells, their publishers, their authors, and the customers who buy them. The BOOK entity has four attributes. Book Number is the unique identifier. A book has exactly one publisher. Publisher Name is the unique identifier of the PUBLISHER entity. A publisher may have (and generally has) published many books that Good Reading carries; however, Good Reading also wants to be able to keep track of some publishers that currently have no books in Good Reading's inventory (note the zero-modality symbol from PUBLISHER

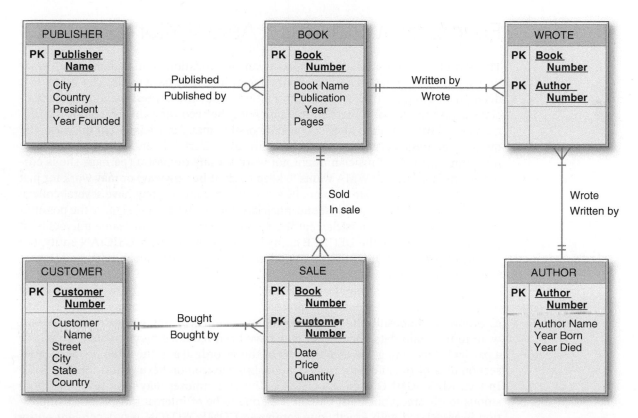

FIGURE 2.10 Good Reading Bookstores entity-relationship diagram

toward BOOK). A book must have at least one author but can have many (where in this case "many" means a few, generally two or three at most). For a person to be of interest to Good Reading as an author, she must have written at least one and possibly many books that Good Reading carries. Note that there is a many-to-many relationship between the BOOK and AUTHOR that is realized in the associative entity WROTE, which has no intersection data. The company wants to keep track of which authors wrote which books, but there are no attributes that further describe that many-to-many relationship. The associative entity SALE indicates that there is a many-to-many relationship between books and customers. A book can be involved in many sales and so can a customer. But a particular sale involves just one book and one customer. Date, Price, and Quantity are intersection data in the many-to-many relationship between the BOOK and CUSTOMER entities.

Does this make sense? Might a customer have bought several copies of the same book on the same date? After all, that's what the presence of the Quantity attribute implies. And might she have then bought more copies of the same book on a later date? Yes to both questions! A grandmother bought a copy of a book for each of three of her grandchildren one day and they liked it so much that she returned and bought five more copies of the same book for her other five grandchildren several days later. By the way, notice that the modality 0 going from book to sale says that a book may not have been involved in any sales (maybe it just came out). The modality of 1 going from customer to book says that for a person to be considered a customer, he must have participated in at least one sale, which is reasonable.

Example: World Music Association

The World Music Association (WMA) is an organization that maintains information about its member orchestras and the recordings they have made. The WMA E-R diagram in Figure 2.11 shows the information about the orchestras and their musicians across the top and the information about the recordings in the rest of the diagram. Each orchestra has at least one and possibly many musicians. (In this case, the modality expressing "at least one" is a technicality. Certainly an orchestra must have many musicians.) A musician might not work for any orchestra (perhaps she is currently unemployed but WMA wants to keep track of her anyway) or may work for just one orchestra. A musician may not be a college graduate or may have several college degrees. A degree belongs to just one musician (for the moment we ignore the possibility that more than one musician earned the same degree from the same university in the same year). Since the DEGREE entity is dependent on the MUSICIAN entity, the unique identifier for DEGREE is the combination of the Musician Number and Degree (e.g. B.A.) attributes.

Looking downward from the ORCHESTRA entity box, an orchestra may have made no recordings of a particular composition or may have made many. In the reverse direction, a composition may not have been recorded by any orchestra (but we still want to maintain data about it) or may have been recorded by many orchestras. For a particular recording, we note the year of the recording and the retail price, as intersection data of the many-to-many relationship between orchestras and compositions. In fact, RECORDING is an associative entity. A composer may have several compositions to his credit but must have at least one to be of interest to WMA. A composition is associated with exactly one composer. COMPOSITION is a dependent entity

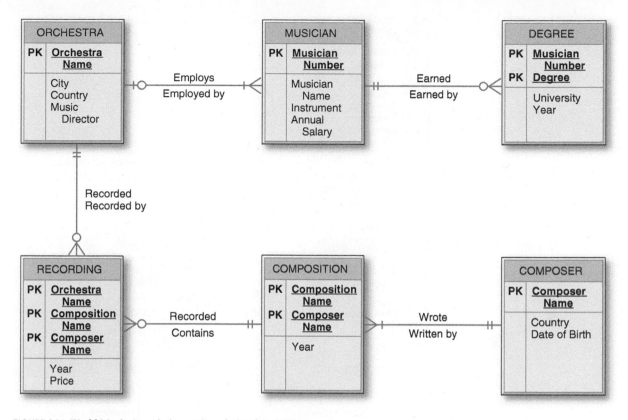

FIGURE 2.11 World Music Association entity-relationship diagram

to COMPOSER, which means that the unique identifier of COMPOSITION is the combination of Composer Name and Composition Name. After all, there could be Beethoven's "Third Symphony" and Mozart's "Third Symphony." This has an important implication for the RECORDING associative entity. To uniquely identify a recording (and attach the year and price intersection data to it) requires an Orchestra Name, Composition Name, and Composer Name.

Example: Lucky Rent-A-Car

Lucky Rent-A-Car's business environment is, obviously, centered on its cars. This is literally true in its E-R diagram, shown in Figure 2.12. A car was manufactured by exactly one manufacturer. A manufacturer manufactured at least one and generally many of Lucky's cars. A car has had many maintenance events (but a brand new car may not have had any, yet). A car may not have been rented to any customers (again, the case of a brand new car) or to many customers. A customer may have rented many cars from Lucky, and to be in Lucky's business environment must have rented at least one. Rental Date, Return Date, and Total Cost are intersection data to the many-to-many relationship between CAR and CUSTOMER, as shown in the associative entity RENTAL.

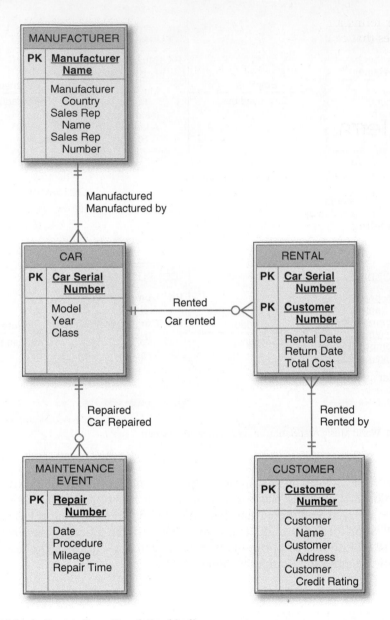

FIGURE 2.12 Lucky Rent-A-Car entity-relationship diagram

Summary

Being able to express entities, attributes, and relationships is an important preliminary step toward database management. The entity-relationship model is a diagramming technique that gives us this capability. The E-R model can display unary relationships (relationships between entities of the same type), binary relationships (relationships between entities of two different types), and ternary relationships (relationships between entities of three different types). Based on the number of distinct entities involved in a relationship, we expand this to one-to-one, one-to-many, and many-to-many unary relationships, one-to-one, one-to-many, and many-to-many binary relationships, and ternary relationships (which we consider to in general be many-to-many-to-many).

Other terms and concepts discussed include cardinality (the *maximum* number of entities that can be involved in a particular relationship), modality (the *minimum* number of entity occurrences that can be involved in a relationship), intersection data (data that describes a many-to-many relationship), and associative entities.

Key Terms

Associative entity	Entity	Intersection data	One-to-one relationship
Attribute	Entity-relationship	Many-to-many	Relationship
Binary relationship	(E-R) diagram	relationship	Ternary relationship
Cardinality	Entity-relationship	Modality	Unary relationship
Data modeling	(E-R) model	One-to-many relationship	Unique identifier

Questions

1. What is data modeling? Why is it important?

2. What is the entity-relationship model?

3. What is a relationship?

4. What are the differences among a unary relationship, a binary relationship, and a ternary relationship?

5. Explain and compare the cardinality of a relationship and the modality of a relationship.

6. Explain the difference between a one-to-one, a one-to-many, and a many-to-many binary relationship.

7. What is intersection data in a many-to-many binary relationship? What does the intersection data describe?

8. Can a many-to-many binary relationship have no intersection data? Explain.

9. Can intersection data be placed in the entity box of one of the two entities in the many-to-many relationship? Explain.

10. What is an associative entity? How does intersection data relate to an associative entity?

11. Describe the three cases of unique identifiers for associative entities.

12. Describe the concept of the unary relationship.

13. Explain how a unary relationship can be described as one-to-one, one-to-many, and many-to-many if only one entity type is involved in the relationship.

14. Describe the ternary relationship concept.

15. Can a ternary relationship have intersection data? Explain.

16. What is a dependent entity? (See the description in the General Hardware example.)

Exercises

1. Draw an entity-relationship diagram that describes the following business environment.

   The city of Chicago, IL, wants to maintain information about its extensive system of high schools, including its teachers and their university degrees, its students, administrators, and the subjects that it teaches.

   Each school has a unique name, plus an address, telephone number, year built, and size in square feet. Students have a student number, name, home address, home telephone number, current grade, and age. Regarding a student's school assignment, the school system is only interested in keeping track of which school

   a student *currently* attends. Each school has several administrators, such as the principal and assistant principals. Administrators are identified by an employee number and also have a name, telephone number, and office number.

   Teachers are also identified by an employee number and each has a name, age, subject specialty such as English (assume only one per teacher), and the year that they entered the school system. Teachers tend to move periodically from school to school and the school system wants to keep track of the *history* of which schools the teacher has taught in, including the current school. Included will be the year in which the teacher entered the school, and the highest pay rate that the teacher attained at the school. The school system wants to keep track of the universities that each teacher attended, including the degrees earned and the years in which they were earned. The school system wants to record each university's name, address, year founded, and Internet URL (address). Some teachers, as department heads, supervise other teachers. The school system wants to keep track of these supervisory relationships but only for teachers' *current* supervisors.

The school system also wants to keep track of the subjects that it offers (e.g. French I, Algebra III). Each subject has a unique subject number, a subject name, the grade level in which it is normally taught, and the year in which it was introduced in the school system. The school system wants to keep track of which teacher taught which student which subject, including the year this happened and the grade received.

2. The following entity-relationship diagram describes the business environment of Video Centers of Europe, Ltd., which is a chain of videotape and DVD rental stores. Write a verbal description of how VCE conducts its business, based on this E-R diagram.

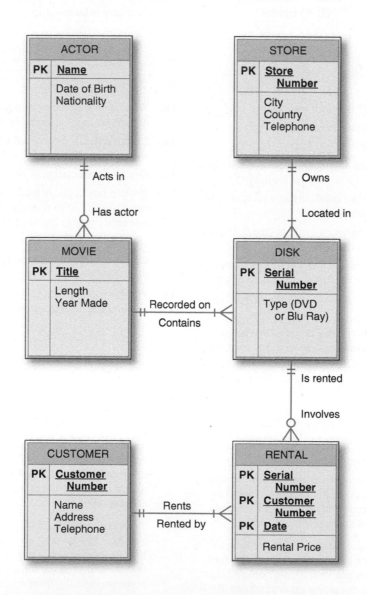

Minicases

1. Draw an entity-relationship diagram that describes the following business environment.

   Happy Cruise Lines has several ships and a variety of cruise itineraries, each involving several ports of call. The company wants to maintain information on the sailors who *currently* work on each of its ships. It also wants to keep track of both its past and future cruises and of the passengers who sailed on the former and are booked on the latter.

   Each ship has at least one and, of course, normally many sailors on it. The unique identifier of each ship is its ship number. Other ship attributes include ship name, weight, year built, and passenger capacity. Each sailor has a unique sailor identification number, as well as a name, date of birth, and nationality. Some of the sailors are in supervisory positions, supervising several other sailors. Each sailor reports to just one supervisor. A cruise is identified by a unique cruise serial number. Other cruise descriptors include a sailing date, a return date, and a departure port (which is also the cruise's ending point). Clearly, a cruise involves exactly one ship; over time a ship sails on many cruises, but there is a requirement to be able to list a new ship that has not yet sailed on any cruises at all. Each cruise stops at at least one and usually several ports of call, each of which is normally host to many cruises, over time. In addition, the company wants to maintain information about ports that it has not yet used in its cruises but may use in the future. A port is identified by its name and the country it is in. Other information about a port includes its population, whether a passport is required for passengers to disembark there, and its current docking fee, which is assumed to be the same for all ships. Passenger information includes a unique passenger number, name, home address, nationality, and date of birth. A cruise typically has many passengers on it (certainly at least one). Hoping for return business, the company assumes that each passenger may have sailed on several of its cruises (and/or may be booked for a future cruise). For a person to be of interest to the company, he or she must have sailed on or be booked on at least one of the company's cruises. The company wants to keep track of how much money each passenger paid (or will pay) for each of their cruises, as well as their satisfaction rating of the cruise, if it has been completed.

2. Draw an entity-relationship diagram that describes the following business environment. The Super Baseball League wants to maintain information about its teams, their coaches, players, and bats. The information about players is historical. For each team, the league wants to keep track of all of the players who have ever played on the team, including the current players. For each player, it wants to know about every team the player ever played for. On the other hand, coach affiliation and bat information is only current.

   The league wants to keep track of each team's team number, which is unique, its name, the city in which it is based, and the name of its manager. Coaches have a name (which is assumed to be unique only within its team) and a telephone number. Coaches have units of work experience that are described by the type of experience and the number of years of that type of experience. Bats are described by their serial numbers (which are unique only within a team) and their manufacturer's name. Players have a player number that is unique across the league, a name, and an age.

   A team has at least one and usually several coaches. A coach works for only one team. Each coach has several units of work experience or may have none. Each unit of work experience is associated with the coach to whom it belongs. Each team owns at least one and generally many bats. Currently and historically, each team has and has had many players. To be of interest to the league, a player must have played on at least one and possibly many teams during his career. Further, the league wants to keep track of the number of years that a player has played on a team and the batting average that he compiled on that team.

The Database Management System Concept

Data has always been the key component of information systems. In the beginning of the modern information systems era, data was stored in simple files. As companies became more and more dependent on their data for running their businesses, shortcomings in simple files became apparent. These shortcomings led to the development of the database management system concept, which provides a solid basis for the modern use of data in organizations of all descriptions.

OBJECTIVES

Define data-related terms such as entity and attribute and storage-related terms such as field, record, and file.

Identify the four basic operations performed on stored data.

Compare sequential access of data with direct access of data.

Discuss the problems encountered in a non-database information systems environment.

List the five basic principles of the database concept.

Describe how data can be considered to be a manageable resource.

List the three problems created by data redundancy.

Describe the nature of data redundancy among many files.

Explain the relationship between data integration and data redundancy in one file.

State the primary defining feature of a database management system.

Explain why the ability to store multiple relationships is an important feature of the database approach.

Explain why providing support for such control issues as data security, backup and recovery, and concurrency is an important feature of the database approach.

Explain why providing support for data Independence is an important feature of the database approach.

Introduction

Before the database concept was developed, all data in information systems (then generally referred to as "data processing systems") was stored in simple linear files. Some applications and their programs required data from only one file. Some applications required data from several files. Some of the more complex applications used data extracted from one file as the search argument (the item to be found) for extracting data from another file. Generally, files were created for a single application and were used only for that application. There was no sharing of files or of data among applications and, as a result, the same data often appeared redundantly in multiple files. In addition to this data redundancy among multiple files, a lack of sophistication in the design of individual files often led to data redundancy within those individual files.

As information systems continued to grow in importance, a number of the ground rules began to change. Hardware became cheaper—much cheaper relative to the computing power that it provided. Software development took on a more standardized, "structured" form. Large backlogs of new applications to be implemented built up, making the huge amount of time spent on maintaining existing programs more and more unacceptable. It became increasingly clear that the lack of a focus on data was one of the major factors in this program maintenance dilemma. Furthermore, the redundant data across multiple files and even within individual files was causing data accuracy nightmares (to be explained further in this chapter), just as companies were relying more and more on their information systems to substantially manage their businesses. As we will begin to see in this chapter, the technology that came to the rescue was the database management system.

Summarizing, the problems included:

- Data was stored in different formats in different files.
- Data was often not shared among different programs that needed it, necessitating the duplication of data in redundant files.
- Little was understood about file design, resulting in redundant data within individual files.
- Files often could not be rebuilt after damage by a software error or a hardware failure.
- Data was not secure and was vulnerable to theft or malicious mischief by people inside or outside the company.
- Programs were usually written in such a manner that if the way that the data was stored changed, the program had to be modified to continue working.
- Changes in everything from access methods to tax tables required programming changes.

This chapter will begin by presenting some basic definitions and concepts about data. Then it will describe the type of file environment that existed before database management emerged. Then it will describe the problems inherent in the file environment and show how the database concept overcame them and set the stage for a vastly improved information systems environment.

Data Before Database Management

As we said in Chapter 1, pieces of data are facts in our environment that are important to us. Usually we have many facts to describe something of interest to us.

For example, let's consider the facts we might be interested in about an employee of ours named John Baker. Our company is a sales-oriented company and John Baker is one of our salespersons. We want to remember that his employee number (which we will now call his salesperson number) is 137. We are also interested in the facts that his commission percentage on the sales he makes is 10%, his home city is Detroit, his home state is Michigan, his office number is 1284, and he was hired in 1995. There are, of course, reasons that we need to keep track of these facts about John Baker, such as generating his paycheck every week. It certainly seems reasonable to collect together all of the facts about Baker that we need and to hold all of them together. Figure 3.1 shows all of these facts about John Baker presented in an organized way.

Salesperson Number	Salesperson Name	City	State	Office Number	Commission Percentage	Year of Hire
137	Baker	Detroit	MI	1284	10	1995

FIGURE 3.1 Facts about salesperson Baker

Records and Files

Since we have to generate a paycheck each week for every employee in our company, not just for Baker, we are obviously going to need a collection of facts like those in Figure 3.1 for every one of our employees. Figure 3.2 shows a portion of that collection.

Let's proceed by revisiting some terminology from Chapter 2, and introducing some additional terminology along with some additional concepts. What we have been loosely referring to as a "thing" or "object" in our environment that we want to keep track of is called an **entity**. Remember that this is the real physical object or event, not the facts about it. John Baker, the real, living, breathing person whom you can go over to and touch, is an entity. A collection of entities of the same type (e.g. all the company's employees) is called an **entity set**. An **attribute** is a property of, a characteristic of, or a fact that we know about an entity. Each characteristic or property of John Baker, including his salesperson number 137, his name, city of Detroit, state of Michigan, office number 1284, commission percentage 10, and year of hire 1995, is an attributes of John Baker. Some attributes have unique values within an entity set.

Salesperson Number	Salesperson Name	City	State	Office Number	Commission Percentage	Year of Hire
119	Taylor	New York	NY	1211	15	2003
137	Baker	Detroit	MI	1284	10	1995
186	Adams	Dallas	TX	1253	15	2001
204	Dickens	Dallas	TX	1209	10	1998
255	Lincoln	Atlanta	GA	1268	20	2003
361	Carlyle	Detroit	MI	1227	20	2001
420	Green	Tucson	AZ	1263	10	1993

FIGURE 3.2 Salesperson file

For example, the salesperson numbers are unique within the salesperson entity set, meaning each salesperson has a different salesperson number. We can use the fact that salesperson numbers are unique to distinguish among the different salespersons.

Using the structure in Figure 3.2, we can define some standard file-structure terms and relate them to the terms entity, entity set, and attribute. Each row in Figure 3.2 describes a single entity. In fact, each row contains all the facts that we know about a particular entity. The first row contains all the facts about salesperson 119, the second row contains all the facts about salesperson 137, and so on. Each row of a structure like this is called a **record**. The columns representing the facts are called **fields**. The entire structure is called a **file**. The file in Figure 3.2, which is about the most basic kind of file imaginable, is often called a simple file or a **simple linear file** (linear because it is a collection of records listed one after the other in a long line). Since the salesperson attribute is unique, the salesperson field values can be used to distinguish the individual records of the file. Speaking loosely at this point, the salesperson number field can be referred to as the **key field** or key of the *file*.

Tying together the two kinds of terminology that we have developed, a record of a file describes an entity, a whole file contains the descriptions of an entire entity set, and a field of a record contains an attribute of the entity described by that record. In Figure 3.2, each row is a record that describes an entity, specifically a single salesperson. The whole file, row by row or record by record, describes each salesperson in the collection of salespersons. Each column of the file represents a different attribute of salespersons. At the row or entity level, the salesperson name field for the third row of the file indicates that the third salesperson, salesperson 186, has Adams as his salesperson name attribute, i.e. he is named Adams.

One last terminology issue is the difference between the terms "type" and "occurrence." Let's talk about it in the context of a record. If you look at a file, like that in Figure 3.2, there are two ways to describe "a record." One, which is referred to as the record type, is a structural description of each and every record in the file. Thus, we would describe the salesperson record type as a record consisting of a salesperson number field, a salesperson name field, a city field, and so forth. This is a general description of what any of the salesperson records looks like. The other way of describing a record is referred to as a record occurrence or a record instance. A specific record of the salesperson file is a record occurrence or instance. Thus, we would say that, for example, the set of values {186, Adams, Dallas, TX, 1253, 15, 2001} is an occurrence of the salesperson record type.

Your Turn

3.1 Entities and Attributes

Entities and their attributes are all around us in our everyday lives. Normally, we don't stop to think about the objects or events in our world formally as entities with their attributes, but they're there.

Question:

Choose an object in your world that you interact with frequently. It might be a university, a person, an automobile, your home, etc. Make a list of some of the chosen entity's attributes. Then, generalize them to "type." For example, you may have a backpack (an entity) that is green in color (an attribute of that entity). Generalize that to the entity set of all backpacks and to the *attribute type* color. Next, go through the same exercise for an event in your life, such as taking a particular exam, your last birthday party and eating dinner last night.

Basic Concepts in Storing and Retrieving Data

Having established the idea of a file and its records, we can now, in simple terms at this point, envision a company's data as a large collection of files. The next step is to discuss how we might want to access data from these files and otherwise manipulate the data in them.

Retrieving and Manipulating Data   There are four fundamental operations that can be performed on stored data, whether it is stored in the form of a simple linear file, such as that of Figure 3.2, or in any other form. They are:

- Retrieve or Read
- Insert
- Delete
- Update

It is convenient to think of each of these operations as basically involving one record at a time, although in practice they can involve several records at once, as we will see later in the book. Retrieving or reading a record means looking at a record's contents without changing them. For example, using the Salesperson file of Figure 3.2, we might read the record for salesperson 204 because we want to find out which year she was hired. Insertion means adding a new record to the file, as when a new salesperson is hired. Deletion means deleting a record from the file, as when a salesperson leaves the company. Updating means changing one or more of a record's field values, for example, if we want to increase salesperson 420's commission percentage from 10 to 15. There is clearly a distinction between retrieving or reading data and the other three operations. Retrieving data allows a user to refer to the data for some business purpose *without changing it*. All of the other three operations involve changing the data. Different topics in this book will focus on one or another of these operations simply because a particular one of the four operations may be more important for a particular topic than the others.

One particularly important concept concerning data retrieval is that, while information systems applications come in a countless number of variations, there are fundamentally only two kinds of access to stored data that any of them require. These two ways of retrieving data are known as **sequential access** and **direct access**.

Sequential Access   The term sequential access means the retrieval of all or a portion of the records of a file one after another, in some sequence, starting from the beginning, until all the required records have been retrieved. This could mean all the records of the file, if that is the goal, or all the records up to some point, such as up to the point that a record being searched for is found. The records will be retrieved in some order and there are two possibilities for this. In **"physical" sequential access**, the records are retrieved one after the other, just as they are stored on the disk device (more on these devices later). In **"logical" sequential access**, the records are retrieved in order based on the values of one or a combination of the fields.

Assuming the records of the Salesperson file of Figure 3.2 are stored on the disk in the order shown in the figure, if they are retrieved in physical sequence they will be retrieved in the order shown in the figure. However, if, for example, they are to be retrieved in logical sequence based on the Salesperson Name field, then the record for Adams would be retrieved first, followed by the record for Baker, followed by the record for Carlyle, and so on in alphabetic order. An example of an application that would require the sequential retrieval of the records of this file would be the weekly payroll processing. If the company wants to generate a payroll check for each salesperson in the order of their salesperson numbers, it can very simply retrieve the records physically sequentially, since that's the order in which they are stored on the disk. If the company wants to produce the checks in the order of the salespersons' names, it will have to perform a **logical sequential retrieval** based on the Salesperson Name field. It can do this either by sorting the records on the Salesperson Name field or by using an index (see below) that is built on this field.

We said that sequential access could involve retrieving a portion of the records of a file. This sense of sequential retrieval usually means starting from the beginning of the file and searching every record, in sequence, until finding a particular record that is being sought. Obviously, this could take a long time for even a moderately large file and so is not a particularly desirable kind of operation, which leads to the concept of direct access.

Direct Access   The other mode of access is direct access. Direct access is the retrieval of a single record of a file or a subset of the records of a file based on one or more values of a field or a combination of fields in the file. For example, in the Salesperson file of Figure 3.2, if we need to retrieve the record for salesperson 204 to find out her year of hire, we would perform a direct access operation on the file specifying that we want the record with a value of 204 in the Salesperson Number field. How do we know that we would retrieve only one record? Because the Salesperson Number field is the unique, key field of the file, there can only be one record (or none) with any one particular value. Another possibility is that we want to retrieve the records for all the salespersons with a commission percentage of 10. The subset of the records retrieved would consist of the records for salespersons 137, 204, and 420.

Direct access is a crucial concept in information systems today. If you telephone a bank with a question about your account, you would not be happy having to wait on the phone while the bank's information system performs a sequential access of its customer file until it finds your record. Clearly this example calls for direct access. In fact, the vast majority of information systems operations that all companies perform today require direct access.

Both sequential access and direct access can certainly be accomplished with data stored in simple files. But simple files leave a lot to be desired. What is the concept of database and what are its advantages?

The Database Concept

The database concept is one of the most powerful, enduring technologies in the information systems environment. It encompasses a variety of technical and managerial issues and features that are at the heart of today's information systems scene. In order to get started and begin to develop the deep understanding of database that we seek, we will focus on five issues that establish a set of basic principles of the database concept:

1. The creation of a **datacentric environment** in which a company's data can truly be thought of as a significant corporate resource. A key feature of this environment is the ability to share data among those inside and outside of the company who require access to it.
2. The ability to achieve **data integration** while at the same time storing data in a non-redundant fashion. This, alone, is the central, defining feature of the database approach.

3. The ability to store data representing entities involved in multiple relationships without introducing **data redundancy** or other structural problems.
4. The establishment of an environment that manages certain data control issues, such as data security, backup and recovery, and concurrency control.
5. The establishment of an environment that permits a high degree of data independence.

Data as a Manageable Resource

Broadly speaking, the information systems environment consists of several components including hardware, networks, applications software, systems software, people, and data. The relative degree of focus placed on each of these has varied over time. In particular, the amount of attention paid to data has undergone a radical transformation. In the earlier days of "data processing," most of the time and emphasis in application development was spent on the programs, as opposed to on the data and data structures. Hardware was expensive and the size of main memory was extremely limited by today's standards. Programming was a new discipline and there was much to be learned about it in order to achieve the goal of efficient processing. Standards for effective programming were unknown. In this environment, the treatment of the data was hardly the highest-priority concern.

At the same time, as more and more corporate functions at the operational, tactical, and strategic levels became dependent on information systems, data increasingly became recognized as an important corporate resource. Furthermore, the corporate community became increasingly convinced that a firm's data about its products, manufacturing processes, customers, suppliers, employees, and competitors could, with proper storage and use, give the firm a significant competitive advantage.

Money, plant and equipment, inventories, and people are all important enterprise resources and, indeed, a great deal of effort has always been expended to manage them. As corporations began to realize that data is also an important enterprise resource, it became increasingly clear that data would have to be managed in an organized way, too, Figure 3.3. What was needed was a **software utility** that could manage and protect data while providing controlled shared access to it so that it could fulfill its destiny

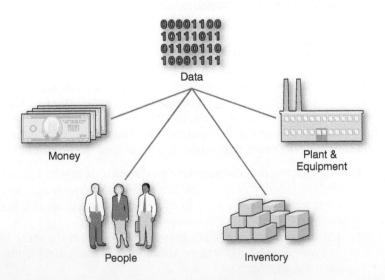

FIGURE 3.3 Corporate resources

as a critical **corporate resource**. Out of this need was born the database management system.

As we look to the future and look back at the developments of the last few years, we see several phenomena that emphasize the importance of data and demand its careful management as a corporate resource. These include reengineering, electronic commerce, and **enterprise resource planning (ERP) systems** that have placed an even greater emphasis on data. In reengineering, data and information systems are aggressively used to redesign business processes for maximum efficiency. At the heart of every electronic commerce Web site is a database through which companies and their customers transact business. Another very important development was that of enterprise resource planning (ERP) systems, which are collections of application programs built around a central shared database. ERP systems very much embody the principles of shared data and of data as a corporate resource.

Data Integration and Data Redundancy

Data integration and data redundancy, each in their own right, are critical issues in the field of database management.

- Data integration refers to the ability to tie together pieces of related data within an information system. If a record in one file contains customer name, address, and telephone data and a record in another file contains sales data about an item that the customer has purchased, there may come a time when we want to contact the customer about the purchased item.
- Data redundancy refers to the same fact about the business environment being stored more than once within an information system. Data integration is clearly a positive feature of a database management system. Data redundancy is a negative feature (except for performance reasons under certain circumstances that will be discussed later in this book).

In terms of the data structures used in database management systems, data integration and data redundancy are tied together and will be discussed together in this section of the book.

Data stored in an information system describes the real-world business environment. Put another way, the data is a reflection of the environment. Over the years that information systems have become increasingly sophisticated, they and the data that they contain have revolutionized the ways that we conduct virtually all aspects of business. But, as valuable as the data is, if the data is duplicated and stored multiple times within a company's information systems facilities, it can result in a nightmare of poor performance, lack of trust in the accuracy of the data, and a reduced level of competitiveness in the marketplace. Data redundancy and the problems it causes can occur within a single file or across multiple files. The problems caused by data redundancy are threefold:

- First, the redundant data takes up a great deal of extra disk space. This alone can be quite significant.
- Second, if the redundant data has to be updated, additional time is needed to do so since, if done correctly, every copy of the redundant data must be updated. This can create a major performance issue.
- Third and potentially the most significant is the potential for **data integrity problems**. The term data integrity refers to the accuracy of the data. Obviously, if the

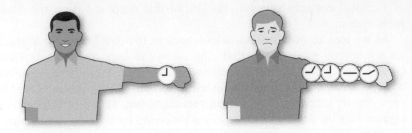

FIGURE 3.4 With several watches the correct time might not be clear

data in an information system is inaccurate, it and the whole information system are of limited value. The problem with redundant data, whether in a single file or across multiple files, occurs when it has to be updated (or possibly when it is first stored). If data is held redundantly and all the copies of the data record being updated are not all correctly updated to the new values, there is clearly a problem in data integrity. There is an old saying that has some applicability here, "The person with one watch always knows what time it is. The person with several watches is never quite sure," Figure 3.4.

Data Redundancy Among Many Files   Beginning with data redundancy across multiple files, consider the following situation involving customer names and addresses. Frequently, different departments in an enterprise in the course of their normal everyday work need the same data. For example, the sales department, the accounts receivable department, and the credit department may need customer name and address data. Often, the solution to this multiple need is redundant data. The sales department has its own stored file that, among other things, contains the customer name and address, and likewise for the accounts receivable and credit departments, Figure 3.5.

One day, customer John Jones, who currently lives at 123 Elm Street, moves to 456 Oak Street. If his address is updated in two of the files but not the third, then the company's data is inconsistent, Figure 3.6. Two of the files indicate that John Jones lives at 456 Oak Street but one file still shows him living at 123 Elm Street. The company can no longer trust its information system. How could this happen? It could have been a software or a hardware error. But more likely it was because whoever received the new information and was responsible for updating one or two of the files simply did

	Sales file	
Customer Number	Customer Name	Customer Address
2746795	John Jones	123 Elm Street

	Accounts Receivable file	
Customer Number	Customer Name	Customer Address
2746795	John Jones	123 Elm Street

	Credit file	
Customer Number	Customer Name	Customer Address
2746795	John Jones	123 Elm Street

FIGURE 3.5 Three files with redundant data

	Sales file	
Customer Number	Customer Name	Customer Address
2746795	John Jones	456 Oak Street

	Accounts Receivable file	
Customer Number	Customer Name	Customer Address
2746795	John Jones	456 Oak Street

	Credit file	
Customer Number	Customer Name	Customer Address
2746795	John Jones	123 Elm Street

FIGURE 3.6 Three files with a data integrity problem

not know of the existence of the third. As mentioned earlier, at various times in information systems history it has not been unusual in large companies for the same data to be held redundantly in sixty or seventy files! Thus, the possibility of data integrity problems is great.

Multiple file redundancy begins as more a managerial issue than single file redundancy, but it also has technical components. The issue is managerial to the extent that a company's management does not encourage data sharing among departments and their applications. But it is technical when it comes to the reality of whether the company's software systems are capable of providing shared access to the data without compromising performance and data security.

Data Integration and Data Redundancy Within One File   Data redundancy in a single file results in exactly the same three problems that resulted from data redundancy in multiple files: wasted storage space, extra time on data update, and the potential for data integrity problems. To begin developing this scenario, consider Figure 3.7, which shows two files from the General Hardware Co. information system. General Hardware is a wholesaler of hardware, tools, and related items. Its customers are hardware stores, home improvement stores, and department stores, or chains of such stores. Figure 3.7a shows the Salesperson file, which has one record for each of General Hardware's salespersons. Salesperson Number is the unique identifying "key" field and as such is underlined in the figure. Clearly, there is no data redundancy in this file. There is one record for each salesperson and each individual **fact** about a salesperson is listed once in the salesperson's record.

Figure 3.7b shows General Hardware's Customer file. Customer Number is the unique key field. Again, there is no data redundancy, but two questions have to be answered regarding the Salesperson Number field appearing in this file. First, why is it there? After all, it seems already to have a good home as the unique identifying field of the Salesperson file. The Salesperson Number field appears in the Customer file to record which salesperson is responsible for a given customer account. In fact, there is a one-to-many relationship between salespersons and customers. A salesperson can and generally does have several customer accounts, while each customer is serviced by only one General Hardware salesperson. The second question involves the data in the Salesperson Number field in the Customer file. For example, salesperson number 137 appears in four of the records (plus once in the first record of the Salesperson file!).

(a) Salesperson file

Salesperson Number	Salesperson Name	Commission Percentage	Year of Hire
137	Baker	10	1995
186	Adams	15	2001
204	Dickens	10	1998
361	Carlyle	20	2001

(b) Customer file

Customer Number	Customer Name	Salesperson Number	HQ City
0121	Main St. Hardware	137	New York
0839	Jane's Stores	186	Chicago
0933	ABC Home Stores	137	Los Angeles
1047	Acme Hardware Store	137	Los Angeles
1525	Fred's Tool Stores	361	Atlanta
1700	XYZ Stores	361	Washington
1826	City Hardware	137	New York
2198	Western Hardware	204	New York
2267	Central Stores	186	New York

FIGURE 3.7 General Hardware Company files

Does this constitute data redundancy? The answer is no. For data to be redundant (and examples of data redundancy will be coming up shortly), the same fact about the business environment must be recorded more than once. The appearance of salesperson number 137 in the first record of the Salesperson file establishes 137 as the identifier of one of the salespersons. The appearance of salesperson number 137 in the first record of the Customer file indicates that salesperson number 137 is responsible for customer number 0121. This is a different fact about the business environment. The appearance of salesperson number 137 in the third record of the Customer file indicates that salesperson number 137 is responsible for customer number 0933. This is yet another distinct fact about the business environment. And so on through the other appearances of salesperson number 137 in the Customer file.

Retrieving data from each of the files of Figure 3.7 individually is straightforward and can be done on a direct basis if the files are setup for direct access. Thus, if there is a requirement to find the name or commission percentage or year of hire of salesperson number 204, it can be satisfied by retrieving the record for salesperson number 204 in the Salesperson file. Similarly, if there is a requirement to find the name or responsible salesperson (by salesperson number!) or headquarters city of customer number 1525, we simply retrieve the record for customer number 1525 in the Customer file.

But, what if there is a requirement to find the *name* of the salesperson responsible for a particular customer account, say for customer number 1525? Can this requirement be satisfied by retrieving data from only one of the two files of Figure 3.7? No, it cannot! The information about which salesperson is responsible for which customers is recorded only in the Customer file and the salesperson names are recorded only in the Salesperson file. Thus, finding the salesperson name will be an exercise in data integration. In order to find the name of the salesperson responsible for a particular customer, first the record for the customer in the Customer file would have to be retrieved. Then, using the salesperson number found in that record, the correct salesperson record can be retrieved from the Salesperson file to find the salesperson name. For example, if there is a need to find the *name* of the salesperson responsible for customer number 1525, the first operation would be to retrieve the record for customer number 1525 in the Customer file. As shown in Figure 3.7b, this would yield salesperson number 361 as the number of the responsible salesperson. Then, accessing the record for salesperson 361 in the Salesperson file in Figure 3.7a determines that the name of the salesperson responsible for customer 1525 is Carlyle. While it's true that the data in the record in the Salesperson file and the data in the record in the Customer file have been integrated, the data integration process has been awfully laborious.

This kind of custom-made, multicommand, multifile access (which, by the way, could easily require more than two files, depending on the query and the files involved) is clumsy, potentially error prone, and expensive in terms of performance. While the two files have the benefit of holding data non-redundantly, what is lacking is a good level of data integration. That is, it is overly difficult to find and retrieve pieces of data in the two files that are related to each other. For example, customer number 1525 and salesperson name Carlyle in the two files in Figure 3.7 are related to each other by virtue of the fact that the two records they are in both include a reference to salesperson number 361. Yet, as shown above, ultimately finding the salesperson name Carlyle by starting with the customer number 1525 is an unacceptably laborious process.

A fair question to ask is, if we knew that data integration was important in this application environment and if we knew that there would be a frequent need to find the name of the salesperson responsible for a particular customer, why were the files structured as in Figure 3.7 in the first place? An alternative arrangement is shown in Figure 3.8. The single file in Figure 3.8 combines the data in the two files of Figure 3.7. Also, the Customer Number field values of both are identical.

The file in Figure 3.8 was created by merging the salesperson data from Figure 3.7a into the records of Figure 3.7b, based on corresponding salesperson numbers. As a result, notice that the number of records in the file in Figure 3.8 is identical to the number of records in the Customer file of Figure 3.7b. This is actually a result of the "direction" of the one-to-many relationship in which each salesperson can be associated with several customers. The data was "integrated" in this merge operation. Notice, for example, that in Figure 3.7b, the record for customer number 1525 is associated with salesperson number 361. In turn, in Figure 3.7a, the record for salesperson number 361 is shown to have the name Carlyle. Those two records were merged, based on the common salesperson number, into the record for customer number 1525 in Figure 3.8. (Notice, by the way, that the Salesperson Number field appears twice in Figure 3.8 because it appeared in each of the files of Figure 3.7. The field values in each of those two fields are identical in each record in the file in Figure 3.8, which must be the case since it was on those identical values that the record merge that created the file in Figure 3.8 was based. That being the case, certainly one of the two Salesperson Number fields in the file in Figure 3.8 could be deleted without any loss of information.)

The file in Figure 3.8 is certainly **well integrated**. Finding the name of the salesperson who is responsible for customer number 1525 now requires a single record access of the record for customer number 1525. The salesperson name, Carlyle, is right there in that record. This appears to be the solution to the earlier multifile access problem. Unfortunately, integrating the two files caused another problem: data redundancy. Notice in Figure 3.8 that, for example, the fact that salesperson number 137 is named Baker is repeated four times, as are his commission percentage and year of hire. This is, indeed, data redundancy, as it repeats the same facts about the business

Customer Number	Customer Name	Salesperson Number	HQ City	Salesperson Number	Salesperson Name	Commission Percentage	Year of Hire
0121	Main St. Hardware	137	New York	137	Baker	10	1995
0839	Jane's Stores	186	Chicago	186	Adams	15	2001
0933	ABC Home Stores	137	Los Angeles	137	Baker	10	1995
1047	Acme Hardware Store	137	Los Angeles	137	Baker	10	1995
1525	Fred's Tool Stores	361	Atlanta	361	Carlyle	20	2001
1700	XYZ Stores	361	Washington	361	Carlyle	20	2001
1826	City Hardware	137	New York	137	Baker	10	1995
2198	Western Hardware	204	New York	204	Dickens	10	1998
2267	Central Stores	186	New York	186	Adams	15	2001

FIGURE 3.8 General Hardware Company combined file

environment multiple times within the one file. If a given salesperson is responsible for several customer accounts, then the data about the salesperson *must* appear in several records in the merged or integrated file. It would make no sense from a logical or a retrieval standpoint to specify, for example, the salesperson name, commission percentage, and year of hire for one customer that the salesperson services and not for another. This would imply a special relationship between the salesperson and that one customer that does not exist and would remove the linkage between the salesperson and his other customers. To be complete, the salesperson data must be repeated for every one of his customers.

The combined file in Figure 3.8 also illustrates what have come to be referred to as anomalies in poorly structured files. The problems arise when two *different kinds of data*, like salesperson and customer data in this example, are merged into one file. Look at the record in Figure 3.8 for customer number 2198, Western Hardware. The salesperson for this customer is Dickens, salesperson number 204. Look over the table and note that Western Hardware happens to be the only customer that Dickens currently has. If Western Hardware has gone out of business or General Hardware has stopped selling to it and they decide to delete the record for Western Hardware from the file, they also lose everything they know about Dickens: his commission percentage, his year of hire, even his name associated with his salesperson number, 204. This situation, which is called the deletion anomaly, occurs because salesperson data doesn't have its own file, as in Figure 3.7a. The only place in the combined file of Figure 3.8 that you can store salesperson data is in the records with the customers. If you delete a customer and that record was the only one for that salesperson, the salesperson's data is gone.

Conversely, in the insertion anomaly, General Hardware can't record data in the combined file of Figure 3.8 about a new salesperson the company just hired until she is assigned at least one customer. After all, the identifying field of the records of the combined file is Customer Number! Finally, the update anomaly notes that the redundant data of the combined file, such as Baker's commission percentage of 10 repeated four times, must be updated each place it exists when it changes (for example, if Baker is rewarded with an increase to a commission percentage of 15).

There appears to be a very significant tradeoff in the data structures between data integration and data redundancy. The two files of Figure 3.7 are non-redundant but have poor data integration. Finding the name of the salesperson responsible for a particular customer account requires a multicommand, multifile access that can be slow and error-prone. The merged file of Figure 3.8, in which the data is very well integrated, eliminates the need for a multicommand, multifile access for this query, but is highly data redundant. Neither of these situations is acceptable. A poor level of data integration slows down the company's information systems and, perhaps, its business! Redundant data can cause data accuracy and other problems. Yet both the properties of data integration and of non-redundant data are highly desirable. And, while the above example appears to show that the two are hopelessly incompatible, over the years a few—very few—ways have been developed to achieve both goals in a single data management system. In fact, this concept is so important that it is the primary defining feature of database management systems:

> A database management system is a software utility for storing and retrieving data that gives the end-user the impression that the data is well integrated even though the data can be stored with no redundancy at all.

Any data storage and retrieval system that does not have this property should not be called a database management system. Notice a couple of fine points in the above definition. It says, "data *can* be stored with no redundancy," indicating that non-redundant storage is feasible but not required. In certain situations, particularly involving performance issues, the database designer may choose to compromise on the issue of data redundancy. Also, it says, "that gives the end-user the *impression* that the data is well integrated." Depending on the approach to database management taken by the particular database management system, data can be physically integrated and stored that way on the disk or it can be integrated at the time that a **data retrieval** query is executed. In either case, the data will, "give the end-user the impression that the data is well integrated." Both of these fine points will be explored further later in this book.

Multiple Relationships

Chapter 2 demonstrated how entities can relate to each other in unary, binary, and ternary one-to-one, one-to-many, and many-to-many relationships. Clearly, a database management system must be able to store data about the entities in a way that reflects and preserves these relationships. Furthermore, this must be accomplished in such a way that it does not compromise the fundamental properties of data integration and non-redundant data storage described above. Consider the following problems with attempting to handle **multiple relationships** in simple linear files, using the binary one-to-many relationship between General Hardware Company's salespersons and customers as an example.

First, the Customer file of Figure 3.7 does the job with its Salesperson Number field. The fact that, for example, salesperson number 137 is associated with four of the customers (it appears in four of the records) while, for example, customer number 1826 has only one salesperson associated with it demonstrates that the one-to-many relationship has been achieved. However, as has already been shown, the two files of this figure lack an efficient data integration mechanism; i.e. trying to link detailed salesperson data with associated customer data is laborious. (Actually, as will be seen later in this book, the structures of Figure 3.7 are quite viable in the relational DBMS environment. In that case, the relational DBMS software will handle the data integration requirement. But without that relational DBMS software, these structures are deficient in terms of data integration.) Also, the combined file of Figure 3.8 supports the one-to-many relationship but, of course, introduces data redundancy.

Figure 3.9 shows a "horizontal" solution to the problem. The Salesperson Number field has been removed from the Customer file. Instead, each record in the Salesperson file lists all the customers, by customer number, that the particular salesperson is responsible for. This could conceivably be implemented as one variable-length field of some sort containing all the associated customer numbers for each salesperson, or it could be implemented as a series of customer number fields. While this arrangement does represent the one-to-many relationship, it is unacceptable for two reasons. One is that the record length could be highly variable depending on how many customers a particular salesperson is responsible for. This can be tricky from a space management point of view. If a new customer is added to a salesperson's record, the new larger size of the record may preclude its being stored in the same place on the disk as it came from, but putting it somewhere else may cause performance problems in future retrievals. The other reason is that once a given salesperson record is retrieved, the person or program that retrieved it would have a difficult time going through all the associated customer numbers looking for the one desired. With simple files like these, the normal expectation is that there will be one value of each field type in each record (e.g. one salesperson number, one salesperson name, and so on). In the arrangement in Figure 3.9, the end-user or supporting software would have to deal with a list of values, i.e. of customer numbers, upon retrieving a salesperson record. This would be an unacceptably complex process.

(a) Salesperson file

Salesperson Number	Salesperson Name	Commission Percentage	Year of Hire	Customer Numbers
137	Baker	10	1995	0121, 0933, 1047, 1826
186	Adams	15	2001	0839, 2267
204	Dickens	10	1998	2198
361	Carlyle	20	2001	1525, 1700

(b) Customer file

Customer Number	Customer Name	HQ City
0121	Main St. Hardware	New York
0839	Jane's Stores	Chicago
0933	ABC Home Stores	Los Angeles
1047	Acme Hardware Store	Los Angeles
1525	Fred's Tool Stores	Atlanta
1700	XYZ Stores	Washington
1826	City Hardware	New York
2198	Western Hardware	New York
2267	Central Stores	New York

FIGURE 3.9 General Hardware Company combined files: One-to-many relationship horizontal variation

Figure 3.10 shows a "vertical" solution to the problem. In a single file, each salesperson record is immediately followed by the records for all of the customers for which the salesperson is responsible. While this does preserve the one-to-many relationship, the complexities involved in a system that has to manage multiple record types in a single file make this solution unacceptable, too.

A database management system must be able to handle all of the various unary, binary, and ternary relationships in a logical and efficient way that does not introduce data redundancy or interfere with data integration. The database management system approaches that are in use today all satisfy this requirement. In particular, the way that the relational approach to database management handles it will be explained in detail.

137	Baker	10	1995	

0121	Main St. Hardware	137	New York
0933	ABC Home Stores	137	Los Angeles
1047	Acme Hardware Store	137	Los Angeles
1826	City Hardware	137	New York

186	Adams	15	2001

0839	Jane's Stores	186	Chicago
2267	Central Stores	186	New York

204	Dickens	10	1998

2198	Western Hardware	204	New York

361	Carlyle	20	2001

1525	Fred's Tool Stores	361	Atlanta
1700	XYZ Stores	361	Washington

FIGURE 3.10 General Hardware Company combined files: One-to-many relationship vertical variation

Security

Backup and Recovery

Concurrency Control

FIGURE 3.11 Three data control issues

Data Control Issues

The people responsible for managing the data in an information systems environment must be concerned with several **data control issues**. This is true regardless of which database management system approach is in use. It is even true if no database management system is in use, that is, if the data is merely stored in simple files. Most prominent among these data control issues are **data security**, **backup and recovery**, and **concurrency control**, Figure 3.11. These are introduced here and will be covered in more depth later in this book. The reason for considering these data control issues in this discussion of the essence of the database management system concept is that such systems should certainly be expected to handle these issues frequently for all the data stored in the system's databases.

Computer security has become a very broad topic with many facets and concerns. These include protecting the physical hardware environment, defending against hacker attacks, encrypting data transmitted over networks, educating employees on the importance of protecting the company's data, and many more. All computer security exposures potentially affect a company's data. Some exposures represent direct threats to data while others are more indirect. For example, the theft of transmitted data is a direct threat to data while a computer virus, depending on its nature, may corrupt programs and systems in such a way that the data is affected on an incidental or delayed basis. The types of direct threats to data include outright theft of the data, unauthorized exposure of the data, malicious corruption of the data, unauthorized updates of the data, and loss of the data. Protecting a company's data assets has become a responsibility that is shared by its operating systems, special security utility software, and its database management systems. All database management systems incorporate features that are designed to help protect the data in their databases.

Data can be lost or corrupted in any of a variety of ways, not just from the data security exposures just mentioned. Entire files, portions of databases, or entire databases can be lost when a disk drive suffers a massive accidental or deliberate failure. At the extreme, all of a company's data can be lost to a disaster such as a fire, a hurricane, or an earthquake. Hackers, computer viruses, or even poorly written application programs can corrupt from a few to all of the records of a file or database. Even an unintentional error in entering data into a single record can be propagated to other records that use its values as input into the creation of their values. Clearly, every company (and even every PC user!) must have more than one copy of every data file and database. Furthermore, some of the copies must be kept in different buildings, or even different cities, to prevent a catastrophe from destroying all copies of the data. The process of using this duplicate data, plus other data, special software, and even specially designed disk devices to recover lost or corrupted data is known as "backup and recovery." As a key issue in data management, backup and recovery must be considered and incorporated within the database management system environment.

In today's multi-user environments, it is quite common for two or more users to attempt to access the same data record simultaneously. If they are merely trying to read the data without updating it, this does not cause a problem. However, if two or more users are trying to update a particular record simultaneously, say a bank account balance or the number of available seats on an airline flight, they run the risk of generating what is known as a "**concurrency problem**." In this situation, the updates can interfere with each other in such a way that the resulting data values will be incorrect. This intolerable possibility must be guarded against and, once again, the database management system must be designed to protect its databases from such an eventuality.

A fundamental premise of the database concept is that these three data control issues—data security, backup and recovery, and concurrency—must be managed by or coordinated with the database management system. This means that when a new application program is written for the database environment, the programmers can concentrate on the details of the application and not have to worry about writing code to manage these data control issues. It means that there is a good comfort level that the potential problems caused by these issues are under control since they are being managed by long-tested components of the DBMS. It means that the functions are standard for all of the data in the environment, which leads to easier management and economies of scale in assigning and training personnel to be responsible for the data. This kind of commonality of control is a hallmark of the database approach.

Data Independence

In the earlier days of "data processing," many decisions involving the way that application programs were written were made in concert with the specific file designs and the choice of file organization and access method used. The program logic itself was dependent upon the way in which the data is stored. In fact, the "**data dependence**" was often so strong that if for any reason the storage characteristics of the data had to be changed, the program itself had to be modified, often extensively. That was a very undesirable characteristic of the data storage and programming environments because of the time and expense involved in such efforts. In practice, storage structures sometimes have to change, to reflect improved storage techniques, application changes, attempts at sharing data, and performance tuning, to name a few reasons. Thus, it is highly desirable to have a data storage and programming environment in which as many types of changes in the data structure as possible would not require changes in the application programs that use them. This goal of "data independence" is an objective of today's database management systems.

DBMS Approaches

We have established a set of principles for the database concept and said that a database management system is a software utility that embodies those concepts. The next question concerns the nature of a DBMS in terms of how it organizes data and how it permits its retrieval. Considering that the database concept is such a crucial component of the information systems environment and that there must be a huge profit motive tied up with it, you might think that many people have worked on the problem over the years and come up with many different approaches to designing DBMSs. It's true that many very bright people have worked on this problem for a long time but, interestingly, you can count the number of different viable approaches that have emerged on the fingers of one hand. In particular, the central issue of providing a non-redundant data environment that also looks as though it is integrated is a very hard nut to crack. Let's just say that we're fortunate that even a small number of practical ways to solve this problem have been discovered.

Basically, there are five major DBMS approaches:

- Hierarchical
- Network
- Relational
- Object-oriented
- NoSQL

The hierarchical and network approaches to database are both called "navigational" approaches because of the way that programs have to "navigate" through hierarchies and networks of data to find the data they need. Both of these technologies were developed in the 1960s and, relative to the other approaches, are somewhat similar in structure. IBM's Information Management System (IMS), a DBMS based on the hierarchical approach, was released in 1969. It was followed in the early 1970s by several network-based DBMSs developed by such computer manufacturers of the time as UNIVAC, Honeywell, Burroughs, and Control Data. There was also a network-based DBMS called Integrated Data Management Store (IDMS) produced by an independent software vendor originally called Cullinane Systems, which was eventually absorbed into Computer Associates. These navigational DBMSs, which were suitable only for mainframe computers, were an elegant solution to the redundancy/integration problem at the time that they were developed. But they were complex, difficult to work with in many respects, and, as we said, required a mainframe computer. Now often called "legacy systems," some of them interestingly have survived to this very day for certain applications that require a lot of data and fast data response times.

Your Turn

3.2 Integrating Data

The need to integrate data is all around us, even in our personal lives. We integrate data many times each day without realizing that that's what we're doing. When we compare the ingredients needed for a recipe with the food "inventory" in our cupboards, we are integrating data. When we think about buying something and relate its price to the money we have in our wallets or in our bank accounts or to the credit remaining on our credit cards, we are integrating data. When we compare our schedules with our children's schedules and perhaps those of others with whom we carpool, we are integrating data. Can you think of other ways in which you integrate data on a daily basis?

Question:

Consider a medical condition for which you or someone you know is being treated. Describe the different ways that you integrate data in taking care of that condition. Hints: Consider your schedule, your doctors' schedules, the amount of prescription medication you have on hand, the inventory of medication at the pharmacy you use, and so on.

The relational database approach became commercially viable in about 1980. After several years of user experimentation, it became the preferred DBMS approach and has remained so ever since. Chapters 4–8 of this book, as well as portions of later chapters, are devoted to the relational approach. The object-oriented approach has proven useful for a variety of niche applications and will be discussed in Chapter 9. It is interesting to note that some key object-oriented database concepts have found their way into some of the mainstream relational DBMSs and some are described as taking a hybrid "object/relational" approach to database. NoSQL database will be described in Chapter 13.

Summary

There are five major components in the database concept. One is the development of a datacentric environment that promotes the idea of data being a significant corporate resource and encourages the sharing of data. Another, which is really the central premise of database management, is the ability to achieve data integration while at the same time storing data in a non-redundant fashion. The third, which at the structural level is actually closely related to the integration/redundancy paradigm, is the ability to store data representing entities involved in multiple relationships without introducing redundancy. Another component is the presence of a set of data controls that address such issues as data security, backup and recovery, and concurrency control. The final component is that of data independence, the ability to modify data structures without having to modify programs that access them.

There are basically five approaches to database management: the early hierarchical and network approaches, the current standard relational approach, and the specialty object-oriented approach, many features of which are incorporated into today's expanded relational database management systems. The latest approach is NoSQL database.

Key Terms

Attribute	Data integration	Entity	Multiple relationships
Backup and recovery	Data integrity problem	Entity set	Physical sequential access
Computer security	Data redundancy	Fact	Record
Concurrency control	Data retrieval	Field	Sequential access
Concurrency problem	Data security	File	Simple linear file
Corporate resource	Datacentric environment	Key field	Software utility
Data control issues	Direct access	Logical sequential access	Well integrated
Data dependence	Enterprise resource	Logical sequential	
Data independence	planning (ERP) system	retrieval	

Questions

1. What is data? Do you think the word "data" should be treated as a singular or plural word? Why?

2. Name some entities and their attributes in a university environment.

3. Name some entities and attributes in an insurance company environment.

4. Name some entities and attributes in a furniture store environment.

5. What is the relationship between:
   a. An entity and a record?
   b. An attribute and a field?
   c. An entity set and a file?

6. What is the difference between a record type and an occurrence of that record? Give some examples.

7. Name the four basic operations on stored data. In what important way is one in particular different from the other three?

8. What is sequential access? What is direct access? Which of the two is more important in today's business environment? Why?

9. Give an example of and describe an application that would require sequential access in:
   a. The university environment.
   b. The insurance company environment.
   c. The furniture store environment.

10. Give an example of and describe an application that would require direct access in:
    a. The university environment.

b. The insurance company environment.

c. The furniture store environment.

11. Should data be considered a true corporate resource? Why or why not? Compare and contrast data to other corporate resources (capital, plant and equipment, personnel, etc.) in terms of importance, intrinsic value, and modes of use.

12. Defend or refute the following statement: "Data is the most important corporate resource because it describes all of the others."

13. What are the two kinds of data redundancy, and what are the three types of problems that they cause in the information systems environment?

14. What factors might lead to redundant data across multiple files? Is the problem managerial or technical in nature?

15. Describe the apparent tradeoff between data redundancy and data integration in simple linear files.

16. In your own words, describe the key quality of a DBMS that sets it apart from other data handling systems.

17. Do you think that the single-file redundancy problem is more serious, less serious, or about the same as the multifile redundancy problem? Why?

18. What are the two defining goals of a database management system?

19. What expectation should there be for a database management system with regard to handling multiple relationships? Why?

20. What are the problems with the "horizontal" and "vertical" solutions to the handling of multiple relationships as described in the chapter?

21. What expectation should there be for a database management system with regard to handling data control issues such as data security, backup and recovery, and concurrency control? Why?

22. What would the alternative be if database management systems were not designed to handle data control issues such as data security, backup and recovery, and concurrency control?

23. What is data independence? Why is it desirable?

24. What expectation should there be for a database management system with regard to data independence? Why?

25. What are the four major DBMS approaches? Which approaches are used the most and least today?

Exercises

1. Consider a hospital in which each doctor is responsible for many patients while each patient is cared for by just one doctor. Each doctor has a unique employee number, name, telephone number, and office number. Each patient has a unique patient number, name, home address, and home telephone number.

a. What kind of relationship is there between doctors and patients?

b. Develop sample doctor and patient data and construct two files in the style of Figure 3.5 in which to store your sample data.

c. Do any fields have to be added to one or the other of the two files to record the relationship between doctors and patients? Explain.

d. Merge these two files into one, in the style of Figure 3.6. Does this create any problems with the data? Explain.

2. The Dynamic Chemicals Corp. keeps track of its customers and its orders. Customers typically have several outstanding orders while each order was generated by a single customer. Each customer has a unique customer number, a customer name, address, and telephone number. An order has a unique order number, a date, and a total cost.

a. What kind of relationship is there between customers and orders?

b. Develop sample customer and order data and construct two files in the style of Figure 3.7 in which to store your sample data.

c. Do any fields have to be added to one or the other of the two files to record the relationship between customers and orders? Explain.

d. Merge these two files into one, in the style of Figure 3.6. Does this create any problems with the data? Explain.

Minicases

1. Answer the following questions based on the following Happy Cruise Lines' data.

(a) Ship table

Ship Number	Ship Name	Year Built	Weight (Tons)
005	Sea Joy	1999	80,000
009	Ocean IV	2003	75,000
012	Prince Al	2004	90,000
020	Queen Shirley	1999	80,000

(b) Crew Member table

Sailor Number	Sailor Name	Ship Number	Home Country	Job Title
00536	John Smith	009	USA	Purser
00732	Ling Chang	012	China	Engineer
06988	Maria Gonzalez	020	Mexico	Purser
16490	Prashant Kumar	005	India	Navigator
18535	Alan Jones	009	UK	Cruise Director
20254	Jane Adams	012	USA	Captain
23981	Rene Lopez	020	Philippines	Captain
27467	Fred Jones	020	UK	Waiter
27941	Alain DuMont	009	France	France
28184	Susan Moore	009	Canada	Wine Steward
31775	James Collins	012	USA	Waiter
32856	Sarah McLachlan	012	Ireland	Cabin Steward

a. Regarding the Happy Cruise Lines Crew Member file.
   i. Describe the file's record type.
   ii. Show a record occurrence.
   iii. Describe the set or range of values that the Ship Number field can take.
   iv. Describe the set or range of values that the Home Country field can take.

b. Assume that the records of the Crew Member file are physically stored in the order shown.
   i. Retrieve all of the records of the file physically sequentially.
   ii. Retrieve all of the records of the file logically sequentially based on the Sailor Name field.
   iii. Retrieve all of the records of the file logically sequentially based on the Sailor Number field.
   iv. Retrieve all of the records of the file logically sequentially based on the Ship Number field.
   v. Perform a direct retrieval of the records with a Sailor Number field value of 27467.
   vi. Perform a direct retrieval of the records with a Ship Number field value of 020.
   vii. Perform a direct retrieval of the records with a Job Title field value of Captain.

c. The value 009 appears as a ship number once in the Ship file and four times in the Crew Member file. Does this constitute data redundancy? Explain.

d. Merge the Ship and Crew Member files based on the common ship number field (in a manner similar to Figure 3.8 for the General Hardware database). Is the merged file an improvement over the two separate files in terms of:
   i. Data redundancy? Explain.
   ii. Data integration? Explain.

e. Explain why the Ship Number field is in the Crew Member file.

f. Explain why ship number 012 appears four times in the Crew Member file.

g. How many files must be accessed to find:
   i. The year that ship number 012 was built?
   ii. The home country of sailor number 27941?
   iii. The name of the ship on which sailor number 18535 is employed?

h. Describe the procedure for finding the weight of the ship on which sailor number 00536 is employed.

i. What is the mechanism for recording the one-to-many relationship between crew members and ships in the Happy Cruise Lines database above?

2. Answer the following questions based on the following Super Baseball League data.

(a) TEAM file

Team Number	Team Name	City	Manager
137	Eagles	Orlando	Smith
275	Cowboys	San Jose	Jones
294	Statesmen	Springfield	Edwards
368	Pandas	El Paso	Adams
422	Sharks	Jackson	Vega

(b) PLAYER file

Player Number	Player Name	Age	Position	Team Number
1209	Steve Marks	24	Catcher	294
1254	Roscoe Gomez	19	Pitcher	422
1536	Mark Norton	32	First Baseman	368
1953	Alan Randall	24	Pitcher	137
2753	John Harbor	22	Shortstop	294
2843	John Yancy	27	Center Fielder	137
3002	Stuart Clark	20	Catcher	422
3274	Lefty Smith	31	Third Baseman	137
3388	Kevin Taylor	25	Shortstop	294
3740	Juan Vidora	25	Catcher	368

a. Regarding the Super Baseball League Player file shown above:
   i. Describe the file's record type.
   ii. Show a record occurrence.
   iii. Describe the set or range of values that the Player Number field can take.

b. Assume that the records of the Player file are physically stored in the order shown.
   i. Retrieve all of the records of the file physically sequentially.
   ii. Retrieve all of the records of the file logically sequentially based on the Player Name field.
   iii. Retrieve all of the records of the file logically sequentially based on the Player Number field.
   iv. Retrieve all of the records of the file logically sequentially based on the Team Number field.
   v. Perform a direct retrieval of the records with a Player Number field value of 3274.
   vi. Perform a direct retrieval of the records with a Team Number field value of 294.
   vii. Perform a direct retrieval of the records with an Age field value of 24.

c. The value 294 appears as a team number once in the Team file and three times in the Player file. Does this constitute data redundancy? Explain.

d. Merge the Team and Player files based on the common Team Number field (in a manner similar to Figure 3.8 for the General Hardware database). Is the merged file an improvement over the two separate tables in terms of:
   i. Data redundancy? Explain.
   ii. Data integration? Explain.

e. Explain why the Team Number field is in the Player file.

f. Explain why team number 422 appears twice in the Player file.

g. How many files must be accessed to find:
   i. The age of player number 1953?
   ii. The name of the team on which player number 3388 plays?
   iii. The number of the team on which player number 3388 plays?

h. Describe the procedure for finding the name of the city in which player number 3002 is based.

i. What is the mechanism for recording the one-to-many relationship between players and teams in the Super Baseball League database above?

CHAPTER 4

Relational Data Retrieval: SQL

As we move forward into the discussion of database management systems, we will cover a wide range of topics and skills including how to design databases, how to modify database designs to improve performance, how to organize corporate departments to manage databases, and others. But first, to whet your appetites for what is to come, we're going to dive right into one of the most intriguing aspects of database management: retrieving data from relational databases using the industry-standard SQL database management language.

Note: Some instructors may prefer to cover relational data retrieval with SQL after logical database design, Chapter 7, or after physical database design, Chapter 8. This chapter, Chapter 4 on relational data retrieval with SQL, is designed to work just as well in one of those positions as it is here.

OBJECTIVES

Write SQL SELECT commands to retrieve relational data using a variety of operators including GROUP BY, ORDER BY, and the built-in functions AVG, SUM, MAX, MIN, COUNT.
Write SQL SELECT commands that join relational tables.
Write SQL SELECT subqueries.
Describe a strategy for writing SQL SELECT statements.
Describe the principles of a relational query optimizer.

Introduction

There are two aspects of data management: data definition and data manipulation. Data definition, which is operationalized with a **data definition language (DDL)**, involves instructing the DBMS software on what tables will be in the database, what attributes will be in the tables, which attributes will be indexed, and so forth. Data manipulation refers to the four basic operations that can and must be performed on data stored in any DBMS (or in any other data storage arrangement, for that matter): data retrieval, data update, insertion of new records, and deletion of existing records. Data manipulation requires a special language with which users can communicate data manipulation commands to the DBMS. Indeed, as a class, these are known as **data manipulation languages (DMLs)**.

A standard language for data management in relational databases, known as **Structured Query Language** or SQL, was developed in the early 1980s. SQL incorporates both DDL and DML features. It was derived from an early IBM research project in relational databases called "System R." SQL has long since been declared a standard by the American National Standards Institute (ANSI) and by the International Standards Organization (ISO). Indeed, several versions of the standards have been issued over the years. Using the standards, many manufacturers have produced versions of SQL that are all quite similar, at least at the level at which we will look at SQL in this book. These SQL versions are found in such mainstream DBMSs as DB2, Oracle, MS Access, Informix, and others. SQL in its various implementations is used very heavily in practice today by companies and organizations of every description.

SQL is a comprehensive database management language. The most interesting aspect of SQL and the aspect that we want to explore in this chapter is its rich data retrieval capability. The other SQL data manipulation features, as well as the SQL data definition features, will be considered in the database design chapters that come later in this book.

Data Retrieval with the SQL SELECT Command

Introduction to the SQL SELECT Command

Data retrieval in SQL is accomplished with the SELECT command. There are a few fundamental ideas about the SELECT command that you should understand before looking into the details of using it. The first point is that the SQL SELECT command is *not* the same thing as the relational algebra Select operator discussed in Chapter 5. It's a bit unfortunate that the same word is used to mean two different things, but that's the way it is. The fact is that the SQL SELECT command is capable of performing relational Select, Project, and Join operations singly or in combination, and much more.

SQL SELECT commands are considered, for the most part, to be "declarative" rather than "**procedural**" in nature. This means that you specify what data you are looking for rather than provide a logical sequence of steps that guide the system in *how* to find the data. Indeed, as we will see later in this chapter, the relational DBMS analyzes the **declarative** SQL SELECT statement and creates an **access path**, a plan for what steps to take to respond to the query. The exception to this, and the reason for the qualifier "for the most part" at the beginning of this paragraph, is that a feature of the SELECT command known as "subqueries" permits the user to specify a certain amount of logical control over the data retrieval process.

Another point is that SQL SELECT commands can be run in either a "**query**" or an "embedded" mode. In the query mode, the user types the command at a workstation and presses the Enter key. The command goes directly to the relational DBMS, which evaluates the query and processes it against the database. The result is then returned to the user at the workstation. Commands entered this way can normally also be stored and retrieved at a later time for repetitive use. In the embedded mode, the SELECT command is embedded within the lines of a higher-level language program and functions as an input or "read" statement for the program. When the program is run and the program logic reaches the SELECT command, the program executes the SELECT command. The SELECT command is sent to the DBMS which, as in the query-mode case, processes it against the database and returns the results, this time to the program that issued it. The program can then use and further process the returned data. The only tricky part to this is that traditional higher-level language programs are designed to retrieve one record at a time. The result of a relational retrieval command is itself, a relation. A relation, if it consists of a single row, can resemble a record, but a relation of several rows resembles, if anything, several records. In the embedded mode, the program that issued the SQL SELECT command and receives the resulting relation back, must treat the rows of the relation as a list of records and process them one at a time.

SQL SELECT commands can be issued against either the actual, physical database tables or against a "logical view" of one table or of several joined tables. Good business practice dictates that in the commercial environment, SQL SELECT commands should be issued against such logical views rather than directly against the **base tables**. As we will see later in this book, this is a simple but effective security precaution.

Finally, the SQL SELECT command has a broad array of features and options and we will only cover some of them at this introductory level. But what is also very important is that our discussion of the SELECT command and the features that we will cover will work in all of the major SQL implementations, such as Oracle, MS Access, SQL Server, DB2, and Informix, possibly with minor syntax variations in some cases.

Basic Functions

The Basic SELECT Format   In the simplest SELECT command, we will indicate from which table of the database we want to retrieve data, which rows of that table we are interested in, and which attributes of those rows we want to retrieve. The basic format of such a SELECT statement is:

```
SELECT<columns>
FROM<table>
WHERE<predicates identifying rows to be included>;
```

We will illustrate the SQL SELECT command with the General Hardware Co. database of Figure 4.1, which is derived from the General Hardware entity-relationship diagram of Figure 2.9. If you have not as yet covered the database design chapters in this book, just keep in mind that some of the columns are present to tie together related data from different tables, as discussed in Chapter 3. For example, the SPNUM column in the CUSTOMER table is present to tie together related salespersons and customers.

(a) SALESPERSON table

SPNUM	SPNAME	COMMPERCT	YEARHIRE	OFFNUM
137	Baker	10	1995	1284
186	Adams	15	2001	1253
204	Dickens	10	1998	1209
361	Carlyle	20	2001	1227

(b) CUSTOMER table

CUSTNUM	CUSTNAME	SPNUM	HQCITY
0121	Main St. Hardware	137	New York
0839	Jane's Stores	186	Chicago
0933	ABC Home Stores	137	Los Angeles
1047	Acme Hardware Store	137	Los Angeles
1525	Fred's Tool Stores	361	Atlanta
1700	XYZ Stores	361	Washington
1826	City Hardware	137	New York
2198	Western Hardware	204	New York
2267	Central Stores	186	New York

(c) CUSTOMER EMPLOYEE table

CUSTNUM	EMPNUM	EMPNAME	TITLE
0121	27498	Smith	Co-Owner
0121	30441	Garcia	Co-Owner
0933	25270	Chen	VP Sales
0933	30441	Levy	Sales Manager
0933	48285	Morton	President
1525	33779	Baker	Sales Manager
2198	27470	Smith	President
2198	30441	Jones	VP Sales
2198	33779	Garcia	VP Personnel
2198	35268	Kaplan	Senior Accountant

(d) PRODUCT table

PRODNUM	PRODNAME	UNITPRICE
16386	Wrench	12.95
19440	Hammer	17.50
21765	Drill	32.99
24013	Saw	26.25
26722	Pliers	11.50

FIGURE 4.1 The General Hardware Company relational database

(continues)

(e) SALES table

SPNUM	PRODNUM	QUANTITY
137	19440	473
137	24013	170
137	26722	688
186	16386	1745
186	19440	2529
186	21765	1962
186	24013	3071
204	21765	809
204	26722	734
361	16386	3729
361	21765	3110
361	26722	2738

(f) OFFICE table

OFFNUM	TELEPHONE	SIZE
1253	901-555-4276	120
1227	901-555-0364	100
1284	901-555-7335	120
1209	901-555-3108	95

FIGURE 4.1 (Continued)
The General Hardware
Company relational database

As is traditional with SQL, the SQL statements will be shown in all capital letters, except for data values taken from the tables. Note that the attribute names in Figure 4.1 have been abbreviated for convenience and set in capital letters to make them easily recognizable in the SQL statements. Also, spaces in the names have been removed. Using the General Hardware database, an example of a simple query that demonstrates the basic SELECT format is:

"Find the commission percentage and year of hire of salesperson number 186."

The SQL statement to accomplish this would be:

```
SELECT COMMPERCT, YEARHIRE
FROM SALESPERSON
WHERE SPNUM=186;
```

How is this command constructed? The desired attributes are listed in the SELECT clause, the required table is listed in the FROM clause, and the restriction or predicate indicating which row(s) is involved is shown in the WHERE clause in the form of an equation. Notice that SELECT statements always end with a single semicolon (;) at the very end of the entire statement.

The result of this statement is:

COMMPERCT	YEARHIRE
15	2001

As is evident from this query, an attribute like SPNUM that is used to search for the required rows, also known as a "**search argument**," does not have to appear in the query result, as long as its absence does not make the result ambiguous, confusing, or meaningless.

To retrieve the entire record for salesperson 186, the statement would change to:

```
SELECT *
FROM SALESPERSON
WHERE SPNUM=186;
```

resulting in:

SPNUM	SPNAME	COMMPERCT	YEARHIRE	OFFNUM
186	Adams	15	2001	1253

The "*" in the SELECT clause indicates that all attributes of the selected row are to be retrieved. Notice that this retrieval of an entire row of the table is, in fact, a relational Select operation (see Chapter 5)! A relational Select operation can retrieve one *or more* rows of a table, depending, in this simple case, on whether the search argument is a unique or non-unique attribute. The search argument is non-unique in the following query:

"List the salesperson numbers and salesperson names of those salespersons who have a commission percentage of 10."

```
SELECT SPNUM, SPNAME
FROM SALESPERSON
WHERE COMMPERCT=10;
```

which results in:

SPNUM	SPNAME
137	Baker
204	Dickens

The SQL SELECT statement can also be used to accomplish a relational Project operation. This is a vertical slice through a table involving all rows and some attributes. Since all of the rows are included in the Project operation, there is no need for a WHERE clause to limit which rows of the table are included. For example,

"List the salesperson number and salesperson name of all of the salespersons."

```
SELECT SPNUM, SPNAME
FROM SALESPERSON;
```

results in:

SPNUM	SPNAME
137	Baker
186	Adams
204	Dickens
361	Carlyle

To retrieve an entire table, that is to design an SQL SELECT statement that places no restrictions on either the rows or the attributes, you would issue:

```
SELECT *
FROM SALESPERSON;
```

and have as the result:

SPNUM	SPNAME	COMMPERCT	YEARHIRE	OFFNUM
137	Baker	10	1995	1284
186	Adams	15	2001	1253
204	Dickens	10	1998	1209
361	Carlyle	20	2001	1227

Comparisons   In addition to equal (=), the standard comparison operators, greater than (>), less than (<), greater than or equal to (>=), less than or equal to (<=), and not equal to (<>) can be used in the WHERE clause.

> "List the salesperson numbers, salesperson names, and commission percentages of the salespersons whose commission percentage is less than 12."

```
SELECT SPNUM, SPNAME, COMMPERCT
FROM SALESPERSON
WHERE COMMPERCT<12;
```

This results in:

SPNUM	SPNAME	COMMPERCT
137	Baker	10
204	Dickens	10

As another example:

> "List the customer numbers and headquarters cities of the customers that have a customer number of at least 1700."

```
SELECT CUSTNUM, HQCITY
FROM CUSTOMER
WHERE CUSTNUM>=1700;
```

results in:

CUSTNUM	HQCITY
1700	Washington
1826	New York
2198	New York
2267	New York

ANDs and ORs   Frequently, there is a need to specify more than one limiting condition on a table's rows in a query. Sometimes, for a row to be included in the result it must satisfy more than one condition. This requires the Boolean AND operator. Sometimes a row can be included if it satisfies one of two or more conditions. This requires the Boolean OR operator.

AND   An example in which two conditions must be satisfied is:

> "List the customer numbers, customer names, and headquarters cities of the customers that are headquartered in New York and that have a customer number higher than 1500."

```
SELECT CUSTNUM, CUSTNAME, HQCITY
FROM CUSTOMER
WHERE HQCITY='New York'
AND CUSTNUM>1500;
```

resulting in:

CUSTNUM	CUSTNAME	HQCITY
1826	City Hardware	New York
2198	Western Hardware	New York
2267	Central Stores	New York

Notice that customer number 0121, which is headquartered in New York, was not included in the results because it failed to satisfy the condition of having a customer number greater than 1500. With the AND operator, it had to satisfy both conditions to be included in the result.

OR   To look at the OR operator, let's change the last query to:

> "List the customer numbers, customer names, and headquarters cities of the customers that are headquartered in New York *or* that have a customer number higher than 1500."

```
SELECT CUSTNUM, CUSTNAME, HQCITY
FROM CUSTOMER
WHERE HQCITY='New York'
OR CUSTNUM>1500;
```

results in:

CUSTNUM	CUSTNAME	HQCITY
0121	Main St. Hardware	New York
1525	Fred's Tool Stores	Atlanta
1700	XYZ Stores	Washington
1826	City Hardware	New York
2198	Western Hardware	New York
2267	Central Stores	New York

Notice that the OR operator really means one or the other *or both*. Customer 0121 is included because it is headquartered in New York. Customers 1525 and 1700 are included because they have customer numbers higher than 1500. Customers 1826, 2198, and 2267 are included because they satisfy both conditions.

Both AND and OR   What if both AND and OR are specified in the same WHERE clause? AND is said to be "higher in precedence" than OR, and so all ANDs are considered before any ORs are considered. The following query, which has to be worded very carefully, illustrates this point:

> "List the customer numbers, customer names, and headquarters cities of the customers that are headquartered in New York or that satisfy the two conditions of having a customer number higher than 1500 and being headquartered in Atlanta."

```
SELECT CUSTNUM, CUSTNAME, HQCITY
FROM CUSTOMER
WHERE HQCITY='New York'
OR CUSTNUM>1500
AND HQCITY='Atlanta';
```

The result of this query is:

CUSTNUM	CUSTNAME	HQCITY
0121	Main St. Hardware	New York
1525	Fred's Tool Stores	Atlanta
1826	City Hardware	New York
2198	Western Hardware	New York
2267	Central Stores	New York

Notice that since the AND is considered *first*, one way for a row to qualify for the result is if its customer number is greater than 1500 and its headquarters city is Atlanta. With the AND taken first, it's that combination *or* the headquarters city has to be New York. Considering the OR operator first would change the whole complexion of the statement. The best way to deal with this, especially if there are several ANDs and ORs in a WHERE clause, is by using parentheses. The rule is that *anything* in parentheses is done *first*. If the parentheses are nested, then whatever is in the innermost parentheses is done first and then the system works from there toward the outermost parentheses. Thus, a "safer" way to write the last SQL statement would be:

```
SELECT CUSTNUM, CUSTNAME, HQCITY
FROM CUSTOMER
WHERE HQCITY='New York'
OR (CUSTNUM>1500
AND HQCITY='Atlanta');
```

If you really wanted the OR to be considered first, you could force it by writing the query as:

```
SELECT CUSTNUM, CUSTNAME, HQCITY
FROM CUSTOMER
WHERE (HQCITY='New York'
OR CUSTNUM>1500)
AND HQCITY='Atlanta';
```

This would mean that, with the AND outside of the parentheses, both of two conditions have to be met for a row to qualify for the results. One condition is that the headquarters city is New York or the customer number is greater than 1500. The other condition is that the headquarters city is Atlanta. Since for a given row, the headquarters city can't be both Atlanta and New York, the situation looks grim. But, in fact, customer number 1525 qualifies. Its customer number is greater than 1500, which satisfies the OR of the first of the two conditions, and its headquarters city is Atlanta, which satisfies the second condition. Thus, both conditions are met for this and only this row.

BETWEEN, IN, and LIKE **BETWEEN**, **IN**, and **LIKE** are three useful operators. BETWEEN allows you to specify a range of numeric values in a search. IN allows you to specify a list of character strings to be included in a search. LIKE allows you to specify partial character strings in a "wildcard" sense.

BETWEEN Suppose that you want to find the customer records for those customers whose customer numbers are between 1000 and 1700 inclusive (meaning that both 1000 and 1700, as well as all numbers in between them, are included). Using the AND operator, you could specify this as:

```
SELECT *
FROM CUSTOMER
WHERE (CUSTNUM>=1000
AND CUSTNUM>=1700);
```

Or, you could use the BETWEEN operator and specify it as:

```
SELECT *
FROM CUSTOMER
WHERE CUSTNUM BETWEEN 1000 AND 1700;
```

With either way of specifying it, the result would be:

CUSTNUM	CUSTNAME	SPNUM	HQCITY
1047	Acme Hardware Store	137	Los Angeles
1525	Fred's Tool Stores	361	Atlanta
1700	XYZ Stores	361	Washington

IN   Suppose that you want to find the customer records for those customers head-quartered in Atlanta, Chicago, or Washington. Using the OR operator, you could specify this as:

```
SELECT *
FROM CUSTOMER
WHERE (HQCITY='Atlanta'
OR HQCITY='Chicago'
OR HQCITY='Washington');
```

Or, you could use the IN operator and specify it as:

```
SELECT *
FROM CUSTOMER
WHERE HQCITY IN ('Atlanta', 'Chicago', 'Washington');
```

With either way of specifying it, the result would be:

CUSTNUM	CUSTNAME	SPNUM	HQCITY
0839	Jane's Stores	186	Chicago
1525	Fred's Tool Stores	361	Atlanta
1700	XYZ Stores	361	Washington

LIKE   Suppose that you want to find the customer records for those customers whose names begin with the letter "A". You can accomplish this with the LIKE operator and the "%" character used as a wildcard to represent any string of characters. Thus, 'A%' means the letter "A" followed by any string of characters, which is the same thing as saying 'any word that begins with "A".'

```
SELECT *
FROM CUSTOMER
WHERE CUSTNAME LIKE 'A%';
```

The result would be:

CUSTNUM	CUSTNAME	SPNUM	HQCITY
0933	ABC Home Stores	137	Los Angeles
1047	Acme Hardware Store	137	Los Angeles

Note that, unlike BETWEEN and IN, there is no easy alternative way in SQL of accomplishing what LIKE can do.

In a different kind of example, suppose that you want to find the customer records for those customers whose names have the letter "a" as the second letter of their names. Could you specify '%a%'? No, because the '%a' portion of it would mean any number of letters followed by "a", which is not what you want. In order to make sure that there is just one character followed by "a", which is the same thing as saying that "a" is the second letter, you would specify '_a%'. The "_" wildcard character means that there will be exactly one letter (any one letter) followed by the letter "a". The "%", as we already know, means that any string of characters can follow afterwards.

```
SELECT *
FROM CUSTOMER
WHERE CUSTNAME LIKE '_a%';
```

The result would be:

CUSTNUM	CUSTNAME	SPNUM	HQCITY
0121	Main St. Hardware	137	New York
0839	Jane's Stores	186	Chicago

Notice that both the words "Main" and "Jane's" have "a" as their second letter. Also notice that, for example, customer number 2267 was not included in the result. Its name, "Central Stores", has an "a" in it but it is not the second letter of the name. Again, the single "_" character in the operator LIKE '_a%' specifies that there will be one character followed by "a". If the operator had been LIKE '%a%', then Central Stores would have been included in the result.

Filtering the Results of an SQL Query Two ways to modify the results of an SQL SELECT command are by the use of **DISTINCT** and the use of **ORDER BY**. It is important to remember that these two devices do not affect what data is retrieved from the database but rather how the data is presented to the user.

DISTINCT There are circumstances in which the result of an SQL query may contain duplicate items and this duplication is undesirable. Consider the following query:

> "Which cities serve as headquarters cities for General Hardware customers?"

This could be taken as a simple relational Project that takes the HQCITY column of the CUSTOMER table as its result. The SQL command would be:

```
SELECT HQCITY
FROM CUSTOMER;
```

which results in:

HQCITY
New York
Chicago
Los Angeles
Los Angeles
Atlanta
Washington
New York
New York
New York

Technically, this is the correct result, but why is it necessary to list New York four times or Los Angeles twice? Not only is it unnecessary to list them more than once, but doing so produces unacceptable clutter. Based on the way the query was stated, the result should have each city listed once. The DISTINCT operator is used to eliminate duplicate rows in a query result. Reformulating the SELECT statement as:

```
SELECT DISTINCT HQCITY
FROM CUSTOMER;
```

results in:

HQCITY

New York
Chicago
Los Angeles
Atlanta
Washington

ORDER BY   The ORDER BY clause simply takes the results of an SQL query and orders them by one or more specified attributes. Consider the following query:

> "Find the customer numbers, customer names, and headquarters cities of those customers with customer numbers greater than 1000. List the results in alphabetic order by headquarters cities."

```
SELECT CUSTNUM, CUSTNAME, HQCITY
FROM CUSTOMER
WHERE CUSTNUM>1000
ORDER BY HQCITY;
```

This results in:

CUSTNUM	CUSTNAME	HQCITY
1525	Fred's Tool Stores	Atlanta
1047	Acme Hardware Store	Los Angeles
1826	City Hardware	New York
2198	Western Hardware	New York
2267	Central Stores	New York
1700	XYZ Stores	Washington

If you wanted to have the customer names *within the same city* alphabetized, you would write:

```
SELECT CUSTNUM, CUSTNAME, HQCITY
FROM CUSTOMER
WHERE CUSTNUM>1000
ORDER BY HQCITY, CUSTNAME;
```

This results in:

CUSTNUM	CUSTNAME	HQCITY
1525	Fred's Tool Stores	Atlanta
1047	Acme Hardware Store	Los Angeles
2267	Central Stores	New York
1826	City Hardware	New York
2198	Western Hardware	New York
1700	XYZ Stores	Washington

The default order for ORDER BY is ascending. The clause can include the term ASC at the end to make ascending explicit or it can include DESC for descending order.

Built-In Functions

A number of so-called "**built-in functions**" give the SQL SELECT command additional capabilities. They involve the ability to perform calculations based on attribute values or to count the number of rows that satisfy stated criteria.

AVG and SUM   Recall that the SALES table shows the lifetime quantity of particular products sold by particular salespersons. For example, the first row indicates that Salesperson 137 has sold 473 units of Product Number 19440 dating back to when she joined the company or when the product was introduced. Consider the following query:

> "Find the average number of units of the different products that Salesperson 137 has sold (i.e. the average of the quantity values in the first three records of the SALES table)."

Using the AVG operator, you would write:

```
SELECT AVG(QUANTITY)
FROM SALES
WHERE SPNUM=137;
```

and the result would be:

AVG(QUANTITY)

443.67

To find the total number of units of all products that she has sold, you would use the SUM operator and write:

```
SELECT SUM(QUANTITY)
FROM SALES
WHERE SPNUM=137;
```

and the result would be:

SUM(QUANTITY)

1331

MIN and MAX   You can also find the minimum or maximum of a set of attribute values. Consider the following query:

> "What is the largest number of units of Product Number 21765 that any individual salesperson has sold?"

Using the MAX operator, you would write:

```
SELECT MAX(QUANTITY)
FROM SALES
WHERE PRODNUM=21765;
```

and the result would be:

MAX(QUANTITY)

      3110

To find the smallest number of units you simply replace MAX with MIN:

```
SELECT MIN(QUANTITY)
FROM SALES
WHERE PRODNUM=21765;
```

and get:

MIN(QUANTITY)

      809

COUNT   COUNT is a very useful operator that counts the number of rows that sat-isfy a set of criteria. It is often used in the context of "how many of something" meet some stated conditions. Consider the following query:

"How many salespersons have sold Product Number 21765?"

Remember that each row of the SALES table describes the history of a particular salesperson selling a particular product. That is, each combination of SPNUM and PRODNUM is unique; there can only be one row that involves a particular SPNUM/PRODNUM combination. If you can count the number of rows of that table that involve Product Number 21765, then you know how many salespersons have a history of selling it. Using the notational device COUNT(*), the SELECT statement is:

```
SELECT COUNT(*)
FROM SALES
WHERE PRODNUM=21765;
```

and the answer is:

COUNT(*)

3

Don't get confused by the difference between SUM and COUNT. As we demon-strated above, SUM adds up a set of attribute values; COUNT counts the number of rows of a table that satisfy a set of stated criteria.

Grouping Rows

Using the built-in functions, we were able to calculate results based on attribute values in several rows of a table. In effect, we formed a *single* "group" of rows and performed some calculation on their attribute values. There are many situations that require such calculations to be made on *several different groups* of rows. This is a job for the **GROUP BY** clause.

GROUP BY   A little earlier we found the total number of units of all products that one particular salesperson has sold. It seems reasonable that at some point we might want to find the total number of units of all products that *each* salesperson has sold. That is, we want to *group together* the rows of the SALES table that belong to *each* salesperson and calculate a value—the sum of the Quantity attribute values in this case—for each such group. Here is how such a query might be stated:

"Find the total number of units of all products sold by each salesperson."

The SQL statement, using the GROUP BY clause, would look like this:

```
SELECT SPNUM, SUM(QUANTITY)
FROM SALES
GROUP BY SPNUM;
```

and the results would be:

SPNUM	SUM(QUANTITY)
137	1331
186	9307
204	1543
361	9577

Notice that GROUP BY SPNUM specifies that the rows of the table are to be grouped together based on having the same value in their SPNUM attribute. All the rows for Salesperson Number 137 will form one group, all of the rows for Salesperson Number 186 will form another group, and so on. The Quantity attribute values in each group will then be summed—SUM(QUANTITY)—and the results returned to the user. But it is not enough to provide a list of sums:

1331
9307
1543
9577

These are indeed the sums of the quantities for each salesperson. But, without identifying which salesperson goes with which sum, they are meaningless! That's why the SELECT clause includes both the SPNUM and the SUM(QUANTITY). Including the attribute(s) specified in the GROUP BY clause in the SELECT clause allows you to properly identify the sums calculated for each group.

An SQL statement with a GROUP BY clause may certainly also include a WHERE clause. Thus, the query:

> "Find the total number of units of all products sold by each salesperson whose salesperson number is at least 150."

would look like:

```
SELECT SPNUM, SUM(QUANTITY)
FROM SALES
WHERE SPNUM>=150
GROUP BY SPNUM;
```

and the results would be:

SPNUM	SUM(QUANTITY)
186	9307
204	1543
361	9577

HAVING   Sometimes there is a need to limit the results of a GROUP BY based on the values calculated for each group with the built-in functions. For example, take the last query above,

> "Find the total number of units of all products sold by each salesperson whose salesperson number is at least 150."

Now modify it with an additional sentence so that it reads:

> "Find the total number of units of all products sold by each salesperson whose salesperson number is at least 150. Include only salespersons whose total number of units sold is at least 5000."

This would be accomplished by adding a **HAVING** clause to the end of the SELECT statement:

```
SELECT SPNUM, SUM(QUANTITY)
FROM SALES
WHERE SPNUM>=150
GROUP BY SPNUM
HAVING SUM(QUANTITY)>=5000;
```

and the results would be:

SPNUM	SUM(QUANTITY)
186	9307
361	9577

with Salesperson Number 204, with a total of only 1543 units sold, dropping out of the results.

Notice that in this last SELECT statement, there are two limitations: One, that the Salesperson Number must be at least 150, appears in the WHERE clause and the other, that the sum of the number of units sold must be at least 5000, appears in the HAVING clause. It is important to understand why this is so. If the limitation is based on *individual attribute values* that appear in the database, then the condition goes in the WHERE clause. This is the case with the limitation based on the Salesperson Number value. If the limitation is based on *the group calculation performed with the built-in function*, then the condition goes in the HAVING clause. This is the case with the limitation based on the sum of the number of product units sold.

The Join

Up to this point, all the SELECT features we have looked at have been shown in the context of retrieving data from a single table. The time has come to look at how the SQL SELECT command can integrate data from two or more tables or "join" them. There are two specifications to make in the SELECT statement to make a join work. One is that the tables to be joined must be listed in the FROM clause. The other is that the join attributes in the tables being joined must be declared and matched to each other in the WHERE clause. And there is one more point. Since two or more tables are involved in a SELECT statement that involves a join, there is the possibility that the same attribute *name* can appear in more than one of the tables. When this happens, these attribute names must be "qualified" with a table name when used in the SELECT statement. All of this is best illustrated in an example.

Consider the following query, which we discussed earlier in this book:

"Find the name of the salesperson responsible for Customer Number 1525."

The SELECT statement to satisfy this query is:

```
SELECT SPNAME
FROM SALESPERSON, CUSTOMER
WHERE SALESPERSON.SPNUM=CUSTOMER.SPNUM
AND CUSTNUM=1525;
```

and the result is:

SPNAME

Carlyle

Let's take a careful look at this last SELECT statement. Notice that the two tables involved in the join, SALESPERSON and CUSTOMER, are listed in the FROM clause. Also notice that the first line of the WHERE clause:

SALESPERSON.SPNUM = CUSTOMER.SPNUM

links the two join attributes: the SPNUM attribute of the SALESPERSON table (SALESPERSON.SPNUM) and the SPNUM attribute of the CUSTOMER table (CUSTOMER.SPNUM). The notational device of having the table name "." the attribute name is known as "qualifying" the attribute name. As we said earlier, this qualification is necessary when the same attribute name is used in two or more tables in a SELECT statement. By the way, notice in the SELECT statement that the attributes SPNAME and CUSTNUM don't have to be qualified because each appears in only one of the tables included in the SELECT statement.

Here is an example of a join involving three tables, assuming for the moment that salesperson names are unique:

> "List the *names* of the products of which salesperson Adams has sold more than 2000 units."

The salesperson name data appears only in the SALESPERSON table and the product name data appears only in the PRODUCT table. The SALES table shows the linkage between the two, including the quantities sold. And so the SELECT statement will be:

```
SELECT PRODNAME
FROM SALESPERSON, PRODUCT, SALES
WHERE SALESPERSON.SPNUM=SALES.SPNUM
AND SALES.PRODNUM=PRODUCT.PRODNUM
AND SPNAME='Adams'
AND QUANTITY>2000;
```

which results in:

PRODNAME

Hammer
Saw

Your Turn

4.1 Queries Galore!

Having a relational database to query in any business environment opens up a new world of information for managers to use to help them run their portion of the business.

Question:

Think about a business environment that you are familiar with from your daily life. It might be a university, a supermarket, a department store, even a sports league. Write a list of ten questions that you would like to be able to ask that would enhance your interaction with that environment. Is it reasonable that a database could be constructed that would support your ability to ask the questions you've come up with? Do you think that you would be able to formulate your questions using SQL? Explain.

Subqueries

A variation on the way that the SELECT statement works is when one SELECT statement is "nested" within another in a format known as a subquery. This can go on through several levels of SELECT statements, with each successive SELECT statement contained in a pair of parentheses. The execution rule is that the innermost SELECT statement is executed first and its results are then provided as input to the SELECT statement at the next level up. This procedure can be an alternative to the join.

Furthermore, there are certain circumstances in which this procedure *must* be used. These latter circumstances are common enough and important enough to include in this treatment of the SQL SELECT command.

Subqueries as Alternatives to Joins   Let's reconsider the first join example given above:

"Find the name of the salesperson responsible for Customer Number 1525."

If you methodically weave through the database tables to solve this, as we discussed earlier in the book, you start at the CUSTOMER table, find the record for Customer Number 1525 and discover in that record that the salesperson responsible for this customer is Salesperson Number 361. You then take that information to the SALES-PERSON table where you look up the record for Salesperson Number 361 and discover in it that the salesperson's name is Carlyle. Using a subquery, this logic can be built into an SQL statement as:

```
SELECT SPNAME
FROM SALESPERSON
WHERE SPNUM=
   (SELECT SPNUM
    FROM CUSTOMER
    WHERE CUSTNUM=1525);
```

and the result will again be:

SPNAME

Carlyle

Follow the way that the description given above of methodically solving the problem is reconstructed as a SELECT statement with a subquery. Since the inner-most SELECT (the indented one), which constitutes the subquery, is considered first, the CUSTOMER table is queried first, the record for Customer Number 1525 is found and 361 is returned as the SPNUM result. How do we know that only one salesperson number will be found as the result of the query? Because CUSTNUM is a *unique attribute*, Customer Number 1525 can only appear in one record and that one record only has room for one salesperson number! Moving along, Salesperson Number 361 is then fed to the outer SELECT statement. This, in effect, makes the main query, that is the outer SELECT, look like:

```
SELECT SPNAME
FROM SALESPERSON
WHERE SPNUM=361;
```

and this results in:

SPNAME

Carlyle

Notice, by the way, that in the SELECT statement, there is only one semicolon at the end of the entire statement, including the subquery.

When a Subquery is Required There is a very interesting circumstance in which a subquery is *required*. This situation is best explained with an example up front. Consider the following query:

> "Which salespersons with salesperson numbers greater than 200 have the lowest commission percentage?" (We'll identify salespersons by their salesperson number.)

This seems like a perfectly reasonable request, and yet it turns out to be deceptively difficult. The reason is that the query really has two very different parts. First, the system has to determine what the lowest commission percentage is for salespersons with salesperson numbers greater than 200. Then, it has to see which of these salespersons has that lowest percentage. It's really tempting to try to satisfy this type of query with an SQL SELECT statement like:

```
SELECT SPNUM, MIN(COMMPERCT)
FROM SALESPERSON
WHERE SPNUM>200;
```

or, perhaps:

```
SELECT SPNUM
FROM SALESPERSON
WHERE SPNUM>200
AND COMMPERCT=MIN(COMMPERCT);
```

But these *will not work*! It's like asking SQL to perform two separate operations and somehow apply one to the other in the correct sequence. This turns out to be asking too much. But there is a way to do it and it involves subqueries. In fact, what we will do is ask the system to determine the minimum commission percentage *first*, in a subquery, and then use that information in the main query to determine which salespersons have it:

```
SELECT SPNUM
FROM SALESPERSON
WHERE SPNUM>200
AND COMMPERCT=
    (SELECT MIN(COMMPERCT)
     FROM SALESPERSON)
     WHERE SPNUM>200);
```

which results in:

SPNUM

204

The minimum commission percentage across all of the salespersons with salesperson numbers greater than 200 is determined *first* in the subquery and the result is 10. The main query then, in effect, looks like:

```
SELECT SPNUM
FROM SALESPERSON
WHERE SPNUM>200
AND COMMPERCT=10;
```

which yields the result of salesperson number 204, as shown.

Actually, this is a very interesting example of a required subquery. What makes it really interesting is why the predicate, SPNUM>200, appears in *both* the main query *and* the subquery. Clearly it has to be in the subquery because you must first find the lowest commission percentage among the salespersons with salesperson numbers greater than 200. But then why does it have to be in the main query, too? The answer is that the only thing that the subquery returns to the main query is a single number, specifically a commission percentage. *No memory is passed on to the main query of how the subquery arrived at that value.* If you remove SPNUM>200 from the main query, so that it now looks like:

```
SELECT SPNUM
FROM SALESPERSON
WHERE COMMPERCT=
   (SELECT MIN(COMMPERCT)
    FROM SALESPERSON)
    WHERE SPNUM>200);
```

you would find every salesperson *with any salesperson number* whose commission percentage is equal to the lowest commission percentage of the salespersons with salesperson numbers greater than 20. (Of course, if for some reason you *do want* to find all of the salespersons, regardless of salesperson number, who have the same commission percentage as the salesperson who has the lowest commission percentage of the salespersons with salesperson numbers greater than 20, then this last SELECT statement is exactly what you should write!)

A Strategy for Writing SQL SELECT Commands

Before we go on to some more examples, it will be helpful to think about developing a strategy for writing SQL SELECT statements. The following is an ordered list of steps:

1. Determine what the result of the query is to be and write the needed attributes and functions in the SELECT clause. This may seem an obvious instruction, but it will really pay to think this through carefully before going on. In fact, it is at this very first step that you must determine whether the query will require a GROUP BY clause or a subquery. If either of these is required, you should start outlining the overall SELECT statement by writing the GROUP BY clause or the nested SELECT for the subquery further down the page (or screen).
2. Determine which tables of the database will be needed for the query and write their names in the FROM clause. Include only those tables that are really necessary for the query. Sometime this can be tricky. For example, you might need an attribute that is the primary key of a table and you might be tempted immediately to include that table in the FROM clause. However, it could be that the attribute in question is a foreign key in another table that is *already* in the FROM clause for other reasons. It is then unnecessary to include the table in which it is the primary key unless, of course, other attributes from that table are needed, too.
3. Begin constructing the WHERE clause by equating the join attributes from the tables that are in the FROM clause. Once this job is out of the way, you can begin considering the row limitations that must be stated in the WHERE clause.

4. Continue filling in the details of the WHERE clause, the GROUP BY clause, and any subqueries.

One final piece of advice: If you are new to writing SQL SELECT commands but you have a programming background, you may be tempted to avoid setting up joins and try writing subqueries instead. Resist this temptation, for two reasons! One is that joins are an essential part of the relational database concept. Embrace them; don't be afraid of them. The other is that writing multiple levels of nested subqueries can be extremely error prone and difficult to debug.

Example: Good Reading Book Stores

The best way to gain confidence in understanding SQL SELECT statements is to write some! And there are some further refinements of the SQL SELECT that we have yet to present. We will use the same three example databases that appeared in previous chapters but, as with the General Hardware database, we will shorten the attribute names. We will state a variety of queries and then give the SELECT statements that will satisfy them, plus commentary as appropriate. You should try to write the SELECT statements yourself before looking at our solutions!

Figure 4.2 is the Good Reading Bookstores relational database. Here is a list of queries for Good Reading Bookstores.

PUBLISHER table				
PUBNAME	CITY	COUNTRY	TELEPHONE	YRFOUND

AUTHOR table			
AUTHORNUM	AUTHORNAME	YEARBORN	YEARDIED

BOOK table				
BOOKNUM	BOOKNAME	PUBYEAR	PAGES	PUBNAME

CUSTOMER table					
CUSTNUM	CUSTNAME	STREET	CITY	STATE	COUNTRY

WRITING table	
BOOKNUM	AUTHORNUM

SALE table				
BOOKNUM	CUSTNUM	DATE	PRICE	QUANTITY

FIGURE 4.2 Good reading Bookstores Relational database

1. "Find the book number, book name, and number of pages of all the books published by London Publishing Ltd. List the results in order by book name."

   This query obviously requires the PUBNAME attribute but it *does not* require the PUBLISHER table. All of the information needed is in the BOOK table, including the PUBNAME attribute, which is there as a foreign key. The SELECT statement is:

   ```
   SELECT BOOKNUM, BOOKNAME, PAGES
   FROM BOOK
   WHERE PUBNAME='London Publishing Ltd.'
   ORDER BY BOOKNAME;
   ```

2. "How many books of at least 400 pages does Good Reading Bookstores carry that were published by publishers based in Paris, France?"

   This is a straightforward join between the PUBLISHER and BOOK tables that uses the built-in function COUNT. All of the attribute names are unique between the two tables, except for PUBNAME, which must be qualified with a table name every time it is used. Notice that "Good Reading Bookstores" does not appear as a condition in the SELECT statement, although it was mentioned in the query. The entire database is about Good Reading Bookstores and no other! There is no BOOKSTORE CHAIN table in the database and there is no STORENAME or CHAINNAME attribute in any of the tables.

   ```
   SELECT COUNT(*)
   FROM PUBLISHER, BOOK
   WHERE PUBLISHER.PUBNAME=BOOK.PUBNAME
   AND CITY='Paris'
   AND COUNTRY='France'
   AND PAGES>=400;
   ```

3. "List the publishers in Belgium, Brazil, and Singapore that publish books written by authors who were born before 1920."

   Sometimes a relatively simple-sounding query can be fairly involved. This query actually requires four tables of the database! To begin with, we need the PUBLISHER table because that's the only place that a publisher's country is stored. But we also need the AUTHOR table because that's where author birth years are stored. The only way to tie the PUBLISHER table to the AUTHOR table is to connect PUBLISHER to BOOK, then to connect BOOK to WRITING, and finally to connect WRITING to AUTHOR. With simple, one-attribute keys such as those in these tables, the number of joins will be one fewer than the number of tables. The FROM clause below shows four tables and the first three lines of the WHERE clause show the three joins. Also, notice that since a publisher may have published more than one book with the stated specifications, DISTINCT is required to prevent the same publisher name from appearing several, perhaps many, times in the result. Finally, since we want to include publishers in three specific countries, we list the three countries as Belgium,

Brazil, *and* Singapore. But, in the SELECT statement, we have to indicate that for a record to be included in the result, the value of the COUNTRY attribute must be Belgium, Brazil, *or* Singapore.

```
SELECT DISTINCT PUBLISHER.PUBNAME
FROM PUBLISHER, BOOK, WRITING, AUTHOR
WHERE PUBLISHER.PUBNAME=BOOK.PUBNAME
AND BOOK.BOOKNUM=WRITING.BOOKNUM
AND WRITING.AUTHORNUM=AUTHOR.AUTHORNUM
AND COUNTRY IN ('Belgium', 'Brazil', 'Singapore')
AND YEARBORN < 1920;
```

4. "How many books did each publisher in Oslo, Norway; Nairobi, Kenya; and Auckland, New Zealand, publish in 2001?"

The keyword here is "each." This query requires a separate total for each publisher that satisfies the conditions. This is a job for the GROUP BY clause. We want to group together the records for each publisher and count the number of records in each group. Each line of the result must include both a publisher name and count of the number of records that satisfy the conditions. This SELECT statement requires both a join and a GROUP BY. Notice the seeming complexity but really the unambiguous beauty of the ANDs and ORs structure regarding the cities and countries.

```
SELECT PUBLISHER.PUBNAME, CITY, COUNTRY, COUNT(*)
FROM PUBLISHER, BOOK
WHERE PUBLISHER.PUBNAME=BOOK.PUBNAME
AND ((CITY='Oslo' AND COUNTRY='Norway')
     OR (CITY='Nairobi' AND COUNTRY='Kenya')
     OR (CITY='Auckland' AND COUNTRY='New Zealand'))
AND PUBYEAR=2001
GROUP BY PUBLISHER.PUBNAME;
```

5. "Which publisher published the book that has the earliest publication year among all the books that Good Reading Bookstores carries?"

All that is called for in this query is the name of the publisher, not the name of the book. This is a case that requires a subquery. First the system has to determine the earliest publication year, then it has to see which books have that earliest publication year. Once you know the books, their records in the BOOK table give you the publisher names. Since more than one publisher may have published a book in that earliest year, there could be more than one publisher name in the result. And, since a particular publisher could have published more than one book in that earliest year, DISTINCT is required to avoid having that publisher's name listed more than once.

```
SELECT DISTINCT PUBNAME
FROM BOOK
WHERE PUBYEAR=
   (SELECT MIN(PUBYEAR)
    FROM BOOK);
```

Example: World Music Association

Figure 4.3 is the World Music Association relational database. Here is a list of queries for the World Music Association.

1. "What is the total annual salary cost for all the violinists in the Berlin Symphony Orchestra?"

```
SELECT SUM(ANNSALARY)
FROM MUSICIAN
WHERE ORCHNAME='Berlin Symphony Orchestra'
AND INSTRUMENT='Violin';
```

2. "Make a single list, in alphabetic order, of all of the universities attended by the cellists in India."

```
SELECT DISTINCT UNIVERSITY
FROM ORCHESTRA, MUSICIAN, DEGREE
WHERE ORCHESTRA.ORCHNAME=MUSICIAN.ORCHNAME
AND MUSICIAN.MUSNUM=DEGREE.MUSNUM
AND INSTRUMENT='Cello'
AND COUNTRY='India'
ORDER BY UNIVERSITY;
```

ORCHESTRA table			
ORCHNAME	CITY	COUNTRY	MUSICDIR

MUSICIAN table				
MUSNUM	MUSNAME	INSTRUMENT	ANNSALARY	ORCHNAME

DEGREE table			
MUSNUM	DEGREE	UNIVERSITY	YEAR

COMPOSER table		
COMPOSERNAME	COUNTRY	DATEBIRTH

COMPOSITION table		
COMPOSITIONNAME	COMPOSERNAME	YEAR

RECORDING table				
ORCHNAME	COMPOSITIONNAME	COMPOSERNAME	YEAR	PRICE

FIGURE 4.3 World Music Association relational database

3. "What is the total annual salary cost for all of the violinists of each orchestra in Canada? Include in the result only those orchestras whose total annual salary for its violinists is in excess of $150,000."

   Since this query requires a separate total for *each* orchestra, the SELECT statement must rely on the GROUP BY clause. Since the condition that the total must be over 150,000 is based on figures calculated by the SUM built-in function, it must be placed in a HAVING clause rather than in the WHERE clause.

```
SELECT ORCHESTRA.ORCHNAME, SUM(ANNSALARY)
FROM ORCHESTRA, MUSICIAN
WHERE ORCHESTRA.ORCHNAME=MUSICIAN.ORCHNAME
AND COUNTRY='Canada'
AND INSTRUMENT='Violin'
GROUP BY ORCHESTRA.ORCHNAME
HAVING SUM(ANNSALARY)>150000;
```

4. "What is the name of the most highly paid pianist?"

   It should be clear that a subquery is required. First the system has to determine what the top salary of pianists is and then it has to find out which pianists have that salary.

```
SELECT MUSNAME
FROM MUSICIAN
WHERE INSTRUMENT='Piano'
AND ANNSALARY=
   (SELECT MAX(ANNSALARY)
    FROM MUSICIAN
    WHERE INSTRUMENT='Piano');
```

This is another example in which a predicate, INSTRUMENT='Piano' in this case, appears in *both* the main query *and* the subquery. Clearly it has to be in the subquery because you must first find out how much money the highest-paid pianist makes. But then why does it have to be in the main query, too? The answer is that the only thing that the subquery returns to the main query is a single number, specifically a salary value. *No memory is passed on to the main query of how the subquery arrived at that value.* If you remove INSTRUMENT='Piano' from the main query so that it now looks like:

```
SELECT MUSNAME
FROM MUSICIAN
WHERE ANNSALARY=
   (SELECT MAX(ANNSALARY)
    FROM MUSICIAN
    WHERE INSTRUMENT='Piano');
```

you would find every musician *who plays any instrument* whose salary is equal to *the highest- paid pianist.* Of course, if for some reason you *do want* to find all of the musicians, regardless of the instrument they play, who have the same salary as the highest-paid pianist, then this last SELECT statement is exactly what you should write.

5. "What is the name of the most highly paid pianist in any orchestra in Australia?"

This is the same idea as the last query but involves two tables, both of which must be joined in both the main query and the subquery. The reasoning for this is the same as in the last query. The salary of the most highly paid pianist in Australia must be determined first in the subquery. Then that result must be used in the main query, where it must be compared *only* to the salaries of Australian pianists.

```
SELECT MUSNAME
FROM MUSICIAN, ORCHESTRA
WHERE MUSICIAN.ORCHNAME=ORCHESTRA.ORCHNAME
AND INSTRUMENT='Piano'
AND COUNTRY='Australia'
AND ANNSALARY=
   (SELECT MAX(ANNSALARY)
    FROM MUSICIAN, ORCHESTRA
    WHERE MUSICIAN.ORCHNAME=ORCHESTRA.ORCHNAME
    AND INSTRUMENT='Piano'
    AND COUNTRY='Australia');
```

Example: Lucky Rent-A-Car

Figure 4.4 is the Lucky Rent-A-Car relational database. Here is a list of queries for Lucky Rent-A-Car.

1. "List the manufacturers whose names begin with the letter "C" or the letter "D" and that are located in Japan."

```
SELECT MANUFNAME
FROM MANUFACTURER
WHERE (MANUFNAME LIKE 'C%'
       OR MANUFNAME LIKE 'D%')
AND COUNTRY='Japan';
```

2. "What was the average mileage of the cars that had tune-ups in August, 2003?"

```
SELECT AVG(MILEAGE)
FROM MAINTENANCE
WHERE PROCEDURE='Tune-Up'
AND DATE BETWEEN 'AUG-01-2003' AND 'AUG-31-2003';
```

The exact format for specifying dates may differ among SQL processors and a given processor may have several options.

3. "How many different car models are made by manufacturers in Italy?"

This query will use an interesting combination of COUNT and DISTINCT that may not work in all SQL processors. In this case it literally counts the different models among the cars made in Italy. Since many different cars are of the same model, DISTINCT is needed to make sure that each model is counted just once.

MANUFACTURER table			
<u>MANUFNAME</u>	COUNTRY	SALESREPNAME	SALESREPPHONE

CAR table				
<u>CARNUM</u>	MODEL	YEAR	CLASS	<u>MANUFNAME</u>

MAINTENANCE table					
<u>REPAIRNUM</u>	<u>CARNUM</u>	DATE	PROCEDURE	MILEAGE	REPAIRTIME

CUSTOMER table			
<u>CUSTNUM</u>	CUSTNAME	CUSTADDR	CUSTPHONE

RENTAL table				
<u>CARNUM</u>	<u>CUSTNUM</u>	<u>RENTALDATE</u>	RETURNDATE	COST

FIGURE 4.4 Lucky Rent-A-Car relational database

```
SELECT COUNT(DISTINCT MODEL)
FROM MANUFACTURER, CAR
WHERE MANUFACTURER.MANUFNAME=CAR.MANUFNAME
AND COUNTRY='Italy';
```

4. "How many repairs were performed on each car manufactured by Superior Motors during the month of March, 2004? Include only cars in the result that had at least three repairs."

```
SELECT CAR.CARNUM, COUNT(*)
FROM CAR, MAINTENANCE
WHERE CAR.CARNUM=MAINTENANCE.CARNUM
AND MANUFNAME='Superior Motors'
AND DATE BETWEEN 'MAR-01-2004' AND 'MAR-31-2004'
GROUP BY CAR.CARNUM
HAVING COUNT(*)>=3;
```

5. "List the cars of any manufacturer that had an oil change in January, 2004, and had at least as many miles as the highest-mileage car manufactured by Superior Motors that had an oil change that same month."

```
SELECT MAINTENANCE.CARNUM
FROM MAINTENANCE
WHERE PROCEDURE='Oil Change'
AND DATE BETWEEN 'JAN-01-2004' AND 'JAN-31-2004'
AND MILEAGE>=
    (SELECT MAX(MILEAGE)
     FROM CAR, MAINTENANCE
     WHERE CAR.CARNUM = MAINTENANCE.CARNUM
     AND PROCEDURE='Oil Change'
     AND DATE BETWEEN 'JAN-01-2004' AND 'JAN-31-2004'
     AND MANUFNAME='Superior Motors');
```

Relational Query Optimizer

Relational DBMS Performance

An ever-present issue in data retrieval is performance: the speed with which the required data can be retrieved. In a typical relational database application environment, and as we've seen in the examples above, many queries require only one table. It is certainly reasonable to assume that such single-table queries using indexes, hashing, and the like, should, more or less, not take any longer in a relational database system environment than in any other kind of file management system. But, what about the queries that involve joins? Recall the detailed explanation of how data integration works earlier in the book that used the Salesperson and Customer tables as an example. These very small tables did not pose much of a performance issue, even if the join was carried out in the worst-case way, comparing every row of one table to every row of the other table, as was previously described. But what if we attempted to join a 1-million-row table with a 3-million-row table? How long do you think that would take—even on a large, fast computer? It might well take much longer than a person waiting for a response at a workstation would be willing to tolerate. This was actually one of the issues that caused the delay of almost ten years from the time the first article on relational database was published in 1970 until relational DBMSs were first offered commercially almost ten years later.

The performance issue in relational database management has been approached in two different ways. One, the tuning of the database structure, which is known as "physical database design," will be the subject of an entire chapter of this book, Chapter 8. It's that important. The other way that the relational database performance issue has been approached is through highly specialized software in the relational DBMS itself. This software, known as a **relational query optimizer**, is in effect an "expert system" that evaluates each SQL SELECT statement sent to the DBMS and determines an efficient way to satisfy it.

Relational Query Optimizer Concepts

All major SQL processors (meaning all major relational DBMSs) include a query optimizer. Using a query optimizer, SQL attempts to figure out the most efficient way of answering a query, before actually responding to it. Clearly, a query that involves only one table should be evaluated to take advantage of aids such as indexes on pertinent attributes. But, again, the most compelling and interesting reason for having a query optimizer in a relational database system is the goal of executing multiple-table data integration or join-type operations without having to go through the worst-case, very time-consuming, exhaustive row-comparison process. Exactly how a specific relational DBMS's query optimizer works is typically a closely held trade secret. Retrieval performance is one way in which the vendors of these products compete with one another. Nevertheless, there are some basic ideas that we can discuss here.

When an SQL query optimizer is presented with a new SELECT statement to evaluate, it seeks out information about the tables named in the FROM clause. This information includes:

- Which attributes of the tables have indexes built over them.
- Which attributes have unique values.
- How many rows each table has.

The query optimizer finds this information in a special internal database known as the "relational catalog," which will be described further in Chapter 10.

The query optimizer uses the information about the tables, together with the various components of the SELECT statement itself, to look for an efficient way to retrieve the data required by the query. For example, in the General Hardware Co. SELECT statement:

```
SELECT SPNUM, SPNAME
FROM SALESPERSON
WHERE COMMPERCT=10;
```

the query optimizer might check on whether the COMMPERCT attribute has an index built over it. If this attribute does have an index, the query optimizer might decide to use the index to find the rows with a commission percentage of 10. However, if the number of rows of the SALESPERSON table is small enough, the query optimizer might decide to read the entire table into main memory and scan it for the rows with a commission percentage of 10.

Another important decision that the query optimizer makes is how to satisfy a join. Consider the following General Hardware Co. example that we looked at above:

```
SELECT SPNAME
FROM SALESPERSON, CUSTOMER
WHERE SALESPERSON.SPNUM=CUSTOMER.SPNUM
AND CUSTNUM=1525;
```

In this case, the query optimizer should be able to recognize that since CUSTNUM is a unique attribute in the CUSTOMER table and only one customer number is specified in the SELECT statement, only a single record from the CUSTOMER table, the one for customer number 1525, will be involved in the join. Once it finds this CUSTOMER record (hopefully with an index), it can match the SPNUM value found in it against the SPNUM values in the SALESPERSON records looking for a match. If it is clever enough to recognize that SPNUM is a unique attribute in the SALESPERSON table, then all it has to do is find the single SALESPERSON record (hopefully with an index) that has that salesperson number and pull the salesperson name (SPNAME) out of it to satisfy the query. Thus, in this type of case, an exhaustive join can be completely avoided.

When a more extensive join operation can't be avoided, the query optimizer can choose from one of several join algorithms. The most basic, known as a Cartesian product, is accomplished algorithmically with a "**nested-loop join**." One of the two tables is selected for the "outer loop" and the other for the "inner loop." Each of the records of the outer loop is chosen in succession and, for each, the inner-loop table is scanned for matches on the join attribute. If the query optimizer can determine that only a subset of the rows of the outer or inner tables is needed, then only those rows need to be included in the **comparisons**.

A more efficient join algorithm than the nested-loop join, the "**merge-scan join**," can be used only if certain conditions are met. The principle is that for the merge-scan join to work, each of the two join attributes either must be in sorted order or must have an index built over it. An index, by definition, is in sorted order and so, one way or the other, each join attribute has a sense of order to it. If this condition is met, then comparing every record of one table to every record of the other table as in a nested-loop join is unnecessary. The system can simply start at the top of each table or index, as the case may be, and move downwards, without ever having to move upwards.

Summary

SQL has become the standard relational database management data definition and data manipulation language. Data retrieval in SQL is accomplished with the SELECT command. SELECT commands can be run in a direct query mode or embedded in higher-level language programs in an **embedded mode**. The SELECT command can be used to retrieve one or more rows of a table, one or more columns of a table, or particular columns of particular rows. There are built-in functions that can sum and average data, find the minimum and maximum values of a set of data, and count the number of rows that satisfy a condition. These built-in functions can also be applied to multiple subsets or groups of rows. The SELECT command can also integrate data by joining two or more tables. Subqueries can be developed for certain specific circumstances. There is a strategy for writing SQL commands successfully.

Performance is an important issue in the retrieval of data from relational databases. All relational database management systems have a relational query optimizer, which is software that looks for a good way to solve each relational query presented to it. While the ways that these query optimizers work are considered trade secrets, there are several standard concepts and techniques that they generally incorporate.

Key Terms

Access path

AND and OR

Base table

BETWEEN

Built-in functions

Comparisons

Data definition language (DDL)

Data manipulation language (DML)

Declarative

DISTINCT

Embedded mode

GROUP BY

HAVING

IN

LIKE

Merge-scan join

ORDER BY

Nested-loop join

Procedural

Query

Relational query optimizer

Search argument

SELECT

Structured Query Language (SQL)

Subquery

Questions

1. What are the four basic operations that can be performed on stored data?

2. What is Structured Query Language (SQL)?

3. Name several of the fundamental SQL commands and discuss the purpose of each.

4. What is the purpose of the SQL SELECT command?

5. How does the SQL SELECT command relate to the relational Select, Project, and Join concepts?

6. Explain the difference between running SQL in query mode and in embedded mode.

7. Describe the basic format of the SQL SELECT command.

8. In a general way, describe how to write an SQL SELECT command to accomplish a relational Select operation.

9. In a general way, describe how to write an SQL SELECT command to accomplish a relational Project operation.

10. In a general way, describe how to write an SQL SELECT command to accomplish a combination of a relational Select operation and a relational Project operation.

11. What is the purpose of the WHERE clause in SQL SELECT commands?

12. List and describe some of the common operators that can be used in the WHERE clause.

13. Describe the purpose of each of the following operators in the WHERE clause:
    a. AND
    b. OR
    c. BETWEEN
    d. IN
    e. LIKE

14. What is the purpose of the DISTINCT operator?

15. What is the purpose of the ORDER BY clause?

16. Name the five SQL built-in functions and describe the purpose of each.

17. Explain the difference between the SUM and COUNT built-in functions.

18. Describe the purpose of the GROUP BY clause. Why must the attribute in the GROUP BY clause also appear in the SELECT clause?

19. Describe the purpose of the HAVING clause. How do you decide whether to place a row-limiting predicate in the WHERE clause or in the HAVING clause?

20. How do you construct a Join operation in an SQL SELECT statement?

21. What is a subquery in an SQL SELECT statement?

22. Describe the circumstances in which a subquery *must* be used.

23. What is a relational query optimizer? Why are they important?

24. How do relational query optimizers work?

25. What information does a relational query optimizer use in making its decisions?

26. What are some of the ways that relational query optimizers can handle joins?

Exercises

1. Consider the following relational database that Best Airlines uses to keep track of its mechanics, their skills, and their airport locations. Mechanic number (MECHNUM), airport name (AIRNAME), and skill number are all unique fields. SIZE is an airport's size in acres. SKILLCAT is a skill category, such as an engine skill, wing skill, and tire skill. YEARQUAL is the year that a mechanic first qualified in a particular skill; PROFRATE is the mechanic's proficiency rating in a particular skill.

MECHANIC Table				
MECHNUM	MECHNAME	AGE	SALARY	AIRNAME

AIRPORT Table				
AIRNAME	CITY	STATE	SIZE	YEAROPENED

SKILL Table		
SKILLNUM	SKILLNAME	SKILLCAT

QUALIFICATION Table			
MECHNUM	SKILLNUM	YEARQUAL	PROFRATE

Write SQL SELECT commands to answer the following queries.

a. List the names and ages of all the mechanics.

b. List the airports in California that are at least 20 acres in size and have been open since 1935. Order the results from smallest to largest airport.

c. List the airports in California that are at least 20 acres in size or have been open since 1935.

d. Find the average size of the airports in California that have been open since 1935.

e. How many airports have been open in California since 1935?

f. How many airports have been open in each state since 1935?

g. How many airports have been open in each state since 1935? Include in your answer only those states that have at least five such airports.

h. List the names of the mechanics who work in California.

i. Fan blade replacement is the name of a skill. List the names of the mechanics who have a proficiency rating of 4 in fan blade replacement.

j. Fan blade replacement is the name of a skill. List the names of the mechanics who work in California who have a proficiency rating of 4 in fan blade replacement.

k. List the total, combined salaries of all of the mechanics who work in each city in California.

l. Find the largest of all of the airports.

m. Find the largest airport in California.

2. Consider the following relational database for the Quality Appliance Manufacturing Co. The database is designed to track the major appliances (refrigerators, washing machines, dishwashers, etc.) that Quality manufactures. It also records information about Quality's suppliers, the parts they supply, the buyers of the finished appliances, and the finished goods inspectors. Note the following facts about this environment:

- Suppliers are the companies that supply Quality with its major components, such as electric motors, for the appliances. Supplier number is a unique identifier.
- Parts are the major components that the suppliers supply to Quality. Each part comes with a part number but that part number is only unique within a supplier. Thus, from Quality's point of view, the unique identifier of a part is the combination of part number and supplier number.
- Each appliance that Quality manufactures is given an appliance number that is unique across all of the types of appliances that Quality makes.
- Buyers are major department stores, home improvement chains, and wholesalers. Buyer numbers are unique.
- An appliance may be inspected by several inspectors. There is clearly a many-to-many relationship among appliances and inspectors, as indicated by the INSPECTION table.
- There are one-to-many relationships between suppliers and parts (Supplier Number is a foreign key in the PART table), parts and appliances (Appliance Number is a foreign key in the PART table), and appliances and buyers (Buyer Number is a foreign key in the APPLIANCE table).

SUPPLIER Table

SUPPLIER NUM	SUPPLIER NAME	CITY	COUNTRY	PRESIDENT

PART Table

PARTNUM	SUPPLIER NUM	PARTTYPE	COST	APPLIANCE NUM

APPLIANCE Table

APPLIANCE NUM	APPLIANCE TYPE	DATE MANUF	BUYERNUM	PRICE

BUYER Table

BUYERNUM	BUYER NAME	CITY	COUNTRY	CREDIT RATING

INSPECTOR Table

INSPECTORNUM	INSPECTOR NAME	SALARY	DATEHIRE

INSPECTION Table

APPLIANCE NUM	INSPECTOR NUM	DATEINSPECTION	SCORE

Write SQL SELECT commands to answer the following queries.

a. List the names, in alphabetic order, of the suppliers located in London, Liverpool, and Manchester, UK.

b. List the names of the suppliers that supply motors (see PARTTYPE) costing between $50 and $100.

c. Find the average cost of the motors (see PARTTYPE) supplied by supplier number 3728.

d. List the names of the inspectors who were inspecting refrigerators (see APPLIANCETYPE) on April 17, 2011.

e. What was the highest inspection score achieved by a refrigerator on November 3, 2011?

f. Find the total amount of money spent on Quality Appliance products by each buyer from Mexico, Venezuela, and Argentina.

g. Find the total cost of the parts used in each dishwasher manufactured on February 28, 2010. Only include in the results those dishwashers that used at least $200 in parts.

h. List the highest paid inspectors.

i. List the highest paid inspectors who were hired in 2009.

j. Among all of the inspectors, list those who earn more than the highest-paid inspector who was hired in 2009.

Minicases

1. Consider the following relational database for Happy Cruise Lines. It keeps track of ships, cruises, ports, and passengers. A "cruise" is a particular sailing of a ship on a particular date. For example, the seven-day journey of the ship Pride of Tampa that leaves on June 13, 2011, is a cruise. Note the following facts about this environment.

   - Both ship number and ship name are unique in the SHIP Table.

   - A ship goes on many cruises over time. A cruise is associated with a single ship.

   - A port is identified by the combination of port name and country.

   - As indicated by the VISIT Table, a cruise includes visits to several ports and a port is typically included in several cruises.

   - Both Passenger Number and Social Security Number are unique in the PASSENGER Table. A particular person has a single Passenger Number that is used for all the cruises she takes.

   - The VOYAGE Table indicates that a person can take many cruises and a cruise, of course, has many passengers.

SHIP Table				
SHIPNUM	SHIPNAME	BUILDER	LAUNCH DATE	WEIGHT

CRUISE Table				
CRUISE NUM	STARTDATE	ENDDATE	DIRECTOR	SHIPNUM

PORT Table			
PORTNAME	COUNTRY	NUMDOCKS	MANAGER

VISIT Table				
CRUISE NUM	PORTNAME	COUNTRY	ARRDATE	DEPDATE

PASSENGER Table				
PASSENGER NUM	PASSENGER NAME	SOCSEC NUM	STATE	COUNTRY

VOYAGE Table			
PASSENGERNUM	CRUISENUM	ROOMNUM	FARE

Write SQL SELECT commands to answer the following queries.

   a. Find the start and end dates of cruise number 35218.

   b. List the names and ship numbers of the ships built by the Ace Shipbuilding Corp. that weigh more than 60,000 tons.

   c. List the companies that have built ships for Happy Cruise Lines.

   d. Find the total number of docks in all the ports in Canada.

   e. Find the average weight of the ships built by the Ace Shipbuilding Corp. that have been launched since 2000.

   f. How many ports in Venezuela have at least three docks?

   g. Find the total number of docks in each country. List the results in order from most to least.

   h. Find the total number of ports in each country.

   i. Find the total number of docks in each country but include only those countries that have at least twelve docks in your answer.

   j. Find the name of the ship that operated on (was used on) cruise number 35218.

   k. List the names, states and countries of the passengers who sailed on The Spirit of Nashville on cruises that began during July, 2011.

   l. Find the names of the company's heaviest ships.

   m. Find the names of the company's heaviest ships that began a cruise between July 15, 2011 and July 31, 2011.

2. Consider the following relational database for the Super Baseball League. It keeps track of teams in the league, coaches and players on the teams,

work experience of the coaches, bats belonging to each team, and which players have played on which teams. Note the following facts about this environment:

- The database keeps track of the history of all the teams that each player has played on and all the players who have played on each team.
- The database only keeps track of the current team that a coach works for.
- Team number, team name, and player number are each unique attributes across the league.
- Coach name is unique only within a team (and we assume that a team cannot have two coaches of the same name).
- Serial number (for bats) is unique only within a team.
- In the Affiliation table, the Years attribute indicates the number of years that a player played on a team; the batting average is for the years that a player played on a team.

TEAM Table			
TEAMNUM	TEAMNAME	CITY	MANAGER

COACH Table		
TEAMNUM	COACHNAME	ADDRESS

WORK EXPERIENCE Table			
TEAMNUM	COACHNAME	EXPERIENCE TYPE	YEARS EXPERIENCE

BATS Table		
TEAMNUM	SERIALNUM	MANUFACTURER

PLAYER Table		
PLAYERNUM	PLAYERNAME	AGE

AFFILIATION Table			
PLAYERNUM	TEAMNUM	YEARS	BATTINGAVG

Write SQL SELECT commands to answer the following queries.

a. Find the names and cities of all of the teams with team numbers greater than 15. List the results alphabetically by team name.

b. List all of the coaches whose last names begin with "D" and who have between 5 and 10 years of experience as college coaches (see YEARSEXPERIENCE and EXPERIENCETYPE).

c. Find the total number of years of experience of Coach Taylor on team number 23.

d. Find the number of different types of experience that Coach Taylor on team number 23 has.

e. Find the total number of years of experience of each coach on team number 23.

f. How many different manufacturers make bats for the league's teams?

g. Assume that team names are unique. Find the names of the players who have played for the Dodgers for at least five years (see YEARS in the AFFILIATION Table).

h. Assume that team names are unique. Find the total number of years of work experience of each coach on the Dodgers, but include in the result only those coaches who have more than eight years of experience.

i. Find the names of the league's youngest players.

j. Find the names of the league's youngest players whose last names begin with the letter "B".

The Relational Database Model: Introduction

In 1970, Dr. Edgar F. (Ted) Codd of IBM published in *Communications of the ACM* a paper entitled "A Relational Model of Data for Large Shared Data Banks." This paper marked the beginning of the field of relational databases. During the 1970s, the relational approach to databases progressed from being a technical curiosity to a subject of serious interest in the information systems community. But it was not until the early 1980s that commercially viable relational database management systems became available. There were two basic reasons for this. One was that, while the relational database was very tempting in concept, its application in a real-world environment was elusive for performance-related reasons. The second reason was that at exactly the time that Codd's paper was published, the earlier hierarchical and network database management systems were just coming onto the commercial scene and were the focus of intense marketing efforts by the software and hardware vendors of the day. Eventually, both of these obstacles were overcome and the **relational model** became and remains the database model of choice.

OBJECTIVES

Explain why the relational database model became practical in about 1980.

Define such basic relational database terms as relation and tuple.

Describe the major types of keys including primary, candidate, and foreign.

Describe how one-to-one, one-to-many, and many-to-many binary relationships are implemented in a relational database.

Describe how relational data retrieval is accomplished using the relational algebra select, project, and join operators.

Understand how the join operator facilitates data integration in relational database.

Introduction

Several factors converged in the early 1980s to begin turning the tide toward relational database. One was that the performance issues that held back its adoption in the 1970s began to be resolved. Another was that, after a decade of use of hierarchical and network database management systems, information systems professionals were interested in an alternative that would move toward simplifying the database design process and produce database structures that were easier to use and understand at all levels. Also, at this time there was increasing interest in a DBMS environment that would allow easier, more intuitive access to the data by an increasingly broad range of personnel. Finally, the early 1980s saw the advent of the **personal computer**. As software developers began trying to create all manner of applications and supporting software utilities for the PC, it quickly became clear that the existing hierarchical and network database approaches would not work in the PC environment, for two reasons. One was that these DBMSs were simply too large to store and use on the early PCs. The other was that they were too complex to be used by the very broad array of non-information-systems professionals at whom the PCs were targeted.

Today, the relational approach to database management is by far the primary database management approach used in all levels of information systems and for most application purposes, from accounting to banking to manufacturing to sales on the World Wide Web. Relational database management is represented today by such products as Microsoft Access and SQL Server, Oracle, Sybase, and IBM's DB2 and Informix. While these and other relational database systems differ in their features and implementations, they all share a common data structure philosophy and a common data access tool: Structured Query Language (SQL) (often pronounced "sequel"). This chapter will focus on the basic concepts of how data is stored and retrieved in a relational database by a relational DBMS. Chapter 6 will discuss some additional relational database concepts. Then, Chapter 7 will describe logical database design and Chapter 8 will go into physical database design.

The Relational Database Concept

Relational Terminology

In spite of the apparent conflict between non-redundant, linear file data storage and data integration demonstrated in Chapter 3, the relative simplicity of simple, linear files or structures that resemble them in a true database environment is very desirable. After all, the linear file arrangement is the most basic and commonly used data structure there is. This is precisely one of the advantages of relational database management.

To begin with, consider the data structure used in relational databases. In a relational database, the data *appears* to be stored in what we have been referring to as simple, linear files. Following the conventions of the area of mathematics on which relational database is based, we will begin calling those simple linear files **relations**, although in common practice they are also referred to as "tables." In the terminology of files, each **row** is called a "record," while in a relation, each row is called a **tuple**. In files, each **column** is called a "field," while in a relation each column is called an **attribute**. In practice, in speaking about relational database, people commonly use the terms relation, table, and file synonymously. Similarly, tuple, row, and record are often used synonymously, as are attribute, column, and field, Figure 5.1. We will use

Attribute
(or Column or Field) ↓   **Relation (or Table or File)**

Student Number	Student Name	Class	Major
03657	Robert Shaw	Senior	Biology
05114	Gloria Stuart	Freshman	English
05950	Fred Simpson	Junior	Mathematics
12746	W. Shin	Junior	English
15887	Pedro Marcos	Senior	History
19462	H. Yamato	Sophomore	French
21682	Mary Jones	Freshman	Chemistry
24276	Steven Baker	Sophomore	History

Tuple
(or Row or Record)

FIGURE 5.1 Relational database terminology

an appropriate term in each particular situation during our discussion. In particular, we will use the term "relation" in this chapter and the next, in which we are talking about relational database concepts. Following common usage, we will generally use the word "table" in the more applied parts of the book, such as in the corporate database stories in each chapter and in the discussion of SQL in Chapter 4.

It is important to note that there are technical differences between the concept of a file and the concept of a relation (which is why we say that in a relational database the data only *appears* to be stored in structures that look like files). The differences include:

- The columns of a relation can be arranged in any order without affecting the meaning of the data. This is not true of a file.
- Similarly, the rows of a relation can be arranged in any order, which is not true of a file.
- Every row/column position, sometimes referred to as a "**cell**," can have only a single value, which is not necessarily true in a file.
- No two rows of a relation are identical, which is not necessarily true in a file.

A relational database is simply a collection of relations that, as a group, contain the data describing a particular business environment.

Primary and Candidate Keys

Primary Keys   Figure 5.2 contains two relations, the SALESPERSON relation and the CUSTOMER relation, from General Hardware Company's relational database. The SALESPERSON relation has four rows, each representing one salesperson. Also, the SALESPERSON relation has four columns, each representing a characteristic of salespersons. Similarly, the CUSTOMER relation has nine rows, each representing a customer, and four columns.

A relation always has a unique **primary key**. A primary key (sometimes shortened in practice to just "the key") is an attribute or group of attributes whose values are unique throughout all rows of the relation. In fact, the primary key represents the characteristic of a collection of entities that uniquely identifies each one. For example, in the situation described by the relations in Figure 5.2, each salesperson has been assigned a unique salesperson number and each customer has been assigned a unique

(a) SALESPERSON relation

Salesperson Number	Salesperson Name	Commission Percentage	Year of Hire
137	Baker	10	1995
186	Adams	15	2001
204	Dickens	10	1998
361	Carlyle	20	2001

(b) CUSTOMER relation

Customer Number	Customer Name	Salesperson Number	HQ City
0121	Main St. Hardware	137	New York
0839	Jane's Stores	186	Chicago
0933	ABC Home Stores	137	Los Angeles
1047	Acme Hardware Store	137	Los Angeles
1525	Fred's Tool Stores	361	Atlanta
1700	XYZ Stores	361	Washington
1826	City Hardware	137	New York
2198	Western Hardware	204	New York
2267	Central Stores	186	New York

FIGURE 5.2 General Hardware Company relational database

customer number. Therefore the Salesperson Number attribute is the primary key of the SALESPERSON relation and the Customer Number attribute is the primary key of the CUSTOMER relation. As in Figure 5.2, we will start marking the primary key attribute(s) with a single, solid underline.

The number of attributes involved in the primary key is always the minimum number of attributes that provide the uniqueness quality. For example, in the SALESPERSON relation, it would make no sense to have the combination of Salesperson Number and Salesperson Name as the primary key because Salesperson Number is unique by itself. However, consider the situation of a SALESPERSON relation that does not include a Salesperson Number attribute, but instead has a First Name attribute, a Middle Name attribute, and a Last Name attribute. The primary key might then be the combination of the First, Middle, and Last Name attributes (assuming this would always produce a unique combination of values. If it did not, then a fourth attribute could be added to the relation and to the primary key as a sequence field to produce, for example, John Alan Smith #1, John Alan Smith #2, and so forth.) Some attribute or combination of attributes of a relation has to be unique and this can serve as the unique primary key, since, by definition, no two rows can be identical. In the worst case, all of the relation's attributes combined could serve as the primary key if necessary (but this situation is uncommon in practice).

Candidate Keys   If a relation has more than one attribute or minimum group of attributes that represents a way of uniquely identifying the entities, then they are each called a candidate key. (Actually, if there is only one unique attribute or minimum

FIGURE 5.3 Candidate keys become either primary or alternate keys

group of attributes it can also be called a candidate key.) For example, in a personnel relation, an employee number attribute and a Social Security Number attribute (each of which is obviously unique) would each be a candidate key of that relation. When there is more than one candidate key, one of them must be chosen to be the primary key of the relation. That is where the term "candidate key" comes from, since each one is a candidate for selection as the primary key. The decision of which candidate key to pick to be the primary key is typically based on which one will be the best for the purposes of the applications that will use the relation and the database. Sometimes the term **alternate key** is used to describe a candidate key that was not chosen to be the primary key of the relation, Figure 5.3.

Foreign Keys and Binary Relationships

Foreign Keys   If, in a collection of relations that make up a relational database, an attribute or group of attributes serves as the primary key of one relation and also appears in another relation, then it is called a foreign key in that other relation. Thus Salesperson Number, which is the primary key of the SALESPERSON relation, is considered a foreign key in the CUSTOMER relation, Figure 5.4. As shown in Figure 5.4, we will start marking the foreign key attribute(s) with a dashed underline. The concept of the foreign key is crucial in relational databases, as the foreign key is the mechanism that ties relations together to represent unary, binary, and ternary relationships. We begin the discussion by considering how binary relationships are stored in relational databases. These are both the most common and the easiest to deal with. The unary and ternary relationships will come later. Recall from the discussion of the entity-relationship model that the three kinds of binary relationships among the entities in the business environment are the one-to-one, one-to-many, and many-to-many

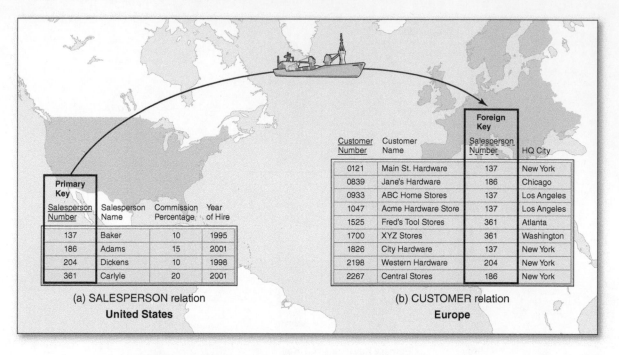

FIGURE 5.4 A foreign key

relationships. The first case is the one-to-many relationship, which is typically the most common of the three.

One-to-Many Binary Relationship   Consider the SALESPERSON and CUS-TOMER relations of Figure 5.2, repeated in Figure 5.4. As one would expect in most sales-oriented companies, notice that each salesperson is responsible for several customers while each customer has a single salesperson as their point of contact with General Hardware. This one-to-many binary relationship can be represented as:

$$\text{Salesperson} \longleftrightarrow\hspace{-0.5em}\rightarrow \text{Customer}$$

For example, the Salesperson Number attribute of the CUSTOMER relation shows that salesperson 137 is responsible for customers 0121, 0933, 1047, and 1826. Looking at it from the point of view of the customer, the same relation shows that the only salesperson associated with customer 0121 is salesperson 137, Figure 5.5. This last point has to be true. After all, there is only one record for each customer in the CUSTOMER relation (the Customer Number attribute is unique since it is the relation's primary key) and there is only one place to put a salesperson number in it. The bottom line is that the Salesperson Number foreign key in the CUSTOMER relation effectively establishes the one-to-many relationship between salespersons and customers.

By the way, notice that, in this case, the primary key of the SALESPERSON relation and the corresponding foreign key in the CUSTOMER relation both have the same *attribute name*, Salesperson Number. This will often be the case but it does not have to be. What is necessary is that both attributes have the same **domain of values**; that is, they must both have values of the same type, such as (in this case) three-digit whole numbers that are the identifiers for salespersons.

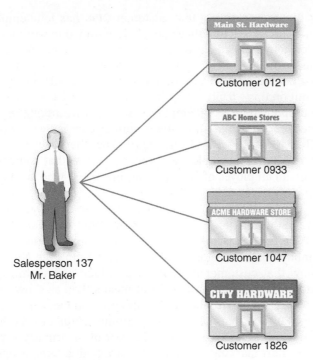

Salesperson 137
Mr. Baker

Customer 0121

Customer 0933

Customer 1047

Customer 1826

FIGURE 5.5 A salesperson and his four customers

It is the presence of a salesperson number in a customer record that indicates which salesperson the customer is associated with. Fundamentally, that is why the Salesperson Number attribute is in the CUSTOMER relation and that is the essence of its being a foreign key in that relation. In Chapter 7, we will discuss database design issues in detail. But, for now, note that when building a one-to-many relationship into a relational database, it will always be the case that the unique identifier of the entity on the "*one* side" of the relationship (Salesperson Number, in this example) will be placed as a foreign key in the relation representing the entity on the "*many* side" of the relationship (the CUSTOMER relation, in this example).

Here's something else about foreign keys. There are situations in which a relation doesn't have a single, unique attribute to serve as its primary key. Then, it requires a combination of two or more attributes to reach uniqueness and serve as its primary key. Sometimes one or more of the attributes in that combination can be a foreign key! Yes, when this happens, a foreign key is actually part of the relation's primary key! This was *not* the case in the CUSTOMER relation of Figure 5.2b. In this relation, the primary key only consists of one attribute, Customer Number, which is unique all by itself. The foreign key, Salesperson Number, is clearly not a part of the primary key.

Here is an example of a situation in which a foreign key is part of a relation's primary key. Figure 5.6 adds the CUSTOMER EMPLOYEE relation, Figure 5.6c, to the General Hardware database. Remember that General Hardware's customers are the hardware stores, home improvement stores, or chains of such stores that it supplies. Figure 5.6c, the CUSTOMER EMPLOYEE relation, lists the employees of each of General Hardware's customers. In fact, there is a one-to-many relationship between customers and customer employees. A customer (like a hardware store) has many employees but an employee, a person, works in only one store:

Customer ◄━━━►► Customer Employee

For example, Figure 5.6c shows that customer 2198 has four employees, Smith, Jones, Garcia, and Kaplan. Each of those people is assumed to work for only one customer company, customer 2198. Following the rule we developed for setting up a one-to-many relationship with a foreign key, the Customer attribute must appear in the CUSTOMER EMPLOYEE relation as a foreign key, and indeed it does.

Now, what about finding a legitimate primary key for the CUSTOMER EMPLOYEE relation? The assumption here is that employee numbers *are unique only within a company*; they are not unique across all of the customer companies. Thus, as shown in the CUSTOMER EMPLOYEE relation in Figure 5.6c, there can be an employee of customer number 0121 who is employee number 30441 in that company's employee numbering system, an employee of customer number 0933 who is employee number 30441 in that company's system, and also an employee of customer number 2198 who is also employee number 30441. That being the case, the Employee Number is not a **unique attribute** in this relation. Neither it nor any other single attribute of the CUSTOMER EMPLOYEE relation is unique and can serve, alone, as the relation's primary key. But the combination of Customer Number and Employee Number is unique. After all, we know that customer numbers are unique and within each customer company, employee numbers are unique. That means that, as shown in Figure 5.6c, the combination of Customer Number and Employee Number can be and is the relation's primary key. Further, that means that Customer Number is both a foreign key in the CUSTOMER EMPLOYEE relation *and* a part of its primary key. As shown in Figure 5.6c, we will start marking attributes that are both a foreign key and a part of the primary key with an underline consisting of a dashed line over a solid line.

Many-to-Many Binary Relationship

Storing the Many-to-Many Binary Relationship   Figure 5.7 expands the General Hardware database by adding two more relations, the PRODUCT relation, Figure 5.7d, and the SALES relation, Figure 5.7e. The PRODUCT relation simply lists the products that General Hardware sells, one row per product, with Product Number as the unique identifier and thus the primary key of the relation. Each of General Hardware's salespersons can sell any or all of the company's products and each product can be sold by any or all of its salespersons. Therefore the relationship between salespersons and products is a many-to-many relationship.

Salesperson ◄◄——————►► Product

So, the database will somehow have to keep track of this many-to-many relationship between salespersons and products. The way that a many-to-many relationship is represented in a relational database is by the creation of an additional relation, in this example, the SALES relation in Figure 5.7e. The SALES relation of Figure 5.7e is intended to record the *lifetime* sales of a particular product by a particular salesperson. Thus, there will be a single row in the relation for each applicable combination of salesperson and product (i.e., when a particular salesperson *has actually sold* some of the particular product). For example, the first row of the SALES relation indicates that salesperson 137 has sold product 19440. Since it is sufficient to record that fact once, the combination of the Salesperson Number and Product Number attributes always produces unique values. So, in general, the new relation created to record the many-to-many relationship will have as its primary key the combined unique identifiers of the two entities in the many-to-many relationship. That's why,

(a) SALESPERSON relation

Salesperson Number	Salesperson Name	Commission Percentage	Year of Hire
137	Baker	10	1995
186	Adams	15	2001
204	Dickens	10	1998
361	Carlyle	20	2001

(b) CUSTOMER relation

Customer Number	Customer Name	Salesperson Number	HQ City
0121	Main St. Hardware	137	New York
0839	Jane's Stores	186	Chicago
0933	ABC Home Stores	137	Los Angeles
1047	Acme Hardware Store	137	Los Angeles
1525	Fred's Tool Stores	361	Atlanta
1700	XYZ Stores	361	Washington
1826	City Hardware	137	New York
2198	Western Hardware	204	New York
2267	Central Stores	186	New York

(c) CUSTOMER EMPLOYEE relation

Customer Number	Employee Number	Employee Name	Title
0121	27498	Smith	Co-Owner
0121	30441	Garcia	Co-Owner
0933	25270	Chen	VP Sales
0933	30441	Levy	Sales Manager
0933	48285	Morton	President
1525	33779	Baker	Sales Manager
2198	27470	Smith	President
2198	30441	Jones	VP Sales
2198	33779	Garcia	VP Personnel
2198	35268	Kaplan	Senior Accountant

FIGURE 5.6 General Hardware Company relational database including the CUSTOMER EMPLOYEE relation

in this example, the Salesperson Number and Product Number attributes both appear in the SALES relation. Each of the two is a foreign key in the SALES relation since each is the primary key of another relation in the database. The combination of these two attributes is unique, and combined they comprise the primary key of the newly created SALES relation.

(a) SALESPERSON relation

Salesperson Number	Salesperson Name	Commission Percentage	Year of Hire
137	Baker	10	1995
186	Adams	15	2001
204	Dickens	10	1998
361	Carlyle	20	2001

(b) CUSTOMER relation

Customer Number	Customer Name	Salesperson Number	HQ City
0121	Main St. Hardware	137	New York
0839	Jane's Stores	186	Chicago
0933	ABC Home Stores	137	Los Angeles
1047	Acme Hardware Store	137	Los Angeles
1525	Fred's Tool Stores	361	Atlanta
1700	XYZ Stores	361	Washington
1826	City Hardware	137	New York
2198	Western Hardware	204	New York
2267	Central Stores	186	New York

(c) CUSTOMER EMPLOYEE relation

Customer Number	Employee Number	Employee Name	Title
0121	27498	Smith	Co-Owner
0121	30441	Garcia	Co-Owner
0933	25270	Chen	VP Sales
0933	30441	Levy	Sales Manager
0933	48285	Morton	President
1525	33779	Baker	Sales Manager
2198	27470	Smith	President
2198	30441	Jones	VP Sales
2198	33779	Garcia	VP Personnel
2198	35268	Kaplan	Senior Accountant

(d) PRODUCT relation

Product Number	Product Name	Unit Price
16386	Wrench	12.95
19440	Hammer	17.50
21765	Drill	32.99
24013	Saw	26.25
26722	Pliers	11.50

(continues)

FIGURE 5.7 General Hardware Company relational database including the PRODUCT and SALES relation

(e) SALES relation

Salesperson Number	Product Number	Quantity
137	19440	473
137	24013	170
137	26722	688
186	16386	1,745
186	19440	2,529
186	21765	1,962
186	24013	3,071
204	21765	809
204	26722	734
361	16386	3,729
361	21765	3,110
361	26722	2,738

FIGURE 5.7 (Continued) General Hardware Company relational database including the PRODUCT and SALES relation

The new SALES relation of Figure 5.7e effectively records the many-to-many relationship between salespersons and products. This is illustrated from the "salesperson side" of the many-to-many relationship by looking at the first three rows of the SALES relation and seeing that salesperson 137 sells products 19440, 24013, and 26722. It is illustrated from the "product side" of the many-to-many relationship by scanning down the Product Number column of the SALES relation, looking for the value 19440, and seeing that product 19440 is sold by salespersons 137 and 186, Figure 5.8.

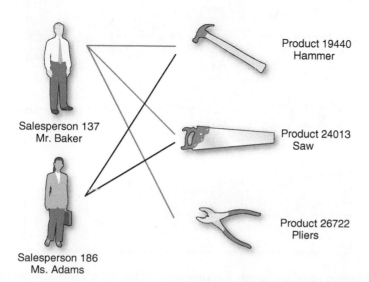

Salesperson 137
Mr. Baker

Salesperson 186
Ms. Adams

Product 19440
Hammer

Product 24013
Saw

Product 26722
Pliers

FIGURE 5.8 Many-to-many relationship between salespersons and products as shown in the SALES relation

Intersection Data   What about the Quantity attribute in the SALES relation? In addition to keeping track of which salespersons have sold which products, General Hardware wants to record *how many* of each particular product each salesperson has sold since the product was introduced or since the salesperson joined the company. So, it sounds like there has to be a "Quantity" attribute. And, an attribute describes an entity, right? Then, which entity does the Quantity attribute describe? Does it describe salespersons the way the Year of Hire does in the SALESPERSON relation? Does it describe products the way Unit Price does in the PRODUCT relation? Each salesperson has exactly one date of hire. Each product has exactly one unit price. But a salesperson doesn't have just one "quantity" associated with her because she sells many products and similarly, a product doesn't have just one "quantity" associated with it because it is sold by many salespersons.

While year of hire is clearly a characteristic of salespersons and unit price is clearly a characteristic of products, "quantity" is a characteristic of *the relationship between salesperson and product.* For example, the fact that salesperson 137 appears in the first row of the SALES relation of Figure 5.7e along with product 19440 indicates that he has a history of selling this product. But do we know more about his history of selling it? Yes! That first row of Figure 5.7e indicates that salesperson 137 has sold 473 units of product 19440. Quantity *describes the many-to-many relationship* between salespersons and products. In a sense it falls at the intersection between the two entities and is thus called "intersection data," Figure 5.9.

Since the many-to-many relationship has its own relation in the database and since it can have attributes, does that mean that we should think of it as a kind of entity? Yes! Many people do just that and refer to it as an "associative entity," a concept we first described when discussing data modeling in Chapter 2!

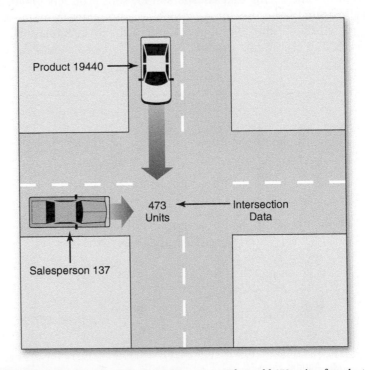

FIGURE 5.9 Intersection data that indicates that salesperson 137 has sold 473 units of product 19440

Additional Many-to-Many Concepts Before leaving the subject of many-to-many relationships, there are a few more important points to make. First, will the combination of the two primary keys representing the two entities in the many-to-many relationship always serve as a unique identifier or primary key in the additional relation representing the many-to-many relationship? The answer is that this depends on the precise nature of the many-to-many relationship. For example, in the situation of the SALES relation in Figure 5.7e, the combination of the two **entity identifier** attributes works perfectly as the primary key, as described above. But, what if General Hardware decides it wants to keep track of each salesperson's *annual* sales of each product instead of their *lifetime* sales? Fairly obviously, a new attribute, Year, would have to be added to the SALES relation, as shown in Figure 5.10. Moreover, as demonstrated by a few sample rows of that relation, the combination of Salesperson Number and Product Number is no longer unique. For example, salesperson 137 sold many units of product 19440 in each of 1999, 2000, and 2001. The first three records of the relation all have the salesperson number, product number combination of 137, 19440. Clearly, the way to solve the problem in this instance is to add the Year attribute to the Salesperson Number and Product Number attributes to form a three-attribute unique primary key. It is quite common in practice to have to add such a "timestamp" to a relation storing a many-to-many relationship in order to attain uniqueness and have a legitimate primary key. Sometimes, as in the example in Figure 5.10, this is accomplished with a Year attribute. A Date attribute is required if the data may be stored two or more times in a year. A Time attribute is required if the data may be stored more than once in a day.

Next is the question of why an additional relation is necessary to represent a many-to-many relationship. For example, could the many-to-many relationship between salespersons and products be represented in either the SALESPERSON or PRODUCT relations? The answer is no! If, for instance, you tried to represent the many-to-many relationship in the SALESPERSON relation, you would have to list all of the products (by Product Number) that a particular salesperson has sold in that salesperson's

SALES relation (modified)			
Salesperson Number	Product Number	Year	Quantity
137	19440	1999	132
137	19440	2000	168
137	19440	2001	173
137	24013	2000	52
137	24013	2001	118
137	26722	1999	140
137	26722	2000	203
137	26722	2001	345
186	16386	1998	250
186	16386	1999	245
186	16386	2000	581
186	16386	2001	669

FIGURE 5.10 Modified SALES relation of the General Hardware Company relational database, including a Year attribute

(a) Additional Product and Quantity columns

Salesperson Number	Salesperson Name	Commission Percentage	Year of Hire	Product	Qty	Product	Qty	Product	Qty	Product	Qty
137	Baker	10	1995	19440	473	24013	170	26722	688		
186	Adams	15	2001	16386	1745	19440	2529	21765	1962	24013	3071
204	Dickens	10	1998	21765	809	26722	734				
361	Carlyle	20	2001	16386	3729	21765	3110	26722	2738		

(b) One additional column for Product and Quantity Pairs

Salesperson Number	Salesperson Name	Commission Percentage	Year of Hire	Product and Quantity Pairs
137	Baker	10	1995	(19440, 473) (24013, 170) (26722, 688)
186	Adams	15	2001	(16386, 1745) (19440, 2529) (21765, 1962) (24013, 3071)
204	Dickens	10	1998	(21765, 809) (26722, 734)
361	Carlyle	20	2001	(16386, 3729) (21765, 3110) (26722, 2738)

FIGURE 5.11 Unacceptable ways of storing a binary many-to-many relationship

record. Furthermore, you would have to carry the Quantity intersection data along with it in some way. For example, in the SALESPERSON relation, the row for salesperson 137 would have to be extended to include products 19440, 24013, and 26722, plus the associated intersection data, Figure 5.11a. Alternatively, one could envision a single additional attribute in the SALESPERSON relation into which all the related product number and intersection data for each salesperson would somehow be stuffed, Figure 5.11b (although, aside from other problems, this would violate the rule that every cell in a relation must have only a single value). In either case, it would be unworkable. Because, in general, each salesperson has been involved in selling different numbers of product types, each record of the SALESPERSON relation would be a different length. Furthermore, additions, deletions, and updates of product/quantity pairs would be a nightmare. Also, trying to access the related data from the "product side," for example, looking for all of the salespersons who have sold a particular product, would be very difficult. And, incidentally, trying to make this work by putting the salesperson data into the PRODUCT relation, instead of putting the product data into the SALESPERSON relation as in Figure 5.11, would generate an identical set of problems. No, the only way that's workable is to create an additional relation to represent the many-to-many relationship. Each combination of a related salesperson and product has its own record, making the insertion, deletion, and update of related items feasible, providing a clear location for intersection data, and avoiding the issue of variable-length records.

Finally, there is the question of whether an additional relation is required to represent a many-to-many relationship if there is no intersection data. For example, suppose that General Hardware wants to track which salespersons have sold which products, but has no interest in how many units of each product they have sold.

The Relational Database Concept   **109**

SALES relation (without intersection data)	
Salesperson Number	Product Number
137	19440
137	24013
137	26722
186	16386
186	19440
186	21765
186	24013
204	21765
204	26722
361	16386
361	21765
361	26722

FIGURE 5.12 The many-to-many SALES relation without intersection data

The SALES relation of Figure 5.7e would then have only the Salesperson Number and Product Number attributes, Figure 5.12. Could this information be stored in some way other than with the additional SALES relation? The answer is that the additional relation is still required. Note that in the explanation above of why an additional relation is necessary in general to represent a many-to-many relationship, the intersection data played only a small role. The issues would still be there, even without intersection data.

One-to-One Binary Relationship   After considering one-to-many and many-to-many binary relationships in relational databases, the remaining binary relationship is the one-to-one relationship. Each of General Hardware's salespersons has exactly one office and each office is occupied by exactly one salesperson, Figure 5.13.

$$\text{Salesperson} \longleftrightarrow \text{Office}$$

Figure 5.14f shows the addition of the OFFICE relation to the General Hardware relational database. The SALESPERSON relation has the Office Number attribute as a foreign key so that the company can look up the record for a salesperson and see to which office she is assigned. Because this is a one-to-one relationship and each salesperson has only one office, the company can also scan down the Office Number column of the SALESPERSON relation, find a particular office number (which can only appear once, since it's a one-to-one relationship), and see which salesperson is assigned to that office. In general, this is the way that one-to-one binary relationships are built into relational databases. The unique identifier, the primary key, of one of the two entities in the one-to-one relationship is inserted into the other entity's relation as a foreign key. The question of which of the two entities is chosen as the "donor" of its primary key and which as the "recipient" will be discussed further when we talk about logical design in Chapter 7.

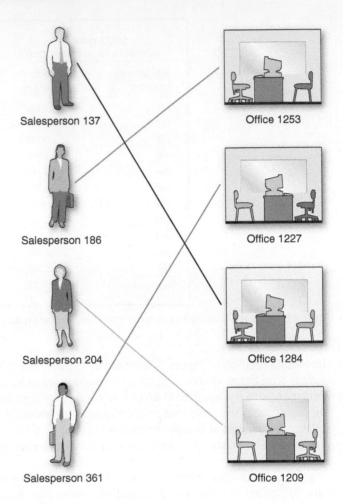

FIGURE 5.13 A one-to-one binary relationship

But there is another interesting question about this arrangement. Could the SALESPERSON and OFFICE relations of Figure 5.14 be combined into one relation? After all, a salesperson has only one office and an office has only one salesperson assigned to it. So, if an office and its unique identifier, Office Number, "belongs" to one particular salesperson, so does that office's Telephone Number and Size. Indeed, when we want to contact a salesperson, we ask for *her phone number*, not for "her office's phone number!" So, could we combine the SALESPERSON and OFFICE relations of Figure 5.14 into the single relation of Figure 5.15? The answer is, it's possible in some cases, but you have to be very careful about making such a decision. In the General Hardware case, how would you store an *unoccupied* office in the database? The relation of Figure 5.15 allows data about an office to be stored only if the office is *occupied*. After all, the primary key of Figure 5.15's relation is Salesperson Number! You can't have a record with office data in it and no salesperson data. A case where it might work is a database of U.S. states and their governors. Every state *always* has exactly one governor and anyone who is a governor *must* be associated with one state. There can't be a state without a governor or a governor without a state.

(a) SALESPERSON relation

Salesperson Number	Salesperson Name	Commission Percentage	Year of Hire	Office Number
137	Baker	10	1995	1284
186	Adams	15	2001	1253
204	Dickens	10	1998	1209
361	Carlyle	20	2001	1227

(b) CUSTOMER relation

Customer Number	Customer Name	Salesperson Number	HQ City
0121	Main St. Hardware	137	New York
0839	Jane's Stores	186	Chicago
0933	ABC Home Stores	137	Los Angeles
1047	Acme Hardware Store	137	Los Angeles
1525	Fred's Tool Stores	361	Atlanta
1700	XYZ Stores	361	Washington
1826	City Hardware	137	New York
2198	Western Hardware	204	New York
2267	Central Stores	186	New York

(c) CUSTOMER EMPLOYEE relation

Customer Number	Employee Number	Employee Name	Title
0121	27498	Smith	Co-Owner
0121	30441	Garcia	Co-Owner
0933	25270	Chen	VP Sales
0933	30441	Levy	Sales Manager
0933	48285	Morton	President
1525	33779	Baker	Sales Manager
2198	27470	Smith	President
2198	30441	Jones	VP Sales
2198	33779	Garcia	VP Personnel
2198	35268	Kaplan	Senior Accountant

(*continues*)

FIGURE 5.14 General Hardware Company relational database including the OFFICE relation

(d) PRODUCT relation

Product Number	Product Name	Unit Price
16386	Wrench	12.95
19440	Hammer	17.50
21765	Drill	32.99
24013	Saw	26.25
26722	Pliers	11.50

(e) SALES relation

Salesperson Number	Product Number	Quantity
137	19440	473
137	24013	170
137	26722	688
186	16386	1,745
186	19440	2,529
186	21765	1,962
186	24013	3,071
204	21765	809
204	26722	734
361	16386	3,729
361	21765	3,110
361	26722	2,738

(f) OFFICE relation

Office Number	Telephone	Size (sq. ft.)
1253	901-555-4276	120
1227	901-555-0364	100
1284	901-555-7335	120
1209	901-555-3108	95

FIGURE 5.14 (Continued) General Hardware Company relational database including the OFFICE relation

Combined SALESPERSON/OFFICE relation

Salesperson Number	Salesperson Name	Commission Percentage	Year of Hire	Office Number	Telephone	Size (sq. ft.)
137	Baker	10	1995	1284	901-555-7335	120
186	Adams	15	2001	1253	901-555-4276	120
204	Dickens	10	1998	1209	901-555-3108	95
361	Carlyle	20	2001	1227	901-555-0364	100

FIGURE 5.15 Combining the SALESPERSON and OFFICE relations into a single relation

Your Turn

5.1 Entities, Keys, and Relationships

Think about a retail store that sells TVs, computers, cameras, DVDs, etc. What entities must it keep track of? What are some of the attributes of those entities? What about relationships among those entities? What do you think would be appropriate primary, candidate, and foreign keys in the relational tables designed to store data about the entities?

Question:

Specifically consider a chain of retail electronics stores. List several of the main entities that the chain must keep track of. What are the relationships between those entities? What would appropriate primary, candidate, and foreign keys be in the relational tables that would store the data about these entities?

At any rate, in practice, there are a variety of reasons for keeping the two relations involved in the one-to-one relationship separate. It may be that because each of the two entities involved is considered sufficiently important in its own right, this separation simply adds clarity to the database. It may be because most users at any one time seek data about only one of the two entities. It may have to do with splitting the data between different geographic sites. It can even be done for system performance in the case where the records would be unacceptably long if the data was all contained in one relation. These issues will be discussed later in this book but it is important to have at least a basic idea of the intricacies of the one-to-one relationship, at this point.

Data Retrieval from a Relational Database

Extracting Data from a Relation

Thus far, the discussion has concentrated on how a relational database is structured. But building relations and loading them with data is only half of the story. The other half is the effort to retrieve the data in a way that is helpful and beneficial to the business organization that built the database. If the database management system did not provide any particular help in this effort, then the problem would revert to simply writing a program in some programming language to retrieve data from the relations, treating them as if they were simple, linear files. But the crucial point is that a major, defining feature of a relational DBMS is the ability to accept high-level **data retrieval** commands, process them against the database's relations, and return the desired data. The data retrieval mechanism is a built-in part of the DBMS and does not have to be written from scratch by every program that uses the database. As we shall soon see, this is true even to the extent of matching related records in different relations (integrating data), as in the earlier example of finding the name of the salesperson on a particular customer account. We shall address what relational retrieval might look like, first in terms of single relations and then across multiple relations.

Since a relation can be viewed as a tabular or rectangular arrangement of data values, it would seem to make sense to want to approach data retrieval horizontally, vertically, or in a combination of the two. Taking a horizontal slice of a relation implies retrieving one or more rows of the relation. In effect, that's an expression for retrieving one or more records or retrieving the data about one or more entities. Taking a vertical slice of a relation means retrieving one or more entire columns of the relation (down through all of its rows). Taken in combination, we can retrieve one or more columns of one or more rows, the minimum of which is a single column of a single row, or a single attribute value of a single record. That's as fine a sense of retrieval as we would ever want.

Using terminology from a database formalism called **relational algebra** and an informal, hypothetical command style for now, there are two commands called Select and Project that are capable of the kinds of horizontal and vertical manipulations just suggested. (Note: The use of the word "Select" here is not the same as its use in the SQL data retrieval language discussed in Chapter 4.)

The Relational Select Operator

Consider the database of Figure 5.14 and its SALESPERSON relation, Figure 5.14a. To begin with, suppose that we want to find the row or record for salesperson number 204. In a very straightforward way, the informal command might be:

Select rows from the SALESPERSON relation in which Salesperson Number = 204. The result would be:

Salesperson Number	Salesperson Name	Commission Percentage	Year of Hire
204	Dickens	10	1998

Notice that the result of the Select operation is itself a relation, in this case consisting of only one row. The result of a relational operation will always be a relation, whether it consists of many rows with many columns or one row with one column (i.e., a single attribute value).

In order to retrieve all of the records with a common value in a particular (non-unique) attribute, for example, all salespersons with a commission percentage of 10, the command looks the same as when dealing with a unique attribute:

Select rows from the SALESPERSON relation in which Commission Percentage = 10. But the result of the operation may include several rows:

Salesperson Number	Salesperson Name	Commission Percentage	Year of Hire
137	Baker	10	1995
204	Dickens	10	1998

If the requirement is to retrieve the entire relation, the command would be:
Select all rows from the SALESPERSON relation.

The Relational Project Operator

To retrieve what we referred to earlier as a vertical slice of the relation requires the **Project operator**. For example, the command to retrieve the number and name of each salesperson in the file might look like:

Project the Salesperson Number and Salesperson Name over the SALESPERSON relation.

The result will be a long narrow relation:

Salesperson Number	Salesperson Name
137	Baker
186	Adams
204	Dickens
361	Carlyle

If we project a nonunique attribute, then a decision must be made on whether or not we want duplicates in the result (although, since the result is itself a relation, technically there should not be any duplicate rows). For example, whether:

Project the Year of Hire over the SALESPERSON relation
produces

Year of Hire
1995
2001
1998
2001

or (eliminating the duplicates in the identical rows) produces

Year of Hire
1995
2001
1998

would depend on exactly how this hypothetical informal command language was implemented.

Combination of the Relational Select and Project Operators

More powerful still is the combination of the Select and Project operators. Suppose we apply them serially, with the relation that results from one operation being used as the input to the next operation. For example, to retrieve the numbers and names of the salespersons working on a 10 % commission, we would issue:

Select rows from the SALESPERSON relation in which Commission Percentage = 10.
Project the Salesperson Number and Salesperson Name over that result.

The first command "selects out" the rows for salespersons 137 and 204. Then the second command "projects" the salesperson numbers and names from those two rows, resulting in:

Salesperson Number	Salesperson Name
137	Baker
204	Dickens

The following combination illustrates the ability to retrieve a single attribute value. Suppose that there is a need to find the year of hire of salesperson number 204. Since Salesperson Number is a unique attribute, only one row of the relation can possibly be involved. Since the goal is to find one attribute value in that row, the result must be just that: a single attribute value. The command is:

Select rows from the SALESPERSON relation in which Salesperson Number = 204. Project the Year of Hire over that result.
The result is the single value:

Year of Hire
1998

Extracting Data Across Multiple Relations: Data Integration

In Chapter 3, the issue of data integration was broached and the concept was defined. First, the data in the Salesperson and Customer files of Figure 3.7 was shown to be non-redundant. Then it was shown that **integrating data** would require extracting data from one file and using that extracted data as a search argument to find the sought-after data in the other file. For example, recall that finding the name of the salesperson who was responsible for customer number 1525 required finding the salesperson number in customer 1525's record in the Customer file (i.e., salesperson number 361) and then using that salesperson number as a search argument in the Salesperson file to discover that the sought-after name was Carlyle. The alternative was the combined file of Figure 3.8 that introduced data redundancy.

A fundamental premise of the database approach is that a DBMS must be able to store data non-redundantly while also providing a data integration facility. But it seems that we may have a problem here. Since relations appear to be largely similar in structure to simple, linear files, do the lessons learned from the files of Figures 3.7 and 3.8 lead to the conclusion that it is impossible to have simultaneously **non-redundant data** storage and data integration with relations in a relational database? In fact, one of the elegant features of relational DBMSs is that they automate the cross-relation data extraction process in such a way that it appears that the data in the relations is integrated while also remaining non-redundant. The data integration takes place at the time that a relational query is processed by the relational DBMS for solution. This is a unique feature of relational databases and is substantially different from the functional equivalents in the older navigational database systems and in some of the newer object-oriented database systems, in both of which the data integration is much more tightly built into the data structure itself. In relational algebra terms, the integration function is known as the Join command.

Now, focus on the SALESPERSON and CUSTOMER relations of Figure 5.14, which outwardly look just like the SALESPERSON and CUSTOMER files of Figure 3.7. Adding the **Join operator** to our hypothetical, informal command style, consider the following commands designed to find the *name* of the salesperson responsible for customer number 1525. Again, this was the query that seemed to be so problematic in Chapter 3.

Join the SALESPERSON relation and the CUSTOMER relation, using the Salesperson Number of each as the join fields.

> Select rows from that result in which Customer Number = 1525.
> Project the Salesperson Name over that last result.

Obviously, the first sentence represents the use of the join command. The join operation will take advantage of the common Salesperson Number attribute, which for this purpose is called the join field, in both relations. The Salesperson Number attribute is, of course, the primary key of the SALESPERSON relation and is a foreign key in the CUSTOMER relation. Remember that the point of the foreign key is to represent a one-to-many (in this case) relationship between salespersons and customers. Some rows of the SALESPERSON relation *are related* to some rows of the CUSTOMER relation by virtue of having the same salesperson number. The Salesperson Number attribute serves to identify each salesperson in the SALESPERSON relation, while the Salesperson Number attribute indicates which salesperson is responsible for a particular customer in the CUSTOMER relation. Thus, the rows of the two relations that have identical Salesperson Number values are *related*. It is these related rows that the join operation will bring together in order to satisfy the query that was posed.

The join operation tries to find matches between the join field values of the rows in the two relations. For example, it finds a match between the Salesperson Number value of 137 in the first row of the SALESPERSON relation and the Salesperson Number value of 137 in the first, third, fourth, and seventh rows of the CUSTOMER relation. When it finds such a pair of rows, it takes all the attribute values from both rows and creates a single new row out of them in the resultant relation. In its most basic form, as shown here, the join is truly an exhaustive operation, comparing every row of one relation to every row of the other relation, looking for a match in the join fields. (Comparing every possible combination of two sets, in this case rows from the two relations, is known as taking the "Cartesian product.") So the result of the join command, the first of the three commands in the example command sequence we're executing, is:

SalesPerson Number	SalesPerson Name	Commission Percentage	Year of Hire	Customer Number	Customer Name	SalesPerson Number	HQ City
137	Baker	10	1995	0121	Main St. Hardware	137	New York
137	Baker	10	1995	0933	ABC Home Stores	137	Los Angeles
137	Baker	10	1995	1047	Acme Hardware Store	137	Los Angeles
137	Baker	10	1995	1826	City Hardware	137	New York
186	Adams	15	2001	0839	Jane's Stores	186	Chicago
186	Adams	15	2001	2267	Central Stores	186	New York
204	Dickens	10	1998	2198	Western Hardware	204	New York
361	Carlyle	20	2001	1525	Fred's Tool Stores	361	Atlanta
361	Carlyle	20	2001	1700	XYZ Stores	361	Washington

Notice that the first and seventh columns are identical in all of their values, row by row. They represent the Salesperson Number attributes from the SALESPERSON and CUSTOMER relations respectively. Remember that two rows from the SALESPERSON and CUSTOMER relations would not be combined together to form a row in the resultant relation unless their two join field values were identical in the first place. This leads to identical values of the two Salesperson Number attributes within each of the rows of the resultant relation. This type of join is called an "**equijoin**." If, as seems reasonable, one of the two identical join columns is eliminated in the process, the result is called a "**natural join**."

Continuing with the command sequence to eventually find the name of the salesperson responsible for customer number 1525, the next part of the command issued is:

Select rows from that result (the relation that resulted from the join) in which Customer Number = 1525.

This produces:

SalesPerson Number	SalesPerson Name	Commission Percentage	Year of Hire	Customer Number	Customer Name	SalesPerson Number	HQ City
361	Carlyle	20	2001	1525	Fred's Tool Stores	361	Atlanta

Finally, we issue the third command
Project the Salesperson Name over that last result.
and get:

SalesPerson Name
Carlyle

Notice that the process could have been streamlined considerably if the relational DBMS had more "intelligence" built into it. The query dealt with only a single customer, customer 1525, and there is only one row for each customer in the CUSTOMER relation, since Customer Number is the unique key attribute. Therefore, the query needed to look at only one row in the CUSTOMER relation, the one for customer 1525. Since this row references only one salesperson, salesperson 361, it follows that, in turn, it needed to look at only one row in the SALESPERSON relation, the one for salesperson 1525. This type of performance issue in relational query processing will be covered later in this book in Chapter 8.

Example: Good Reading Book Stores

Figure 5.16 shows the relational database for the Good Reading Book Stores example described earlier. Since publishers are in a one-to-many relationship to books, the primary key of the PUBLISHER Relation, Publisher Name, is inserted into the BOOK relation as a foreign key. There are two many-to-many relationships. One, between books and authors, keeps track of which authors wrote which books. Recall that a book can have multiple authors and a particular author may have written or partly

PUBLISHER relation

Publisher Name	City	Country	Telephone	Year Founded

AUTHOR relation

Author Number	Author Name	Year Born	Year Died

BOOK relation

Book Number	Book Name	Publication Year	Pages	Publisher Name

CUSTOMER relation

Customer Number	Customer Name	Street	City	State	Country

WRITING relation

Book Number	Author Number

SALE relation

Book Number	Customer Number	Date	Price	Quantity

FIGURE 5.16 Good Reading Bookstores relational database

written many books. The other many-to-many relationship, between books and customers, records which customers bought which books.

The WRITING relation handles the many-to-many relationship between books and authors. The primary key is the combination of Book Number and Author Number. There is no intersection data! Could there be a reason for having intersection data in this relation? If, for example, this database belonged to a publisher instead of a bookstore chain, an intersection data attribute might be Royalty Percentage, i.e. the percentage of the royalties to which a particular author is entitled for a particular book. The SALE relation takes care of the many-to-many relationship between books and customers. Certainly Book Number and Customer Number are part of the primary key of the SALE relation, but is the combination of the two the entire primary key? The answer is that this depends on whether the assumption is made that a given customer can or cannot buy copies of a given book on different days. If the assumption is that a customer can only buy copies of a particular book on one single day, then the combination of Book Number and Customer Number is fine as the primary key. If the assumption is that a customer may indeed buy copies of a given book on different days, then the Date attribute must be part of the primary key to achieve uniqueness.

Example: World Music Association

Figure 5.17 shows the relational database for the World Music Association example described earlier. There is a one-to-many relationship from orchestras to musicians and, in turn, a one-to-many relationship from musicians to degrees. Thus, the primary key of the ORCHESTRA relation, Orchestra Name, appears in the MUSICIAN relation as a foreign key. In turn, the primary key of the MUSICIAN relation, Musician Number, appears in the DEGREE relation as a foreign key. In fact, since the DEGREE attribute is unique only within a musician, the Musician Number attribute and the Degree attribute together serve as the compound primary key of the DEGREE relation. A similar situation exists between composers and compositions. The one-to-many relationship from composers to compositions requires that the primary key of the COMPOSER relation, Composer Name, appear as a foreign key in the COMPOSITION relation. Since composition names are unique only within composers, the combination of Composition Name and Composer Name serves as the compound primary key of the COMPOSITION relation.

ORCHESTRA relation			
Orchestra Name	City	Country	Music Director

MUSICIAN relation				
Musician Number	Musician Name	Instrument	Annual Salary	Orchestra Name

DEGREE relation			
Musician Number	Degree	University	Year

COMPOSER relation		
Composer Name	Country	Date of Birth

COMPOSITION relation		
Composition Name	Composer Name	Year

RECORDING relation				
Orchestra Name	Composition Name	Composer Name	Year	Price

FIGURE 5.17 World Music Association relational database

The many-to-many relationship between orchestras and compositions indicates which orchestras have recorded which compositions and which compositions have been recorded by which orchestras. As a many-to-many relationship, it requires that an additional relation be created. The primary key of this new RECORDING relation has three attributes: Orchestra Name, Composition Name, and Composer Name. Orchestra Name is the unique identifier of orchestras. The combination of Composition Name and Composer Name is the unique identifier of compositions. The combination of Orchestra Name, Composition Name, and Composer Name is the unique identifier of the RECORDING relation. The Year and Price attributes are intersection data in the RECORDING relation. If a particular orchestra could have recorded a particular composition multiple times in different years (although we assume that this is limited to once per year), Year must also be part of the primary key of the RECORDING relation to provide uniqueness.

Example: Lucky Rent-A-Car

Figure 5.18 shows the relational database for the Lucky Rent-A-Car example described earlier. There is a one-to-many relationship from manufacturers to cars and another one-to-many relationship from cars to maintenance events. The former requires the manufacturer primary key, Manufacturer Name, to be placed in the CAR relation as a foreign key. The latter requires the car primary key, Car Serial Number, to be placed in

MANUFACTURER relation

Manufacturer Name	Manufacturer Country	Sales Rep Name	Sales Rep Telephone

CAR relation

Car Serial Number	Model	Year	Class	Manufacturer Name

MAINTENANCE relation

Repair Number	Car Serial Number	Data	Procedure	Mileage	Repair Time

CUSTOMER relation

Customer Number	Customer Name	Customer Address	Customer Telephone

RENTAL relation

Car Serial Number	Customer Number	Rental Date	Return Date	Total Cost

FIGURE 5.18 Lucky Rent-A-Car relational database

the MAINTENANCE relation as a foreign key. The many-to-many relationship among cars and customers requires the creation of a new relation, the RENTAL relation. Each record of the RENTAL relation records the rental of a particular car by a particular customer. Note that the combination of the Car Serial Number and Customer Number attributes is not sufficient as the primary key of the RENTAL relation. A given customer might have rented a given car more than once. Adding Rental Date to the primary key achieves the needed uniqueness.

Summary

The relational approach to database management is by far the primary database management approach used in all levels of information systems applications today. The basic structural component of a relational database is the relation, which *appears* to be a simple linear file but has some technical differences.

Every relation has a unique primary key consisting of one or more attributes that have unique values in that relation. Multiple such unique attributes or combinations of attributes that have the uniqueness property are called candidate keys. The candidate keys that are not chosen to be the one primary key are called alternate keys. If the primary key of one relation in the database also appears in another relation of the database, it called a foreign key in that second relation. Foreign keys tie relations together in the sense that they implement relationships between the entities represented by the relations. A one-to-many relationship is implemented by adding the primary key on the "*one* side" of the relationship to the relation representing the "*many* side" of the relationship. Many-to-many relationships are implemented by constructing an additional relation that includes the primary keys of the two entities in the many-to-many relationship. Additional attributes that describe the many-to-many relationship are called intersection data.

Three basic relational algebra commands permit data retrieval from a relational database. The Select command retrieves one or more rows of a relation. The Project command retrieves one or more columns of a relation. The Join command accomplishes data integration by tying together relations that have a common primary key/ foreign key pair. These three commands can be used in combination to retrieve the specific data required in a particular query.

Key Terms

Alternate key	Entity identifier	Personal computer (PC)	Row
Attribute	Equijoin	Primary key	Select operator
Candidate key	Foreign key	Project operator	Tuple
Cell	Integrating data	Relation	Unique attribute
Column	Join operator	Relational algebra	
Data retrieval	Natural join	Relational database	
Domain of values	Non-redundant data	Relational model	

Questions

1. Why was the commercial introduction of relational database delayed during the 1970s? What factors encouraged its introduction in the early 1980s?

2. How does a relation differ from an ordinary file?

3. Define the terms "tuple" and "attribute."

4. What is a relational database?

5. What are the characteristics of a candidate key?

6. What is a primary key? What is an alternate key?

7. Define the term "foreign key."

8. In your own words, describe how foreign keys are used to set up one-to-many binary relationships in relational databases.

9. Describe why an additional relation is needed to represent a many-to-many relationship in a relational database.

10. Describe what intersection data is, what it describes, and why it does not describe a single entity.

11. What is a one-to-one binary relationship?

12. Describe the purpose and capabilities of:
    a. The relational Select operator.
    b. The relational Project operator.
    c. The relational Join operator.

13. Describe how the join operator works.

Exercises

1. The main relation of a motor vehicle registration bureau's relational database includes the following attributes:

Vehicle Identification Number	License Plate Number	Owner Serial Number	Manufacturer	Model	Year	Color

The Vehicle Identification Number is a unique number assigned to the car when it is manufactured. The License Plate Number is, in effect, a unique number assigned to the car by the government when it is registered. The Owner Serial Number is a unique identifier of each owner. Each owner can own more than one vehicle. The other attributes are not unique. What is/are the candidate key(s) of this relation? If there is more than one candidate key, choose one as the primary key and indicate which is/are the alternate key(s).

2. A relation consists of attributes A, B, C, D, E, F, G, and H.

   No single attribute has unique values.
   The combination of attributes A and E is unique.
   The combination of attributes B and D is unique.
   The combination of attributes B and G is unique.
   Select a primary key for this relation and indicate and alternate keys.

3. In the General Hardware Corp. relational database of Figure 5.14:
   a. How many foreign keys are there in each of the six relations?
   b. List the foreign keys in each of the six relations.

4. Identify the relations that support many-to-many relationships, the primary keys of those relations, and any intersection data in the General Hardware Corp. database.

5. Consider the General Hardware Corp. relational database. Using the informal relational command language described in this chapter, write commands to:
   a. List the product name and unit price of all of the products.
   b. List the employee names and titles of all the employees of customer 2198.
   c. Retrieve the record for office number 1284.
   d. Retrieve the records for customers headquartered in Los Angeles.
   e. Find the size of office number 1209.
   f. Find the name of the salesperson assigned to office number 1209.
   g. List the product name and quantity sold of each product sold by salesperson 361.

6. Consider the General Hardware Corp. relational database and the data stored in it, as shown in Figure 5.14. Find the answer to each of the following queries (written in the informal relational command language described in this chapter).
   a. Select rows from the CUSTOMER EMPLOYEE relation in which Customer Number = 2198.

b. Select rows from the CUSTOMER EMPLOYEE relation in which Customer Number = 2198. Project Employee Number and Employee Name over that result.

c. Select rows from the PRODUCT relation in which Product Number = 21765.

d. Select rows from the PRODUCT relation in which Product Number = 21765. Project Unit Price over that result.

e. Join the SALESPERSON and CUSTOMER relations using the Salesperson Number attribute of each as the join fields. Select rows from that result in which Salesperson Name = Baker. Project Customer Name over that result.

f. Join the PRODUCT relation and the SALES relation using the Product Number attribute of each as the join fields. Select rows in which Product Name = Pliers. Project Salesperson Number and Quantity over that result.

7. For each of Exercise 6, describe in words what the query is trying to accomplish.

Minicases

1. Consider the following relational database for Happy Cruise Lines. It keeps track of ships, cruises, ports, and passengers. A "cruise" is a particular sailing of a ship on a particular date. For example, the seven-day journey of the ship Pride of Tampa that leaves on June 13, 2009, is a cruise. Note the following facts about this environment.

   - Both ship number and ship name are unique in the SHIP Relation.

   - A ship goes on many cruises over time. A cruise is associated with a single ship.

   - A port is identified by the combination of port name and country.

   - As indicated by the VISIT Relation, a cruise includes visits to several ports, and a port is typically included in several cruises.

   - Both Passenger Number and Social Security Number are unique in the PASSENGER Relation. A particular person has a single Passenger Number that is used for all of the cruises that she takes.

   - The VOYAGE Relation indicates that a person can take many cruises and a cruise, of course, has many passengers.

CRUISE Relation				
Cruise Number	Start Date	End Date	Cruise Director	Ship Number

PORT Relation			
Port Name	Country	Number of Docks	Port Manager

VISIT Relation				
Cruise Number	Port Name	Country	Arrival Date	Departure Date

PASSENGER Relation				
Passenger Number	Passenger Name	Social Security Number	Home Address	Telephone Number

VOYAGE Relation			
Passenger Number	Cruise Number	Stateroom Number	Fare

SHIP Relation				
Ship Number	Ship Name	Ship Builder	Launch Date	Gross Weight

   a. Identify the candidate keys of each relation.

   b. Identify the primary key and any alternate keys of each relation.

   c. How many foreign keys does each relation have?

d. Identify the foreign keys of each relation.

e. Indicate any instances in which a foreign key serves as part of the primary key of the relation in which it is a foreign key. Why does each of those relations require a multi-attribute primary key?

f. Identify the relations that support many-to-many relationships, the primary keys of those relations, and any intersection data.

g. Using the informal relational command language described in this chapter, write commands to:

  i. Retrieve the record for passenger number 473942.

  ii. Retrieve the record for the port of Nassau in the Bahamas.

  iii. List all of the ships built by General Shipbuilding, Inc.

  iv. List the port name and number of docks of every port in Mexico.

  v. List the name and number of every ship.

  vi. Who was the cruise director on cruise number 38232?

  vii. What was the gross weight of the ship used for cruise number 39482?

  viii. List the home address of every passenger on cruise number 17543.

2 Super Baseball League Consider the following relational database for the Super Baseball League. It keeps track of teams in the league, coaches and players on the teams, work experience of the coaches, bats belonging to each team, and which players have played on which teams. Note the following facts about this environment:

  • The database keeps track of the history of all of the teams that each player has played on and all of the players who have played on each team.

  • The database keeps track of only the current team that a coach works for.

  • Team Number, Team Name, and Player Number are each unique attributes across the league.

  • Coach Name is unique only within a team (and we assume that a team cannot have two coaches of the same name).

  • Serial Number (for bats) is unique only within a team.

  • In the AFFILIATION relation, the Years attribute indicates that number of years that a player played on a team; the Batting Average is for the years that a player played on a team.

TEAM Relation			
Team Number	Team Name	City	Manager

COACH Relation		
Team Number	Coach Name	Coach Telephone

WORK EXPERIENCE Relation			
Team Number	Coach Name	Experience Type	Years Of Experience

BATS Relation		
Team Number	Serial Number	Manufacturer

PLAYER Relation		
Number Player	Name Player	Age

AFFILIATION Relation			
Player Number	Team Number	Years	Batting Average

a. Identify the candidate keys of each relation.

b. Identify the primary key and any alternate keys of each relation.

c. How many foreign keys does each relation have?

d. Identify the foreign keys of each relation.

e. Indicate any instances in which a foreign key serves as part of the primary key of the relation in which it is a foreign key. Why does each of those relations require a multi-attribute primary key?

f. Identify the relations that support many-to-many relationships, the primary keys of those relations, and any intersection data.

g. Assume that we add the following STADIUM relation to the Super Baseball League relational database. Each team has one home stadium, which is what is represented in this relation. Assume that a stadium can serve as the home stadium for only one team. Stadium Name is unique across the league.

STADIUM Relation			
Stadium Name	Year Built	Size	Team Team Number

What kind of binary relationship exists between the STADIUM relation and the TEAM relation? Could the data from the two relations be combined into one without introducing data redundancy? If so, how?

h. Using the informal relational command language described in this chapter, write commands to:

   i. Retrieve the record for team number 12.

   ii. Retrieve the record for coach Adams on team number 12.

   iii. List the player number and age of every player.

   iv. List the work experience of every coach.

   v. List the work experience of every coach on team number 25.

   vi. Find the age of player number 42459.

   vii. List the serial numbers and manufacturers of all of the Vultures' (the name of a team) bats.

   viii. Find the number of years of college coaching experience that coach Taylor of the Vultures has.

The Relational Database Model: Additional Concepts

Chapter 5 defined the basic terminology of relational database and then demonstrated some fundamental ideas about constructing relations in relational databases and manipulating data in them. The discussion focused on relationships between two different entity types, i.e. binary relationships. This chapter will go beyond binary relationships into unary and ternary relationships. It will then address the important issue of referential integrity.

OBJECTIVES

Describe how unary and ternary relationships are implemented in a relational database.

Explain the concept of referential integrity.

Describe how the referential integrity restrict, cascade, and set-to-null delete rules operate in a relational database.

Introduction

The previous chapter talked about how binary relationships, i.e. those involving two entity types, can be constructed in relational databases so that the data can be integrated while data redundancy is avoided. Unary relationships, with one entity type, and ternary relationships, with three entity types, while perhaps not quite as common as binary relationships, are also facts of life in the real world and so must also be handled properly in relational databases.

Referential integrity addresses a particular issue that can arise between two tables in a relational database. The issue has to do with a foreign key value in one table being able to find a matching primary key value in another table during a join operation. Interestingly, in the older hierarchical and network database management systems, the equivalents of primary and foreign keys were linked by physical address pointers and so were always tied together. But, in relational databases, the tables are basically independent of each other. So, if there are no controls in place, the proper foreign key-primary key matches can be lost when data is updated or records are deleted.

This chapter will address the issues of unary relationships, ternary relationships, and referential integrity, all of which will move us much closer to modeling real-world business environments properly in relational databases.

Relational Structures for Unary and Ternary Relationships

Unary One-to-Many Relationships

Let's continue with the General Hardware Co. example of Figure 5.14, reprinted here for convenience as Figure 6.1. Suppose that General Hardware's salespersons are organized in such a way that some of the salespersons, *in addition to* having their customer responsibilities, serve as the sales managers of other salespersons, Figure 6.2. A salesperson reports to exactly one sales manager, but each salesperson who serves as a sales manager typically has several salespersons reporting to him. Thus, there is a one-to-many relationship within the set or entity type of salespersons.

Salesperson who is also a sales manager ◄────►► Salesperson

This is known as a unary one-to-many relationship. It is unary because there is only one entity type involved. It is one-to-many because among the individual entity occurrences, i.e. among the salespersons, a particular salesperson reports to one salesperson who is his sales manager while a salesperson who is a sales manager may have several salespersons reporting to her. Note that, in general, this arrangement can involve as few as two levels of **entity occurrences** or can involve many levels in a hierarchical arrangement. In general, in a company, an employee can report to a manager who in turn reports to a higher-level manager, and so on up to the CEO.

Assume that the General Hardware Co. has two levels of sales managers, resulting in a three-level hierarchy. That is, each salesperson reports to a sales manager (who is himself a salesperson) and each sales manager reports to one of several chief sales managers (who is herself a salesperson). Figure 6.3 shows two levels of sales managers plus the salespersons who report to them. For example, salespersons 142, 323, and 411 all report to salesperson (and sales manager) 137. Salespersons 137 and 439, both of whom are sales managers, report to salesperson 186 who is a chief sales manager. As you go upward in the hierarchy, each salesperson is associated with exactly one other salesperson. As you go downward in the hierarchy from any salesperson/sales manager, each salesperson/sales manager is associated with many salespersons below, except for the bottom-level salespersons who are not sales managers and thus have no one reporting to them.

Figure 6.4, which is an expansion of the General Hardware Co. SALESPERSON relation in Figure 6.1a, demonstrates how this type of relationship is reflected in a relational database. A one-to-many unary relationship requires the addition of one column to the relation that represents the single entity involved in the unary relationship. In Figure 6.4, the Sales Manager Number attribute is the new attribute that has been added to the SALESPERSON relation. The domain of values of the new column is the same as the domain of values of the relation's primary key. Thus, the values in the new Sales Manager Number column will be three-digit whole numbers representing

(a) SALESPERSON relation

Salesperson Number	Salesperson Name	Commission Percentage	Year of Hire	Office Number
137	Baker	10	1995	1284
186	Adams	15	2001	1253
204	Dickens	10	1998	1209
361	Carlyle	20	2001	1227

(b) CUSTOMER relation

Customer Number	Customer Name	Salesperson Number	HQ City
0121	Main St. Hardware	137	New York
0839	Jane's Stores	186	Chicago
0933	ABC Home Stores	137	Los Angeles
1047	Acme Hardware Store	137	Los Angeles
1525	Fred's Tool Stores	361	Atlanta
1700	XYZ Stores	361	Washington
1826	City Hardware	137	New York
2198	Western Hardware	204	New York
2267	Central Stores	186	New York

(c) COUSTMER EMPLOYEE relation

Customer Number	Employee Number	Employee Name	Title
0121	27498	Smith	Co-Owner
0121	30441	Garcia	Co-Owner
0933	25270	Chen	VP Sales
0933	30441	Levy	Sales Manager
0933	48285	Morton	President
1525	33779	Baker	Sales Manager
2198	27470	Smith	President
2198	30441	Jones	VP Sales
2198	33779	Garcia	VP Personnel
2198	35268	Kaplan	Senior Accountant

(d) PRODUCT relation

Product Number	Product Name	Unit Price
16386	Wrench	12.95
19440	Hammer	17.50
21765	Drill	32.99
24013	Saw	26.25
26722	Pliers	11.50

(continues)

FIGURE 6.1 General Hardware Company relational database

(e) SALES relation

Salesperson Number	Product Number	Quantity
137	19440	473
137	24013	170
137	26722	688
186	16386	1745
186	19440	2529
186	21765	1962
186	24013	3071
204	21765	809
204	26722	734
361	16386	3729
361	21765	3110
361	26722	2738

(f) OFFICE relation

Office Number	Telephone	Size (sq. ft.)
1253	901-555-4276	120
1227	901-555-0364	120
1284	901-555-7335	120
1209	901-555-3108	95

FIGURE 6.1 (Continued) General Hardware Company relational database

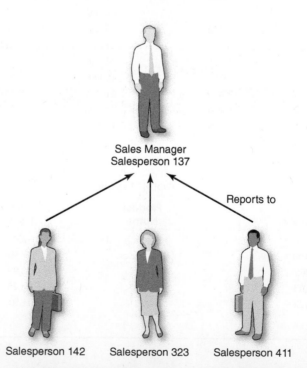

Sales Manager
Salesperson 137

Reports to

Salesperson 142   Salesperson 323   Salesperson 411

FIGURE 6.2 Salespersons 142, 323, and 411 reporting to salesperson 137 who is their sales manager

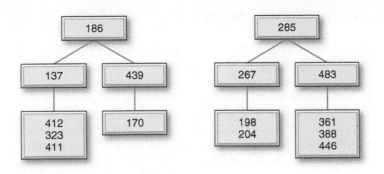

FIGURE 6.3 General Hardware Company salesperson reporting hierarchy

the unique identifiers for salespersons, just like the values in the Salesperson Number column. The value in the new column for a particular row represents the value of the next entity "upward" in the unary one-to-many hierarchy. For example, in the row for salesperson number 323, the sales manager value is 137 because salesperson 323's sales manager is salesperson/sales manager 137, as shown in Figure 6.3. Similarly, the row for salesperson 137, who happens also to be a sales manager, shows salesperson number 186 in its Sales Manager Number column. Salesperson/sales manager 137 reports to chief sales manager 186, also as shown in Figure 6.3. The sales manager column value for salesperson/chief sales manager 186 is blank because the reporting structure happens to end with each chief sales manager; i.e. there is nothing "above" salesperson 186 in Figure 6.3.

Note that a unary one-to-one relationship, for example, one salesperson backing-up another (see Figure 2.7a) is handled in a manner similar to Figure 6.4. The difference is that the Sales Manager Number column would be replaced by a Back-Up Number column and a particular salesperson number would appear at most once in that column.

SALESPERSON relation				
Salesperson Number	Salesperson Name	Commission Percentage	Year of Hire	Sales Manager Number
137	Baker	10	1995	186
142	Smith	15	2001	137
170	Taylor	18	1992	439
186	Adams	15	2001	
198	Wang	20	1990	267
204	Dickens	10	1998	267
267	Perez	22	2000	285
285	Costello	10	1996	
323	McNamara	15	1995	137
361	Carlyle	20	2001	483
388	Goldberg	20	1997	483
411	Davidson	18	1992	137
439	Warren	10	1996	186
446	Albert	10	2001	483
483	Jones	15	1995	285

FIGURE 6.4 General Hardware Company SALESPERSON relation including Sales Manager Number attribute

Unary Many-to-Many Relationships

The unary many-to-many relationship is a special case that has come to be known as the "bill of materials" problem. Among the entity occurrences of a single entity type, which is what makes this "unary," each particular entity occurrence can be related to many other occurrences and each of those latter occurrences can, in turn, be related to many other occurrences. Put another way, every entity occurrence can be related to many other occurrences, which, if you think about it, makes this a many-to-many relationship because only one entity type is involved. (Yes, that sounds a little strange, but keep reading.) The general idea is that in a complex item, say an automobile engine, small parts are assembled together to make a small component or assembly. Then some of those small components or assemblies (and maybe some small parts) are assembled together to make medium-sized components or assemblies, and so on until the final, top-level "component" is the automobile engine. The key concept here is that an assembly at any level is considered to be both a part made up of smaller units and a unit that can be a component of a larger part. Parts and assemblies at all levels are all considered occurrences of the same entity type and they all have a unique identifier in a single domain of values.

Certainly, this requires an example! Figure 6.5 illustrates this concept using an expansion of General Hardware Co.'s product set.

Product ◀◀ ——— ▶▶ Product

The numbers in parentheses are product numbers. Assume, as is quite reasonable, that General Hardware not only sells individual tools but also sells sets of tools. Both individual tools and sets of tools are considered to be "products," which also makes sense. As shown in Figure 6.5, General Hardware carries several types (or perhaps sizes) of wrenches, hammers, and drills. Various combinations of wrenches and hammers are sold as wrench and hammer sets. Various combinations of these sets and other tools such as drills are sold as even larger sets. Very importantly, notice the many-to-many nature of this arrangement. For example, the Master Wrench Set (product number 44), looking to its left, *is comprised of* three different wrenches, including Wrench Model A (#11). Conversely, Wrench Model A, looking to its right, *is a component of* two different wrench sets, both the Deluxe Wrench Set (#43) and the Master Wrench Set (#44). This demonstrates the many-to-many nature of products. Similarly, both the Supreme Tool Set (#53) and the Grand Tool Set (#56) are, obviously, comprised of several smaller sets and tools, while the Deluxe Hammer Set (#48) is a component of both the Supreme Tool Set (#53) and the Grand Tool Set (#56).

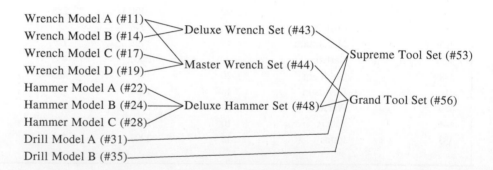

FIGURE 6.5 General Hardware Company product bill of materials

PRODUCT relation		
Product Number	Product Name	Unit Price
11	Wrench Model A	12.50
14	Wrench Model B	13.75
17	Wrench Model C	11.62
19	Wrench Model D	15.80
22	Hammer Model A	17.50
24	Hammer Model B	18.00
28	Hammer Model C	19.95
31	Drill Model A	31.25
35	Drill Model B	38.50
43	Deluxe Wrench Set	23.95
44	Master Wrench Set	35.00
48	Deluxe Hammer Set	51.00
53	Supreme Tool Set	100.00
56	Grand Tool Set	109.95

FIGURE 6.6 General Hardware Company modified PRODUCT relation

How can this unary many-to-many relationship be represented in a relational database? First of all, note that Figure 6.6 is a modification and expansion of the PRODUCT relation in the General Hardware Co. relational database of Figure 6.1d. Note that the product numbers matching the product numbers in Figure 6.5 have been reduced to two digits for simplicity in the explanation. Every individual unit item and every set in Figure 6.5 has its own row in the relation in Figure 6.6 because every item and set in Figure 6.5 is a *product* that General Hardware has for sale.

Now, here is the main point. Just as a binary many-to-many relationship requires the creation of an additional relation in a relational database, so does a unary many-to-many relationship. The new additional relation is shown in Figure 6.7. It consists of two attributes. The domain of values of *each* column is that of the Product Number

Assembly	Part
43	11
43	14
44	11
44	17
44	19
48	22
48	24
48	28
53	43
53	48
53	31
56	44
56	48
56	35

FIGURE 6.7 General Hardware Company unary many-to-many relation

column in the PRODUCT relation of Figure 6.6. The relation of Figure 6.7 represents, in a tabular format, the way that the assemblies of Figure 6.5 are constructed. The first two rows of Figure 6.7 literally say that product (assembly) number 43 (the Deluxe Wrench Set) is comprised of products 11 and 14, as indicated in Figure 6.5. Next, product (assembly) 44 is comprised of products 11, 17, and 19. Moving to the last three rows of the relation, product (assembly) 56 is comprised of products 44 and 48, both of which happen to be assemblies, and product 35. Again, notice the many-to-many relationship as it is represented in the relation of Figure 6.7. The first two rows indicate that assembly 43 *is comprised of* two parts. Conversely, the first and third rows indicate that part 11 *is a component of* two different assemblies.

Ternary Relationships

A ternary relationship is a relationship that involves three different entity types. If the entity types are A, B, and C, then we might illustrate this as:

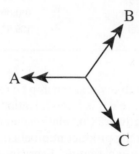

To demonstrate this concept in the broadest way using the General Hardware Co. database, let's slightly modify part of the General Hardware premise. The assumption has always been that there is a one-to-many relationship between salespersons and customers. A salesperson is responsible for several customers, while a customer is in contact with (is sold to by) exactly one of General Hardware's salespersons. For the purposes of describing a general ternary relationship, we change that premise temporarily to a many-to-many relationship between salespersons and customers. That is, we now assume that any salesperson can make a sale to any customer and any customer can buy from any salesperson.

With that change, consider the ternary relationship among salespersons, customers, and products. Such a relationship allows us to keep track of which salesperson sold which product to which customer. This is very significant. In this environment, a salesperson can sell many products and a salesperson can sell to many customers. A product can be sold by many salespersons and can be sold to many customers. A customer can buy many products and can buy from many salespersons. All of this leads to a lot of different possibilities for any given sale. So, it is very important to be able to tie down a particular sale by noting and recording which salesperson sold which product to which customer. For example, we might store the fact that salesperson 137 sold some of product number 24013 to customer 0839, Figure 6.8.

Relations a, b, and c of Figure 6.9 show the SALESPERSON, CUSTOMER, and PRODUCT relations, respectively, from the General Hardware relational database of Figure 6.1, except for one change. Since there is no longer a one-to-many relationship between salespersons and customers, the Salesperson Number foreign key in the

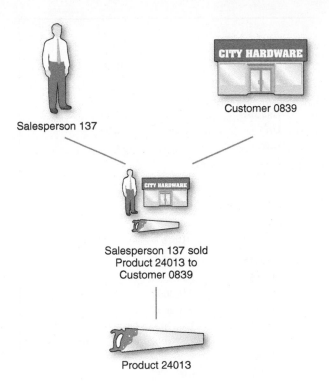

Salesperson 137

Customer 0839

Salesperson 137 sold
Product 24013 to
Customer 0839

Product 24013

FIGURE 6.8 A ternary relationship

(a) SALESPERSON relation

Salesperson Number	Salesperson Name	Commission Percentage	Year of Hire
137	Baker	10	1995
186	Adams	15	2001
204	Dickens	10	1998
361	Carlyle	20	2001

(b) CUSTOMER relation

Customer Number	Customer Name	HQ City
0121	Main St. Hardware	New York
0839	Jane's Stores	Chicago
0933	ABC Home Stores	Los Angeles
1047	Acme Hardware Store	Los Angeles
1525	Fred's Tool Stores	Atlanta
1700	XYZ Stores	Washington
1826	City Hardware	New York
2198	Western Hardware	New York
2267	Central Stores	New York

(continues)

FIGURE 6.9 A portion of General Hardware Company relational database modified to demonstrate a ternary relationship

(c) PRODUCT relation

Product Number	Product Name	Unit Price
16386	Wrench	12.95
19440	Hammer	17.50
21765	Drill	32.99
24013	Saw	26.25
26722	Pliers	11.50

(d) SALES relation

Salesperson Number	Customer Number	Product Number	Date	Quantity
137	0839	24013	2/21/2002	25
361	1700	16386	2/27/2002	70
137	2267	19440	3/1/2002	40
204	1047	19440	3/1/2002	15
186	0839	26722	3/12/2002	35
137	1700	16386	3/17/2002	65
361	0121	21765	3/21/2002	40
204	2267	19440	4/03/2002	30
204	0839	19440	4/17/2002	20

FIGURE 6.9 (Continued)
A portion of General Hardware Company relational database modified to demonstrate a ternary relationship

CUSTOMER relation has been removed! The three relations are now all quite independent with no foreign keys in any of them.

Figure 6.9d, the SALES relation, shows how this ternary relationship is represented in a relational database. Similarly to how we created an additional relation to accommodate a binary many-to-many relationship, an additional relation has to be created to accommodate a ternary relationship, and that relation is Figure 6.9d. Clearly, as in the binary many-to-many case, the primary key of the additional relation will be (at least) the combination of the primary keys of the entities involved in the relationship. Thus, in Figure 6.9d, the Salesperson Number, Customer Number, and Product Number attributes all appear as foreign keys and the combination of the three serves as part of the primary key. Why just "part of" the primary key? Because in this example, a particular salesperson may have sold a particular product to a particular customer more than once on different dates. Thus the Date attribute must also be part of the primary key. (We assume that this combination of the three could not have happened more than once on the same date. If it could, then there would also need to be a "time" attribute in the key.) Recall that this need for an additional attribute in the primary key also came up when we discussed binary many-to-many relationships in the last chapter. Finally, the Quantity attribute in Figure 6.9d is intersection data, just as it would be in a binary many-to-many relationship. The quantity of the product that the salesperson sold to the customer is clearly an attribute of the ternary relationship, not of any one of the entities.

There is one more important point to make about ternary relationships. In the process of describing the ternary relationship, you may have noticed that, taken two at a time, every pair of the three entities, salespersons, customers, and products, are in a binary many-to-many relationship. In general, this would be shown as:

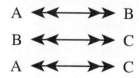

The question is: are these three many-to-many relationships the equivalent of the ternary relationship? Do they provide the same information that the ternary relationship does? The answer is, no!

Again, consider salespersons, customers, and products. You might know that a particular salesperson has made sales to a particular customer. You might also know that a particular salesperson has sold certain products at one time or another. And, you might know that a particular customer has bought certain products. But all of that is not the same thing as knowing that a particular salesperson sold a particular product to a particular customer. Still skeptical? Look at Figure 6.10. Parts a, b, and c of the figure clearly illustrate three many-to-many relationships. They are between (a) salespersons and customers, (b) customers and products, and (c) salespersons and products. Part a shows, among other things, that salesperson 137 sold something to customer 0839. Part b shows that customer 0839 bought product 19440. Does that mean that we can infer that salesperson 137 sold product 19440 to customer 0839? No! That's a possibility and, indeed, part c of the figure shows that salesperson 137 did sell product 19440. But part c of the figure also shows that salesperson 204 sold product 19440. Is it possible that salesperson 204 sold it to customer 0839? According to part a, salesperson 204 sold *something* to customer 0839, but it doesn't indicate what. You can go around and around Figure 6.10 and never conclude with certainty that salesperson 137 sold product 19440 to customer 0839. That would require a ternary relationship and a relation like the one in Figure 6.9d. Notice that the last row of Figure 6.9d shows, without a doubt, that it was salesperson 204 who sold product 19440 to customer 0839.

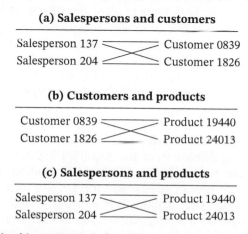

FIGURE 6.10 Ternary relationship counter-example

Your Turn

6.1 Ternary Relationships

Ternary relationships are all around us. Think about an automobile dealership. Certainly the dealership management wants to keep track of which car was sold to which customer by which salesperson. Certainly this is important for billing, accounting, and commission purposes. But also, in that kind of high-priced product environment, it's simply good business to keep track of such information for future marketing and customer relationship reasons.

Question:

Consider a hospital environment involving patients, doctors, nurses, procedures, medicines, hospital rooms, etc. Make a list of five ternary relationships in this environment. Remember that each one has to make sense from a business point of view.

Referential Integrity

The Referential Integrity Concept

Thus far in this chapter and the previous one, we have been concerned with how relations are constructed and how data can be retrieved from them. Data retrieval is the operation that clearly provides the ultimate benefit from maintaining a database, but it is not the only operation needed. Certainly, we should expect that, as with any data storage scheme, in addition to retrieving data we must be prepared to perform such data maintenance operations as inserting new records (or rows of a relation), deleting existing records, and updating existing records. All database management systems provide the facilities and commands to accomplish these data maintenance operations. But there are some potential pitfalls in these operations that must be dealt with.

The problem is that the logically related (by foreign keys) but physically independent nature of the relations in a relational database exposes the database to the possibility of a particular type of data integrity problem. This problem has come to be known as a **referential integrity** problem because it revolves around the circumstance of trying to *refer* to data in one relation in the database, based on values in another relation. (Actually, referential integrity is an issue in all of the DBMS approaches, not just the relational approach. We discuss this issue here because we are focusing on relational databases and the concept is much easier to explain in the context of an example, again the General Hardware database.) Also, while referential integrity problems can surface in any of the three operations that result in changes to the database—insert, delete, and update records—we will generally use the case of delete to explain the concept while mentioning insert and update where appropriate.

First, consider the situation of **record deletion** in the two relations of Figure 6.11, which is a repeat of Figure 5.2. Suppose that salesperson 361, Carlyle, left the company and his record was deleted from the SALESPERSON relation. The problem is that there are still two records in the CUSTOMER relation (the records for customers 1525 and 1700) that *refer* to salesperson 361, i.e. that have the value 361 in the Salesperson Number foreign key attribute. It is as if Carlyle left the company and his customers have not as yet been reassigned to other salespersons. If a relational join command was issued to join the two relations in order to (say) find the name of the salesperson responsible for customer 1525, there would be a problem. The relational DBMS would pick up the salesperson number value 361 in the record for customer

(a) SALESPERSON relation			
Salesperson Number	Salesperson Name	Commission Percentage	Year of Hire
137	Baker	10	1995
186	Adams	15	2001
204	Dickens	10	1998
361	Carlyle	20	2001

(b) CUSTOMER relation			
Customer Number	Customer Name	Salesperson Number	HQ City
0121	Main St. Hardware	137	New York
0839	Jane's Stores	186	Chicago
0933	ABC Home Stores	137	Los Angeles
1047	Acme Hardware Store	137	Los Angeles
1525	Fred's Tool Stores	361	Atlanta
1700	XYZ Stores	361	Washington
1826	City Hardware	137	New York
2198	Western Hardware	204	New York
2267	Central Stores	186	New York

FIGURE 6.11 General Hardware Company SALESPERSON and CUSTOMER relations

1525 in the CUSTOMER relation, but would not be able to match 361 to a record in the SALESPERSON relation because there no longer is a record for salesperson 361 in the SALESPERSON relation—it was deleted! Notice that the problem arose because the deleted record, a salesperson record, was on the "*one* side" of a one-to-many relationship. What about the customer records on the "*many* side" of the one-to-many relationship? Suppose customer 1047, Acme Hardware Store, is no longer one of General Hardware's customers. Deleting the record for customer 1047 in the CUSTOMER relation has no referential integrity exposure. Nothing else in these two relations refers to customer 1047.

Similar referential integrity arguments can be made for the record insertion and update operations, but the issue of whether the exposure is on the "*one* side" or the "*many* side" of the one-to-many relationship changes! Again, in the case of deletion, the problem occurred when a record was deleted on the "*one* side" of the one-to-many relationship. But, for insertion, if a new salesperson record is inserted into the Salesperson relation, i.e. a new record is inserted into the "*one* side" of the one-to-many relationship, there is no problem. All it means is that a new salesperson has joined the company but, as yet, has no customer responsibility. On the other hand, if a new customer record is inserted into the CUSTOMER relation, i.e. a new record is inserted into the "*many* side" of the one-to-many relationship, and it happens to include a salesperson number that does not have a match in the SALESPERSON relation, that would cause the same kind of problem as the deletion example above. Similarly, the update issue would concern updating a foreign key value, i.e. a salesperson number in the CUSTOMER relation with a new salesperson number that has no match in the SALESPERSON relation.

The early relational DBMSs did not provide any control mechanisms for referential integrity. Programmers and users were on their own to keep track of it and this upset many people. This was particularly the case because referential integrity issues in the older hierarchical and network DBMSs were more naturally controlled by the nature of the hierarchical and network data structures on which they were based, at the expense of some flexibility in database design. Modern relational DBMS's provide sophisticated control mechanisms for referential integrity with so-called "**delete rules**," "**insert rules**," and "**update rules**." These rules are specified between pairs of relations. We will take a look at the three most common delete rules, "**restrict**," "**cascade**," and "**set-to-null**," to illustrate the problem.

Three Delete Rules

Delete Rule: Restrict   Again, consider the two relations in Figure 6.11. If the delete rule between the two relations is restrict and an attempt is made to delete a record on the "*one* side" of the one-to-many relationship, the system will forbid the delete to take place if there are any matching foreign key values in the relation on the "*many* side." For example, if an attempt is made to delete the record for salesperson 361 in the SALESPERSON relation, the system will not permit the deletion to take place because the CUSTOMER relation records for customers 1525 and 1700 include salesperson number 361 as a foreign key value, Figure 6.12. This is as if to say, "You can't delete a salesperson record as long as there are customers for whom that salesperson is responsible." Clearly, this is a reasonable and necessary course of action in many business situations.

Delete Rule: Cascade   If the delete rule between the two relations is cascade and an attempt is made to delete a record on the "*one* side" of the relationship, not only will that record be deleted but all of the records on the "*many* side" of the relationship that have a matching foreign key value will also be deleted. That is, the deletion will *cascade* from one relation to the other. For example, if an attempt is made to delete the record for salesperson 361 in the SALESPERSON relation and the delete rule is cascade, that salesperson record will be deleted and so too, automatically, will the records for customers 1525 and 1700 in the CUSTOMER relation because they have 361 as a foreign key value, Figure 6.13. It is as if the assumption is that when a salesperson leaves the company, she always takes all of her customers along with her. While that might be a bit of a stretch in this case, there are many other business situations where it is not a

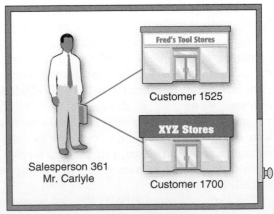

Fred's Tool Stores

Customer 1525

XYZ Stores

Customer 1700

Salesperson 361
Mr. Carlyle

Delete Rule: Restrict

FIGURE 6.12 Delete rule: Restrict

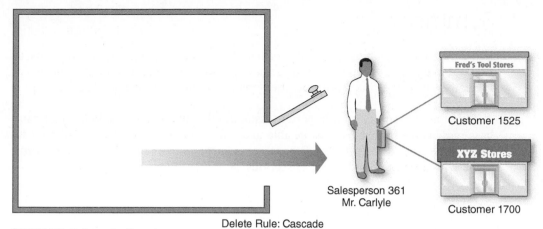

Delete Rule: Cascade

FIGURE 6.13 Delete rule: Cascade

stretch at all. For example, think about a company that has a main employee relation with name, home address, telephone number, etc., plus a second relation that lists and describes the several skills of each employee. Certainly, when an employee leaves the company you would expect to delete both his record in the main employee relation and all his records in the skills relation.

Delete Rule: Set-to-Null   If the delete rule between the two relations is set-to-null and an attempt is made to delete a record on the "*one* side" of the one-to-many relationship, that record will be deleted and the matching foreign key values in the records on the "*many* side" of the relationship will be changed to null. For example, if an attempt is made to delete the record for salesperson 361 in the SALESPERSON relation, that record will be deleted, and the Salesperson Number attribute values in the records for customers 1525 and 1700 in the CUSTOMER relation will be changed from 361 to null, Figure 6.14. This is as if to say, "You can delete a salesperson record and, we will indicate that, temporarily at least, their former customers are without a salesperson." Obviously this is the appropriate response in many business situations.

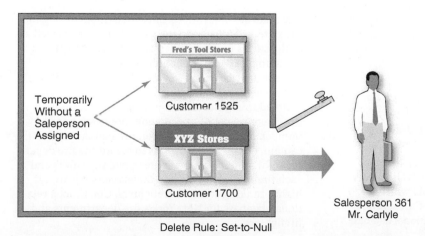

Delete Rule: Set-to-Null

FIGURE 6.14 Delete rule: Set-to-Null

Summary

Relational databases must be capable of handling unary and ternary relationships, as well as binary relationships. All of these have to promote data integration while avoiding data redundancy. As this chapter demonstrated, the relational database concept is up to this task.

Referential integrity is an important issue in relational databases. Relational database management systems must be able to allow users to specify referential integrity controls between related tables. Otherwise, changes to one table that are not coordinated with a related table may cause serious data integrity problems.

Key Terms

Cascade delete rule

Delete rules

Entity occurrence

Insert rules

Record deletion

Referential integrity

Restrict delete rule

Set-to-null delete rule

Update rules

Questions

1. Describe the concept of the unary one-to-many relationship.
2. How is a unary one-to-many relationship constructed in a relational database?
3. Describe the concept of the unary many-to-many relationship.
4. How is a unary many-to-many relationship constructed in a relational database?
5. Describe the concept of the ternary relationship.
6. How is a ternary relationship constructed in a relational database?
7. Is a ternary relationship the equivalent of the three possible binary relationships among the three entities involved? Explain.
8. Describe the problem of referential integrity.
9. Compare and contrast the three delete rules: restrict, cascade, and set-to-null.

Exercises

1. Leslie's Auto Sales has a relational database with which it maintains data on its salespersons, its customers, and the automobiles it sells. Each of these three entity types has a unique attribute identifier. The attributes that it stores are as follows:
    - Salesperson Number (unique), Salesperson Name, Salesperson Telephone, Years with Company
    - Customer Number (unique), Customer Name, Customer Address, Value of Last Purchase from Us
    - Vehicle Identification Number (unique), Manufacturer, Model, Year, Sticker Price. Leslie's also wants to keep track of which salesperson sold which car to which customer, including the date of the sale and the negotiated price. Construct a relational database for Leslie's Auto Sales.

2. The State of New York certifies firefighters throughout the state and must keep track of all of them, as well as of the state's fire departments. Each fire department has a unique department number, a name that also identifies its locale (city, county, etc.), the year it was established, and its main telephone number. Each certified firefighter has a unique firefighter number, a name, year of certification, home telephone number, and a rank (firefighter, fire lieutenant, fire captain, etc.). The state wants to record the fire department for which each firefighter currently works and each firefighter's supervisor. Supervisors are always higher-ranking certified firefighters. Construct a relational database for New York's fire departments and firefighters.

3. The ABC Consulting Corp. contracts for projects that, depending on their size and skill requirements, can be assigned to an individual consultant or to a team of consultants. A consultant or a team can work on several projects simultaneously. Several employees can be organized into a team. Larger teams can consist of a combination of smaller teams, sometimes with additional individual consultants added. This pattern can continue to larger and larger teams. ABC wants to keep track of its consultants, teams, and projects, including which consultant or team is responsible for each project. Each consultant has a unique employee number, plus a name, home address, and telephone number. Each project has a unique project number, plus a name, budgeted cost, and due date. Construct a relational database for ABC Consulting. Hint: You may want to develop an attribute called "responsible party" that can be either a team or an individual consultant. Each project has one responsible party that is responsible for its completion. Or you may want to think of an individual consultant as a potential "team of one" and have the responsibility for each project assigned to a "team" that could then be an individual consultant or a genuine team.

4. Consider the General Hardware Corp. database of Figure 6.1. Describe the problem of referential integrity in terms of the CUSTOMER and CUSTOMER EMPLOYEE relations if the record for customer 2198 in the CUSTOMER relation is deleted. (Assume that no delete rules exist.)

5. In the General Hardware Corp. database of Figure 6.1, what would happen if:
   a. The delete rule between the CUSTOMER and CUSTOMER EMPLOYEE relations is restrict and an attempt is made to delete the record for customer 2198 in the CUSTOMER relation?
   b. The delete rule between the CUSTOMER and CUSTOMER EMPLOYEE relations is cascade and an attempt is made to delete the record for customer 2198 in the CUSTOMER relation?
   c. The delete rule between the CUSTOMER and CUSTOMER EMPLOYEE relations is set-to-null and an attempt is made to delete the record for customer 2198 in the CUSTOMER relation?
   d. The delete rule between the CUSTOMER and CUSTOMER EMPLOYEE relations is restrict and an attempt is made to delete the record for employee 33779 of customer 2198 in the CUSTOMER EMPLOYEE relation?
   e. The delete rule between the CUSTOMER and CUSTOMER EMPLOYEE relations is cascade and an attempt is made to delete the record for employee 33779 of customer 2198 in the CUSTOMER EMPLOYEE relation?
   f. The delete rule between the CUSTOMER and CUSTOMER EMPLOYEE relations is set-to-null and an attempt is made to delete the record for employee 33779 of customer 2198 in the CUSTOMER EMPLOYEE relation?

Minicases

1. Happy Cruise Lines
   a. Look at the Happy Cruise Lines database of Chapter 5, Minicase 1 but, for this question, consider *only* the SHIP, PORT, and PASSENGER relations. The company wants to keep track of which passengers visited which ports on which ships on which dates. Reconstruct these three relations as necessary and/or add additional relation(s) as necessary to store this information.
   b. Consider the following data from the SHIP and CRUISE relations of the Happy Cruise Lines database of Chapter 5, Minicase 1:

SHIP Relation				
Ship Number	Ship Name	Ship Builder	Launch Date	Gross Weight
005	Sea Joy	Jones	1999	80,000
009	Ocean IV	Ajax	2003	75,000
012	Prince Al	Ajax	2004	90,000
020	Queen Shirley	Master	1999	80,000

CRUISE Relation				
Cruise Number	Start Date	End Date	Cruise Director	Ship Number
21644	7/5/2002	7/12/2002	Smith	009
23007	8/14/2002	8/24/2002	Chen	020
24288	3/28/2003	4/4/2003	Smith	009
26964	7/1/2003	7/11/2003	Gomez	020
27045	7/15/2003	7/22/2003	Adams	012
28532	8/17/2003	8/24/2003	Adams	012
29191	12/20/2003	12/27/2003	Jones	009
29890	1/15/2004	1/22/2004	Levin	020

What would happen if:

i. The delete rule between the SHIP and CRUISE relations is restrict and an attempt is made to delete the record for ship number 012 in the SHIP relation?

ii. The delete rule between the SHIP and CRUISE relations is restrict and an attempt is made to delete the record for ship number 005 in the SHIP relation?

iii. The delete rule between the SHIP and CRUISE relations is cascade and an attempt is made to delete the record for ship number 012 in the SHIP relation?

iv. The delete rule between the SHIP and CRUISE relations is cascade and an attempt is made to delete the record for ship number 005 in the SHIP relation?

v. The delete rule between the SHIP and CRUISE relations is set-to-null and an attempt is made to delete the record for ship number 012 in the SHIP relation?

vi. The delete rule between the SHIP and CRUISE relations is set-to-null and an attempt is made to delete the record for ship number 005 in the SHIP relation?

vii. The delete rule between the SHIP and CRUISE relations is restrict and an attempt is made to delete the record for cruise number 26964 in the CRUISE relation?

viii. The delete rule between the SHIP and CRUISE relations is cascade and an attempt

is made to delete the record for cruise number 26964 in the CRUISE relation?

ix. The delete rule between the SHIP and CRUISE relations is set-to-null and an attempt is made to delete the record for cruise number 26964 in the CRUISE relation?

2. Super Baseball League

a. In the Super Baseball League database of Chapter 5, Minicase 2, assume that instead of having coaches who are different from players, now some of the players serve as coaches to other players. A player/coach can have several players whom he coaches. Each player is coached by only one player/coach. Reconstruct the database structure to reflect this change.

b. In the Super Baseball League database of Chapter 5, Minicase 2, assume that the TEAM relation has a record for team number 17 and that the COACH relation has records for three coaches on that team. What would happen if:

i. The delete rule between the TEAM and COACH relations is restrict and an attempt is made to delete the record for team 17 in the TEAM relation?

ii. The delete rule between the TEAM and COACH relations is cascade and an attempt is made to delete the record for team 17 in the TEAM relation?

iii. The delete rule between the TEAM and COACH relations is set-to-null and an attempt is made to delete the record for team 17 in the TEAM relation?

iv. The delete rule between the TEAM and COACH relations is restrict and an attempt is made to delete the record for one of team 17's coaches in the COACH relation?

v. The delete rule between the TEAM and COACH relations is cascade and an attempt is made to delete the record for one of team 17's coaches in the COACH relation?

vi. The delete rule between the TEAM and COACH relations is set-to-null and an attempt is made to delete the record for one of team 17's coaches in the COACH relation?

Logical Database Design

Logical database design is the process of deciding how to arrange the attributes of the entities in a given business environment into database structures, such as the tables of a relational database. The goal of logical database design is to create well-structured tables that properly reflect the company's business environment. The tables will be able to store data about the company's entities in a non-redundant manner and foreign keys will be placed in the tables so that all the relationships among the entities will be supported. Physical database design, which will be treated in the next chapter, is the process of modifying the logical database design to improve performance.

OBJECTIVES

Describe the concept of logical database design.
Design relational databases by converting entity-relationship diagrams into relational tables.
Describe the data normalization process.
Perform the data normalization process.
Test tables for irregularities using the data normalization process.
Learn basic SQL commands to build *data structures*.
Learn basic SQL commands to manipulate data.

Introduction

Historically, a number of techniques have been used for logical database design. In the 1970s, when the hierarchical and network approaches to database management were the only ones available, a technique known as **data normalization** was developed. While data normalization has some very useful features, it was difficult to apply in that environment. Data normalization can also be used to design relational databases and, actually, is a better fit for relational databases than it was for the hierarchical and network databases. But, as the relational approach to database management and the entity-relationship approach to data modeling both blossomed in the 1980s, a very natural and pleasing approach to logical database design evolved in which rules were developed to convert E-R diagrams into relational tables. Optionally, the result of this process can then be tested with the data normalization technique. Thus, this chapter on the logical design of relational databases will proceed in three parts: first, the conversion of E-R diagrams into relational tables, then the data normalization technique, and finally the use of the data normalization technique to test the tables resulting from the **E-R diagram conversions**.

Converting E-R Diagrams into Relational Tables

Introduction

Converting entity-relationship diagrams to relational tables is surprisingly straight-forward, with just a few simple rules to follow. Basically, each entity will convert to a table, plus each many-to-many relationship or associative entity will convert to a table. The only other issue is that during the conversion, certain rules must be followed to ensure that foreign keys appear in their proper places in the tables. We will demonstrate these techniques by methodically converting the E-R diagrams of Chapter 2 into relational tables.

Converting a Simple Entity

Figure 7.1 repeats the simple entity box in Figure 2.1. Figure 7.2 shows a relational table that can store the data represented in the entity box. The table simply contains the attributes that were specified in the entity box. Notice that Salesperson Number is

FIGURE 7.1 The entity box from Figure 2.1

SALESPERSON			
Salesperson Number	Salesperson Name	Commission Percentage	Year of Hire

FIGURE 7.2 Conversion of an E-R diagram entity box to a relational table

underlined to indicate that it is the unique identifier of the entity, and the primary key of the table. Clearly, the more interesting issues and rules come about when, as almost always happens, entities are involved in relationships with other entities.

Converting Entities in Binary Relationships

One-to-One Binary Relationship   Figure 7.3 repeats the one-to-one binary relationship of Figure 2.4a. There are three options for designing tables to represent this data, as shown in Figure 7.4. In Figure 7.4a, the two entities are combined into one relational table. On the one hand, this is possible because the one-to-one relationship means that for one salesperson, there can only be one associated office and conversely, for one office there can be only one salesperson. So a particular salesperson and office combination can fit together in one record, as shown in Figure 7.4a. On the other hand, this design is not a good choice for two reasons. One reason is that the very fact that salesperson and office were drawn in two different entity boxes in the E-R diagram of Figure 7.3 means that they are thought of separately in this business environment and thus should be kept separate in the database. The other reason is the modality of zero at the salesperson in Figure 7.3. Reading that diagram from right to left, it says that an office might have no one assigned to it. Thus, in the table in Figure 7.4a, there could be a few or possibly many record occurrences that have values for the office number, telephone, and size attributes but have the four attributes pertaining to salespersons empty or null! This could result in a lot of wasted storage space, but it is worse than that. If Salesperson Number is declared to be the primary key of the table, this scenario would mean that there would be records with no primary key values, a situation which is clearly not allowed.

Figure 7.4b is a better choice. There are separate tables for the salesperson and office entities. In order to record the relationship, i.e. which salesperson is assigned to which office, the Office Number attribute is placed as a foreign key in the SALESPERSON table. This connects the salespersons with the offices to which they are assigned. Again, look at the modalities in the E-R diagram in Figure 7.3. Reading from left to right, each salesperson is assigned to exactly one office (indicated by the two "ones" adjacent to the office entity). That translates directly into each record in the SALESPERSON table of Figure 7.4b having a value (and a single value, at that) for its Office Number foreign key attribute. That's good! But what about the problem of unassigned offices mentioned in the previous paragraph? In Figure 7.4b, unassigned offices will each have a record in the OFFICE table, with Office Number as the primary key, which is fine. Their office numbers will simply not appear as foreign key values in the SALESPERSON table.

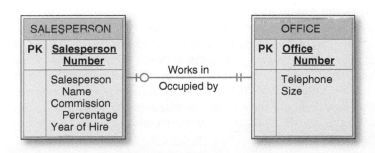

FIGURE 7.3 The one-to-one (1-1) binary relationship from Figure 2.4a

SALESPERSON/OFFICE						
<u>Salesperson Number</u>	Salesperson Name	Commission Percentage	Year of Hire	<u>Office Number</u>	Telephone	Size

a. One-to-one binary relationship converted to a single relational table.

SALESPERSON				
<u>Salesperson Number</u>	Salesperson Name	Commission Percentage	Year of Hire	<u>Office Number</u>

OFFICE		
<u>Office Number</u>	Telephone	Size

b. One-to-one binary relationship converted to two relational tables, with the foreign key in the SALESPERSON table.

SALESPERSON			
<u>Salesperson Number</u>	Salesperson Name	Commission Percentage	Year of Hire

OFFICE			
<u>Office Number</u>	Telephone	<u>Salesperson Number</u>	Size

c. One-to-one binary relationship converted to two relational tables, with the foreign key in the OFFICE table.

FIGURE 7.4 Conversion of an E-R diagram with two entities in a one-to-one binary relationship into one or two relational tables

Finally, instead of placing Office Number as a foreign key in the SALESPERSON table, could you instead place Salesperson Number as a foreign key in the OFFICE table, Figure 7.4c? Recall that, reading the E-R diagram of Figure 7.3 from right to left, the modality of zero adjacent to the salesperson entity says that an office might be empty, i.e. it might not be assigned to any salesperson. But then, some or perhaps many records of the OFFICE table of Figure 7.4c would have no value or a null in their Salesperson Number foreign key attribute positions. Why bother having to deal with this situation when the design in Figure 7.4b avoids it?

Certainly, it follows that if the modalities were reversed, meaning that the zero modality was adjacent to the office entity box and the one modality was adjacent to the salesperson entity box, then the design in Figure 7.4c would be the preferable one. This would mean that every office must have a salesperson assigned to it but a salesperson may or may not be assigned to an office. Perhaps lots of the salespersons travel most of the time and don't need offices. By the way, while we're in "what if" mode, what if the modality was zero *on both sides*? Then there would be a judgment call to make between the designs of Figure 7.4b and Figure 7.4c. If the goal is to minimize the number of null values in the foreign key, then you have to decide whether it is more likely that a salesperson is not assigned to an office (Figure 7.4c is preferable) or that an office is empty (Figure 7.4b is preferable).

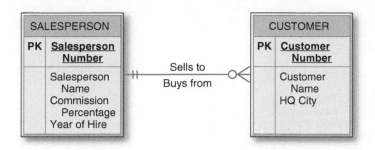

FIGURE 7.5 The one-to-many (1-M) binary relationship from Figure 2.4b

SALESPERSON			
Salesperson Number	Salesperson Name	Commission Percentage	Year of Hire

CUSTOMER			
Customer Number	Customer Name	HQ City	Salesperson Number

FIGURE 7.6 Conversion of an E-R diagram with two entities in a one-to-many binary relationship into two relational tables

One-to-Many Binary Relationship   Figure 7.5 (copied from Figure 2.4b) shows an E-R diagram for a one-to-many binary relationship. Figure 7.6 shows the conversion of this E-R diagram into two relational tables. This is, perhaps, the simplest case of all. The rule is that the unique identifier of the entity on the "*one* side" of the one-to-many relationship is placed as a foreign key in the table representing the entity on the "*many* side." In this case, the Salesperson Number attribute is placed in the CUSTOMER table as a foreign key. Each salesperson has one record in the SALESPERSON table, as does each customer in the CUSTOMER table. The Salesperson Number attribute in the CUSTOMER table links the two and, since the E-R diagram tells us that every customer must have a salesperson, there are no empty attributes in the CUSTOMER table records.

Many-to-Many Binary Relationship   Figure 7.7 shows the E-R diagram with the many-to-many binary relationship from Figure 2.5. The equivalent diagram from Figure 2.6, using an associative entity, is shown in Figure 7.8. An E-R diagram with two entities in a many-to-many relationship converts to three relational tables, as shown in Figure 7.9. Each of the two entities converts to a table with its own attributes but with no foreign keys (regarding this relationship). The SALESPERSON table and the PRODUCT table in Figure 7.9 each contain only the attributes shown in the salesperson and product entity boxes of Figures 7.7 and 7.8.

In addition, there must be a third "many-to-many" table for the many-to-many relationship, the reasons for which were explained in Chapter 5. The primary key of this additional table is the combination of the unique identifiers of the two entities in the many-to-many relationship. Additional attributes consist of the intersection data, Quantity in this example. Also as explained in Chapter 5, there are circumstances in which additional attributes, such as date and timestamp attributes, must be added to the primary key of the many-to-many table to achieve uniqueness.

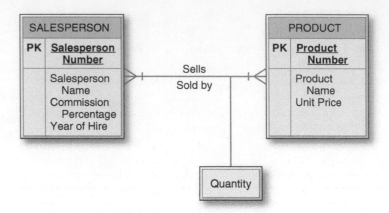

FIGURE 7.7 The many-to-many binary relationship
from Figure 2.5

FIGURE 7.8 The
associative entity
from Figure 2.6

FIGURE 7.9 Conversion of an
E-R diagram in Figure 7.7
(and Figure 7.8) with two
entities in a many-to-many
binary relationship into three
relational tables

SALESPERSON			
Salesperson Number	Salesperson Name	Commission Percentage	Year of Hire

PRODUCT		
Product Number	Product Name	Unit Price

SALE		
Salesperson Number	Product Number	Quantity

Converting Entities in Unary Relationships

One-to-One Unary Relationship   Figure 7.10 repeats the E-R diagram with a one-to-one unary relationship from Figure 2.7a. In this case, with only one entity type involved and with a one-to-one relationship, the conversion requires only one table, as shown in Figure 7.11. For a particular salesperson, the Backup Number attribute represents the salesperson number of his backup person, i.e. the person who handles his accounts when he is away for any reason.

One-to-Many Unary Relationship   The one-to-many unary relationship situation is very similar to the one-to-one unary case. Figure 7.12 repeats the E-R diagram from Figure 2.7b. Figure 7.13 shows the conversion of this diagram into a relational database. Some employees manage other employees. An employee's manager is recorded in the Manager Number attribute in the table in Figure 7.13. The manager numbers are actually salesperson numbers since some salespersons are sales managers who manage other salespersons. This arrangement works because each employee has only one manager. For any particular SALESPERSON record, there can only be one value

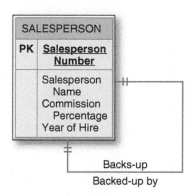

FIGURE 7.10 The one-to-one (1-1) unary relationship from Figure 2.7a

SALESPERSON				
Salesperson Number	Salesperson Name	Commission Percentage	Year of Hire	Backup Number

FIGURE 7.11 Conversion of the E-R diagram in Figure 7.10 with a one-to-one unary relationship into a relational table

FIGURE 7.12 The one-to-many (1-M) unary relationship from Figure 2.7b

SALESPERSON				
Salesperson Number	Salesperson Name	Commission Percentage	Year of Hire	Manager Number

for the Manager Number attribute. However, if you scan down the Manager Number column, you will see that a particular value may appear several times because a person can manage several other salespersons.

Many-to-Many Unary Relationship   Figure 7.14 shows the E-R diagram for the many-to-many unary relationship of Figure 2.7c. As Figure 7.15 indicates, this relationship requires two tables in the conversion. The PRODUCT table has no foreign keys. The COMPONENT table indicates which items go into making up which other items, as was described in the bill-of-materials discussion in Chapter 6. This table also contains any intersection data that may exist in the many-to-many relationship. In this example, the Quantity attribute indicates how many of a particular item go into making up another item.

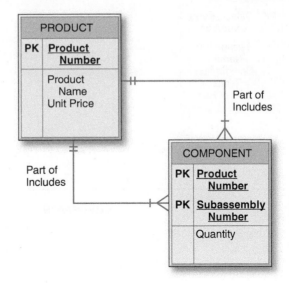

FIGURE 7.14 The many-to-many unary relationship from Figure 2.7c

PRODUCT		
Product Number	Product Name	Unit Price

COMPONENT		
Product Number	Subassembly Number	Quantity

FIGURE 7.15 Conversion of the E-R diagram in Figure 7.14 with a many-to-many unary relationship into two relational tables

The fact that we wind up with two tables in this conversion is really not surprising. The general rule is that in the conversion of a many-to-many relationship of *any* degree (unary, binary, or ternary), the number of tables will be equal to the number of entity types (one, two, or three, respectively) plus one more table for the many-to-many relationship. Thus, the conversion of the many-to-many unary relationship required two tables, the many-to-many binary relationship three tables, and, as will be shown next, the many-to-many ternary relationship four tables.

Converting Entities in Ternary Relationships

Finally, Figure 7.16 repeats the E-R diagram with the ternary relationship from Figure 2.8. Figure 7.17 shows the four tables necessary for the conversion to relational tables. Notice that the primary key of the SALE table, which is the table added for the many-to-many relationship, is the combination of the unique identifiers of the three entities involved, plus the Date attribute. In this case, with the premise being that a particular salesperson can have sold a particular product to a particular customer *on different days*, the Date attribute is needed in the primary key to achieve uniqueness.

Designing the General Hardware Co. Database

Having explored the specific E-R diagram-to-relational database conversion rules, let's look at a few examples, beginning with the General Hardware Co. Figure 7.18 is the General Hardware E-R diagram. It is convenient to begin the database design process

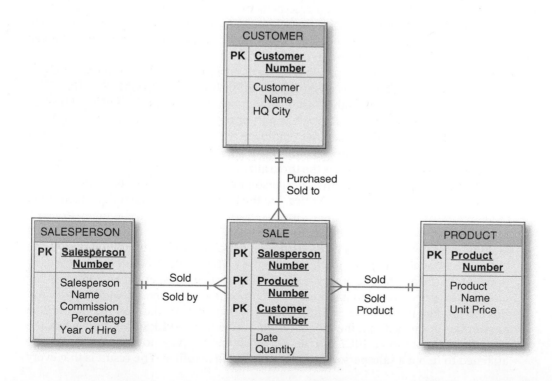

FIGURE 7.16 The ternary relationship from Figure 2.8

SALESPERSON			
<u>Salesperson Number</u>	Salesperson Name	Commission Percentage	Year of Hire

CUSTOMER		
<u>Customer Number</u>	Customer Name	HQ City

PRODUCT		
<u>Product Number</u>	Product Name	Unit Price

SALE				
<u>Salesperson Number</u>	<u>Customer Number</u>	<u>Product Number</u>	Date	Quantity

FIGURE 7.17 Conversion of the E-R diagram in Figure 7.16 with three entities in a ternary relationship into four relational tables

with an important, central E-R diagram entity, such as salesperson, that has relationships with several other entities. Thus, the relational database in Figure 7.19 includes a SALESPERSON table with the four salesperson attributes shown in Figure 7.18's salesperson entity box (plus the Office Number attribute, to which we will return shortly). To the right of the salesperson entity box in the E-R diagram, there is a one-to-many relationship ("Sells To") between salespersons and customers. The database then includes a CUSTOMER table with the Salesperson Number attribute as a foreign key, because salesperson is on the "*one* side" of the one-to-many relationship and customer is on the "*many* side" of the one-to-many relationship.

Customer employee is a dependent entity of customer and there is a one-to-many relationship between them. Because of this relationship, the CUSTOMER EMPLOYEE table in the database includes the Customer Number attribute as a foreign key. Furthermore, the Customer Number attribute is part of the primary key of the CUSTOMER EMPLOYEE table because customer employee is a dependent entity and we're told that employee numbers are unique only within a customer.

The PRODUCT table contains the three attributes of the product entity. The many-to-many relationship between the salesperson and product entities is represented by the SALES table in the database. Notice that the combination of the unique identifiers (Salesperson Number and Product Number) of the two entities in the many-to-many relationship is the primary key of the SALES table. Finally, the office entity has its table in the database with its three attributes, which brings us to the presence of the Office Number attribute as a foreign key in the SALESPERSON table. This is needed to maintain the one-to-one binary relationship between salesperson and office. A fair question is, since the relationship is "one" on both sides, why did we decide to put the foreign key in the SALESPERSON table rather than in the OFFICE table? The answer lies in the fact that the modality adjacent to SALESPERSON is zero while the modality adjacent to OFFICE is one. An office may or may not have a salesperson assigned to it, but a salesperson *must* be assigned to an office. The result is that every

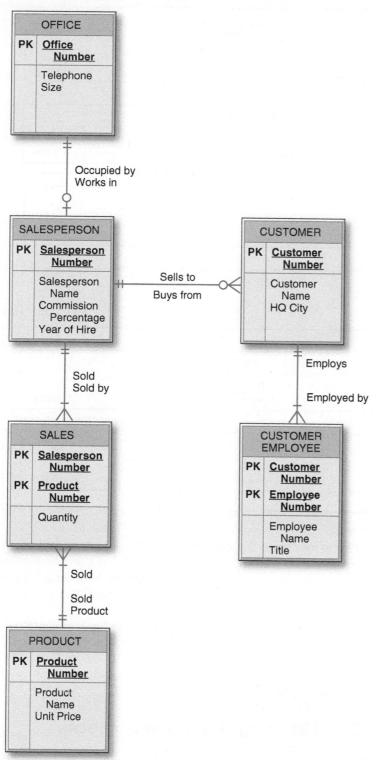

FIGURE 7.18 The General Hardware Company
E-R diagram

SALESPERSON				
<u>Salesperson Number</u>	Salesperson Name	Commission Percentage	Year of Hire	<u>Office Number</u>

CUSTOMER			
<u>Customer Number</u>	Customer Name	<u>Salesperson Number</u>	HQ City

CUSTOMER EMPLOYEE			
<u>Customer Number</u>	<u>Employee Number</u>	Employee Name	Title

PRODUCT		
<u>Product Number</u>	Product Name	Unit Price

SALES		
<u>Salesperson Number</u>	<u>Product Number</u>	Quantity

OFFICE		
<u>Office Number</u>	Telephone	Size

FIGURE 7.19 The General Hardware Company relational database

salesperson must have an associated office number; the Office Number attribute in the SALESPERSON table can't be null. If we reversed it and put the Salesperson Number attribute in the OFFICE table, many of the Salesperson Number attribute values could be null since the zero modality going from office to salesperson tells us that an office can be empty.

One last thought: Why did the PRODUCT table end-up without any foreign keys? Because it is not the "target" (it is not on the "*many* side") of any one-to-many binary relationship. It is also not involved in a one-to-one binary relationship that would require the presence of a foreign key. Finally, it is not involved in a unary relationship that would require repeating the primary key in the table.

Designing the Good Reading Bookstores Database

The Good Reading Bookstores' E-R diagram is repeated in Figure 7.20. Beginning with the central book entity and looking to its left, we see that there is a one-to-many relationship between books and publishers. A publisher publishes many books but a book is published by just one publisher. The Good Reading Bookstores relational

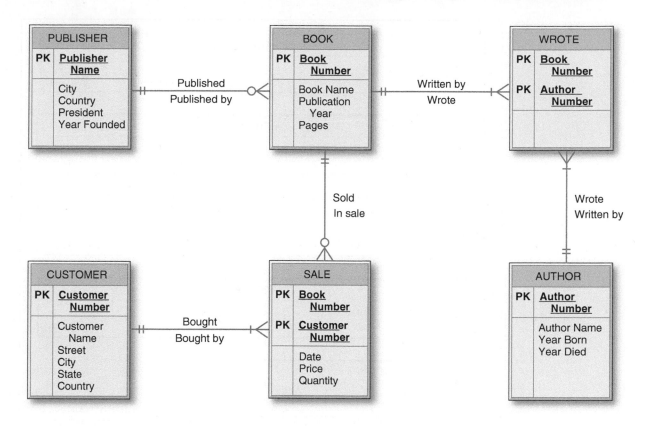

FIGURE 7.20 Good Reading Bookstores entity-relationship diagram

database of Figure 7.21 shows the BOOK and PUBLISHER tables. Publisher Name is a foreign key in the BOOK table because publisher is on the "*one* side" of the one-to-many relationship and book is on the "*many* side." Next is the AUTHOR table, which is straightforward. The many-to-many binary relationship between books and authors is reflected in the WRITING table, which has no intersection data. Finally, there is the customer entity and the many-to-many relationship between books and customers. Correspondingly, the relational database includes a CUSTOMER table and a SALE table to handle the many-to-many relationship. Notice the Date, Price, and Quantity attributes appearing in the SALE table as intersection. Also notice that since a customer can buy the same book on more than one day, the Date attribute must be part of the primary key to achieve uniqueness.

Your Turn

7.1 The E-R Diagram Conversion Logical Design Technique

In Your Turn in Chapter 2, you created an entity-relationship diagram for your university environment.

Question:

Using the logical design techniques just described, convert your university E-R diagram into a logical database design.

PUBLISHER

Publisher Name	City	Country	Telephone	Year Founded

AUTHOR

Author Number	Author Name	Year Born	Year Died

BOOK

Book Number	Book Name	Publication Year	Pages	Publisher Name

CUSTOMER

Customer Number	Customer Name	Street	City	State	Country

WRITING

Book Number	Author Number

SALE

Book Number	Customer Number	Date	Price	Quantity

FIGURE 7.21 The Good Reading Bookstores relational database

Designing the World Music Association Database

Looking at the World Music Association E-R diagram in Figure 7.22, it appears that the orchestra entity would be a good central starting point for the database design process. Thus, the relational database in Figure 7.23 begins with the ORCHESTRA table. The Orchestra Name foreign key in the MUSICIAN table reflects the one-to-many relationship from orchestra to musician. Since degree is a dependent entity of musician in a one-to-many relationship and degrees (e.g. B.A.) are unique only within a musician, not only does Musician Number appear as a foreign key in the DEGREE table but also it must be part of that table's primary key. A similar situation exists between the composer and composition entities, as shown in the COMPOSER and COMPOSITION tables in the database. Finally, the many-to-many relationship between orchestra and composition is converted into the RECORDING table. Notice that the primary key of the RECORDING table begins with the Orchestra Name attribute and then continues with both the Composition Name and Composer Name attributes. This is because the primary key of one of the two entities in the many-to-many relationship, composition, is the combination of those two latter attributes.

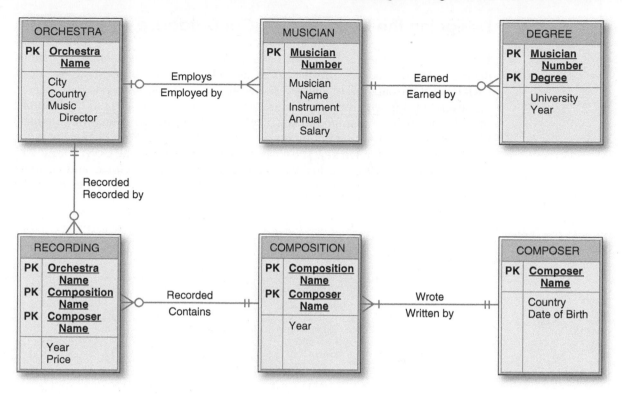

FIGURE 7.22 World Music Association entity-relationship diagram

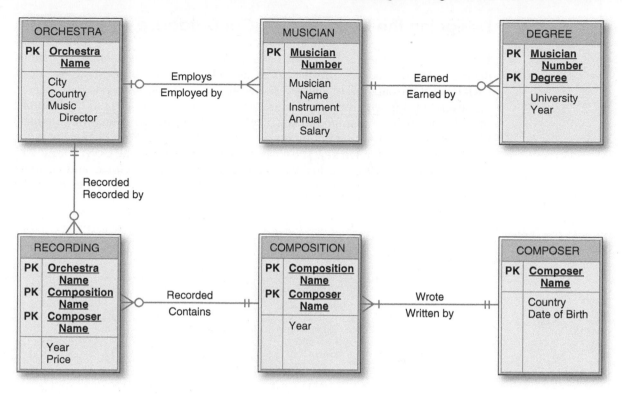

FIGURE 7.23 The World Music Association relational database

Designing the Lucky Rent-A-Car Database

Figure 7.24 shows the Lucky Rent-A-Car E-R diagram. The conversion to a relational database structure begins with the car entity and its four attributes, as shown in the CAR table of the database in Figure 7.25. Because car is on the *many* side" of a one-to-many relationship with the manufacturer entity, the CAR table also has the Manufacturer Name attribute as a foreign key. The straightforward one-to-many relationship from car to maintenance event produces a MAINTENANCE EVENT table with Car Serial Number as a foreign key. The customer entity converts to the CUSTOMER table with its four attributes. The many-to-many relationship between car and customer converts to the RENTAL table. Car Serial Number, the unique identifier of the car

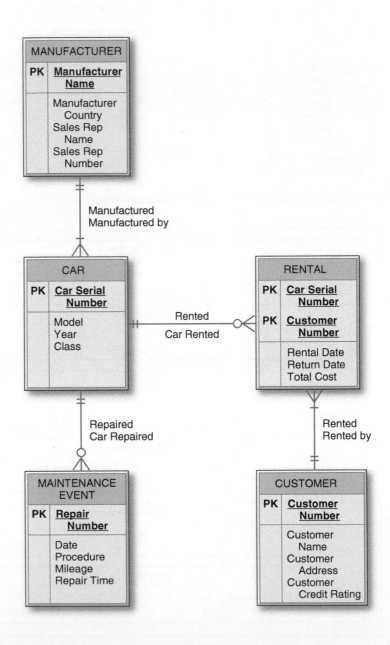

FIGURE 7.24 Lucky Rent-A-Car entity-relationship diagram

MANUFACTURER			
<u>Manufacturer Name</u>	Manufacturer Country	Sales Rep Name	Sales Rep Telephone

CAR				
<u>Car Serial Number</u>	Model	Year	Class	<u>Manufacturer Name</u>

MAINTENANCE					
<u>Repair Number</u>	<u>Car Serial Number</u>	Date	Procedure	Mileage	Repair Time

CUSTOMER			
<u>Customer Number</u>	Customer Name	Customer Address	Customer Telephone

RENTAL				
<u>Car Serial Number</u>	<u>Customer Number</u>	<u>Rental Date</u>	Return Date	Total Cost

FIGURE 7.25 The Lucky Rent-A-Car relational database

entity, and Customer Number, the unique identifier of the customer entity, plus the Rental Date intersection data attribute form the three-attribute primary key of the RENTAL table, with Return Date and Total Cost as additional intersection data attributes. Rental Date has to be part of the primary key to achieve uniqueness because a particular customer may have rented a particular car on several different dates.

The Data Normalization Process

Data normalization was the earliest formalized database design technique and at one time was the starting point for logical database design. Today, with the popularity of the Entity-Relationship model and other such diagramming tools and the ability to convert its diagrams to database structures, data normalization is used more as a check on database structures produced from E-R diagrams than as a full-scale database design technique. That's one of the reasons for learning about data normalization. Another reason is that the data normalization process is another way of demonstrating and learning about such important topics as data redundancy, foreign keys, and other ideas that are so central to a solid understanding of database management.

Data normalization is a methodology for organizing attributes into tables so that redundancy among the non-key attributes is eliminated. Each of the resultant tables deals with a single data focus, which is just another way of saying that each resultant table will describe a single entity type or a single many-to-many relationship. Furthermore, foreign keys will appear exactly where they are needed. In other words, the output of the data normalization process is a properly structured relational database.

Introduction to the Data Normalization Technique

The input required by the data normalization process has two parts. One is a list of all the attributes that must be incorporated into the database: that is, all of the attributes in all of the entities involved in the business environment under discussion plus all of the intersection data attributes in all of the many-to-many relationships between these entities. The other input, informally, is a list of all of the defining associations among the attributes. Formally, these defining associations are known as functional dependencies. And what are defining associations or functional dependencies? They are a means of expressing that the value of one particular attribute is associated with a specific single value of another attribute. If we know that one of these attributes has a particular value, then the other attribute *must* have some other value. For example, for a particular Salesperson Number, 137, there is exactly one Salesperson Name, Baker, associated with it. Why is this true? In this example, a Salesperson Number uniquely identifies a salesperson and, after all, a person can have only one name! And this is true for every person! Informally, we might say that Salesperson Number *defines* Salesperson Name. If I give you a Salesperson Number, you can give me back the one and only name that goes with it. (It's a little like the concept of independent and dependent variables in mathematics. Take a value of the independent variable, plug it into the formula and you get back the specific value of the dependent variable associated with that independent variable.) These defining associations are commonly written with a right-pointing arrow like this:

$$\text{Salesperson Number} \longrightarrow \text{Salesperson Name}$$

In the more formal terms of functional dependencies, Salesperson Number, in general the attribute on the left side, is referred to as the determinant. Why? Because its value *determines* the value of the attribute on the right side. Conversely, we also say that the attribute on the right is *functionally dependent* on the attribute on the left.

Data normalization is best explained with an example and this is a good place to start one. In order to demonstrate the main points of the data normalization process, we will modify part of the General Hardware Co. business environment and focus on the salesperson and product entities. Let's assume that salespersons are organized into departments and each department has a manager who is not herself a salesperson. Then the list of attributes we will consider is shown in Figure 7.26. The list of defining associations or functional dependencies is shown in Figure 7.27.

Salesperson Number
Salesperson Name
Commission Percentage
Year of Hire
Department Number
Manager Name
Product Number
Product Name
Unit Price
Quantity

FIGURE 7.26 List of attributes for salespersons and products

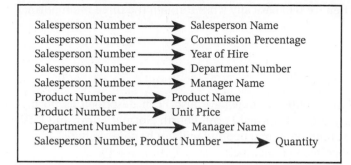

FIGURE 7.27 List of defining associations (functional dependencies) for the attributes of salespersons and products

Notice a couple of fine points about the list of defining associations in Figure 7.27. The last association:

$$\text{Salesperson Number, Product Number} \longrightarrow \text{Quantity}$$

shows that the *combination* of two or more attributes may possibly define another attribute. That is, the combination of a particular Salesperson Number and a particular Product Number defines or specifies a particular Quantity. Put another way, in this business context, we know how many units of a particular product a particular salesperson has sold. Another point, which will be important in demonstrating one step of the data normalization process, is that Manager Name is defined, independently, by two different attributes: Salesperson Number and Department Number:

$$\text{Salesperson Number} \longrightarrow \text{Manager Name}$$
$$\text{Department Number} \longrightarrow \text{Manager Name}$$

Both these defining associations are true! If I identify a salesperson by his Salesperson Number, you can tell me who his manager is. Also, if I state a department number, you can tell me who the manager of the department is. How did we wind up with two different ways to define the same attribute? Very easily! It simply means that during the systems analysis process, both these equally true defining associations were discovered and noted. By the way, the fact that I know the department that a salesperson works in:

$$\text{Salesperson Number} \longrightarrow \text{Department Number}$$

(and that each of these two attributes independently define Manager Name) will also be an issue in the data normalization process. More about this later.

Steps in the Data Normalization Process

The data normalization process is known as a "decomposition process." Basically, we are going to line up all the attributes that will be included in the relational database and start subdividing them into groups that will eventually form the database's tables. Thus, we are going to "decompose" the original list of all of the attributes into subgroups. To do this, we are going to step through a number of normal forms. First, we will demonstrate what unnormalized data looks like. After all, if data can exist in several different normal forms, then there should be the possibility that data is in none of the normal forms, too! Then we will basically work through the three main normal forms in order:

First Normal Form
Second Normal Form
Third Normal Form

There are certain "exception conditions" that have also been described as normal forms. These include the Boyce-Codd Normal Form, Fourth Normal Form, and Fifth Normal Form. They are less common in practice and will not be covered here.

Here are three additional points to remember:

1. Once the attributes are arranged in third normal form (and if none of the exception conditions are present), the group of tables that they comprise is, in fact, a well-structured relational database with no data redundancy.
2. A group of tables is said to be in a particular normal form if every table in the group is in that normal form.
3. The data normalization process is progressive. If a group of tables is in second normal form it is also in first normal form. If they are in third normal form they are also in second normal form.

Unnormalized Data   Figure 7.28 shows the salesperson and product-related attributes listed in Figure 7.26 arranged in a table with sample data. The salesperson and product data is taken from the General Hardware Co. relational database of Figure 5.14, with the addition of Department Number and Manager Name data. Note that salespersons 137, 204, and 361 are all in department number 73 and their manager is Scott. Salesperson 186 is in department number 59 and his manager is Lopez.

The table in Figure 7.28 is unnormalized. The table has four records, one for each salesperson. But, since each salesperson has sold several products and there is only

SALESPERSON/PRODUCT table									
Salesperson Number	Product Number	Salesperson Name	Commission Percentage	Year of Hire	Department Number	Manager Name	Product Name	Unit Price	Quantity
137	19440	Baker	10	1995	73	Scott	Hammer	17.50	473
	24013						Saw	26.25	170
	26722						Pliers	11.50	688
186	16386	Adams	15	2001	59	Lopez	Wrench	12.95	1745
	19440						Hammer	17.50	2529
	21765						Drill	32.99	1962
	24013						Saw	26.25	3071
204	21765	Dickens	10	1998	73	Scott	Drill	32.99	809
	26722						Pliers	11.50	734
361	16386	Carlyle	20	2001	73	Scott	Wrench	12.95	3729
	21765						Drill	32.99	3110
	26722						Pliers	11.50	2738

FIGURE 7.28 The salesperson and product attributes, unnormalized with sample data

| SALESPERSON/PRODUCT table | | | | | | | | | |
| Salesperson Number | Product Number | Salesperson Name | Commission Percentage | Year of Hire | Department Number | Manager Name | Product Name | Unit Price | Quantity |

FIGURE 7.29 The salesperson and product attributes in first normal form

one record for each salesperson, several attributes of each record must have multiple values. For example, the record for salesperson 137 has three product numbers, 19440, 24013, and 26722, in its Product Number attribute, because salesperson 137 has sold all three of those products. Having such multivalued attributes is not permitted in first normal form, and so this table is unnormalized.

First Normal Form   The table in Figure 7.29 is the first normal form representation of the data. The attributes under consideration have been listed out in one table and a primary key has been established. As the sample data of Figure 7.30 shows, the number of records has been increased (over the unnormalized representation) so that every attribute of every record has just one value. The multivalued attributes of Figure 7.28 have been eliminated. Indeed, the definition of first normal form is a table in which every attribute value is atomic, that is, no attribute is multivalued.

The combination of the Salesperson Number and Product Number attributes constitutes the primary key of this table. What makes this combination of attributes a legitimate primary key? First of all, the business context tells us that the combination of the two provides unique identifiers for the records of the table and that there is no single attribute that will do the job. That, of course, is how we have been approaching primary keys all along. Secondly, in terms of data normalization, according to the list of defining associations or functional dependencies of Figure 7.27, every attribute in the table is either part of the primary key or is defined by one or both attributes of the primary key. Salesperson Name, Commission Percentage, Year of Hire, Department Number, and Manager Name are each defined by Salesperson Number. Product Name

SALESPERSON/PRODUCT table									
Salesperson Number	Product Number	Salesperson Name	Commission Percentage	Year of Hire	Department Number	Manager Name	Product Name	Unit Price	Quantity
137	19440	Baker	10	1995	73	Scott	Hammer	17.50	473
137	24013	Baker	10	1995	73	Scott	Saw	26.25	170
137	26722	Baker	10	1995	73	Scott	Pliers	11.50	688
186	16386	Adams	15	2001	59	Lopez	Wrench	12.95	1475
186	19440	Adams	15	2001	59	Lopez	Hammer	17.50	2529
186	21765	Adams	15	2001	59	Lopez	Drill	32.99	1962
186	24013	Adams	15	2001	59	Lopez	Saw	26.25	3071
204	21765	Dickens	10	1998	73	Scott	Drill	32.99	809
204	26722	Dickens	10	1998	73	Scott	Pliers	11.50	734
361	16386	Carlyle	20	2001	73	Scott	Wrench	12.95	3729
361	21765	Carlyle	20	2001	73	Scott	Drill	32.99	3110
361	26722	Carlyle	20	2001	73	Scott	Pliers	11.50	2738

FIGURE 7.30 The salesperson and product attributes in first normal form with sample data

and Unit Price are each defined by Product Number. Quantity is defined by the combination of Salesperson Number and Product Number.

Are these two different ways of approaching the primary key selection equivalent? Yes! If the combination of a particular Salesperson Number and a particular Product Number is unique, then it identifies exactly one record of the table. And, if it identifies exactly one record of the table, then that record shows the single value of each of the non-key attributes that is associated with the unique combination of the key attributes.

But that is the same thing as saying that each of the non-key attributes is defined by or is functionally dependent on the primary key! For example, consider the first record of the table in Figure 7.30.

Sales-person Number	Product Number	Sales-person Name	Commission Percentage	Year of Hire	Depart-ment Number	Manager Name	Product Name	Unit Price	Quantity
137	19440	Baker	10	1995	73	Scott	Hammer	17.50	473

The combination of Salesperson Number 137 and Product Number 19440 is unique. There is only one record in the table that can have that combination of Salesperson Number and Product Number values. Therefore, if someone specifies those values, the only Salesperson Name that can be associated with them is Baker, the only Commission Percentage is 10, and so forth. But that has the same effect as the concept of functional dependency. Since Salesperson Name is functionally dependent on Salesperson Number, given a particular Salesperson Number, say 137, there can be only one Salesperson Name associated with it, Baker. Since Commission Percentage is functionally dependent on Salesperson Number, given a particular Salesperson Number, say 137, there can be only one Commission Percentage associated with it, 10. And so forth.

First normal form is merely a starting point in the normalization process. As can immediately be seen from Figure 7.30, there is a great deal of data redundancy in first normal form. There are three records involving salesperson 137 (the first three records) and so there are three places in which his name is listed as Baker, his commission percentage is listed as 10, and so on. Similarly, there are two records involving product 19440 (the first and fifth records) and this product's name is listed twice as Hammer and its unit price is listed twice as 17.50. Intuitively, the reason for this is that attributes of two different kinds of entities, salespersons and products, have been mixed together in one table.

Second Normal Form   Since data normalization is a decomposition process, the next step will be to decompose the table of Figure 7.29 into smaller tables to eliminate some of its data redundancy. And, since we have established that at least some of the redundancy is due to mixing together attributes about salespersons and attributes about products, it seems reasonable to want to separate them out at this stage. Informally, what we are going to do is to look at each of the non-key attributes of the table in Figure 7.29 and, on the basis of the defining associations of Figure 7.27, decide which attributes of the key are really needed to define it. For example, Salesperson Name really only needs Salesperson Number to define it; it does not need Product Number. Product Name needs only Product Number to define it; it does not need Salesperson Number. Quantity indeed needs both attributes, according to the last defining association of Figure 7.27.

More formally, second normal form, which is what we are heading for, does not allow *partial functional dependencies*. That is, in a table in second normal form, every non-key attribute must be *fully functionally dependent* on the entire key of that table. In plain language, a non-key attribute cannot depend on only part of the key, in the way that Salesperson Name, Product Name, and most of the other non-key attributes of Figure 7.29 do.

Figure 7.31 shows the salesperson and product attributes arranged in second normal form. There is a SALESPERSON Table in which Salesperson Number is the sole primary key attribute. Every non-key attribute of the table is fully defined just by Salesperson Number, as can be verified in Figure 7.27. Similarly, the PRODUCT Table has Product Number as its sole primary key attribute and the non-key attributes of the table are dependent just on it. The QUANTITY Table has the combination of Salesperson Number and Product Number as its primary key because its non-key attribute, Quantity, requires both of them together to define it, as indicated in the last defining association of Figure 7.27.

Figure 7.32 shows the sample salesperson and product data arranged in the second normal form structure of Figure 7.31. Indeed, much of the data redundancy visible in Figure 7.30 has been eliminated. Now, only once is salesperson 137's name listed as Baker, his commission percentage listed as 10, and so forth. Only once is product 19440's name listed as Hammer and its unit price listed as 17.50.

Second normal form is thus a great improvement over first normal form. But, has all of the redundancy been eliminated? In general, that depends on the particular list of attributes and defining associations. It is possible, and in practice it is often the case, that second normal form is completely free of data redundancy. In such a case, the second normal form representation is identical to the third normal form representation.

A close look at the sample data of Figure 7.32 reveals that the second normal form structure of Figure 7.31 has not eliminated all the data redundancy. At the right-hand end of the SALESPERSON Table, the fact that Scott is the manager of department 73 is repeated three times and this certainly constitutes redundant data. How could this have happened? Aren't all the non-key attributes fully functionally dependent on Salesperson Number? They are, but that is not the nature of the problem. It's true that Salesperson Number defines both Department Number and Manager Name and that's reasonable. If I'm focusing in on a particular salesperson, I should know what department she is in and what her manager's name is. But, as indicated in the next-to-last defining association of Figure 7.27, one of those two attributes defines the other: given a department number, I can tell you who the manager of that department is.

SALESPERSON Table					
Salesperson Number	Salesperson Name	Commission Percentage	Year of Hire	Department Number	Manager Name

PRODUCT Table		
Product Number	Product Name	Unit Price

QUANTITY Table		
Salesperson Number	Product Number	Quantity

FIGURE 7.31 The salesperson and product attributes in second normal form

SALESPERSON Table

Salesperson Number	Salesperson Name	Commission Percentage	Year of Hire	Department Number	Manager Name
137	Baker	10	1995	73	Scott
186	Adams	15	2001	59	Lopez
204	Dickens	10	1998	73	Scott
361	Carlyle	20	2001	73	Scott

PRODUCT Table

Product Number	Product Name	Unit Price
16386	Wrench	12.95
19440	Hammer	17.50
21765	Drill	32.99
24013	Saw	26.25
26722	Pliers	11.50

QUANTITY Table

Salesperson Number	Product Number	Quantity
137	19440	473
137	24013	170
137	26722	688
186	16386	1745
186	19440	2529
186	21765	1962
186	24013	3071
204	21765	809
204	26722	734
361	16386	3729
361	21765	3110
361	26722	2738

FIGURE 7.32 The salesperson and product attributes in second normal form with sample data

In the SALESPERSON Table, one of the non-key attributes, Department Number, defines another one of the non-key attributes, Manager Name. This is what is causing the problem.

Third Normal Form   In third normal form, non-key attributes are not allowed to define other non-key attributes. Stated more formally, third normal form does not allow *transitive dependencies* in which one non-key attribute is functionally dependent on another.

Again, there is one example of this in the second normal form representation in Figure 7.31. In the SALESPERSON table, Department Number and Manager

SALESPERSON Table				
Salesperson Number	Salesperson Name	Commission Percentage	Year of Hire	Department Number

DEPARTMENT Table	
Department Number	Manager Name

PRODUCT Table		
Product Number	Product Name	Unit Price

QUANTITY Table		
Salesperson Number	Product Number	Quantity

FIGURE 7.33 The salesperson and product attributes in third normal form

Name are both non-key attributes and, as shown in the next-to-last association in Figure 7.27, Department Number defines Manager Name. Figure 7.33 shows the third normal form representation of the attributes. Note that the SALESPERSON Table of Figure 7.31 has been further decomposed into the SALESPERSON and DEPART-MENT Tables of Figure 7.33. The Department Number and Department Manager attributes, which were the problem, were split off to form the DEPARTMENT Table, but a copy of the Department Number attribute (the primary key attribute of the new DEPARTMENT Table) was left behind in the SALESPERSON Table. If this had not been done, there no longer would have been a way to indicate which department each salesperson is in.

The sample data for the third normal form structure of Figure 7.33 is shown in Figure 7.34. Now, the fact that Scott is the manager of department 73 is shown only once, in the second record of the DEPARTMENT Table. Notice that the Department Number attribute in the SALESPERSON Table continues to indicate which department a salesperson is in.

There are several important points to note about the third normal form structure of Figure 7.33:

1. It is completely free of data redundancy.
2. All foreign keys appear where needed to logically tie together related tables.
3. It is the same structure that would have been derived from a properly drawn entity-relationship diagram of the same business environment.

Finally, there is one exception to the rule that in third normal form, non-key attributes are not allowed to define other non-key attributes. The rule does not hold if the defining non-key attribute is a candidate key of the table. Let's say, just for the sake of argument here, that the Salesperson Name attribute is unique. That makes Salesperson Name a candidate key in Figure 7.33's SALESPERSON Table. But, if Salesperson Name is unique, then it must define Commission Percentage, Year of Hire, and Department Number just as the unique Salesperson Number attribute does. Since it was not chosen to be the primary key of the table, Salesperson Name is technically a non-key attribute

SALESPERSON Table

Salesperson Number	Salesperson Name	Commission Percentage	Year of Hire	Department Number
137	Baker	10	1995	73
186	Adams	15	2001	59
204	Dickens	10	1998	73
361	Carlyle	20	2001	73

DEPARTMENT Table

Department Number	Manager Name
59	Lopez
73	Scott

PRODUCT Table

Product Number	Product Name	Unit Price
16386	Wrench	12.95
19440	Hammer	17.50
21765	Drill	32.99
24013	Saw	26.25
26722	Pliers	11.50

QUANTITY Table

Salesperson Number	Product Number	Quantity
137	19440	473
137	24013	170
137	26722	688
186	16386	1745
186	19440	2529
186	21765	1962
186	24013	3071
204	21765	809
204	26722	734
361	16386	3729
361	21765	3110
361	26722	2738

FIGURE 7.34 The salesperson and product attributes in third normal form with sample data

that defines other non-key attributes. Yet it does not appear from the sample data of Figure 7.34 to be causing any data redundancy problems. Since it was a candidate key, its defining other non-key attributes is not a problem.

Example: General Hardware Co.

If the entire General Hardware Co. example, including the newly added Department Number and Manager Name attributes, were organized for the data normalization process, the list of defining associations or functional dependencies of Figure 7.27 would be expanded to look like Figure 7.35. Several additional interesting functional dependencies in this expanded list are worth pointing out. First, although Salesperson Number is a determinant, defining several other attributes, it is in turn functionally dependent on another attribute, Customer Number:

$$\text{Customer Number} \longrightarrow \text{Salesperson Number}$$

As we have already established, this functional dependency makes perfect sense. Given a particular customer, I can tell you who the salesperson is who is responsible for that customer. This is part of the one-to-many relationship between salespersons and customers. The fact that, in the reverse direction, a particular salesperson has several customers associated with him makes no difference in this functional dependency analysis. Also, the fact that Salesperson Number is itself a determinant, defining several other attributes, does not matter. Next:

$$\text{Customer Number, Employee Number} \longrightarrow \text{Employee Name}$$
$$\text{Customer Number, Employee Number} \longrightarrow \text{Title}$$

Remember that in the General Hardware business environment, employee numbers are unique only within a customer company. Thus, this functional dependency correctly shows that the combination of the Customer Number and Employee Number attributes is required to define the Employee Name and Title attributes.

Figure 7.36 shows the General Hardware Co. attributes, including the added Department Number and Manager Name attributes, arranged in first normal form. Moving to

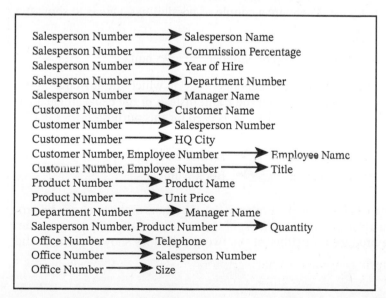

FIGURE 7.35 List of defining associations (functional dependencies) for the attributes of the General Hardware Company example

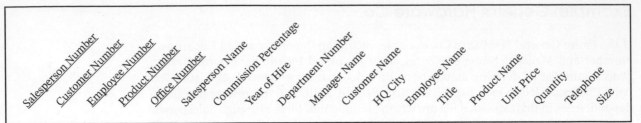

FIGURE 7.36 The General Hardware Company attributes in first normal form

second normal form would produce the database structure in Figure 7.19, except that the Department Number and Manager Name attributes would be split out in moving from second to third normal form, as previously shown.

Example: Good Reading Bookstores

In the General Hardware Co. example, the reason that the table representing the many-to-many relationship between salespersons and products

Salesperson Number	Product Number	Quantity

fell out so easily in the data normalization process was because of the presence of the functional dependency needed to define the intersection data attribute, Quantity:

$$\text{Salesperson Number, Product Number} \longrightarrow \text{Quantity}$$

A new twist in the Good Reading Bookstores example is the presence of the many-to-many relationship between the book and author entities with no intersection data. This is shown in the WRITING Table of Figure 7.21. The issue is how to show this in a functional dependencies list. There are a couple of possibilities. One is to show the two attributes defining "null":

$$\text{Book Number, Author Number} \longrightarrow \text{null}$$

The other is to show paired "multivalued dependencies" in which the attribute on the left determines a *list* of attribute values on the right, instead of the usual single attribute value on the right. A double-headed arrow is used for this purpose:

$$\text{Book Number} \longrightarrow\!\!\!\!\!\longrightarrow \text{Author Number}$$
$$\text{Author Number} \longrightarrow\!\!\!\!\!\longrightarrow \text{Book Number}$$

These literally say that given a book number, a list of authors of the book can be produced and that given an author number, a list of the books that an author has written or co-written can be produced. In either of the two possibilities shown, the null and the paired multivalued dependencies, the notation in the functional dependency list can be used as a signal to split the attributes off into a separate table in moving from first to second normal form.

The other interesting point in the Good Reading Bookstores example involves the many-to-many relationship of the SALE Table in Figure 7.21. Recall that Date and Price were intersection data attributes that, because of the requirements of the company, had to be part of the primary key of the table. This would be handled very simply and naturally with a functional dependency that looks like this:

$$\text{Book Number, Customer Number, Date, Price} \longrightarrow \text{Quantity}$$

The complete list of functional dependencies is shown in Figure 7.37. First normal form for the Good Reading Bookstores example would consist of the list of its attributes with the following attributes in the primary key:

Publisher Name
Author Number
Book Number
Customer Number
Date

Moving from first to second normal form, including incorporating the rule described above for the many-to-many relationship with no intersection data, would directly yield the tables of Figure 7.21. As there are no instances of a non-key attribute defining another non-key attribute, this arrangement is already in third normal form.

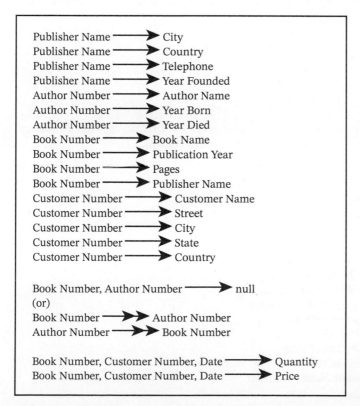

FIGURE 7.37 List of defining associations (functional dependencies) for the attributes of the Good Reading Bookstores example

Example: World Music Association

The World Music Association example is straightforward in terms of data normalization. The complete list of functional dependencies is shown in Figure 7.38. Since degree is unique only within a musician and composition name is unique only within a composer, note that three of the functional dependencies are:

$$\text{Musician Number, Degree} \longrightarrow \text{University}$$
$$\text{Musician Number, Degree} \longrightarrow \text{Year}$$
$$\text{Composition Name, Composer Name} \longrightarrow \text{Year}$$

The primary key attributes in first normal form are:

Orchestra Name
Musician Number
Degree
Composer Name
Composition Name

With this in mind, proceeding from first to second normal form will produce the tables in Figure 7.23. These are free of data redundancy and are, indeed, also in third normal form.

Example: Lucky Rent-A-Car

Figure 7.39 lists the Lucky Rent-A-Car functional dependencies. The primary key attributes in first normal form are:

Manufacturer Name
Car Serial Number
Repair Number
Customer Number
Rental Date

Once again, the conversion from first to second normal form results in a redundancy-free structure, Figure 7.25, that is already in third normal form.

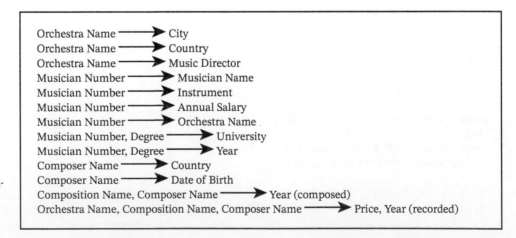

FIGURE 7.38 List of defining associations (functional dependencies) for the attributes of the World Music Association example

Orchestra Name $\longrightarrow$ City
Orchestra Name $\longrightarrow$ Country
Orchestra Name $\longrightarrow$ Music Director
Musician Number $\longrightarrow$ Musician Name
Musician Number $\longrightarrow$ Instrument
Musician Number $\longrightarrow$ Annual Salary
Musician Number $\longrightarrow$ Orchestra Name
Musician Number, Degree $\longrightarrow$ University
Musician Number, Degree $\longrightarrow$ Year
Composer Name $\longrightarrow$ Country
Composer Name $\longrightarrow$ Date of Birth
Composition Name, Composer Name $\longrightarrow$ Year (composed)
Orchestra Name, Composition Name, Composer Name $\longrightarrow$ Price, Year (recorded)

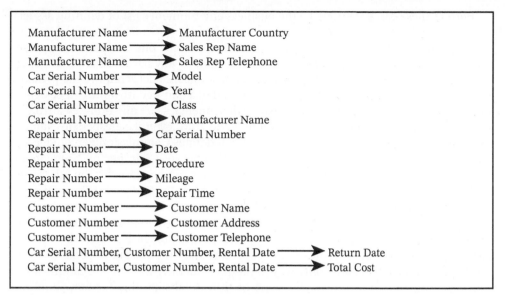

Manufacturer Name ⟶ Manufacturer Country
Manufacturer Name ⟶ Sales Rep Name
Manufacturer Name ⟶ Sales Rep Telephone
Car Serial Number ⟶ Model
Car Serial Number ⟶ Year
Car Serial Number ⟶ Class
Car Serial Number ⟶ Manufacturer Name
Repair Number ⟶ Car Serial Number
Repair Number ⟶ Date
Repair Number ⟶ Procedure
Repair Number ⟶ Mileage
Repair Number ⟶ Repair Time
Customer Number ⟶ Customer Name
Customer Number ⟶ Customer Address
Customer Number ⟶ Customer Telephone
Car Serial Number, Customer Number, Rental Date ⟶ Return Date
Car Serial Number, Customer Number, Rental Date ⟶ Total Cost

FIGURE 7.39 List of defining associations (functional dependencies) for the attributes of the Lucky Rent-A-Car example

Your Turn

7.2 The Data Normalization Technique

In Your Turn in Chapter 2, you created an entity-relationship diagram for your university environment.

Question:

Develop a set of functional dependencies for your university environment. Then design a database for your university environment using the data normalization technique.

Testing Tables Converted from E-R Diagrams with Data Normalization

As we said earlier, logical database design is generally performed today by converting entity-relationship diagrams to relational tables and then checking those tables against the data normalization technique rules. Since we already know that the databases in Figures 7.19, 7.21, 7.23, and 7.25 (for the four example business environments we've been working) with are in third normal form, there really isn't much to check. As one example, consider the General Hardware Co. database of Figure 7.19.

The basic idea in checking the structural worthiness of relational tables with the data normalization rules is to:

1. Check to see if there are any partial functional dependencies. That is, check whether any non-key attributes are dependent on or are defined by only part of the table's primary key.
2. Check to see if there are any transitive dependencies. That is, check whether any non-key attributes are dependent on or are defined by any other non-key attributes (other than candidate keys).

Both of these can be verified by the business environment's list of defining associations or functional dependencies.

In the SALESPERSON Table of Figure 7.19, there is only one attribute, Salesperson Number, in the primary key. Therefore there cannot be any partial functional dependencies. By their very definition, partial functional dependencies require the presence of more than one attribute in the primary key, so that a non-key attribute can be dependent on *only part of the key*! As for transitive dependencies, are any non-key attributes determined by any other non-key attributes? No! And, even if Salesperson Name is assumed to be a unique attribute and therefore it defines Commission Percentage and Year of Hire, this would be an allowable exception because Salesperson Name, being unique, would be a candidate key. The same analysis can be made for the other General Hardware tables with single-attribute primary keys: the CUSTOMER, PRODUCT, and OFFICE tables of Figure 7.19.

Figure 7.19's CUSTOMER EMPLOYEE Table has a two-attribute primary key because Employee Number is unique only within a customer. But then, by the very same logic, the non-key attributes Employee Name and Title *must* be dependent on the *entire* key, because that is the only way to uniquely identify who we are talking about when we want to know a person's name or title. Analyzing this further, Employee Name cannot be dependent on Employee Number alone because it is not a unique attribute. Functional dependency requires uniqueness from the determining side. And, obviously, Employee Name cannot be dependent on Customer Number alone. A customer company has lots of employees, not just one. Therefore, Employee Name and Title must be dependent on the entire primary key and the rule about no partial functional dependencies is satisfied. Since the non-key attributes Employee Name and Title do not define each other, the rule about no transitive dependencies is also satisfied and thus the table is clearly in third normal form.

In the SALES Table of Figure 7.19, there is a two-attribute primary key and only one non-key attribute. This table exists to represent the many-to-many relationship between salespersons and products. The non-key attributes, just Quantity in this case, constitute intersection data. *By the definition of intersection data* these non-key attributes *must* be dependent on the entire primary key. In any case, there would be a line in the functional dependency list indicating that Quantity is dependent on the combination of the two key attributes. Thus, there are no partial functional dependencies in this table. Interestingly, since there is only one non-key attribute, transitive dependencies cannot exist. After all, there must be at least two non-key attributes in a table for one non-key attribute to be dependent on another.

Your Turn

7.3 Checking Your Logical Design with Normalization

In Your Turn 7-1 (the first Your Turn in this chapter), you designed a database for your university

environment by converting an E-R diagram to a relational database.

Question:

Check the resulting relational database design using the data normalization technique.

Building the Data Structure with SQL

SQL has data definition commands that allow you to take the database structure you just learned how to design with the logical database design techniques and implement it for use with a relational DBMS. This process begins by the creation of "base tables." These are the actual physical tables in which the data will be stored on the disk. The command that creates base tables and tells the system what attributes will be in them is called the **CREATE TABLE** command. Using the CREATE TABLE command, you can also specify which attribute is the primary key. As an example, here is the command to create the General Hardware Company SALESPERSON table we have been working with shown in Figure 7.19. (Note that the syntax of these commands varies somewhat among the various relational DBMS products on the market. The commands shown in this chapter, which are based on the ORACLE DBMS, are designed to give you a general idea of the command structures. You should check the specific syntax required by the DBMS you are using.)

```
CREATE TABLE SALESPERSON
(SPNUM CHAR(3) PRIMARY KEY,
SPNAME CHAR(12)
COMMPERCT DECIMAL(3,0)
YEARHIRE CHAR(4)
OFFNUM CHAR(3));
```

Notice that the CREATE TABLE command names the table SALESPERSON and lists the attributes in it (with abbreviated attribute names that we have created for brevity). Each attribute is given an attribute type and length. So SPNUM, the Salesperson Number, is specified as CHAR(3). It is three characters long (yes, it's a number, but it's not subject to calculations so it's more convenient to specify it as a character attribute). On the other hand, COMMPERCT, the Commission Percentage, is specified as DECIMAL(3,0), meaning that it is a three-position number with no decimal positions. Thus it could be a whole number from 0–999, although we know that it will always be a whole number from 0–100 since it represents a commission percentage. Finally, the command indicates that SPNUM will be the primary key of the table.

If a table in the database has to be discarded, the command is the **DROP TABLE** command.

```
DROP TABLE SALESPERSON;
```

A logical view (sometimes just called a "view") is derived from one or more base tables. A view may consist of a subset of the columns of a single table, a subset of the rows of a single table, or both. It can also be the join of two or more base tables. The creation of a view in SQL does *not* entail the physical duplication of data in a base table into a new table. Instead, the view is a mapping onto the base table(s). It's literally a "view" of some part of the physical, stored data. Views are built using the **CREATE VIEW** command. Within this command, you specify the base table(s) on which the view is to be based and the attributes and rows of the table(s) that are to be included in the view. Interestingly, these specifications are made within the CREATE VIEW command using the SELECT statement, which is also used for data retrieval.

For example, to give someone access to only the Salesperson Number, Salesperson Name, and Year of Hire attributes of the SALESPERSON table, you would specify:

```
CREATE VIEW EMPLOYEE AS
SELECT SPNUM, SPNAME, YEARHIRE
FROM SALESPERSON;
```

The name of the view is EMPLOYEE, which can then be used in other SQL commands as if it were a table name. People using EMPLOYEE as a table name would have access to the Salesperson Number, Salesperson Name, and Year of Hire attributes of the SALESPERSON table but would not have access to the Commission Percentage or Office Number attributes (in fact, they would not even know that these two attributes exist!).

Views can be discarded using the **DROP VIEW** command:

```
DROP VIEW EMPLOYEE;
```

Manipulating the Data with SQL

Once the tables have been created, the focus changes to the standard data manipulation operations of updating existing data, inserting new rows in tables, and deleting existing rows in tables. (Data retrieval is discussed in Chapter 4.) The commands are **UPDATE, INSERT**, and **DELETE**. In the UPDATE command, you have to identify which row(s) of a table are to be updated based on data values within those rows. Then you have to specify which columns are to be updated and what the new data values of those columns in those rows will be. For example, consider the SALESPERSON table in Figure 7.34. If salesperson 204's commission percentage has to be changed from the current 10% to 12%, the command would be:

```
UPDATE SALESPERSON
SET COMMPERCT = 12
WHERE SPNUM = '204';
```

Notice that the command first specifies the table to be updated in the UPDATE clause, then specifies the new data in the SET clause, then specifies the affected row(s) in the WHERE clause.

Your Turn

7.4 SQL Data Definition and Data Manipulation Statements

By now, from the previous Your Turns in this chapter, you have a well-structured relational database design for your university environment.

Question:

Take one of your university tables and write SQL commands to create the table, create a view of the table, and update, insert, and delete records in the table.

In the INSERT command, you have to specify a row of data to enter into a table. To add a new salesperson into the SALESPERSON table whose salesperson number is 489, name is Quinlan, commission percentage is 15, year of hire is 2011, and department number is 59, the command would be:

```
INSERT INTO SALESPERSON
VALUES
('489','Quinlan',15,'2011','59');
```

In the DELETE command you have to specify which row(s) of a table are to be deleted based on data values within those rows. To delete the row for salesperson 186 the command would be:

```
DELETE FROM SALESPERSON
WHERE SPNUM = '186';
```

Summary

Logical database design is the process of creating a database structure that is free of data redundancy and that promotes data integration. There are two techniques for logical database design. One technique involves taking the entity-relationship diagram that describes the business environment and going through a series of steps to convert it to a well-structured relational database structure. The other technique is the data normalization technique. Furthermore, the data normalization technique can be used to check the results of the E-R diagram conversion for errors.

SQL is both a data definition language and a data manipulation language. Included in the basic data definition commands are CREATE TABLE, DROP TABLE, CREATE VIEW, and DROP VIEW. Included in the basic data manipulation commands are UPDATE, INSERT, and DELETE.

Key Terms

CREATE TABLE	**DROP TABLE**	**First normal form**	**Third normal form**
CREATE VIEW	**DROP VIEW**	**INSERT**	**UPDATE**
Data normalization	**Entity-relationship**	**Logical database design**	
DELETE	**diagram conversion**	**Second normal form**	

Questions

1. What is logical database design?
2. What is physical database design and how does it relate to logical database design?
3. In general terms, describe the main logical database design techniques and how they relate to one another.
4. Based on an entity-relationship diagram, how can you determine how many tables there will be in the corresponding relational database?
5. Describe the process for converting entities in each of the following relationships into relational database structures:
   a. One-to-one binary relationship.
   b. One-to-many binary relationship.
   c. Many-to-many binary relationship.
   d. One-to-one unary relationship.
   e. One-to-many unary relationship.

f. Many-to-many unary relationship.

g. Ternary relationship.

6. Describe the data normalization process including its specific steps. Why is it referred to as a "decomposition process?"

7. Explain the following terms:
   a. Functional dependency.
   b. Determinant.

8. What characterizes unnormalized data? Why is such data problematic?

9. What characterizes tables in first normal form? Why is such data problematic?

10. What is a partial functional dependency? What does the term "fully functionally dependent" mean?

11. What is the rule for converting tables in first normal form to tables in second normal form?

12. What is the definition of data in second normal form?

13. What is a transitive dependency?

14. What is the rule for converting tables in second normal form to tables in third normal form?

15. What is the definition of data in third normal form?

16. What are the characteristics of data in third normal form?

17. How can data normalization be used to check the results of the E-R diagram-to-relational database conversion process?

18. What SQL command do you use to produce a new table structure? What SQL command do you use to discard a table?

19. What is a view? What SQL commands do you use to produce a new view and to discard one that is no longer needed?

20. What are the SQL data manipulation commands and what are their functions?

Exercises

1. Convert the Video Centers of Europe, Ltd., entity-relationship diagram in Exercise 2.2 into a well-structured relational database.

2. Convert the Central Hospital entity-relationship diagram on the page 182 into a well-structured relational database.

3. Video Centers of Europe, Ltd., is a chain of movie DVD rental stores. It must maintain data on the DVDs it has for rent, the movies recorded on the DVDs, its customers, and the actual rental. Each DVD for rent has a unique serial number. Movie titles and customer numbers are also unique identifiers. Assume that each movie has exactly one "star." Note the difference in the year that the movie was originally filmed and the date that a DVD—an actual disk—was manufactured. Some of the attributes and functional dependencies in this environment are as follows:

Attributes

DVD Number

Manufacture Date

Movie Title

Star

Year Filmed

Length [in minutes]

Customer Number

Customer Name

Customer Address

Rental Date

Return Date

Fee Paid

Functional Dependencies

DVD Number ⟶ Movie Title

DVD Number ⟶ Star

DVD Number ⟶ Manufacture Date

Movie Title ⟶ Star

Movie Title ⟶ Length

Movie Title ⟶ Year Filmed

Customer Number ⟶ Customer Name

Customer Number ⟶ Customer Address

DVD Number, Customer Number,
    Rental Date ⟶ Return Date, Fee Paid

For each of the following tables, first write the table's current normal form (as 1NF, 2NF, or 3NF). Then, take those tables that are currently in 1NF or 2NF and reconstruct them as well-structured 3NF tables. Primary key attributes are underlined. Do not assume any functional dependencies other than those shown.

a. <u>Movie Title</u>, Star, Length, Year Filmed

b. <u>DVD Number</u>, <u>Customer Number</u>, <u>Rental Date</u>, Customer Name, Return Date, Fee Paid

c. <u>DVD Number</u>, Manufacture Date, Movie Title, Star

    d. <u>Movie Title</u>, <u>Customer Number</u>, Star, Length, Customer Name, Customer Address

    e. <u>DVD Number</u>, <u>Customer Number</u>, <u>Rental Date</u>, Return Date, Fee Paid

4. The U.S. government wants to keep track of information about states, governors, cities, and mayors. In addition, it wants to maintain data on the various federal agencies and the annual grants each agency gives to the individual states. Each federal agency is headed by an administrator. Agency names and state names are unique but city names are unique only within a state. The attributes and functional dependencies in this environment are as follows:

Attributes

State

Governor ID Number

Governor Name

State Flower

City

Mayor ID Number

Mayor Name

City Hall Address

Mayor Telephone

Federal Agency

Administrator

Annual Grant

Functional Dependencies

State ⟶ Governor ID Number

State ⟶ Governor Name

State ⟶ State Flower

State, City ⟶ Mayor ID Number

State, City ⟶ Mayor Name

State, City ⟶ City Hall Address

State, City ⟶ Mayor Telephone

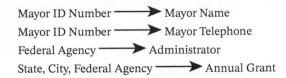

Mayor ID Number ⟶ Mayor Name

Mayor ID Number ⟶ Mayor Telephone

Federal Agency ⟶ Administrator

State, City, Federal Agency ⟶ Annual Grant

For each of the following tables, first write the table's current normal form (as 1NF, 2NF, or 3NF). Then, reconstruct those tables that are currently in 1NF or 2NF as well-structured 3NF tables. Primary key attributes are underlined. Do not assume any functional dependencies other than those shown.

    a. <u>State</u>, <u>City</u>, Governor Name, Mayor ID Number, Mayor Name, Mayor Telephone

    b. <u>State</u>, <u>City</u>, Mayor Name, Mayor Telephone

    c. <u>State</u>, <u>City</u>, <u>Federal Agency</u>, Governor Name, Administrator, Annual Grant

    d. <u>State</u>, <u>City</u>, Governor Name, State Flower, Mayor Telephone

    e. <u>State</u>, <u>City</u>, City Hall Address, Mayor ID Number, Mayor Name, Mayor Telephone

5. Consider the General Hardware relational database shown in Figure 7.19.

    a. Write an SQL command to create the CUSTOMER table.

    b. Write an SQL command to create a view of the CUSTOMER table that includes only the Customer Number and HQ City attributes.

    c. Write an SQL command to discard the OFFICE table.

    d. Assume that Customer Number 8429 is the responsibility of Salesperson Number 758. Write an SQL command to change that responsibility to Salesperson Number 311.

    e. Write an SQL command to add a new record to the CUSTOMER table for Customer Number 9442. The Customer Name is Smith Hardware Stores, the responsible salesperson is Salesperson Number 577, and the HQ City is Chicago.

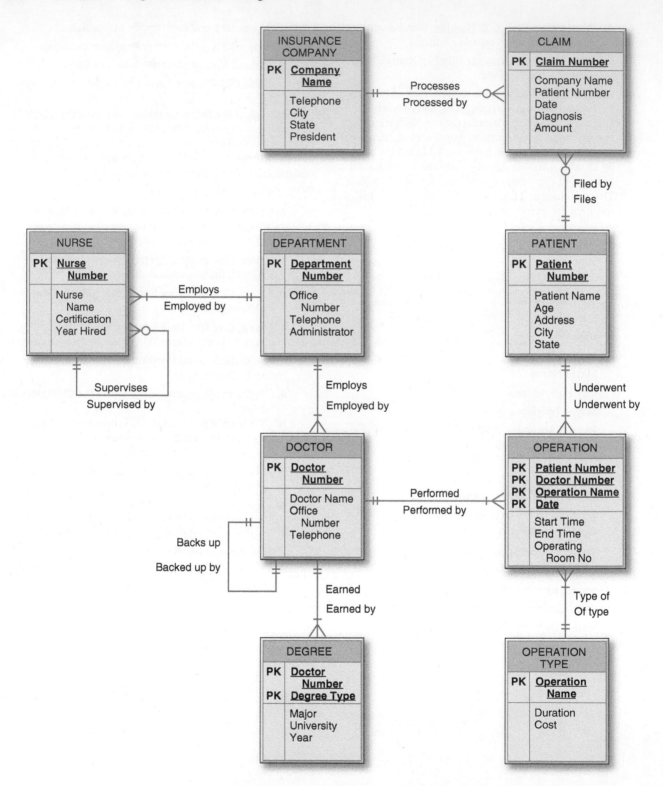

Central Hospital entity-relationship diagram

Minicases

1. Happy Cruise Lines. Convert the Happy Cruise Lines entity-relationship diagram on the next page into a well-structured relational database.

2. Super Baseball League. The Super Baseball League wants to keep track of information about its players, its teams, and the minor league teams (which we will call minor league "clubs" to avoid using the word "team" twice). Minor league clubs are not part of the Super Baseball League but players train in them with the hope of eventually advancing to a team in the Super Baseball League. The intent in this problem is to keep track only of the *current* team on which a player plays in the Super Baseball League. However, the minor league club data must be *historic* and include all of the minor league clubs for which a player has played. Team names, minor league club names, manager names, and stadium names are assumed to be unique, as, of course, is player number.

   Design a well-structured relational database for this Super Baseball League environment using the data normalization technique. Progress from first to second normal form and then from second to third normal form justifying your design decisions at each step based on the rules of data normalization. The attributes and functional dependencies in this environment are as follows:

Attributes

Player Number
Player Name
Player Age
Team Name
Manager Name
Stadium Name
Minor League Club Name
Minor League Club City
Minor League Club Owner
Minor League Club Year Founded
Start Date
End Date
Batting Average

Functional Dependencies

Player Number $\longrightarrow$ Player Name
Player Number $\longrightarrow$ Age
Player Number $\longrightarrow$ Team Name
Player Number $\longrightarrow$ Manager Name
Player Number $\longrightarrow$ Stadium Name
Minor League Club Name $\longrightarrow$ City
Minor League Club Name $\longrightarrow$ Owner
Minor League Club Name $\longrightarrow$ Year Founded
Team Name $\longrightarrow$ Manager Name
Team Name $\longrightarrow$ Stadium Name
Player Number, Minor League Club Name $\longrightarrow$
    Start Date, End Date, Batting Average

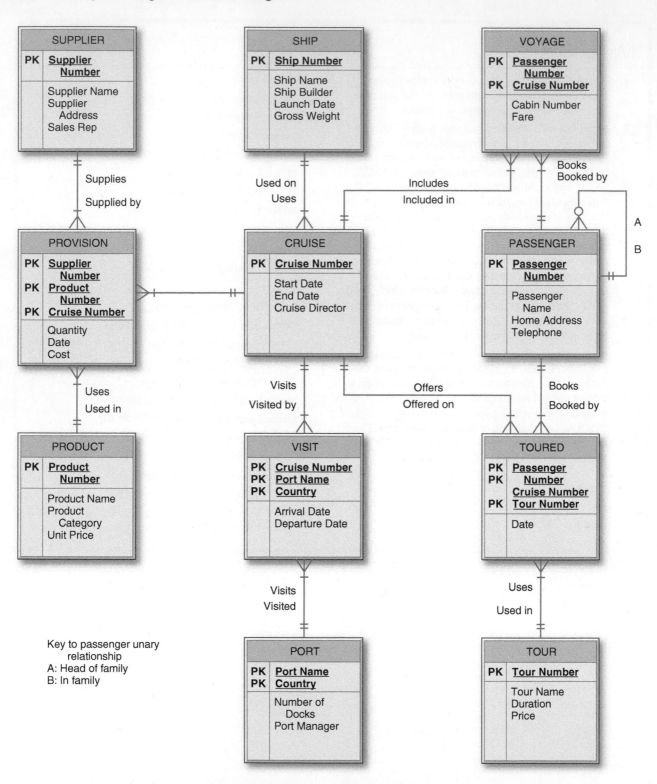

Happy Cruise Lines entity-relationship diagram

SUPPLIER

PK	**Supplier Number**
	Supplier Name
	Supplier Address
	Sales Rep

SHIP

PK	**Ship Number**
	Ship Name
	Ship Builder
	Launch Date
	Gross Weight

VOYAGE

PK	**Passenger Number**
PK	**Cruise Number**
	Cabin Number
	Fare

Supplies
Supplied by

Used on
Uses

Includes
Included in

Books
Booked by

A
B

PROVISION

PK	**Supplier Number**
PK	**Product Number**
PK	**Cruise Number**
	Quantity
	Date
	Cost

CRUISE

PK	**Cruise Number**
	Start Date
	End Date
	Cruise Director

PASSENGER

PK	**Passenger Number**
	Passenger Name
	Home Address
	Telephone

Uses
Used in

Visits
Visited by

Offers
Offered on

Books
Booked by

PRODUCT

PK	**Product Number**
	Product Name
	Product Category
	Unit Price

VISIT

PK	**Cruise Number**
PK	**Port Name**
PK	**Country**
	Arrival Date
	Departure Date

TOURED

PK	**Passenger Number**
PK	**Cruise Number**
PK	**Tour Number**
	Date

Visits
Visited

Uses
Used in

Key to passenger unary relationship
A: Head of family
B: In family

PORT

PK	**Port Name**
PK	**Country**
	Number of Docks
	Port Manager

TOUR

PK	**Tour Number**
	Tour Name
	Duration
	Price

Physical Database Design

If computers ran at infinitely fast speeds and data stored on disks could be found and brought into primary memory for processing literally instantly, then logical database design would be the only kind of database design to talk about. Well-structured, redundancy-free third normal form tables are the ideal relational database structures and, in a world of infinite speeds, would be practical, too. But, as fast as computers have become, their speeds are certainly not infinite and the time necessary to find data stored on disks and bring it into primary memory for processing are crucial issues in whether an application runs as fast as it must. For example, if you telephone your insurance company to ask about a claim you filed and the customer service agent takes two minutes to find the relevant records in the company's information system, you might well become frustrated with the company and question its ability to handle your business competently. Data storage, retrieval, and processing speeds do matter. Regardless of how elegant an application and its database structures are, if the application runs so slowly that it is unacceptable in the business environment, it will be a failure. This chapter addresses how to take a well-structured relational database design and modify it for improved **performance**.

OBJECTIVES

Describe the principles of file organizations and access methods.

Describe how disk storage devices work.

Describe the concept of physical database design.

List and describe the inputs to the physical database design process.

Describe a variety of physical database design techniques ranging from adding indexes to denormalization.

Introduction

Database performance can be adversely affected by a wide variety of factors, as shown in Figure 8.1. Some factors are a result of application requirements and often the most obvious culprit is the need for joins. Joins are an elegant solution to the need for data integration, but they can be unacceptably slow in many cases. Also, the need to calculate and retrieve the same totals of numeric data over and over again can cause performance problems. Another type of factor is very large volumes of data. Data is the lifeblood of an information system, but when there is a lot of it, care must be taken to store and retrieve it efficiently to maintain acceptable performance. Certain factors involving the structure of the data, such as the amount of direct access provided and the presence of clumsy, multi-attribute primary keys, can certainly affect performance. If related data in different tables that must be retrieved together is physically dispersed on rotating **disks**, retrieval performance will be slower than if the data is stored physically close together on the disk. Finally, the business environment often presents significant performance challenges. We want data to be shared and to be widely used for the benefit of the business. However, a very large number of access operations to the same data can cause a bottleneck that can ruin the performance of an application environment. And giving people access to more data than they need to see can be a security risk.

Physical database design is the process of modifying a database structure to improve the performance of the run-time environment. That is, we are going to modify the third normal form tables produced by the logical database design techniques to speed up the applications that will use them. A variety of kinds of modifications can be made, ranging from simply adding indexes to making major changes to the table structures. Some of the changes, while making some applications run faster, may make other applications that share the data run slower. Some of the changes may even compromise the principle of avoiding data redundancy! We will investigate and explain a number of physical database design techniques in this chapter, pointing out the advantages and disadvantages of each.

In order to discuss physical database design, we will begin with a review of disk storage devices, file organizations, and access methods.

Factors Affecting Application and Database Performance

- Application Factors
  - Need for Joins
  - Need to Calculate Totals
- Data Factors
  - Large Data Volumes
- Database Structure Factors
  - Lack of Direct Access
  - Clumsy Primary Keys
- Data Storage Factors
  - Related Data Dispersed on Disk
- Business Environment Factors
  - Too Many Data Access Operations
  - Overly Liberal Data Access

FIGURE 8.1 Factors affecting application and database performance

Disk Storage

The Need for Disk Storage

Computers execute programs and process data in their main or primary memory. Primary memory is very fast and certainly does permit direct access, but it has several drawbacks:

- It is relatively expensive.
- It is not transportable (that is, you can't remove it from the computer and carry it away with you, as you can an external hard drive).
- It is volatile. When you turn the computer off you lose whatever data is stored in it.

Because of these shortcomings, the vast volumes of data and the programs that process them are held on secondary memory devices. Data is loaded from secondary memory into primary memory when required for processing (as are programs when they are to be executed). A loose analogy can be drawn between primary and secondary memory in a computer system and a person's brain and a library, Figure 8.2. The brain cannot possibly hold all of the information a person might need, but (let's say) a large library can. So when a person needs some particular information that's not in her brain at the moment, she finds a book in the library that has the information and, by reading it, transfers the information from the book to her brain. Secondary memory devices in use today include compact disks and magnetic tape, but by far the predominant secondary memory technology in use today is magnetic disk, or simply "disk."

Note: At the time of this writing, rotating disks are in the process of largely being replaced by **"solid state disks"** (SSDs). Since rotating disks are still in use, we will continue to describe them and how they affect database performance, while also pointing out the differences between rotating disk and solid state disk technologies in this regard.

How Rotating Disk Storage Works

The Structure of Rotating Disk Devices   Rotating disk devices, commonly called "disk drives," come in a variety of types and capacities ranging from a single aluminum or ceramic disk or **"platter"** to large multi-platter units that hold many billions of bytes of data. Some disk devices, like "external hard drives," are designed to be removable and transportable from computer to computer; others, such as the **"fixed"** or **"hard"** disk drives in PCs and the disk drives associated with larger computers, are designed to be non-removable. The platters have a metallic coating that can be

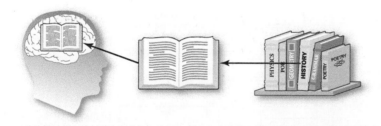

FIGURE 8.2 Primary and secondary memory are like a brain and a library

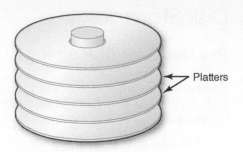

FIGURE 8.3 The platters of a disk are mounted on a central spindle

magnetized and this is how the data is stored, bit by bit. Disks are very fast in storage and retrieval times (although not nearly as fast as primary memory), provide a direct access capability to the data, are less expensive than primary memory units on a byte-by-byte basis, and are non-volatile (when you turn off the computer or unplug the external drive, you don't lose the data on the disk).

It is important to see how data is arranged on disks to understand how they provide a direct access capability. It is also important because certain decisions on how to arrange file or database storage on a disk can seriously affect the performance of the applications using the data.

In the large disk devices used with mainframe computers and mid-sized "servers" (as well as the hard drives or fixed disks in PCs), several disk platters are stacked together and mounted on a central spindle, with some space between them, Figure 8.3. In common usage, even a multi-platter arrangement like this is simply referred to as "the disk." Each of the two surfaces of a platter is a recording surface on which data can be stored. (Note: In some of these devices, the upper surface of the topmost platter and the lower surface of the bottommost platter are not used for storing data. We will assume this situation in the following text and figures.) The platter arrangement spins at high speed in the disk drive. The basic disk drive (there are more complex variations) has an "access-arm mechanism" with arms that can reach in between the disks, Figure 8.4. At the end of each arm are two "read/write heads," one for storing and retrieving data from the recording surface above the arm and the other for the surface below the arm, as shown in the figure. It is important to understand that the entire access-arm mechanism always moves as a unit in and out among the disk platters, so that the read/write heads are always p aligned exactly one above the other in a straight line. The platters spin at high velocity on the central spindle, all together as a single unit. The spinning of the platters and the ability of the access-arm mechanism to move in and out allows the read/write heads to be located over any piece of data on the entire unit, many times each second, and it is this mechanical system that provides the direct access capability.

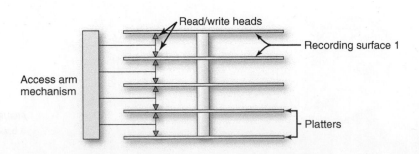

FIGURE 8.4 A disk drive with its access arm
mechanism and read/write heads

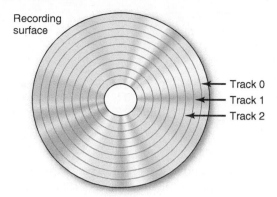
Recording surface

Track 0
Track 1
Track 2

FIGURE 8.5 Tracks on a recording surface

Tracks   On a recording surface, data is stored, serially by bit (bit by bit, byte by byte, field by field, record by record), in concentric circles known as tracks, Figure 8.5. There may be fewer than one hundred or several hundred tracks on each recording surface, depending on the particular device. Typically, each track holds the same amount of data. The tracks on a recording surface are numbered track 0, track 1, track 2, and so on. How would you store the records of a large file on a disk? You might assume that you would fill up the first track on a particular surface, then fill up the next track on the surface, then the next, and so on until you have filled an entire surface. Then you would move on to the next surface. At first, this sounds reasonable and perhaps even obvious. But it turns out it's problematic. Every time you move from one track to the next on a surface, the device's access-arm mechanism has to move. That's the only way that the read/write head, which can read or write only one track at a time, can get from one track to another on a given recording surface. But the access-arm mechanism's movement is a slow, mechanical motion compared to the electronic processing speeds in the computer's CPU and main memory. There is a better way to store the file!

Cylinders   Figure 8.6 shows the disk's access-arm mechanism positioned so that the read/write head for recording surface 0 is positioned at that surface's track 76. Since the entire access-arm mechanism moves as a unit and the read/write heads are always one over the other in a line, the read/write head for recording surface 1 is positioned at that surface's track 76, too. In fact, each surface's read/write head is positioned over its track 76. If you picture the collection of each surface's track 76, one above the other, they seem to take the shape of a **cylinder**, Figure 8.7. Indeed, each collection of tracks,

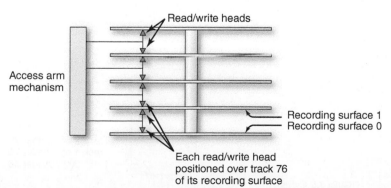
Read/write heads

Access arm mechanism

Recording surface 1
Recording surface 0

Each read/write head positioned over track 76 of its recording surface

FIGURE 8.6 Each read/write head positioned over track 76 of its recording surface

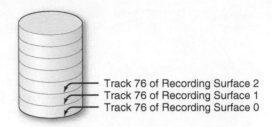

FIGURE 8.7 The collection of each recording surface's track 76 looks like a cylinder.
This collection of tracks is called cylinder 76

one from each recording surface, one directly above the other, is known as a cylinder. Notice that the number of cylinders in a disk is equal to the number of tracks on any one of its recording surfaces.

If we want to number the cylinders in a disk, which seems like a reasonable thing to do, it is certainly convenient to give a cylinder the number corresponding to the track numbers it contains. Thus, the cylinder in Figure 8.7, which is made up of track 76 from each recording surface, will be numbered and called cylinder 76. There is one more point to make. So far, the numbering we have looked at has been the numbering of the tracks on the recording surfaces, which also led to the numbering of the cylinders. But, once we have established a cylinder, it is also necessary to number the tracks within the cylinder, Figure 8.8. Typically, these are numbered 0, 1, . . ., n, which corresponds to the numbers of the recording surfaces. What will "n" be? That's the same question as how many tracks are there in a cylinder, but we've already answered that question. Since each recording surface "contributes" one track to each cylinder, the number of tracks in a cylinder is the same as the number of recording surfaces in a disk. The bottom line is to remember that we are going to number the tracks across a recording surface and then, *perpendicular to that*, we are also going to number the tracks in a cylinder.

Why is the concept of the cylinder important? Because in storing or retrieving data on a disk, you can move from one track of a cylinder to another *without having to move the access-arm mechanism*. The operation of turning off one read/write head and turning on another is an electrical switch that takes almost no time compared to the time it takes to move the access-arm mechanism. Thus, the ideal way to store data on a disk is to fill one cylinder and then move on to the next cylinder, and so on. This speeds up the applications that use the data considerably. Incidentally, it may seem that this is important only when reading files sequentially, as opposed to when performing the more important direct access operations. But, we will see later that in many database situations closely related pieces of data will have to be accessed together, so that storing them in such a way that they can be retrieved quickly can be a big advantage.

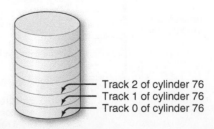

FIGURE 8.8 Cylinder 76's tracks

Steps in Finding and Transferring Data   Summarizing the way these rotating disk devices work, there are four major steps or timing considerations in the transfer of data from a disk to primary memory:

1. **Seek Time**: The time it takes to move the access-arm mechanism to the correct cylinder from its current position.
2. **Head Switching**: Selecting the read/write head to access the required track of the cylinder.
3. **Rotational Delay**: Waiting for the desired data on the track to arrive under the read/write head as the disk is spinning. On average, this takes half the time of one full rotation of the disk. That's because, as the disk is spinning, at one extreme the needed data might have just arrived under the read/write head at the instant the head was turned on, while at the other extreme you might have just missed it and have to wait for a full rotation. On the average, this works out to half a rotation.
4. **Transfer Time**: The time to move the data from the disk to primary memory once steps 1–3 have been completed.

One last point. Another term for a record in a file is a logical record. Since the rate of processing data in the CPU is much faster than the rate at which data can be brought in from secondary memory, it is often advisable to transfer several consecutively stored logical records at a time. Once such a physical record or block of several logical records has been brought into primary memory from the disk, each logical record can be examined and processed as necessary by the executing program.

File Organizations and Access Methods

The Goal: Locating a Record

Depending on application requirements, we might want to retrieve the records of a file on either a sequential or a direct-access basis. Disk devices can store records in some logical sequence, if we wish, and can access records in the middle of a file. But that's still not enough to accomplish direct access. Direct access requires the combination of a direct access device and the proper accompanying software.

Say that a file consists of many thousands or even a few million records. Further, say that there is a single record that you want to retrieve and you know the value of its unique identifier, its key. The question is, how do you know where it is on the disk? The disk device may be capable of going directly into the middle of a file to pull out a record, but how does it know where that particular record is? Remember, what we're trying to avoid is having it read through the file in sequence until it finds the record being sought. It's not magic (nothing in a computer ever is) and it is important to have a basic understanding of each of the steps in working with simple files, including this step, before we talk about databases. This brings us to the subject known as "file organizations and access methods," which refers to how we store the records of a file on the disk and how we retrieve them. We refer to the way that we store the data for subsequent retrieval as the **file organization**. The way that we retrieve the data, based on it being stored in a particular file organization, is called the **access method**. (Note in passing that the terms "file organization" and "access method" are often used synonymously, but this is technically incorrect.)

What we are primarily concerned with is how to achieve direct access to the records of a file, since this is the predominant mode of file operation, today. In terms of file organizations and access methods, there are basically two ways of achieving direct access. One involves the use of a tool known as an "**index**." The other is based on a way of storing and retrieving records known as a "**hashing method**." The idea is that if we know the value of a field of a record we want to retrieve, the index or hashing method will pinpoint its location in the file and tell the hardware mechanisms of the disk device where to find it.

The Index

The interesting thing about the concept of an index is that, while we are interested in it as a tool for direct access to the records in files, the principle involved is exactly the same as of the index in the back of a book. After all, a book is a storage medium for information about some subject. And, in both books and files, we want to be able to find some portion of the contents "directly" without having to scan sequentially from the beginning of the book or file until we find it. With a book, there are really three choices for finding a particular portion of the contents. One is a sequential scan of every page starting from the beginning of the book and continuing until the desired content is found. The second is using the table of contents. The table of contents in the front of the book summarizes what is in the book by major topics, and it is written in the same order as the material in the book. To use the table of contents, you have to scan through it from the beginning and, because the items it includes are summarized and written at a pretty high level, there is a good chance that you won't find what you're looking for. Even if you do, you will typically be directed to a page in the vicinity of the topic you're looking for, not to the exact page. The third choice is to use the index at the back of the book. The index is arranged alphabetically by item. As humans, we can do a quick, efficient search through the index, using the fact that the items in it are in alphabetic order, to quickly home in on the topic of interest. Then what? Next to the located item in the index appears a page number. Think of the page number as the address of the item you're looking for. In fact, it is a "direct pointer" to the page in the book where the material appears. You proceed directly to that page and find the material there, Figure 8.9.

FIGURE 8.9 The index in a book

The index in the back of a book has three key elements that are also characteristic of information systems indexes:

- The items of interest are copied over into the index but the original text is not disturbed in any way.
- The items copied over into the index are sorted (alphabetized in the index at the back of a book).
- Each item in the index is associated with a "pointer" (in a book index this is a page number) pointing to the place in the text where the item can be found.

Simple Linear Index   The indexes used in information systems come in a variety of types and styles. We will start with what is called a "simple linear index," because it is relatively easy to understand and is very close in structure to the index in the back of a book. On the right-hand side of Figure 8.10 is the Salesperson file. As before, it is in order by the unique Salesperson Number field. It is reasonable to assume that the records in this file are stored on the disk in the sequence shown in Figure 8.10. (We note in passing that retrieving the records in physical sequence, as they are stored on the disk, would also be retrieving them in logical sequence by salesperson number, since they were ordered on salesperson number when they were stored.) Figure 8.10 also shows that we have numbered the records of the file with a "Record Number" or a "Relative Record Number" ("relative" because the record number is relative to the beginning of the file). These record numbers are a handy way of referring to the records of the file and using such record numbers is considered another way of "physically" locating a record in a file, just as a cylinder and track address is a physical address.

On the left-hand side of Figure 8.10 is an index built over the Salesperson Name field of the Salesperson file. Notice that the three rules for building an index in a book were observed here, too. The indexed items were copied over from the file to the index and the file was not disturbed in any way. The items in the index were sorted. Finally, each indexed item was associated with a physical address, in this case the relative record number (the equivalent of a page number in a book) of the record of the Salesperson file from which it came. The first "index record" shows Adams 3 because the record of the Salesperson file with salesperson name Adams is at relative record location 3 in the Salesperson file. Notice the similarity between this index and the index in the back of a book. Just as you can quickly find an item you are looking for in a book's index because the items are in alphabetic order, a programmed procedure could quickly find one of the salespersons' names in the index because they are in sorted order. Then, just as the item that you found in the book's index has a page number next to it telling you

Index			Salesperson File		
Salesperson Name	Record Address		Record Number	Salesperson Number	Salesperson Name	City
Adams	3		1	119	Taylor	New York
Baker	2		2	137	Baker	Detroit
Carlyle	6		3	186	Adams	Dallas
Dickens	4		4	204	Dickens	Dallas
Green	7		5	255	Lincoln	Atlanta
Lincoln	5		6	361	Carlyle	Detroit
Taylor	1		7	420	Green	Tucson

FIGURE 8.10 Salesperson file on the right with index built over the Salesperson Name field, on the left

Index		Salesperson File			
City	Record Address	Record Number	Salesperson Number	Salesperson Name	City
Atlanta	5	1	119	Taylor	New York
Dallas	3	2	137	Baker	Detroit
Dallas	4	3	186	Adams	Dallas
Detroit	2	4	204	Dickens	Dallas
Detroit	6	5	255	Lincoln	Atlanta
New York	1	6	361	Carlyle	Detroit
Tucson	7	7	420	Green	Tucson

FIGURE 8.11 Salesperson file on the right with index built over the City field, on the left

where to look for the detailed information you seek, the index record in the index of Figure 8.10 has the relative record number of the record of the Salesperson file that has the information, i.e. the record, that you are looking for.

Figure 8.11, with an index built over the City field, demonstrates another point about indexes. An index can be built over a field with non-unique values.

Figure 8.12 shows the Salesperson file with an index built over the Salesperson Number field. This is an important concept known as an "indexed-sequential file." In an indexed-sequential file, the file is stored on the disk in order based on a set of field values (in this case the salesperson numbers) and an index is built *over that same field*. This allows both sequential and direct access by the key field, which can be an advantage when applications with different retrieval requirements share the file. The odd thing about this index is that since the Salesperson file was already in sequence by the Salesperson Number field, when the salesperson numbers were copied over into the index they were already in sorted order! Further, for the same reason, the record addresses are also in order. In fact, in Figure 8.12, the Salesperson Number field in the Salesperson file, with the list of relative record numbers next to it, appears to be identical to the index. But then, why bother having an index built over the Salesperson Number field at all? In principle, the reason is that when the search algorithm processes the salesperson numbers, they have to be in primary memory. Again in principle, it would be much more efficient to bring the smaller index into primary memory for this purpose than to bring the entire Salesperson file in just to process the Salesperson Number field.

Why, in the last couple of sentences, did we keep using the phrase, "in principle?" The answer to this is closely tied to the question of whether simple linear indexes are

Index		Salesperson File			
Salesperson Number	Record Address	Record Number	Salesperson Number	Salesperson Name	City
119	1	1	119	Taylor	New York
137	2	2	137	Baker	Detroit
186	3	3	186	Adams	Dallas
204	4	4	204	Dickens	Dallas
255	5	5	255	Lincoln	Atlanta
361	6	6	361	Carlyle	Detroit
420	7	7	420	Green	Tucson

FIGURE 8.12 Salesperson file on the right with index built over the Salesperson Number field, on the left

practical for use in even moderately sized information systems applications. And the answer is that they are not. One reason (and here is where the "in principle" in the last paragraph come in) is that, even if the simple linear index is made up of just two columns, it would still be clumsy to try to move all or even parts of it into primary memory to use it in a search. At best, it would require many read operations to the disk on which the index is located. The second reason has to do with inserting new disk records. Look once again at the Salesperson file and the index in Figure 8.10. Say that a new salesperson named French is hired and assigned salesperson number 452. Her record can be inserted at the end of the Salesperson file, where it would become record number 8. But the index would have to be updated, too: an index record, French 8, would have to be inserted between the index records for Dickens and Green to maintain the crucial alphabetic or sorted sequence of the index, Figure 8.13. The problem is that there is no obvious way to accomplish that insertion unless we move all the index records from Green to Taylor down one record position. In even a moderate-size file, that would clearly be impractical!

Indeed, the simple linear index is not a good solution for indexing the records of a file. This leads us to another kind of index that *is suitable* for indexing even very large files, the *B+-tree index*.

Your Turn

8.1 Simple Linear Indexes

When we think of indexes (other than those used to access data in computers), most people would agree that those thoughts would be limited to the indexes in the backs of books. But, if we want to and it makes sense, we can create indexes to help us find objects in our world other than items inside books. (By the way, have you ever seen a directory in a department store that lists its departments alphabetically and then, next to each department name, indicates the floor it's on? That's an index, too!)

Question:

Choose a set of objects in your world and develop a simple linear index to help you find them when you need to. For example, you may have CDs or DVDs on different shelves of a bookcase or in different rooms of your house. In this example, what would be the identifier in the index for each CD or DVD? What would be the physical location in the index? Think of another set of objects and develop an index for them.

Index			Salesperson File			
Salesperson Name	Record Address		Record Number	Salesperson Number	Salesperson Name	City
Adams	3		1	119	Taylor	New York
Baker	2		2	137	Baker	Detroit
Carlyle	6		3	186	Adams	Dallas
Dickens	4		4	204	Dickens	Dallas
Green	7		5	255	Lincoln	Atlanta
Lincoln	5		6	361	Carlyle	Detroit
Taylor	1		7	420	Green	Tucson
			8	452	French	New York
French 8	?					

FIGURE 8.13 Salesperson file with the insertion of a record for #452 French. But how can you squeeze the index record into the proper sequence?

B+-Tree Index   The B+-tree index, in its many variations (and there are many, including one called the B*-tree), is far and away the most common data-indexing system in use today. Assume that the Salesperson File now includes records for several hundred salespersons. Figure 8.14 is a variation of how the B+-tree index works. The figure shows the salesperson records arranged in sequence by the Salesperson Number field on ten cylinders (numbered 1–10) of a rotating disk. (The B+ tree principles are the same in a solid state disk as in a rotating disk, but obviously without cylinders and tracks.) Above the ten cylinders is an arrangement of special index records in what is known as a "tree." There is a single index record, known as the "root," at the top, with "branches" leading down from it to other "nodes." Sometimes the lowest-level nodes are called "leaves." For the terminology, think of it as a real tree turned upside-down with the roots clumped into a single point at the top, Figure 8.15. Alternatively, you can think of it as a family tree, which normally has this same kind of top-to-bottom orientation.

Notice the following about the index records in the tree:

- The index records contain salesperson number key values copied from certain of the salesperson records.
- Each key value in the tree is associated with a pointer that is the address of either a lower-level index record or a cylinder containing the salesperson records.

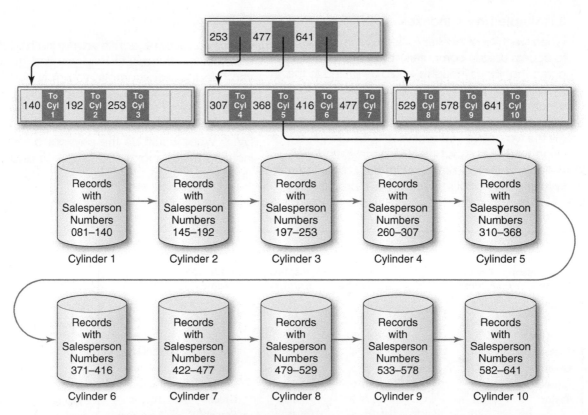

FIGURE 8.14 Salesperson file with a B+-tree index

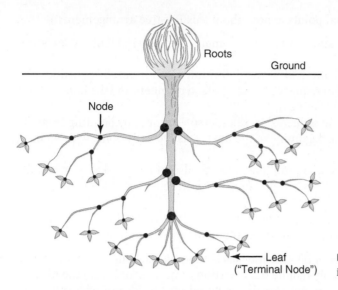

Roots

Ground

Node

Leaf
("Terminal Node")

FIGURE 8.15 A real tree, upside down, with the roots clumped together into a single point

- Each index record, at every level of the tree, contains space for the same number of key value/pointer pairs (four in this example). This index record capacity is arbitrary, but once it is set, it must be the same for every index record at every level of the index.
- Each index record is at least half full (in this example each record actually contains at least two key value/pointer pairs).

How are the key values in the index tree constructed and how are the pointers arranged? The lowest level of the tree contains the highest key value of the salesperson records on each of the 10 data cylinders. That's why there are 10 key values in the lowest level of the index tree. Each of those 10 key values has a pointer to the data cylinder from which it was copied. For example, the leftmost index record on the lowest level of the tree contains key values 140, 192, and 253, which are the highest key values on cylinders 1, 2, and 3, respectively. The root index record contains the highest key value of each of the index records at the next (which happens to be the last in this case) level down. Looking down from the root index record, notice that 253 is the highest key value of the first index record at the next level down, and so on for key values 477 and 641 in the root.

Let's say that you want to perform a direct access for the record for salesperson 361. A stored search routine would start at the root and scan its key values from left to right, looking for the first key value greater than or equal to 361, the key value for which you are searching. Starting from the left, the first key value in the root greater than or equal to 361 is 477. The routine would then follow the pointer associated with key value 477 to the second of the three index records at the next level. The search would be repeated in that index record, following the same rules. This time, key value 368 is the first one from the left that is higher than or equal to 361. The routine would then follow the pointer associated with key value 368 to cylinder 5. Additional search cues within the cylinder could then point to the track and possibly even the position on the track at which the record for salesperson 361 is to be found.

There are several additional points to note about this B+-tree arrangement:

- The tree index is small and can be kept in main memory indefinitely for a frequently accessed file.
- The file and index of Figure 8.14 fit the definition of an indexed-sequential file, because the file is stored in sequence by salesperson numbers and the index is built over the Salesperson Number field.
- The file can be retrieved in sequence by salesperson number by pointing from the end of one cylinder to the beginning of the next, as is typically done, without even using the tree index.
- B+-tree indexes can be and are routinely used to also index non-key, non-unique fields, although the tree can be deeper and/or the structures at the end of the tree can be more complicated.
- In general, the storage unit for groups of records can be (as in the above example) but need not be the cylinder or any other physical device sub-unit.

The final point to make about B+-tree indexes is that, unlike simple linear indexes, they are designed to comfortably handle the insertion of new records into the file and the deletion of records. The principle for this is based on the idea of unit splits and contractions, both at the record storage level and at the index tree level. For example, say that a new record with salesperson number 365 must be inserted. Starting from the root and following the same procedure for a record search, the computer determines that this record should be located on Cylinder 5 in order to maintain the sequence of the records based on the salesperson number key. If there is room on the track on the cylinder that it should go into to maintain the sequence, the other records can be shifted over and there is no problem. If the track it should go into is full but another track on the cylinder has been left empty as a reserve, then the set of records on the full track plus the one for 365 can be "split," with half of them staying on the original track and the other half moving to the reserve track. There would also have to be a mechanism to maintain the proper sequence of tracks within the cylinder, as the split may have thrown it off.

But suppose that cylinder 5 is completely full. Then the collection of records on the entire cylinder has to be split between cylinder 5 and an empty reserve cylinder, say cylinder 11, Figure 8.16. That's fine, except that the key value of 368 in the tree index's lowest level still points to cylinder 5 while the record with key value 368 is now on cylinder 11. Furthermore, there is no key value/pointer pair representing cylinder 11 in the tree index, at all! If the lowest-level index record containing key value 368 had room, a pointer to the new cylinder could be added and the keys in the key value/pointer pairs adjusted. But, as can be seen in Figure 8.14, there is no room in that index record.

Records
with
Salesperson
Numbers
310–330

Cylinder 5

Records
with
Salesperson
Numbers
332–368

Cylinder 11

FIGURE 8.16 The records of cylinder 5 plus the newly added record, divided between cylinder 5 and an empty reserve cylinder, cylinder 11

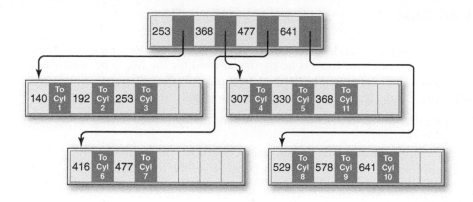

FIGURE 8.17 The B+-tree index after the cylinder 5 split

Figure 8.17 shows how this situation is handled. The index record into which the key for the new cylinder should go (the middle of the three index records at the lower level), which happens to be full, is split into two index records. The now five instead of four key values and their associated pointers are divided, as equally as possible, between them. But, in Figure 8.14, there were three key values in the record at the next level up (which happens to be the root), and now there are four index records instead of the previous three at the lower level. As shown in Figure 8.17, the empty space in the root index record is used to accommodate the new fourth index record at the lower level. What would have happened if the root index record had already been full? It would have been split in half and a new root at the next level up would have been created, expanding the index tree from two levels of index records to three levels.

Remember the following about indexes:

- An index can be built over any field of a file, whether or not the file is in physical sequence based on that or any other field. The field need not have unique values.
- An index can be built on a single field but it can also be built on a combination of fields. For example, an index could be built on the combination of City and State in the Salesperson file.
- In addition to its direct access capability, an index can be used to retrieve the records of a file in logical sequence based on the indexed field. For example, the index in Figure 8.10 could be used to retrieve the records of the Salesperson file in sequence by salesperson name. Since the index is in sequence by salesperson name, a simple scan of the index from beginning to end lists the relative record numbers of the salesperson records in order by salesperson name.
- Many separate indexes into a file can exist simultaneously, each based on a different field or combination of fields of the file. The indexes are quite independent of each other.
- When a new record is inserted into a file, an existing record is deleted, or an indexed field is updated, all of the affected indexes must be updated.

Creating an Index with SQL   Creating an index with SQL entails naming the index, specifying the table being indexed, and specifying the column on which the index is being created. So, for example, to create index A in Figure 8.21, which is an index built on the Salesperson Number attribute of the SALESPERSON table, you would write:

```
CREATE INDEX A ON SALESPERSON(SPNUM);
```

Hashed Files

There are many applications in which all file accesses must be done on a direct basis, speed is of the essence, and there is no particular need for the file to be organized in sequence by the values of any of its fields. An approach to file organization and access that fills this bill is the hashed file. The basic ideas include:

- The number of records in a file is estimated and enough space is reserved on a disk to hold them.
- Additional space is reserved for additional "overflow" records.
- To determine where to insert a particular record of the file, the record's key value is converted by a "hashing routine" into one of the reserved record locations on the disk.
- To subsequently find and retrieve the record, the same hashing routine is applied to the key value during the search.

Say, for example, that our company has 50 salespersons and that we have reserved enough space on the disk for their 50 records. There are many hashing routines but the most common is the "**division-remainder method**." In the division-remainder method, we divide the key value of the record that we want to insert or retrieve by the number of record locations that we have reserved. Remember long division, with its "quotient" and "remainder?" We perform the division, discard the quotient, and use the remainder to tell us where to locate the record. Why the remainder? Because the remainder is tailor-made for pointing to one of the storage locations. If, as in this example, we have 50 storage locations and divide a key value by that number, 50, we will get a remainder that is a whole number between 0 and 49. The value of the quotient doesn't matter. If we number the 50 storage locations 0–49 and store a record at the location dictated by its "hashed" key value, we have clearly developed a way to store and then locate the records, and a very fast way, at that! There's only one problem. More than one key value can hash to the same location. When this happens, we say that a "**collision**" has occurred, and the two key values involved are known as "synonyms."

Figure 8.18 shows a storage area that can hold 50 salesperson records plus space for **overflow records**. (We will not go into how to map this space onto the cylinders and tracks of a disk, but it can be done easily.) The main record storage locations are numbered 0–49; the overflow locations begin at position 50. An additional field for a "synonym pointer" has been added to every record location. Let's start by storing the record for salesperson 186. Dividing 186 by the number of record locations (50) yields a quotient of 3 (which we don't care about) and a remainder of 36. So, as shown in the figure, we store the record for salesperson 186 at record location 36. Next, we want to store the record for salesperson 361. This time, the hashing routine gives a remainder of 11 and, as shown in the figure, that's where the record goes. The next record to be stored is the record for salesperson 436. The hashing routine produces a remainder of 36. The procedure tries to store the record at location 36, but finds that another record is already stored there.

To solve this problem, the procedure stores the new record at one of the overflow record locations, say number 50. It then indicates this by storing that location number in the synonym pointer field of record 36. When another collision occurs with the insertion of salesperson 236, this record is stored at the next overflow location and its location is stored at location 50, the location of the last record that "hashed" to 36.

Record Location	Salesperson Number	Salesperson Name	. . .	Synonym Pointer
0				
11	361	Carlyle	. . .	
36	186	Adams	. . .	50
49				
50	436	James	. . .	51
51	236	Stein	. . .	−1
52				
53				
54				

FIGURE 8.18 The Salesperson file stored as a hashed file

Subsequently, if an attempt is made to retrieve the record for salesperson 186, the key value hashes to 36 and, indeed, the record for salesperson 186 is found at location 36. If an attempt is made to retrieve the record for salesperson 436, the key hashes to 36 but another record (the one for salesperson 186) is found at location 36. The procedure then follows the synonym pointer at the end of location 36 to location 50, where it finds the record for salesperson 436. A search for salesperson 236's record would follow the same sequence. Key value 236 would hash to location 36 but another record would be found there. The synonym pointer in the record at location 36 points to location 50, but another record, 436, is found there, too. The synonym pointer in the record at location 50 points to location 51, where the desired record is found.

There are a few other points to make about hashed files:

- It should be clear that the way that the hashing algorithm scatters records within the storage space disallows any sequential storage based on a set of field values.
- A file can only be hashed once, based on the values of a single field or a single combination of fields. This is because the essence of the hashing concept includes the physical placement of the records based on the result of the hashing routine. A record can't be located in one place based on the hash of one field and at the same time be placed somewhere else based on the hash of another field. It can't be in two places at once!
- If a file is hashed on one field, direct access based on another field can be achieved by building an index on the other field.
- Many hashing routines have been developed. The goal is to minimize the number of collisions and synonyms, since these can obviously slow down retrieval performance. In practice, several hashing routines are tested on a file to determine the best "fit." Even a relatively simple procedure like the division-remainder method can be fine-tuned. In this method, experience has shown that once the number of storage locations has been determined, it is better to choose a slightly higher

number, specifically the next prime number or the next number not evenly divisible by any number less than 20.

- A hashed file must occasionally be reorganized after so many collisions have occurred that performance is degraded to an unacceptable level. A new storage area with a new number of storage locations is chosen and the process starts all over again.
- Figure 8.18 shows a value of −1 in the synonym pointer field of the record for salesperson 236 at storage location 51. This is an end-of-chain marker. It is certainly possible that a search could be conducted for a record, say with key value 386, that does not exist in the file. 386 would hash to 36 and the chain would be followed to location 50 and then to location 51. Some signal has to then be set up at the end of the chain to indicate that there are no more records stored in the file that hash to 36, so that the search can be declared over and a "not found" condition indicated. (A negative number is a viable signal because there can't be a negative record location!)

Inputs to Physical Database Design

Physical database design starts where logical database design ends. That is, the well-structured relational tables produced by the conversion from entity-relationship diagrams or by the data normalization process form the starting point for physical database design. But these tables are only part of the story. In order to determine how best to modify the tables to improve application performance, a wide range of factors must be considered. The factors will help determine which modification techniques to apply and how to apply them. And, at that, the process is as much art as science. The choices are so numerous and the possible combinations of modifications are so complex that even the experienced designer hopes for a satisfactory but not a perfect solution.

Figure 8.19 lists the inputs to physical database design and thus the factors that are important to it. These naturally fall into several subgroups. First, we will take a look at

Inputs into the Physical Database Design Process
- The Tables Produced by the Logical Database Design Process
- Business Environment Requirements
  - Response Time Requirements
  - Throughput Requirements
- Data Characteristics
  - Data Volume Assessment
  - Data Volatility
- Application Characteristics
  - Application Data Requirements
  - Application Priorities
- Operational Requirements
  - Data Security Concerns
  - Backup and Recovery Concerns
- Hardware and Software Characteristics
  - DBMS Characteristics
  - Hardware Characteristics

FIGURE 8.19 Inputs into the physical database design process

each of these physical design inputs and factors, one by one. Then we will describe a variety of physical database design techniques, explaining how the various inputs and factors influence each of these techniques.

The Tables Produced by the Logical Database Design Process

The tables produced by the logical database design process (which for simplicity we will refer to as the "logical design") form the starting point of the physical database design process. These tables are "pure" in that they reflect all of the data in the business environment, they have no data redundancy, and they have in place all the foreign keys that are needed to establish all the relationships in the business environment. Unfortunately, they may present a variety of problems when it comes to performance, as we previously described. Again, for example, without indexes or hashing, there is no support for direct access. Or it is entirely possible that a particular query may require the join of several tables, which may cause an unacceptably slow response from the database. So, it is clear that these tables, in their current form, are very likely to produce unacceptable performance and that is why we must go on modifying them in physical database design.

Business Environment Requirements

Beyond the logical design, the requirements of the business environment lead the list of inputs and factors in physical database design. These include response time requirements and throughput requirements.

Response Time Requirements   **Response time** is the delay from the time that the Enter Key is pressed to execute a query until the result appears on the screen. One of the main factors in deciding how extensively to modify the logical design is the establishment of the response time requirements. Do the major applications that will use the database require two-second response, five-second response, ten-second response, etc.? That is, how long a delay will a customer telephoning your customer service representatives tolerate when asking a question about her account? How fast a response do the managers in your company expect when looking for information about a customer or the sales results for a particular store or the progress of goods on an assembly line? Also, different types of applications differ dramatically in response time requirements. Operational environments, including the customer service example, tend to require very fast response. "Decision support" environments, such as the data warehouse environment discussed in Chapter 13 tend to have relaxed response time requirements.

Throughput Requirements   **Throughput** is the measure of how many queries from simultaneous users must be satisfied in a given period of time by the application set and the database that supports it. Clearly, throughput and response time are linked. The more people who want access to the same data at the same time, the more pressure on the system to keep the response time from dropping to an unacceptable level. And the more potential pressure there is on response time, the more important the physical design task becomes.

Data Characteristics

How much data will be stored in the database and how frequently different parts of it will be updated are important in physical design as well.

Data Volume Assessment   How much data will be in the database? Roughly, how many records is each table expected to have? Some physical design decisions will hinge on whether a table is expected to have 300, 30,000, or 3,000,000 records.

Data Volatility   **Data volatility** describes how often stored data is updated. Some data, such as active inventory records that reflect the changes in goods constantly being put into and taken out of inventory, is updated frequently. Some data, such as historic sales records, is never updated (except for the addition of data from the latest time period to the end of the table). How frequently data is updated, the volatility of the data, is an important factor in certain physical design decisions.

Application Characteristics

The nature of the applications that will use the data, which applications are the most important to the company, and which data will be accessed by each application form yet another set of inputs and factors in physical design.

Application Data Requirements   Exactly which database tables does each application require for its processing? Do the applications require that tables be joined? How many applications and which specific applications will share particular database tables? Are the applications that use a particular table run frequently or infrequently? Questions like these yield one indication of how much demand there will be for access to each table and its data. More heavily used tables and tables frequently involved in joins require particular attention in the physical design process.

Application Priorities   Typically, tables in a database will be shared by different applications. Sometimes, a modification to a table during physical design that's proposed to help the performance of one application hinders the performance of another application. When a conflict like that arises, it's important to know which of the two applications is the more critical to the company. Sometimes this can be determined on an increased profit or cost-saving basis. Sometimes it can be based on which application's sponsor has greater political power in the company. But, whatever the basis, it is important to note the relative priority of the company's applications for physical design choice considerations.

Operational Requirements: Data Security, Backup, and Recovery

Certain physical design decisions can depend on such data management issues as data security and backup and recovery. Data security, which will be discussed in Chapter 11, can include such concerns as protecting data from theft or malicious destruction and making sure that sensitive data is accessible only to those employees of the company who have a "need to know." Backup and recovery, which will also be discussed in Chapter 11, ranges from recovering a table or a database that has been corrupted or lost due to hardware or software failure to recovering an entire information system after a natural disaster. Sometimes, data security and backup and recovery concerns can affect physical design decisions.

Your Turn

8.2 Physical Database Design Inputs

Consider a university information systems environment or another information systems environment of your choice. Think about a set of 5–10 applications that constitute the main applications in this environment.

Question:

For each of these 5–10 applications, specify the response time requirements and the throughput requirements. What would the volumes be of the database tables needed to support these applications? How volatile would you expect the data to be? What concerns would you have about the security and privacy of the data?

Hardware and Software Characteristics   Finally, the hardware and software environments in which the databases will reside have an important bearing on physical design.

DBMS Characteristics   All relational database management systems are certainly similar in that they support the basic, even classic at this point, relational model. However, relational DBMSs may differ in certain details, such as the exact nature of their indexes, attribute data type options, SQL query features, etc., that must be known and taken into account during physical database design.

Hardware Characteristics   Certain hardware characteristics, such as processor speeds and disk data transfer rates, while not directly parts of the physical database design process, are associated with it. Simply put, the faster the hardware, the more tolerant the system can be of a physical design that avoids relatively severe changes in the logical design.

Another issue in this regard is the changing characteristics of secondary storage devices and options, including the gradual replacement of rotating disks with solid state disks and the use of server farms.

Physical Database Design Techniques

Figure 8.20 lists several physical database design categories and techniques within each. The order of the categories is significant. Depending on how we modify the logical design to try to make performance improvements, we may wind up introducing new complications or even reintroducing data redundancy. Also, as noted in Figure 8.20, the first three categories do not change the logical design while the last four categories do. So, the order of the categories is roughly from least to most disruptive of the original logical design. And, in this spirit, the only techniques that introduce data redundancy (storing **derived data**, **denormalization**, duplicating tables, and adding **subset tables**) appear at the latter part of the list.

Physical design categories and techniques that DO NOT change the logical design

- Adding External Features
  - Adding Indexes
  - Adding Views
- Reorganizing Stored Data
  - Clustering Files
- Splitting a Table into Multiple Tables
  - Horizontal Partitioning
  - Vertical Partitioning
  - Splitting-Off Large Text Attributes

Physical design categories and techniques that Do change the logical design

- Changing Attributes in a Table
  - Substituting Foreign Keys
- Adding Attributes to a Table
  - Creating New Primary Keys
  - Storing Derived Data
- Combining Tables
  - Combine Tables in One-to-One Relationships
  - Alternatives for Repeating Groups
  - Denormalization
- Adding New Tables
  - Duplicating Tables
  - Adding Subset Tables

FIGURE 8.20 Physical database design categories and techniques

Adding External Features

This first category of physical design changes, adding external features, doesn't change the logical design at all! Instead, it involves adding features to the logical design, specifically indexes and views. While certain tradeoffs have to be kept in mind when adding these external features, there is no introduction of data redundancy.

Adding Indexes   Since the name of the game is performance and since today's business environment is addicted to finding data on a direct-access basis, the use of indexes in relational databases is a natural. There are two questions to consider.

The first question is: which attributes or combinations of attributes should you consider indexing in order to have the greatest positive impact on the application environment? Actually, there are two sorts of possibilities. One category is attributes that are likely to be prominent in direct searches. These include:

- Primary keys.
- **Search attributes**, i.e. attributes whose values you will use to retrieve particular records. This is true especially when the attribute can take on many different values. (In fact, there is an argument that says that it is not beneficial to build an index on an attribute that has only a small number of possible values.)

The other category is attributes that are likely to be major players in operations such as joins that will require direct searches internally. Such operations also include the SQL ORDER BY and GROUP BY commands described in Chapter 4. It should be clear that a particular attribute might fall into both of these categories!

The second question is: what potential problems can be caused by building too many indexes? If it were not for the fact that building too many indexes can cause problems in certain kinds of databases, the temptation would be to build a large number of indexes for maximum direct-access benefit. The issue here is the volatility of the data. Indexes are wonderful for direct searches. But when the data in a table is updated, the system must take the time to update the table's indexes, too. It will do this automatically, but it takes time. If several indexes must be updated, this multiplies the time to update the table several times over. What's wrong with that? If there is a lot of update activity, the time that it takes to make the updates *and update all the indexes* could slow down the operations that are just trying to read the data for query applications, degrading query response time down to an unacceptable level!

One final point about building indexes: if the **data volume**, the number of records in a table, is very small, then there is no point in building any indexes on it at all (although some DBMSs will always require an index on the primary key). The point is that if the table is small enough, it is more efficient to just read the whole table into main memory and search by scanning it!

Figure 8.21 repeats the General Hardware Co. relational database, to which we will add some indexes. We start by building indexes, marked indexes A–F, on the primary key attribute(s) of each table. Consider the SALESPERSON and CUSTOMER tables. If the application set requires joins of the SALESPERSON and CUSTOMER tables, the Salesperson Number attribute of the CUSTOMER table would be a good choice for an index, index G, because it is the foreign key that connects those two tables in the join. If we frequently need to find salesperson records on a direct basis by Salesperson *Name*, then that attribute should have an index, index H, built on it. Consider the SALES table. If we have an important, frequently run application that has to find the total sales for all or a range of the products, then the needed GROUP BY command would run more efficiently if the Product Number attribute was indexed, index I.

Adding Views   Another external feature that doesn't change the logical design is the view. In relational database terminology, a **view** is what is more generally known in database management as a "**logical view.**" It is a mapping onto a physical table that allows an end user to access only part of the table. The view can include a subset of the table's columns, a subset of the table's rows, or a combination of the two. It can even be based on the join of two tables *No data is physically duplicated when a view is created.* It is literally a way of viewing just part of a table. For example, in the General Hardware Co. SALESPERSON table, a view can be created that includes only the Salesperson Number, Salesperson Name, and Office Number attributes. A particular person can be given access to the view and then sees only these three columns. He is not even aware of the existence of the other two attributes of the physical table.

A view is an important device in protecting the security and privacy of data, an issue that we listed among the factors in physical database design. Using views to limit the access of individuals to only the parts of a table that they really need to do their work is clearly an important means of protecting a company's data. As we will see later, the combination of the view capability and the SQL GRANT command forms a powerful data protection tool.

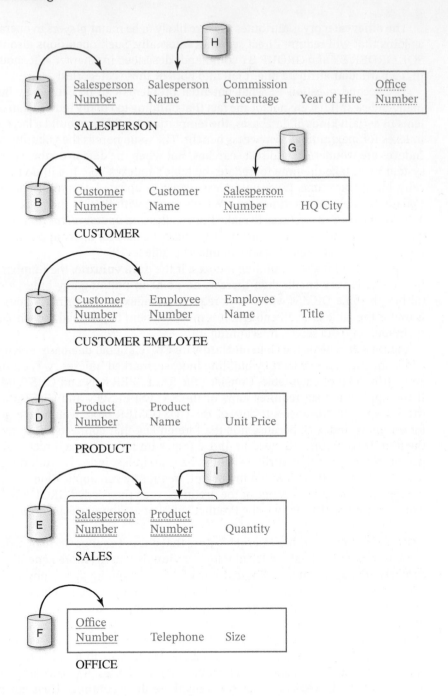

FIGURE 8.21 The General Hardware Company
relational database with some indexes

Reorganizing Stored Data

The next level of change in physical design involves reorganizing the way data is stored on the disk without changing the logical design at all and thus without introducing data redundancy. This is particularly true with rotating disk technology but may also affect solid state disks. We present an example of this type of modification.

137	Baker	10	1995

	0121	Main St. Hardware	137	New York
	0933	ABC Home Stores	137	Los Angeles
	1047	Acme Hardware Store	137	Los Angeles
	1826	City Hardware	137	New York

186	Adams	15	2001

	0839	Jane's Stores	186	Chicago
	2267	Central Stores	186	New York

204	Dickens	10	1998

	2198	Western Hardware	204	New York

361	Carlyle	20	2001

	1525	Fred's Tool Stores	361	Atlanta
	1700	XYZ Stores	361	Washington

FIGURE 8.22 Clustering files with the SALESPERSON and CUSTOMER tables

Clustering Files   Suppose that in the General Hardware Co. business environment, it is important to be able to frequently and quickly retrieve all of the data in a salesperson record together with all of the records of the customers for which that salesperson is responsible. Clearly, this requires a join of the SALESPERSON and CUSTOMER tables. Just for the sake of argument, assume that this retrieval, including the join, does not work quickly enough to satisfy the response time or throughput requirements. One solution, assuming that the DBMS in use supports it, might be the use of "clustered files."

Figure 8.22 shows the General Hardware salesperson and customer data from Figure 5.14 arranged as clustered files. The logical design has not changed. Logically, the DBMS considers the SALESPERSON and CUSTOMER tables just as they appear in Figure 5.14. But physically, they have been arranged on the disk in the interleaved fashion shown in Figure 8.22. Each salesperson record is followed physically on the disk by the customer records with which it is associated. That is, each salesperson record is followed on the disk by the records of the customers for whom that salesperson is responsible. For example, the salesperson record for salesperson 137, Baker, is followed on the disk by the customer records for customers 0121, 0933, 1047, and 1826. Note that the salesperson number 137 appears as a foreign key in each of those four customer records. So, if a query is posed to find a salesperson record, say Baker's record, and all his associated customer records, performance will be improved because all five records are right near each other on the disk, even though logically they come from two separate tables. Without the clustered files, Baker's record would be on one part of the disk with all of the other salesperson records and the four customer records would be on another part of the disk with the other customer records, resulting in slower retrieval for this kind of two-table, integrated query.

The downside of this clustering arrangement is that retrieving subsets of *only* salesperson records or *only* customer records is slower than without clustering. Without clustering, all the salesperson records are near each other on the disk, which helps when retrieving subsets of them. With clustering, the salesperson records are scattered over a much larger area on the disk because they're interspersed with all of those customer records, slowing down the retrieval of subsets of just salesperson records.

Splitting a Table into Multiple Tables

The three physical design techniques in this category arrange for particular parts of a table, either groups of particular rows or groups of particular columns, to be stored separately, on different areas of a disk or on different disks. In Chapter 12, when we discuss distributed database, we will see that this concept can even be extended to storing particular parts of a table in different cities.

Horizontal Partitioning   In **horizontal partitioning**, the rows of a table are divided into groups and the groups are stored separately, on different areas of a disk or on different disks. This may be done for several reasons. One is to manage the different groups of records separately for security or backup and recovery purposes. Another is to improve data retrieval performance when, for example, one group of records is accessed much more frequently than other records in the table. For example, suppose that the records for sales managers in the CUSTOMER EMPLOYEE table of Figure 5.14c must be accessed more frequently than the records of other customer employees. Separating out the frequently accessed group of records, as shown in Figure 8.23, means that they can be stored near each other in a concentrated space on the disk, which will speed up their retrieval. The records can also be stored on an otherwise infrequently used disk, so that the applications that use them don't have to compete excessively with other applications that need data on the same disk. The downside of this horizontal partitioning is that it can make a search of the entire table or the retrieval of records from more than one partition more complex and slower.

Vertical Partitioning   A table can also be subdivided by columns, producing the same advantages as horizontal partitioning. In this case, the separate groups, each made up of different columns of a table, are created because different users or applications require different columns. For example, as shown in Figure 8.24, it might be beneficial to split up the columns of the SALESPERSON table of Figure 5.14a so that the Salesperson Name and Year of Hire columns are stored separately from the others. But note that in creating these vertical partitions, *each partition must have a*

Customer Number	Employee Number	Employee Name	Title
0933	30441	Levy	Sales Manager
1525	33779	Baker	Sales Manager

Customer Number	Employee Number	Employee Name	Title
0121	27498	Smith	Co-Owner
0121	30441	Garcia	Co-Owner
0933	25270	Chen	VP Sales
0933	48285	Morton	President
2198	27470	Smith	President
2198	30441	Jones	VP Sales
2198	33779	Garcia	VP Personnel
2198	35268	Kaplan	Senior Accountant

FIGURE 8.23 Horizontal partitioning of the CUSTOMER EMPLOYEE table

Salesperson Number	Salesperson Name	Year of Hire
137	Baker	1995
186	Adams	2001
204	Dickens	1998
361	Carlyle	2001

Salesperson Number	Commission Percentage
137	10
186	15
204	10
361	20

FIGURE 8.24 Vertical partitioning of the SALESPERSON table

copy of the primary key, Salesperson Number in this example. Otherwise, in **vertical partitioning**, how would you track which rows in each partition go together to logically form the rows of the original table? In fact, this point leads to an understanding of the downside of vertical partitioning. A query that involves the retrieval of complete records—i.e. data that is in more than one vertical partition—actually requires that the vertical partitions be *joined* to reunite the different parts of the original records.

Splitting Off Large Text Attributes   A variation on vertical partitioning involves splitting off large **text attributes** into separate partitions. Sometimes the records of a table have several numeric attributes and a long text attribute that provides a description of the data in each record. It might well be that frequent access of the numeric data is necessary and that the long text attribute is accessed only occasionally. The problem is that the presence of the long text attribute tends to spread the numeric data over a larger disk area and thus slows down retrieval of the numeric data. The solution is to split off the text attribute, *together with a copy of the primary key*, into a separate vertical partition and store it elsewhere on the disk.

Changing Attributes in a Table

Up to this point, none of the physical design techniques discussed have changed the logical design. They have all involved adding external features such as indexes and views, or physically moving records or columns on the disk as with clustering and partitioning. The first physical design technique category that changes the logical design involves substituting a different attribute for a foreign key.

Substituting Foreign Keys   Consider the SALESPERSON and CUSTOMER tables of Figure 8.21. We know that Salesperson Number is a unique attribute and serves as the primary key of the SALESPERSON table. Say, for the sake of argument, that the Salesperson Name attribute is also unique, meaning that both Salesperson Number and Salesperson Name are candidate keys of the SALESPERSON table. Salesperson Number has been chosen to be the primary key and Salesperson Name is an alternate key.

FIGURE 8.25 Substituting another candidate key for a foreign key

CUSOTMER			
Customer Number	Customer Name	Salesperson *Name*	HQ City

Now, assume that there is a frequent need to retrieve data about customers, including the *name* of the salesperson responsible for that customer. The CUSTOMER table contains the *number* of the Salesperson who is responsible for a customer but not the name. By now, we know that solving this problem requires a join of the two tables, based on the common Salesperson Number attribute. But, if this is a frequent or critical query that requires high speed, we can improve the performance by *substituting* Salesperson Name for Salesperson Number as the foreign key in the CUSTOMER table, as shown in Figure 8.25. With Salesperson Name now contained in the CUSTOMER table, we can retrieve customer data, including the *name* of the responsible salesperson, *without having to do a performance-slowing join.* Finally, since Salesperson Name is a candidate key of the SALESPERSON table, using it as a foreign key in the CUSTOMER table still retains the ability to join the two tables when this is required for other queries.

Adding Attributes to a Table

Another means of improving database performance entails modifying the logical design by adding attributes to tables. Here are two ways to do this.

Creating New Primary Keys   Sometimes a table simply does not have a single unique attribute that can serve as its primary key. A two-attribute primary key, such as the combination of state and city names, might be OK. But in some circumstances the primary key of a table might consist of two, three, or more attributes and the performance implications of this may well be unacceptable. For one thing, indexing a multi-attribute key would likely be clumsy and slow. For another, having to use the multi-attribute key as a foreign key in the other tables in which such a foreign key would be necessary would probably also be unacceptably complex.

The solution is to invent a new primary key for the table that consists of a single new attribute. The new attribute will be a unique serial number attribute, with an arbitrary unique value assigned to each record of the table. This new attribute will then also be used as the foreign key in the other tables in which such a foreign key is required. In the General Hardware database of Figure 8.21, recall that the two-attribute primary key of the CUSTOMER EMPLOYEE table, Customer Number and Employee Number, is necessary because customer numbers are unique only within each customer company. Suppose that General Hardware decides to invent a new attribute, Customer Employee Number, which will be its own set of employee numbers for these people that will be *unique across all of the customer companies.* Then, the current two-attribute primary key of the CUSTOMER EMPLOYEE table can be replaced by this one new attribute, as shown in Figure 8.26. If the Customer Number, Employee Number combination had been placed in other tables in the database as a foreign key (it wasn't), then the two-attribute combination would be replaced by this new single attribute, too. Notice that Customer Number is still necessary as a foreign key because that's how we know which customer company a person works for. Arguably, the old

CUSTOMER EMPLOYEE				
Customer Employee Number	Customer Number	Employee Number	Employee Name	Title

Employee Number attribute may still be required because that is still their employer's internal identifier for them.

Storing Derived Data   Some queries require performing calculations on the data in the database and returning the calculated values as the answers. If these same values have to be calculated over and over again, perhaps by one person or perhaps by many people, then it might make sense to calculate them once and store them in the database. Technically, this is a form of data redundancy, although a rather subtle form. If the "raw" data is ever updated without the stored, calculated values being updated as well, the accuracy or integrity of the database will be compromised.

To illustrate this point, let's add another attribute to General Hardware's CUSTOMER table. This attribute, called Annual Purchases in Figure 8.27a, is the expected amount of merchandise, in dollars, that a customer will purchase from General Hardware in a year. Remember that there is a one-to-many relationship from salespersons to customers, with each salesperson being responsible for several (or many) customers. Suppose that there is a frequent need to quickly find the total amount of merchandise each *salesperson* is expected to account for in a year, i.e. the sum of the Annual Purchases attribute for all of the particular salesperson's customers. This sum could be recalculated each time it is requested for any particular salesperson, but that might take too long. The other choice is to calculate the sum for each salesperson and store it in the database, recognizing that whenever a customer's Annual Purchases value changes, the sum for the customer's salesperson has to be updated, too.

CUSTOMER				
Customer Number	Customer Name	Salesperson Number	IIQ City	*Annual Purchases*

a. Annual Purchases attribute added to the CUSTOMER table.

SALESPERSON					
Salesperson Number	Salesperson Name	Commission Percentage	Year of Hire	Office Number	Total Annual Customer Purchases

CUSTOMER				
Customer Number	Customer Name	Salesperson Number	HQ City	Annual Purchases

b. Total Annual Customer Purchases attribute added to the SALESPERSON table as derived data.

FIGURE 8.27 Adding derived data

The question then becomes, where do we store the summed annual purchases amount for each salesperson? Since the annual purchases figures are in the CUSTOMER table, your instinct might be to store the sums there. But where in the CUSTOMER table? You can't store them in individual customer records, because each sum involves *several* customers. You could insert special "sum records" in the CUSTOMER table but they wouldn't have the same attributes as the customer records themselves and that would be very troublesome. Actually, the answer is to store them in the SALESPERSON table. Why? Because there is one sum for each salesperson—again, it's the sum of the annual purchases of all of that salesperson's customers. So, the way to do it is to add an additional attribute, the Total Annual Customer Purchases attribute, to the SALESPERSON table, as shown in Figure 8.27b.

Combining Tables

Three techniques are described below, all of which involve combining two tables into one. Each technique is used in a different set of circumstances. It should be clear that all three share the same advantage: if two tables are combined into one, then there must surely be situations in which the presence of the new single table lets us avoid joins that would have been necessary when there were two tables. Avoiding joins is generally a plus for performance. But at what price? Let's see.

Combine Tables in One-to-One Relationships   Remember the one-to-one relationship between salespersons and offices in the General Hardware environment? Figure 8.28 shows the two tables combined into one. After all, if a salesperson can have only one office and an office can have only one salesperson assigned to it, there can be nothing wrong with combining the two tables. Since a salesperson can have only one office, a salesperson can be associated with only one office number, one (office) telephone, and one (office) size. A like argument can be made from the perspective of an office. Office data can still be accessed on a direct basis by simply creating an index on the Office Number attribute in the combined table.

Again, the advantage is that if we ever have to retrieve detailed data about a salesperson *and* his office in one query, it can now be done without a join. There are two negatives. One is that the tables are no longer logically, as well as physically, independent. If we want information just about offices, there is no longer an OFFICE table to go to. The data is still there, but we have to be aware that it is buried in the SALESPERSON/OFFICE table. The other negative is that retrievals of salesperson data *alone* or of office data *alone* could be slower than before because the longer combined SALESPERSON/OFFICE records spread the combined data over a larger area of the disk.

Alternatives for Repeating Groups   Suppose that we change the business environment so that every salesperson has exactly two customers, identified respectively as their "large" customer and their "small" customer, based on annual purchases. The structure of Figure 8.21 would still work just fine. But, because these **"repeating**

FIGURE 8.28 Combined SALESPERSON/OFFICE table showing the merger of two tables in a one-to-one relationship

SALESPERSON/OFFICE						
Salesperson Number	Salesperson Name	Commission Percentage	Year of Hire	Office Number	Telephone	Size

SALESPERSON/CUSTOMERS										
Salesperson Number	Salesperson Name	Commission Percentage	Year of Hire	Office Number	Large Customer Number	Large Customer Name	Large Customer HQ City	Small Customer Number	Small Customer Name	Small Customer HQ City

FIGURE 8.29 Merging of repeating groups into another table

groups" of customer attributes, one "group" of attributes (Customer Number, Customer Name, etc.) for each customer are so well controlled they can be folded into the SALESPERSON table. What makes them so well controlled is that there are exactly two for each salesperson and they can even be distinguished from each other as "large" and "small." This arrangement is shown in Figure 8.29. Note that the foreign key attribute of Salesperson Number from the CUSTOMER table is no longer needed.

Once again, this arrangement avoids joins when salesperson and customer data must be retrieved together. But, as with the one-to-one relationship case above, retrievals of salesperson data *alone* or of customer data *alone* could be slower than before because the longer combined SALESPERSON/CUSTOMER records spread the combined data over a larger area of the disk. And retrieving customer data alone is now more difficult. In the one-to-one relationship case, we could simply create an index on the Office Number attribute of the combined table. But in the combined table of Figure 8.29, there are *two* customer number attributes in each salesperson record. Retrieving records about customers alone would clearly take greater skill than before.

Denormalization   In the most serious database performance dilemmas, when everything else that can be done in terms of physical design has been done, it may be necessary to take pairs of related third normal form tables, and combine them, introducing possibly massive data redundancy. Why would anyone in their right mind want to do this? Because if after everything else has been done to improve performance, response times and throughput are still unsatisfactory for the business environment, eliminating run-time joins by recombining tables may mean the difference between a usable system and a lot of wasted money on a database (and application) development project that will never see the light of day. Clearly, if the physical designers decide to go this route, they must put procedures in place to manage the redundant data as they updated over time.

Figure 8.30 shows the denormalized SALESPERSON and CUSTOMER tables combined into one. The surviving table of the two in the one-to-many relationship will always be the table on the "*many* side" of the relationship. You can attach one set of salesperson data to a customer record; you cannot attach many sets of customer data to a single salesperson record without creating an even worse mess. The sample salesperson and customer data from Figure 5.14 is denormalized in Figure 8.31. (Figure 8.31 is identical to Figure 3.8. We used it in Chapter 3 to make a point about

CUSTOMER							
Customer Number	Customer Name	Salesperson Number	HQ City	Salesperson Number	Salesperson Name	Commission Percentage	Year of Hire

FIGURE 8.30 The denormalized SALESPERSON and CUSTOMER tables as the new CUSTOMER table

CUSTOMER							
Customer Number	Customer Name	Salesperson Number	HQ City	Salesperson Number	Salesperson Name	Commission Percentage	Year of Hire
0121	Main St. Hardware	137	New York	137	Baker	10	1995
0839	Jane's Stores	186	Chicago	186	Adams	15	2001
0933	ABC Home Stores	137	Los Angeles	137	Baker	10	1995
1047	Acme Hardware Store	137	Los Angeles	137	Baker	10	1995
1525	Fred's Tool Stores	361	Atlanta	361	Carlyle	20	2001
1700	XYZ Stores	361	Washington	361	Carlyle	20	2001
1826	City Hardware	137	New York	137	Baker	10	1995
2198	Western Hardware	204	New York	204	Dickens	10	1998
2267	Central Stores	186	New York	186	Adams	15	2001

FIGURE 8.31 The denormalized salesperson and customer data from Figure 5.12

data redundancy when we were exploring that subject.) Since a salesperson can have several customers, a particular salesperson's data will be repeated for each customer he has. Thus, the table shows that salesperson number 137's name is Baker *four times*, his commission percentage is 10 *four times*, and his year of hire was 1995 *four times*. The performance improvement had better be worth it, because the integrity exposure is definitely there.

Adding New Tables

Finally, there is the concept of simply duplicating data. Sometimes the final performance issue is that trying to maintain response time and throughput with the number of applications and users trying to share the same data is beyond the capabilities of the hardware, the software, and all the other physical design techniques. At the risk of overt data redundancy (which hopefully you will attempt to manage), the only recourse is to duplicate the data.

Duplicating Tables   Clearly, the direct approach is to duplicate tables and have different applications access the duplicates. This is exactly the opposite of the central database management concept of sharing data.

Adding Subset Tables   A somewhat less severe technique is to duplicate only those portions of a table that are most heavily accessed. These "subset" tables can then be assigned to different applications to ease the performance crunch. Data redundancy is still the major drawback, although obviously there is not as much of it as when the entire table is duplicated.

Example: Good Reading Book Stores

Consider the Good Reading Book Stores database of Figure 5.16. Recall that there is a one-to-many relationship between the PUBLISHER and BOOK tables. A book is published by exactly one publisher but a publisher publishes many books. That's why the Publisher Name attribute is in the BOOK table as a foreign key. A reasonable assumption is that there are several hundred publishers and many thousands of different books. If the various stores in the Good Reading chain carry different books to satisfy their individual clienteles, then there could be thousands of publishers and hundreds of thousands of different books.

Assume that at Good Reading's headquarters, there is a frequent need to find very quickly the details of a book, based on either its book number or its title, together with details about its publisher. As stated, this would clearly require a join of the PUBLISHER and BOOK tables. If the join takes too long, resulting in unacceptable response times, throughput, or both, what are the possibilities in terms of physical design to improve the situation? Here are several suggestions, although each has its potential drawbacks, as previously discussed.

- The Book Number attribute and the Book Title attributes in the PUBLISHER table can each have an index built on them to provide direct access, since the problem says that books are going to be searched for based on one of these two attributes.
- The two join attributes, the Publisher Name attribute of the PUBLISHER table and the Publisher Name attribute of the BOOK table, can each have an index built on them to help speed up the joint operation.
- If the DBMS permits it, the two tables can be clustered, with the book records associated with a particular publisher stored near that publisher's record on the disk.
- The two tables can be denormalized, with the appropriate publisher data being appended to each book record (and the PUBLISHER table being eliminated), as:

Book Number	Book Title	Publication Year	Pages	Publisher Name	City	Country	Telephone	Year Founded

What if it's important to be able to find quickly the *number of different books* that Good Reading carries from a particular publisher? This information could be found by using the SQL COUNT function to count up the number of that publisher's books when the query is asked. However, if this proves too slow, as it well might, then the number of books from each publisher can be calculated and stored as an additional attribute of "derived data" in the PUBLISHER table as:

Publisher Name	City	Country	Telephone	Year Founded	Number of Books

Example: World Music Association

Consider the World Music Association (WMA) relational database of Figure 5.17. WMA has a problem: there are many more retrieval requests for information about recordings by Beethoven and Mozart than for recordings by other composers. Since those records are scattered throughout the RECORDING table, performance tends to be slower than desired. A solution is to partition the RECORDING table horizontally into two partitions, one with the records for recordings by Beethoven and Mozart and the other with all the other records of the table. These two partitions can be stored on different parts of the same disk or on different disks. Performance will be improved with the Beethoven and Mozart records separated out and concentrated together on a restricted disk area.

There is also an application need to frequently and quickly retrieve salary data for the musicians on an individual and group basis. In the MUSICIAN table, the salary data is mixed in with other data (potentially much more data in each record than is shown in this example), which tends to slow down retrieval speeds. A solution is to create a vertical partition for the Annual Salary attribute, separating it from the rest of the attributes of the table. Remember that a copy of the primary key, in this case Musician Number, must accompany the non-key attribute(s) being split off into a separate vertical partition. Thus, one vertical partition will consist of the Musician Number and Annual Salary attributes while the other will consist of Musician Number and all of the non-key attributes except for the Annual Salary attribute. Storing these two vertical partitions on different parts of a disk or on different disks will enhance performance under the application circumstances described.

Assume that the COMPOSITION table has an additional attribute called "Description":

Composition Name	Composer Name	Year	Description

Description is a long text attribute that allows written descriptions of compositions to be stored in the database. While this is certainly useful, WMA has several applications that require frequent fast access to the other attributes of the table. The bulky description data tends to spread the records over a wider area of the disk than would otherwise be the case. Again, this is really a special case of the vertical partitioning scenario. The solution is to break out the description data, together with a copy of the primary key, and store it elsewhere on the disk or on a different disk.

The next example involves the MUSICIAN table, and for this example we want to assume that the Musician Name attribute is unique. This means that now both Musician Number and Musician Name are candidate keys of the table and Musician Number has been chosen to be the primary key. It seems that there is an important application that requires the fast and frequent retrieval of musician names together with their college-degree data, but without their musician numbers. As currently structured, this would clearly require repeated joins of the MUSICIAN and DEGREE tables, which might cause unacceptable performance problems. Since the Musician *Name* attribute is unique and is a candidate key of the MUSICIAN table, a solution to this problem is to replace the Musician Number foreign-key attribute in the DEGREE table with Musician Name:

Musician *Name*	Degree	University	Year

With Musician Name already in the DEGREE table, the retrieval situation described does not require a join. Plus, the DEGREE table can still tie degrees uniquely to musicians, since Musician Name is unique.

Another possible solution to the more general problem of retrieving both detailed data about musicians *and* their degrees at the same time involves the concept of repeating groups. We know that there is a one-to-many relationship between musicians and degrees since a musician can have several degrees but a degree is associated with only one musician. Suppose we assume that a musician can have at most three degrees. We can then eliminate the DEGREE table entirely by merging its data into the MUSICIAN table:

Musician Number	Musician Name	Instrument	Annual Salary	Orchestra Name	Degree #1	University #1	Year #1	Degree #2	University #2	Year #2	Degree #3	University #3	Year #3

This is possible because of the small fixed maximum number of degrees and because of the ability to distinguish among them, in this case in a time sequence based on when they were awarded or by level, say bachelor's degree first, master's degree second. Clearly, in this case, there will be null attribute values since not every musician has three degrees. Further, there may be more programmer involvement since inserting new degree data or even retrieving degree data may require more informed and careful operations. But it certainly eliminates the join between the MUSICIAN table and the now defunct DEGREE table, and may be the modification necessary for acceptable performance.

Example: Lucky Rent-A-Car

Consider the Lucky Rent-A-Car database of Figure 5.18. One issue with this company is the privacy of their customers' data. Some of their employees may need to access the entire CUSTOMER table, while others may need, for example, customer number and customer name data but not the more personal data, such as customer address and customer telephone. A restriction can be set up to accomplish this using views. One view can be created that includes the entire table; another can be created that includes only the Customer Number and Customer Name attributes. Using these two views in the SQL GRANT command (discussed in Chapter 11), different employees or groups of employees can be given full access to the CUSTOMER table or restricted access to only part of it.

The RENTAL table represents the many-to-many relationship among cars and customers, recording who rented which car on a particular date. The primary key is thus Car Serial Number, Customer Number, and Rental Date. Recall that Rental Date must be part of the primary key because a particular customer could have rented a particular car on more than one occasion. This three-attribute primary key is clumsy. An index built on it would be long and clumsy too, and if it had to be used as a foreign key in another table, that would be clumsy, too. A solution is to add a new Rental Number attribute that will serve as a unique key of the table:

Rental Number	Car Serial Number	Customer Number	Rental Date	Return Date	Total Cost

Next, assume that the following table, which has data about the president of each manufacturer, has been added to the database:

Manufacturer Name	President Name	President Address	President Telephone	President email

Since each company has exactly one president, there is a one-to-one relationship between manufacturers, represented by the existing MANUFACTURER table, and presidents, represented by the new PRESIDENT table. As is usually the case in such situations, it makes sense to represent the two different entities in two different tables. However, if we ever need to retrieve both detailed manufacturer data and detailed president data, we will have to execute a join. If we have to do this frequently and with significant speed, it may make sense to combine the two tables together:

Manufacturer Name	Manufacturer Country	Sales Rep Name	Sales Rep Telephone	President Name	President Address	President Telephone	President email

After all, since a company has only one president, it also has only one president name, one president address, and so forth. This arrangement makes for a bulkier table that will be spread out over a larger disk area than either table alone, possibly slowing down certain retrievals. But it will avoid the join needed to retrieve manufacturer and president detailed data together.

Finally, here are examples of the physical design technique of adding new tables. Lucky Rent-A-Car's CAR table is accessed very frequently—so frequently, in fact, that it has become a performance bottleneck. The company has decided to duplicate the table and put each of the two copies on different disk devices so that some applications can access one disk and other applications the other disk. This will improve throughput. However, these two duplicate tables must be kept identical at all times and any changes made to them must be made to both copies simultaneously. Notice that while the CAR table may have to be read frequently for Lucky's rental operations, it has to be updated only when new cars are added to Lucky's inventory or existing cars are taken out of inventory. This makes the duplicate-table technique practical, since frequent changes that require the updating of both tables simultaneously would slow down the entire environment significantly.

In the CUSTOMER table, some large corporate customers' records are accessed much more frequently than the rest of the customer records. To help ease this performance bottleneck and to gather these customer records together in one disk area to further enhance performance, a subset table of *copies* of just these records can be created and stored elsewhere on the disk or on a different disk. Again, the issue of simultaneous updates of the duplicate data must be considered. Note the difference between creating a subset table and creating a horizontal partition. In the case of subset tables, a copy of the records is left behind in the original table; in the case of horizontal partitioning, no copy is left behind.

Summary

Data is all around us but we normally don't think about it unless we have to use it to keep track of objects that are important to us. The objects and events we come into contact with and their attributes can be noted in structures as simple as lists, which, by extension, we can think of as files and their records.

Moving on to storing data in computers, four basic operations have to be performed: retrieving stored data, inserting new data, deleting stored data, and updating stored data. Applications requiring these operations, in particular the operation of retrieving stored data, may require data to be accessed sequentially while other applications— most of the applications we deal with today—may require data to be accessed on a direct basis.

Disk devices are the predominant secondary memory devices in use today. They are capable of providing both sequential and direct access to data. Rotating disk devices consist of one or more platters on which data can be stored magnetically, mounted on a central spindle. The data is stored on each platter surface in a pattern of concentric circles called tracks. Tracks located one above another on successive surfaces comprise a cylinder. These rotating disk devices are gradually being replaced by solid state disks (SSDs).

The arrangement of data on disks is based on a file organization that in turn allows data to be retrieved using an access method. Two such methods for direct access are indexes and hashing. A simple linear index consists of two columns: an ordered list of the identifiers of the records being indexed, each of which is associated in the second column with its physical location on the disk. A more practical arrangement and the one in common use in today's computers is the B+-tree, in which the index is constructed in a hierarchical arrangement. Hashing is a way of arranging the records on the disk based on a mathematical calculation on each record's identifier; retrieval is accomplished using the same mathematical calculation.

Physical database design is the modification of the database structure to improve performance. A variety of factors involving the database structure or its use can adversely affect system performance. In addition to the logical design results, inputs to the physical design process include response time requirements, throughput requirements, and a variety of other data and application characteristics and operational requirements.

Physical database design techniques fall into two categories: techniques that do not change the logical design and techniques that do change the logical design. The former include adding external features such as indexes, reorganizing stored data on the disk, and splitting a table into multiple tables. The latter include adding attributes to a table or changing attributes in a table, combining tables, and adding new tables.

Key Terms

Access method	Disk	Overflow records	Subset tables
B+-tree index	Division-remainder	Performance	Text attribute
Clustering files	method	Physical database design	Throughput
Collision	File organization	Platter	Track
Cylinder	Fixed disk drive	Repeating groups	Transfer time
Data volatility	Hashing method	Response time	Vertical partitioning
Data volume	Head switching	Rotational delay	View
Database performance	Horizontal partitioning	Search attribute	
Denormalization	Index	Seek time	
Derived data	Logical view	Solid state disks (SSD)	

Questions

1. Describe the following disk concepts or components.
   a. Platter and recording surface.
   b. Track.
   c. Cylinder.
   d. Read/write head.
   e. Access-arm mechanism.

2. Why is it important to store files on a cylinder-by-cylinder basis?

3. Describe the four steps in the transfer of data from disk to primary memory.

4. What is a file organization? What is an access method? What do they accomplish?

5. What is an index? Compare the concept of the index in a book to an index in an information system.

6. Describe the idea of the simple linear index. What are its shortcomings?

7. What is an indexed-sequential file?

8. Describe the idea of the B+-tree index. What are its advantages over the simple linear index?

9. Describe how a direct search works using a B+-tree index.

10. Describe what happens to the index tree when you insert new records into a file with a B+-tree index.

11. Answer the following general questions about indexes:
    a. Can an index be built over a non-unique field?
    b. Can an index be built over a field if the file is not stored in sequence by that field?
    c. Can an index be built over a combination of fields as well as over a single field?
    d. Is there a limit to the number of indexes that can be built for a file?
    e. How is an index affected when a change is made to a file? Does every change to a file affect every one of its indexes?
    f. Can an index be used to achieve sequential access? Explain.

12. Describe the idea of the hashed file. What are its advantages and disadvantages in comparison to indexes?

13. Describe how a direct search works in a hashed file using the division-remainder method of hashing.

14. What is a collision in a hashed file? Why do collisions occur? Why are they of concern in the application environment?

15. What is physical database design?

16. Describe why physical database design is necessary.

17. Explain why the need to perform joins is an important factor affecting application and database performance.

18. Why does the degree to which data is dispersed over a disk affect application and database performance?

19. Explain why the volume of data access operations can adversely affect application and database performance.

20. Which "input" is the starting point for physical database design?

21. Describe how response time requirements and throughput requirements determine the overall performance level of the application and database environment.

22. Describe the characteristics of the data in the database that must be considered as inputs to the physical database design process. Why are they important?

23. Describe the characteristics of the applications that must be considered as inputs to the physical database design process. Why are they important?

24. Why do DBMS and hardware characteristics have to be taken into account in the physical design process?

25. Explain the statement, "Some physical database design techniques change the logical design and some do not."

26. What attributes should be considered as candidates for having indexes built on them? What is the potential problem with building too many indexes?

27. What is a "view"? Which factors affecting application and database performance can be dealt with by using views? Explain.

28. Describe the "**clustering files**" technique. What advantage is gained by using it? What is its disadvantage?

29. What is the difference between horizontal and vertical partitioning? What is their common advantage? Are their disadvantages the same or different? Explain.

30. Describe the physical design technique of substituting foreign keys. Under what circumstances would you use it?

31. Under what circumstances would you want to create a new single-attribute primary key in a table? What would it accomplish?

32. Under what circumstances would you want to store derived data in a table? What would it accomplish?

33. Combining tables that are in a one-to-one relationship, combining tables involving well controlled repeating groups, and denormalization all lead to the same performance advantage. What is it? Why is it important?

34. What is denormalization? Denormalization, while improving performance under certain circumstances, also leads to a serious problem. How does denormalization improve performance and what is this major drawback?

35. Duplicating entire tables or parts of tables ("subset tables") obviously introduces data redundancy. What is the advantage of doing this? Do you think it's worth the introduction of redundancy? Explain.

Exercises

1. A fixed disk consists of six platters. The upper surface of the topmost platter and the lower surface of the bottommost platter are not used for recording data. There are 120 tracks on each recording surface. How many of each of the following are there in the disk:

  a. Recording surfaces?

  b. Cylinders?

  c. Tracks per cylinder?

2. A fixed disk has 80 cylinders. The tracks in each cylinder are numbered 0–11. The upper surface of the topmost platter and the lower surface of the bottommost platter are not used for recording data. How many of each of the following are there in the disk:

  a. Recording surfaces?

  b. Platters?

  c. Tracks per recording surface?

3. Consider the B+-tree index, below:

  a. A record has just been added to Cylinder 6, causing a cylinder split. The highest key value on Cylinder 6 is now 2156, the highest key value on Cylinder 20, and the empty reserve cylinder that received half of Cylinder 6's records is now 2348. Update the tree index accordingly.

  b. A record has just been added to Cylinder 10, causing a cylinder split. The highest key value on Cylinder 10 is now 3780, the highest key value on Cylinder 25, and the empty reserve cylinder that received half of Cylinder 10's records is now 3900. Update the tree index accordingly. (Note: This question is intended to be independent of the question in part a. Start each of parts a and b from the figure shown.)

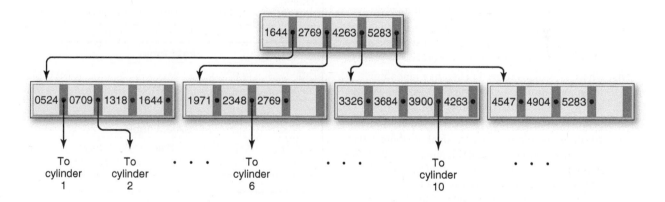

4. A hashed file has space for 70 records. Relative record numbers of 0–69 label each of the 70 record positions. In addition, there is space for several overflow (synonym) records. Draw a picture of the file and, using the division-remainder method, store records with each of the following four digit keys, taking collisions into account as necessary:

  a. 4000.

  b. 5207.

  c. 0360.

  d. 1410.

5. Consider the following relational database that Best Airlines uses to keep track of its mechanics, their skills, and their airport locations. Mechanic number, airport name, and skill number are all unique fields. Size is an airport's size in acres. Skill Category is the type of skill, such as an engine skill, wing skill, and tire skill. Year Qualified is the year that a mechanic first qualified in a particular skill; Proficiency Rating is the mechanic's proficiency rating in a particular skill.

MECHANIC Table

Mechanic Number	Mechanic Name	Telephone	Salary	Airport Name

AIRPORT Table

Airport Name	City	State	Size	Year Opened

SKILL Table

Skill Number	Skill Name	Skill Category

QUALIFICATION Table

Mechanic Number	Skill Number	Year Qualified	Proficiency Rating

Analyze each of the following situations and, using the physical database design techniques discussed in this chapter, state how you would modify the logical design shown to improve performance or otherwise accommodate it.

a. There is a high-priority need to quickly find any particular airport's data given only the airport's city and state.

b. There is a frequent need to find the total salary of all of the mechanics at any particular airport.

c. There is a high-priority need to quickly find any particular mechanic's data together with the data about the airport at which she works.

d. There is a frequent need to list the names and telephone numbers of the mechanics who work at any particular airport, together with the airport's city and state.

e. Assume that there is an additional attribute called Skill Description in the SKILL table. This attribute is used to store lengthy descriptions of each skill. The problem is that its presence in the SKILL table is slowing down access to the rest of the data in the table, which is accessed much more frequently.

f. The need to access data about the ten largest airports in the country is much more frequent than the need to access data about the rest of the airports.

6. Consider the following relational database for the Quality Appliance Manufacturing Co. The database is designed to track the major appliances (refrigerators, washing machines, dishwashers, etc.) that Quality manufactures. It also records information about Quality's suppliers, the parts they supply, the buyers of the finished appliances, and the finished goods inspectors. Note the following facts about this environment:

- Suppliers are the companies that supply Quality with its major components, such as electric motors, for the appliances. Supplier number is a unique identifier.

- Parts are the major components that the suppliers supply to Quality. Each part comes with a part number but that part number is unique only within a supplier. Thus, from Quality's point of view, the unique identifier of a part is the combination of part number and supplier number.

- Each appliance that Quality manufactures is given an appliance number that is unique across all of the types of appliances that Quality makes.

- Buyers are major department stores, home improvement chains, and wholesalers. Buyer numbers are unique.

- An appliance may be inspected by several inspectors. There is clearly a many-to-many relationship between appliances and inspectors.

- There are one-to-many relationships between suppliers and parts (Supplier Number is a foreign key in the PART table), parts and appliances (Appliance Number is a foreign key in the PART table), and appliances and buyers (Buyer Number is a foreign key in the APPLIANCE table).

SUPPLIER Table

Supplier Number	Supplier Name	City	Country	Telephone

PART Table

Part Number	Supplier Number	Part Type	Cost	Appliance Number

APPLIANCE Table

Appliance Number	Appliance Type	Date of Manufacture	Buyer Number	Price

BUYER Table

Buyer Number	Buyer Name	City	Country	Credit Rating

INSPECTOR Table

Inspector Number	Inspector Name	Salary	Date of Hire

INSPECTION Table

Appliance Number	Inspector Number	Date of Inspection	Score

Analyze each of the following situations and, using the physical database design techniques discussed in this chapter, state how you would modify the logical design shown to improve performance or otherwise accommodate it.

a. The Appliance Type attribute in the APPLIANCE table indicates whether an appliance is a refrigerator, washing machine, etc. Refrigerator records are accessed much more frequently than those for the other appliance types and there are strict response time requirements for accessing them.

b. There is a frequent and very high-priority need to quickly retrieve detailed data about an appliance together with detailed data about who bought it.

c. Because of the large number of people trying to access the PART table and the fast response time needed, the PART table has become a bottleneck and the required response time is not being achieved.

d. Assume that the Buyer Name attribute in the BUYER table is unique. There is a high-priority need to quickly retrieve the following data about appliances: appliance number, appliance type, date of manufacture, and buyer *name*.

e. In the APPLIANCE table, there is a much more frequent need with strict response time requirements to access the price data (of course together with the appliance number) than to access the rest of the data in the table.

Minicases

1. Happy Cruise Lines.

Consider the Happy Cruise Lines Sailor file shown below. It lists all the sailors on the company's cruise ships by their unique sailor identification number, their name, the unique identification number of the ship they currently work on, their home country, and their job title.

Sailor file				
Sailor Number	Sailor Name	Ship Number	Home Country	Job Title
00536	John Smith	009	USA	Purser
00732	Ling Chang	012	China	Engineer
06988	Maria Gonzalez	020	Mexico	Purser
16490	Prashant Kumar	005	India	Navigator
18535	Alan Jones	009	UK	Cruise Director
20254	Jane Adams	012	USA	Captain
23981	Rene Lopez	020	Philippines	Captain
27467	Fred Jones	020	UK	Waiter
27941	Alain DuMont	009	France	Captain
28184	Susan Moore	009	Canada	Wine Steward
31775	James Collins	012	USA	Waiter
32856	Sarah McLachlan	012	Ireland	Cabin Steward

a. Create a simple linear index for the Sailor file based on:

   i. The Sailor Name field.

   ii. The Sailor Number field.

   iii. The Ship Number field.

   iv. The combination of the Ship Number and the Job Title fields.

b. Construct a B+-tree index of the type shown in this chapter for the Sailor file, *assuming now that there are many more records than are shown above.* The file and the index have the following characteristics:

The file is stored on nine cylinders of the disk. The highest key values on the nine cylinders, in order, are:

Cylinder 1: 02653
Cylinder 2: 07784
Cylinder 3: 13957
Cylinder 4: 18002
Cylinder 5: 22529
Cylinder 6: 27486
Cylinder 7: 35800
Cylinder 8: 41633
Cylinder 9: 48374

Each index record can hold four key value/pointer pairs.

There are three index records at the lowest level of the tree index.

c. The same as part b above, but now there are four index records at the lowest level of the tree index.

d. The same as part b above, but each index record can hold two key value/pointer pairs and there are five index records at the lowest level of the tree index.

2. The Super Baseball League.

Consider the Super Baseball League Player file shown below. It lists all of the players in the league by their unique player identification number, their name, age, the year they joined the league, and the team on which they are currently playing.

Player file				
Player Number	Player Name	Age	First Year	Team Number
1538	Fred Williams	23	2003	12
1882	Tom Parker	29	2000	35
2071	Juan Gomez	33	1990	12
2364	Steve Smith	24	2002	20
2757	Tim Jones	37	1988	18
3186	Dave Lester	29	1998	18
3200	Rod Smith	25	2002	20
3834	Chico Lopez	24	2003	12
4950	Chris Vernon	26	2003	15
5296	Barry Morton	30	1995	35

a. Create a simple linear index for the Player file based on:

    i. The Team Number field.

    ii. The Player Name field.

    iii. The Player Number field.

    iv. The combination of the Team Number and the Player Number fields.

b. Construct a B+-tree index of the type shown in this chapter for the Player file, *assuming that there are now many more records than are shown above*. The file and the index have the following characteristics:

The file is stored on eight cylinders of the disk. The highest key values on the eight cylinders, in order, are:

Cylinder 1: 1427
Cylinder 2: 1965
Cylinder 3: 2848
Cylinder 4: 3721
Cylinder 5: 4508
Cylinder 6: 5396
Cylinder 7: 6530
Cylinder 8: 7442

Each index record can hold four key value/pointer pairs.

There are three index records at the lowest level of the tree index.

c. The same as part b above, but now there are four index records at the lowest level of the tree index.

d. The same as part b above, but each index record can hold two key value/pointer pairs and there are four index records at the lowest level of the tree index.

3. Consider the following relational database for Happy Cruise Lines. It keeps track of ships, cruises, ports, and passengers. A "cruise" is a particular sailing of a ship on a particular date. For example, the seven-day journey of the ship Pride of Tampa that leaves on June 13, 2003, is a cruise. Note the following facts about this environment:

- Both ship number and ship name are unique in the SHIP Table.

- A ship goes on many cruises over time. A cruise is associated with a single ship.

- A port is identified by the combination of port name and country.

- As indicated by the VISIT Table, a cruise includes visits to several ports and a port is typically included in several cruises.

- Both Passenger Number and Social Security Number are unique in the PASSENGER Table. A particular person has a single Passenger Number that is used for all of the cruises that she takes.

- The VOYAGE Table indicates that a person can take many cruises and a cruise, of course, has many passengers.

SHIP Table				
Ship Number	Ship Name	Ship Builder	Launch Date	Gross Weight

CRUISE Table				
Cruise Number	Start Date	End Date	Cruise Director	Ship Number

PORT Table

Port Name	Country	Number of Docks	Port Manager

VISIT Table

Cruise Number	Port Name	Country	Arrival Date	Departure Date

PASSENGER Table

Passenger Number	Passenger Name	Social Security Number	Home Address	Telephone Number

VOYAGE Table

Passenger Number	Cruise Number	Stateroom Number	Fare

Analyze each of the following situations and, using the physical database design techniques discussed in this chapter, state how you would modify the logical design shown to improve performance or otherwise accommodate it.

a. There is a need to list cruises by cruise number but there is also a periodic need to list all of the cruises in order by start date.

b. There is a frequent need to quickly retrieve the data about a cruise together with the data about the ship used on the cruise.

c. There is a frequent need to quickly retrieve cruise data based on departure date.

d. Data about passengers from California must be accessed quickly and much more frequently than data about passengers from anywhere else.

e. There is a frequent need to quickly retrieve a list of the port managers of the ports at which the ship on any particular cruise will stop.

f. There is a frequent need to quickly find the total number of passengers who were on any particular cruise.

g. There is a frequent need to find the start and end dates of cruises as quickly as possible.

h. There is a frequent need to find cruise data based on ship *name*. Hint: The Ship Name attribute is unique.

4. Consider the following relational database for the Super Baseball League. It keeps track of teams in the league, coaches and players on the teams, work experience of the coaches, bats belonging to each team, and which players have played on which teams. Note the following facts about this environment:

- The database keeps track of the history of all the teams that each player has played on and all the players who have played on each team.
- The database keeps track of only the current team that a coach works for.
- Team number, team name, and player number are each unique attributes across the league.
- Coach name is unique only within a team (and we assume that a team cannot have two coaches of the same name).
- Serial number (for bats) is unique only within a team.
- In the Affiliation table, the years attribute indicates the number of years that a player played on a team; the batting average is for the years that a player played on a team.

TEAM Table

Team Number	Team Name	City	Manager

COACH Table

Team Number	Coach Name	Coach Telephone

WORK EXPERIENCE Table

Team Number	Coach Name	Experience Type	Years of Experience

BATS Table

Team Number	Serial Number	Manufacturer

PLAYER Table

Player Number	Player Name	Age

AFFILIATION Table

Player Number	Team Number	Years	Batting Average

Analyze each of the following situations and, using the physical database design techniques discussed in this chapter, state how you would modify the logical design shown to improve performance or otherwise accommodate it.

a. There is a frequent need to quickly find the total number of years that any particular player has played in the league (i.e. the total number of years played for all of the teams a player played for).

b. There is a need to retrieve AFFILIATION table records directly based on batting averages.

c. The three-attribute primary key of the WORK EXPERIENCE table has been found to be cumbersome to use in queries and awkward to index.

d. There is a frequent very high-priority need to quickly retrieve player name and age data together with the teams (identified by team number) they have played on, the number of years they played on the teams, and the batting averages they compiled.

e. Assume that we add the following Stadium table to the Super Baseball League relational database. Each team has one home stadium, which is what is represented in this table. Assume that a stadium can serve as the home stadium for only one team. Stadium name is unique across the league.

STADIUM Table			
Stadium Name	Year Built	Size	Team Number

There is a frequent high-priority need to quickly retrieve detailed team and stadium data together.

Object-Oriented Database Management

Traditional information systems and the applications within them have always maintained a clear separation between their programs and their data. Programs and data structures are designed separately, implemented separately, and stored separately on disk. Relational databases fit very well into this arrangement. For a long time the emphasis was on the programs, with the data structures and ultimately the data stored in them being a secondary consideration. From a managerial point of view, the concept of data as a corporate resource has made significant inroads into changing the IS environment from this program-centric mentality into a more datacentric one.

On the technical side, an alternative approach to information systems and IS development, which comes under the broad heading of "object orientation," began during the 1980s. This approach is, by its nature, more datacentric. It began with object-oriented programming, then object-oriented systems analysis and object-oriented systems design, and finally object-oriented database management, complete with object-oriented database management systems (OODBMS). A variety of OODBMSs have been developed and marketed commercially. We will take a brief look at the essential points of object-oriented database management in this chapter, but, as we do, it is important to bear in mind that the commercial OODBMSs vary widely in the OODBMS features that they support either partially or fully.

OBJECTIVES

List several limitations in the relational database model.

Describe the object-oriented database concept.

Model data using such complex relationships as generalization and aggregation, and such concepts as inheritance and polymorphism.

Describe the benefits of encapsulation.

Describe the value of developing abstract data types.

Explain what an object/relational database is.

Introduction

Relational tables certainly seem to do a good job of storing data for information systems, as we've seen in concept and in a variety of examples. So, what's missing? The answer to this question is a bit complicated. Many people would say that nothing is missing from the relational model (or, for that matter, in this context, from the hierarchical and network models that came before it)! Others would point out that for certain kinds of complex applications, the relational model lacks support for the more complex data model features they need. There is even an argument that all applications could benefit from certain additional features in terms of data integrity.

Let's take a look at "what's missing" from the relational model. The answer to this question will also serve as an introduction to the main features of the object-oriented database model.

- While the relational model is fine for dealing with unary, binary, and ternary relationships among entities, it does not directly provide support for more complex but important relationships among different subcategories or specialized categories of particular entities. This is known as "generalization" or **"generalization/specialization"** in the object-oriented database model. Nor does the relational model directly provide support for situations in which particular entities are constructed from other component entities. This is known as **"aggregation"** in the object-oriented database model.

- As in all traditional information systems, the separation of programs and databases exposes the data in the databases to being updated by a variety of programs. Of course, we assume that these programs are thoroughly tested and debugged. But with many people writing programs that can affect particular data, there is always the question whether a hidden mistake can pop up unexpectedly and cause errors in the data. This becomes even more serious as the sharing of data among different applications increases. What might be desirable is to have a system in which only a limited, controlled set of program segments is allowed to update particular data. Application programs would then make requests for the execution of these program segments to update the data. This could go a long way toward improving the integrity of the data.

- The relational model supports only a limited number of relatively simplistic numeric and character-oriented data types. These are sufficient for most standard accounting, inventory, and other traditional business applications. But this model does not directly support the more complex data types that we increasingly encounter such as graphic images, photo images, video clips, audio clips, long text documents, and such mathematical constructs as matrices. The object-oriented database model, with its "abstract data type" feature, allows the creation of all these data types and any others that are needed.

There are several other features or advantages of the object-oriented database concept. One is that each unit of data or "object" has an object identifier that is permanent and unique among all objects of all types in the system. Another is that some OODBMSs are implemented as pointer-based systems, meaning that related objects are "connected" by their storage addresses, as opposed to the foreign key/join arrangement in relational databases. Arguments have been made that this pointer-based approach provides better performance than the multi-table join approach of relational databases when related data must be brought together. (Ironically, relational databases replaced the pointer-based approach of the earlier hierarchical and network DBMSs.) Finally, it is argued that OODBMSs are the most natural data storage vehicles when using object-oriented programming languages, such as C++, Smalltalk, and Java.

Terminology

Earlier, we defined an entity as an object or event in our environment that we want to keep track of. An entity set was defined as a collection of entities of the same type. Entities have properties that we called attributes. We then defined a data structure known as a record that contains all of the facts (the attributes) that we know about a given entity. The records about all of the entities in an entity set were collected together in a file. Finally, we spoke of a record type as a general description of all of the records in a file, essentially a list of the kinds of attributes that describe each of the entities. And we spoke of a record occurrence as a specific set of attribute values that describe one of the entities.

Object-oriented data modeling has its own features and its own terminology, but it still must describe the entities, the objects, and events in the real business environment. Having said that, the first point to recognize is that in object-oriented modeling, the term **object** is used to describe an advanced data structure that includes an entity's attributes *plus* **methods** or **operations** or **procedures** (program code!) that can operate on and modify the object's attribute values. This is obviously a major departure from the strict separation of data and program code that we're used to. In the same spirit in which we organized the records that described similar entities into a file, the objects that describe similar entities are known collectively as an **object class** or, simply, a **class**. Conversely, an instance or an occurrence of a class is an object.

This terminology is in keeping with the standard diagramming notation for object-oriented systems development known as the **Unified Modeling Language (UML)**. Introduced in 1997 by the Object Management Group (OMG), UML has nine standard diagrams that describe such features as the system's data, its business processes, its intended results, the components of its program code, and its hardware and software architectures. For our purposes, we will focus on the UML **Class Diagram**, which describes the system's data, including attributes of and relationships among the "objects." As before, we will demonstrate these OODBMS concepts in the context of the General Hardware Co. example, as well as the other three running examples we have used. Some of the details of the examples will have to be changed in order to demonstrate the object-oriented concepts and we will point out those changes carefully as they occur.

Complex Relationships

In our earlier discussion of data modeling using the entity-relationship model that led to relational database design, we saw the importance of being able to model unary, binary, and ternary one-to-one, one-to-many, and many-to-many relationships. The first question, then, is: can we model such relationships in UML class diagrams and can they be implemented in the OODBMS concept? The answer is definitely yes. It had better be yes because, as we know by now, those are fundamental relationships in any business environment. The point, however, is that UML class diagrams and ultimately OODBMS implementations go beyond those fundamental relationships to other more specifically targeted kinds of relationships known as generalization and aggregation.

Generalization

Generalization, also known as "generalization/specialization," is a relationship that recognizes that some kinds of entities can be subdivided into smaller, more specialized groups. All of the entities may have some common characteristics but each of the smaller groups may have certain unique characteristics, as well. For example, all movies have a producer and a director, but only animated movies have animation artists. All boats have hulls, owners, and registration numbers, but only sailboats have sails. All retail stores have names, addresses, and occupancy licenses, but only restaurants have health inspection scores and restaurant critic ratings; only gas stations have underground storage tanks; only supermarkets have produce departments and meat departments.

The General Hardware Co. entity-relationship diagram of Figure 2.9 is reproduced here as Figure 9.1. Remember that General Hardware is a wholesaler that supplies retail stores such as hardware stores, home improvement chains, etc. Thus far, the only products that we've assumed General Hardware sells its customers are tools. But now, General Hardware has decided to expand its product line beyond tools to include light fixtures and lumber. Figure 9.2 shows a generalization diagram that represents General Hardware's expanded product line and recognizes that while all of the products share some common attributes, different kinds of products have additional unique attributes. Each box in Figure 9.2 represents a class and has three sections separated by horizontal lines. At the top, in capital letters, is the class name. In the middle are the class attributes. At the bottom are the class operations (although we're not showing any operations yet). The upward-pointing arrows indicate generalizations. The diagram shows that there are three *kinds* of products: TOOLs, LIGHT FIXTUREs, and LUMBER. Furthermore, there are two kinds of tools: POWER TOOLs and NON-POWER TOOLs.

Inheritance of Attributes

The PRODUCT class indicates that all products have three common attributes: Product Number, Product Name, and Unit Price. In fact, we say that all of the classes *below* PRODUCT inherit the attributes shown in PRODUCT; that is, they include these

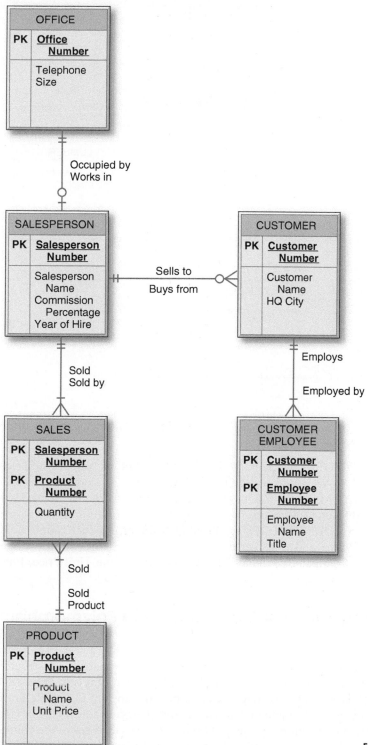

FIGURE 9.1 The General Hardware Company E-R diagram

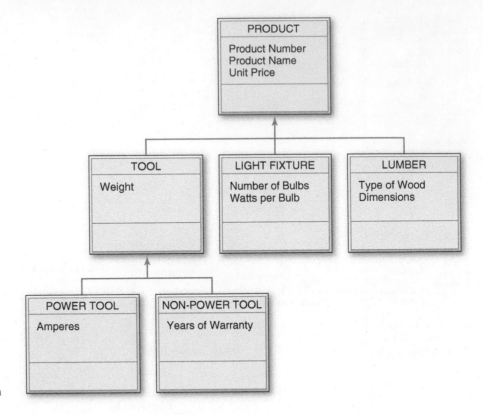

FIGURE 9.2 General Hardware Company product generalization diagram

attributes among their own. In general, attributes are inherited downwards in these generalization diagrams. So,

- the attributes for POWER TOOLs are Product Number, Product Name, Unit Price (all from PRODUCT), Weight (from TOOL), and Amperes.
- the attributes for NON-POWER TOOLs are Product Number, Product Name, Unit Price, Weight, and Years of Warranty.
- the attributes for LIGHT FIXTUREs are Product Number, Product Name, Unit Price, Number of Bulbs, and Watts Per Bulb.
- the attributes for LUMBER are Product Number, Product Name, Unit Price, Type of Wood, and Dimensions.

Operations, Inheritance of Operations, and Polymorphism

Figure 9.3 shows the addition of some operations to the diagram in Figure 9.2. Actually, there are three kinds of operations: constructor, query, and update. A constructor operation creates a new instance of a class, i.e. a new object. An example in Figure 9.3 is Add Lumber, which is an operation that will add a new instance of LUMBER, i.e. a new object, to the database when General Hardware starts carrying a new type or size of lumber in its wholesale inventory. A query operation returns data about the values of an object's attributes but does not update them. Calculate Discount in the PRODUCT class is an example of a query operation. The operation calculates a discount for a particular customer buying a particular product and returns the result to the user who issued the query, but does not store the result in the database. An update operation

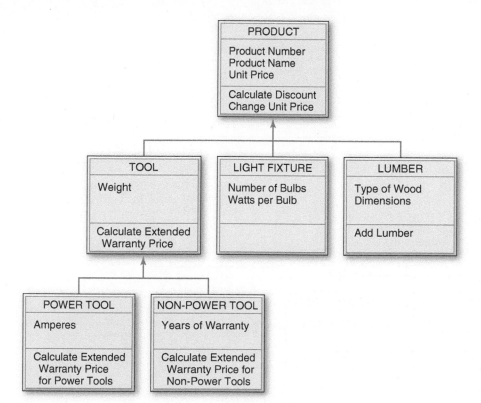

FIGURE 9.3 General Hardware Company product generalization diagram with operations

updates an object's attribute values. Change Unit Price in the PRODUCT class is an example of an update operation. From time to time a product's unit price has to be changed and the result stored in the database as the new unit price.

Notice that Calculate Discount is an operation that applies to all products because operations are inherited downwards in the same way that attributes are. In fact, since there is nothing more said about the discount further down the hierarchy, we conclude that the discount is calculated *in the same way* for all kinds of products. On the other hand, the diagram indicates that the Calculate Extended Warranty Price for TOOLs is performed differently for POWER TOOLs and for NON-POWER TOOLs. The operation is initially specified in the TOOLs box but operation names in the POWER TOOL and NON-POWER TOOL boxes indicate that it changes in some way when it is inherited down to those boxes. Perhaps, the presence of an electric motor in the power tools requires a different kind of calculation. This modification or refinement of operations as they are inherited downwards is called **polymorphism**. (Note: Technically, the operations that are performed differently in the lower-level objects can have the same name—simply Calculate Extended Warranty Price in this example—even though they will perform differently for the different kinds of objects.)

Aggregation

Figure 9.4 shows the addition of the FRAME and BULBS classes, connected to the LIGHT FIXTURE class with a diamond-shaped symbol. This is not further generalization but is another type of relationship known as aggregation. In generalization, lower-level classes are kinds of upper-level classes (e.g. POWER TOOLs and NON-POWER

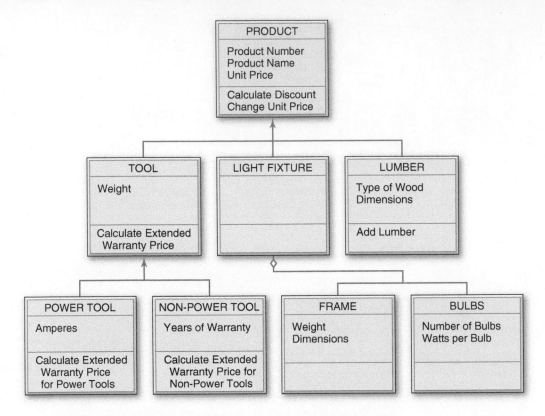

FIGURE 9.4 General Hardware Company product diagram with aggregation

TOOLs are both *kinds of* TOOLs). In aggregation, a class is shown to be composed of other classes. FRAMEs and BULBS are not kinds of LIGHT FIXTUREs; rather, each is *a part of* a LIGHT FIXTURE. As shown in Figure 9.4, the component classes can each have their own special attributes and conceivably, operations, too.

The General Hardware Co. Class Diagram

Figure 9.5 shows the complete General Hardware Co. UML Class Diagram. The upper portion of the diagram is largely the same as the entity-relationship diagram of Figure 9.1. In converting the entity boxes to class boxes, we added some operations and changed some of the notation. In terms of one-to-one, one-to-many, and many-to-many relationships, in this notation "1" means exactly one, "0..1" means zero or one, "0..*" means zero-to-many, and "1..*" means one-to-many. Also note that the many-to-many relationship between SALESPERSON and PRODUCT requires an additional class (similar in concept to an associative entity) to show the nature of the many-to-many relationship, including any intersection data. This SALE class is attached to the connective line between the SALESPERSON and PRODUCT classes with a dashed line.

It is important to stop here for a moment and ask whether an ordinary relational database together with application programming could be used to implement all the various kinds of relationships in Figure 9.5. The answer is yes, it could. But the point is that it would be up to the database designer and especially the application programmer *to manage* the various kinds of relationships in the database with the application code.

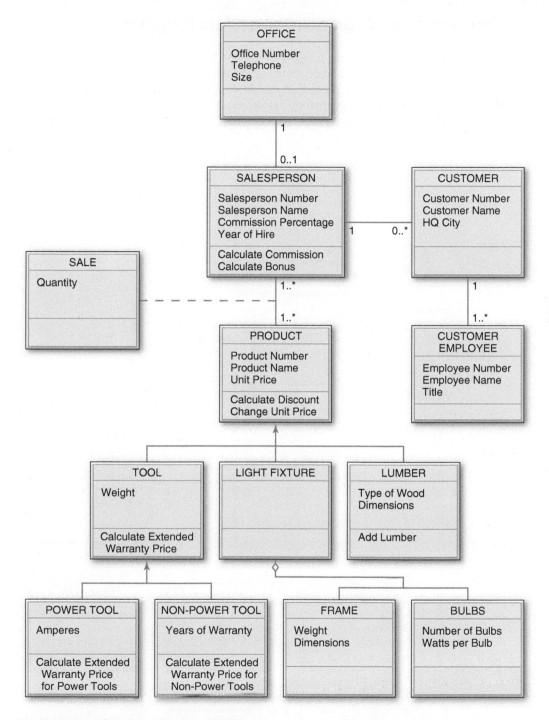

FIGURE 9.5 General Hardware Company class diagram

This is different from an OODBMS, which is designed to handle all of these relationships among its natural features. To stretch a term a bit, in the OODBMS concept, the database management system "understands" all these kinds of relationships and is capable of directly managing the data involved in them.

The Good Reading Bookstores Class Diagram

Good Reading Bookstores has decided to expand its product line to include periodicals (newspapers and magazines), music CDs, and movie videos/DVDs. The upper portion of Figure 9.6 is the class-diagram version of the entity-relationship diagram of Figure 2.10, except that several changes have been made to reflect the change in product line. The BOOK entity type has become the PRODUCT class since there can

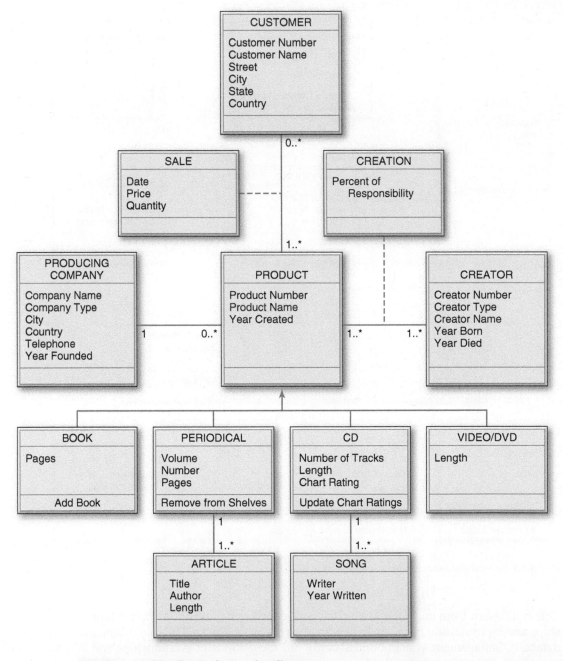

FIGURE 9.6 Good Reading Bookstores class diagram

now be several kinds of products, not just books. Similarly, PUBLISHER has become PRODUCING COMPANY to reflect that we are now dealing with publishers, music studios, and movie studios, and AUTHOR has become CREATOR to reflect that we are now dealing with authors, singers, and movie producers and directors.

A generalization hierarchy has been created under PRODUCT indicating that there are four kinds of products: BOOK, PERIODICAL, CD, and VIDEO/DVD. The three attributes in the PRODUCT class, Product Number, Product Name, and Year Created, are inherited downwards to all four of the subordinate classes. *In addition*, a book has a number of pages, a periodical has a volume, a number, and a number of pages, a CD has a number of tracks, a total length in minutes, and a chart rating (the current popularity of the CD), and a video/DVD has a length in minutes. The BOOK class has a constructor-type operation, Add Book, that adds new BOOK instances, i.e. BOOK objects, as new books are published and added to the store's inventory. PERIODICAL has a query-type operation associated with it that calculates the date when each periodical is to be removed from the store shelves if it has not been purchased by then. CD has an update-type operation associated with it that changes the value of a CD's Chart Rating attribute on a weekly basis as new industry-wide popularity charts come out.

Notice that the PERIODICAL class, and only this class, is associated with the ARTICLE class. Similarly, the CD class, and only this class, is associated with the SONG class. These are reasonable restrictions since only periodicals have articles and only CDs have songs. But, this suggests an interesting point about generalization that we have not seen before. Thus far, the reason for setting up subordinate classes in a generalization hierarchy was to allow the subordinate classes to have distinct attributes and operations that the other subordinate classes don't have. Now, we see that there is a second reason for setting up subordinate classes: to be able to associate only selected subordinate classes with other classes!

The World Music Association Class Diagram

The upper portion of Figure 9.7 is the class diagram version of the World Music Association entity-relationship diagram of Figure 2.11, with one major change. Instead of considering only symphonies, which were associated with orchestras, we are going to consider many kinds of compositions. Of course, different kinds of compositions are performed by different kinds of musical groups. So, the ORCHESTRA entity type in the E-R diagram of Figure 2.11 has become the GROUP class and a generalization hierarchy has been constructed with subordinate classes ORCHESTRA, CHAMBER GROUP, and JAZZ GROUP.

Your Turn

9.1 Generalization/Specialization and Aggregation

Many objects in the world can be broken down into subordinate categories, i.e. "specialized," or, in the opposite direction, "generalized." Other objects can be created from component parts, i.e. "aggregated."

Question:

Develop a generalization/specialization diagram for objects in your university environment or another business environment of your choice. Develop an aggregation diagram for objects in the same business environment. Can you combine the two diagrams into one in a way that makes sense?

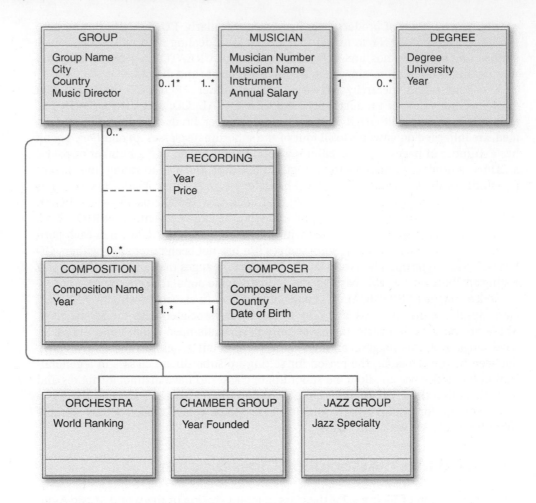

FIGURE 9.7 World Music Association class diagram

The Lucky Rent-A-Vehicle Class Diagram

Lucky Rent-A-Car has expanded to become Lucky Rent-A-Vehicle! In addition to renting cars, Lucky is now renting limousines, trucks, airplanes, and helicopters. The upper part of the Lucky class diagram of Figure 9.8 looks very much like the Lucky entity-relationship diagram of Figure 2.12. The only difference is the change from the CAR entity-type to the VEHICLE class.

There is a two-level generalization hierarchy under VEHICLE. At the first level are the LAND (vehicle) and AIR (vehicle) classes. Then, at the next level down, a LAND vehicle can be a CAR, LIMOUSINE, or TRUCK, while an AIR vehicle can be an AIR-PLANE or a HELICOPTER. Each CAR object will have nine attributes: Body Style and Color, plus four attributes inherited from VEHICLE and another three attributes inherited from LAND. Similarly, each LIMOUSINE will have nine attributes, each TRUCK will have eight attributes, each AIRPLANE will have eleven attributes, and each HELICOPTER will have nine attributes.

There is an update operation for all LAND vehicles to update their mileage attribute that is calculated in the same way for all three types of LAND vehicles; i.e. there is no polymorphism associated with this operation. On the other hand, the diagram indicates that there is polymorphism in the way that the Calculate Next Overhaul Date is

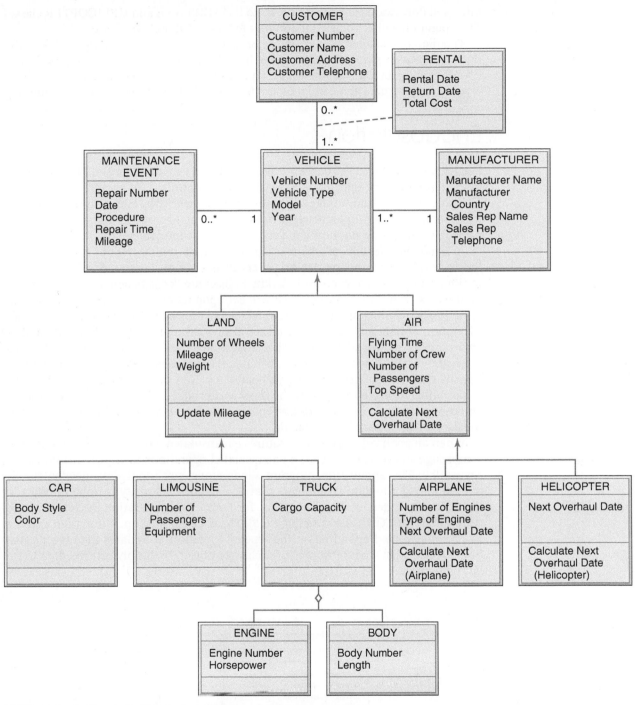

FIGURE 9.8 Lucky Rent-A-Car Vehicle class diagram

inherited downward from the AIR class to the AIRPLANE and HELICOPTER classes. The operation will be somewhat different for each of those two classes.

The diamond-shaped symbol on the branch under the TRUCK class indicates that there is an aggregation diagram under it. Indeed, each TRUCK is composed of an ENGINE and a BODY, each with its own attributes. Notice that the company is interested in keeping data about engines and bodies for trucks but not for cars or limos.

Encapsulation

Earlier, we introduced the concept that it might, in general, be a good idea to permit particular data to be updated only by a limited, controlled set of program segments. This would have the advantage of improving data integrity by eliminating the possibility of some less-than-fully-debugged or otherwise rogue program updating the data in some inaccurate way. But how can such a concept be implemented?

A fascinating feature of object-oriented database management that implements these ideas is called **encapsulation**. In encapsulation, as illustrated in Figure 9.9, the attributes of a class' or even an individual object are "encapsulated," stored together on the disk, with the operations that will act upon them. Yes, the program segments are actually stored within the database, which is a radical departure from the complete separation of data and programs that we always assumed in the relational database environment (as well as in the earlier navigational database environment). Furthermore, the OODBMS will permit the attributes of the encapsulated objects to be updated only by the encapsulated update-type operations. New class instances or objects will be permitted to be created only by the class' encapsulated constructor-type operations. Query-type operations would also be encapsulated but since they do not update data, the data integrity issue is not a factor.

When an application program requires encapsulated data for any reason, it sends a **message** to one of the object's encapsulated operations to trigger it into action, Figure 9.9. The application program sends along any input data needed for the operation (e.g. the number of years that an extended warranty is to be in effect for the Calculate Extended Warranty Price for Power Tools operation in General Hardware's POWER TOOL class in Figure 9.5). The encapsulated operation then executes its program code. Depending on the type of operation, it updates the object's attribute values, adds a new instance of a class or object, or simply returns data to satisfy a query.

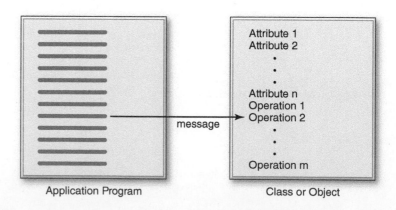

FIGURE 9.9 An application program sends a message that triggers an encapsulated operation in an object

Application Program

Class or Object

Abstract Data Types

Data has traditionally fitted into one of a small number of simple data types consisting of a few variations of character and numeric data. These are adequate to handle the kinds of attributes that we usually think of as being stored in a database. Names, addresses, descriptions, and so forth are stored as character data types. Attributes involving money and other numeric data that includes fractional amounts are stored as decimal numbers. Serial numbers or quantity attributes that count a number of items are stored as integers. Furthermore, these simple data types have operations associated with them in the programming languages that use them. We take it for granted that we can add, subtract, multiply, and divide data stored in the numeric data types, but these operations are indeed associated with numeric data types and they are specifically not associated with character-type data.

Another interesting feature of object-oriented database management is the ability to create new, **abstract data types** and operations that are associated with them. But what kinds of data might require these new and perhaps exotic data types? Figure 9.10 illustrates some of them. In today's increasingly rich data environments, we may want to store static images, line drawings, video clips, and audio clips. For example, consider adding an attribute called "Picture," to the TOOL class of General Hardware's class diagram in Figure 9.5, so that one of the attributes of each tool is a photo of it. (This particular data type has been called a "binary large object" or "BLOB.") Associated operations might include zoom and rotate. Consider adding an attribute called "Flight" to the HELICOPTER class of Lucky Rent-A-Vehicle's class diagram in Figure 9.8 in order to include a video clip of each helicopter flying. Associated operations might include pause or fast-forward. Or consider adding an attribute called "Music" to the CD class of Good Reading Bookstore's class diagram in Figure 9.6 to include an audio clip of one of a CD's songs. An associated operation might be adjust volume. It is worth emphasizing that part of the beauty of this concept is that the attributes that use these new data types are treated exactly like the less exotic attributes that merely use the simple character, decimal, and integer data types.

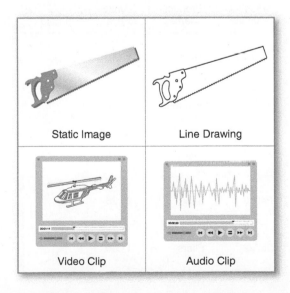

FIGURE 9.10 Abstract data types

Object/Relational Database

When OODBMSs first became commercially available in the 1980s, they found some limited use in niche applications like storing an electric power company's power grid in a data format that could take advantage of the unique features of the object-oriented data approach. But, as we know by now, these OODBMSs didn't overwhelm relational databases and displace them. For, in spite of their new bells and whistles, the OODBMSs were lacking in several areas, including the superior SQL query capabilities that everyone had become accustomed to with relational databases. Yet their advanced features were too tempting to ignore.

Eventually, perhaps inevitably, relational databases and *object-oriented databases* came together in the form of hybrid relational database management systems with added object-oriented features. At first, these were called "extended relational" database systems, but as they became more formalized they became known as **"object/relational" database** systems. Imagine the General Hardware Co. data stored as an object/relational database. A data structure for storing data about tools would essentially be a relational table that would include columns for Product Number, Product Name, Unit Price, Weight, and *Photo* (a photo of the tool), which would be stored as a static image-type of attribute, Figure 9.11. The attribute Photo could then appear in SQL statements just like the other attributes and could be processed as such, returning the photo to the user in a query or even matching a photo against the photos already in the table.

Summary

The relational database model is certainly powerful and has proven to be highly resilient as the standard for data storage and retrieval. However, for certain kinds of complex applications, the relational model is lacking in support for certain useful data model features. The object-oriented model fills this gap. The object-oriented model

Product Number	Product Name	Unit Price	Photo
16386	Wrench	12.95	
19440	Hammer	17.50	
21765	Drill	32.99	
24013	Saw	26.25	
26722	Pliers	11.50	

FIGURE 9.11 The TOOL table in an object/relational database

provides support for more complex but important relationships among different sub-categories or specialized categories of particular entities. This is known as "generalization" or "generalization/specialization." It also supports situations in which particular entities are constructed from other component entities, known as "aggregation." Further, the object-oriented database model with its "abstract data type" feature supports graphic images, photo images, video clips, audio clips, long text documents, and such mathematical constructs as matrices. The object-oriented model also supports "encapsulation," in which a controlled set of program segments is stored with the data and is the only code allowed to update that particular data. Today, object-oriented database management systems have largely given way to the incorporation of these object-oriented features rated into mainstream relational database management systems.

Key Terms

Abstract data type	Generalization/spe-	Object class	Operation
Aggregation	cialization	Object-oriented	Polymorphism
Class	Inheritance	data modeling	Procedure
Class diagram	Message	Object-oriented database	Unified Modeling
Complex relationships	Method	Object/relational	Language (UML)
Encapsulation	Object	database	

Questions

1. Name and briefly describe three deficiencies in the relational database model.

2. In object-oriented terminology, what is an object? What is a class?

3. Describe the advanced relationship known as "generalization." What are its benefits?

4. Describe how attributes are inherited in a generalization hierarchy.

5. What is an "operation?" Can operations be inherited? What is polymorphism?

6. Describe the advanced relationship known as "aggregation." What are its benefits?

7. What is encapsulation in object-oriented databases? What are its benefits?

8. What is an abstract data type (ADT)? What is the significance of a database system that is capable of creating ADTs?

9. What is an object/relational database management system? What are its advantages?

Exercises

1. Draw an object-oriented class diagram, including traditional unary, binary, and ternary relationships, as well as generalization and aggregation relationships as needed, to represent the following business environment. Include all of the attributes and operations listed in the description.

The Houston, TX, city government wants to develop an information system to keep track of all the buildings in the city for both taxation and fire department dispatch purposes. The city will track the address, year built, and owner of record of every building. It will also record the station number, address, and telephone number of each fire station. Each fire station has primary responsibility for a given set of buildings.

There are four types of buildings: single-family homes, apartment buildings, stores, and office buildings. The city wants to record the number of apartments in each apartment building, and the type of goods and annual sales volume of each store. It wants to record the number of floors in each office building. It must also keep track of the companies in each office building. An office building can have several or many companies in it; a company can have offices in several buildings. Each company has a name, telephone number, and unique tax identification number. The city also wants to store the number of square feet that a particular company occupies in a particular office building. Single-family homes are made up of three parts: the house itself, a garage, and a shed. The city wants to keep track of the number of bedrooms, number of baths, and total floor space in the house, the capacity of the garage in number of cars, and the capacity of the shed in volume (cubic feet). There is also a tax calculation formula that differs for each of the four building types.

2. Draw an object-oriented class diagram, including traditional unary, binary, and ternary relationships, as well as generalization and aggregation relationships as needed, to represent the following business environment. Include all the attributes and operations listed in the description.

   Reliable Home Warranty Company contracts with homeowners to repair their major appliances, electrical systems, and plumbing, all for a single annual fee. When a homeowner needs a repair, he calls Reliable and speaks to a dispatcher who sends a qualified technician from a participating repair company. The participating repair company then charges Reliable for the repair. Each dispatcher has an employee number, name, home address, and home telephone number. Each homeowner has a contract number, name, home address, home telephone number, and contract renewal date. Each job has a unique job number, date, and time.

Each job is handled by one dispatcher and (obviously) involves one homeowner.

There are three kinds of jobs: appliance repair, electrical repair, and plumbing repair. For an appliance repair, the company wants to record the appliance type, its model number, its serial number, and the name of the appliance repair company assigned. In addition, Reliable wants to keep track of the manufacturer of the appliance. For each appliance manufacturer it lists the manufacturer name, headquarters address, and telephone number for parts ordering. There is a calculation for the charge that the appliance repair company makes to Reliable based on the type of appliance and the time spent. For a plumbing repair, Reliable keeps track of the name of the plumbing company and the length of time for the repair, but beyond that it makes a distinction between inside repairs and outside repairs such as to sewer lines or septic tanks. Charges from the plumbing company to Reliable are based on a specific plumbing charge formula, but are calculated differently depending on whether the repair is an inside or outside repair. Also, for outside repairs, Reliable must record the distance from the house to the main sewer line or septic tank. For an electrical repair, Reliable tracks the length of time for the repair and the amount and type of wire used in the repair. There is a formula for calculating electrical repair charges based on time and the specialized materials used. Reliable must also keep certain information about the electrical contracting company assigned to the repair. This information includes the contractor's license number, name, address, and liability insurer. A particular electrical contracting company can be involved in many repairs.

Minicases

1. In Minicase 1 of Chapter 2, you were asked to draw an entity-relationship diagram describing Happy Cruise Lines' business environment. We now report that Happy Cruise Lines has been acquired by Mega-Ship Lines, Inc., which has a fleet of oil tankers, container ships, and automobile transport ships. Thus, with the addition of Happy's cruise ships, MegaShip Lines will have four kinds of ships.

   a. Draw an object-oriented generalization diagram, including aggregation relationships as needed, to represent MegaShip's new business environment, with the following attributes and

   operations. All of MegaShip's ships have ship number, ship name, year built, weight, miles traveled, and next overhaul date attributes. In addition, cruise ships have passenger capacity and next health inspection date; oil tankers have oil capacity, container ships have number of containers, and automobile transport ships have number of automobile attributes. An operation determines the next overhaul date for all of the ships in the same manner. Another operation determines the next health inspection date for cruise ships. An operation calculates the next date for a ship to be refueled. This operation is the same for oil tankers, container ships, and automobile transport ships, but is different for cruise ships because of safety precautions regarding the passengers. Oil tankers are composed of a hull, one or more engines, and one or more oil storage tanks. An attribute of hull is length, an attribute of engine is horsepower, and an attribute of oil storage tank is capacity.

b. Add the information given about cruise ships, cruises, etc., in Chapter 2, Exercise 1, to the diagram in part a, constructing a complete object-oriented class diagram.

2. In Minicase 2 of Chapter 2, you were asked to draw an entity-relationship diagram describing the Super Baseball League's business environment. We now report that the Super Baseball League has been absorbed into the Sensational Sports Federation (SSF). SSF divides its sports into two categories: team sports and individual sports. There are three team sports: baseball, basketball, and football, and two individual sports: golf and tennis. The central entity in each of these five sports is a "participant." In the team sports a participant is a team; in the individual sports a participant is an individual player. Every SSF participant (team or individual) has a participant number, participant name, sport (e.g. baseball, golf, etc.), and year affiliated with SSF. In addition, every team has a number of players, a home city and state, and a mascot. Every player in the individual sports has a name, home address, home telephone number, and annual income. Furthermore, golfers have a handicap; tennis players have a world ranking.

a. Draw an object-oriented generalization diagram, to represent SSF's business environment.

b. Add the information given about baseball teams and associated entities in Exercise 2 of Chapter 2, to the diagram in part a, constructing a complete object-oriented class diagram.

c. Add several operations to the class diagram in part b, demonstrating polymorphism with some of them.

Data Administration, Database Administration, and Data Dictionaries

Advanced technologies are only as effective as the people who guide them. This is true of jet airliners, x-ray imaging devices, nuclear power plants, and certainly computers! In the late 1960s, as early navigational database management systems were starting to come into use, a few forward-looking companies began to recognize the need for a department whose job it would be to manage the DBMS and its environment. As the years went on, some of these groups gained responsibility over data in non-DBMS files as well. In addition, some of them advanced from managing data only on an operational basis to performing in addition strategic planning, policy setting, and other broader-based duties. This chapter will describe the functions and groups that companies create to manage their data and their database environment.

OBJECTIVES

Define and compare data administration and database administration.

List and describe the advantages of data administration and database administration.

List and describe the responsibilities of data administration and database administration.

Explain the concept of metadata.

List and describe such metadata realizations as passive and active data dictionaries, relational DBMS catalogs, and data repositories.

Introduction

The "people side" of database management has two parts: data administration and database administration. **Data administration** is a planning and analysis function that is responsible for setting data policy and standards, for promoting the company's data as a competitive resource, for accounting for the use of data, and for providing liaison support to systems analysts during application development. The **database administration** function is more operationally oriented and is responsible for the day-to-day monitoring and management of the company's various active databases, as well as for providing liaison support to program designers during application development. Database administration typically carries out many of the policies set by data administration. This chapter will also describe a class of software tools, known generically as "data dictionaries," that the data administration and database administration functions can use to help manage their company's data.

The Advantages of Data and Database Administration

The initial question is, why do companies need these data and database administration departments? What value do they add? Are they just additional "cost centers" that don't produce revenue? Indeed, at one time or another, most companies have struggled with these questions. But in today's heavily data-intensive, information-dependent business environment, these functions are recognized as being more important than ever. The reasons, as listed in Figure 10.1, are explained next.

Data as a Shared Corporate Resource

Data is a corporate resource that has taken its rightful place alongside money, plant and equipment, personnel, and other corporate resources. Virtually all aspects of business have become dependent on their information systems and the data flowing through them. Today's organizations could not function without their vast stores of personnel data, customer data, product data, supplier data, and so forth. Indeed, data may well be the most important corporate resource because, by its very nature, it describes all of the others. Furthermore, the effective use of its data can give a company a significant competitive advantage. Whether it is used for supply chain management, customer

---

- Data as a shared corporate resource
- Efficiency in job specialization
- Operational management of data
- Managing externally acquired databases
- Managing data in the decentralized environment

FIGURE 10.1 The advantages of data and database administration

service, or advanced marketing applications, a company's data can have a real impact on its share of the marketplace and on its bottom-line profitability.

But all resources tend to be scarce (is there ever enough money to go around?) and there is typically internal competition for them. Data is no exception. As more and more corporate functions seek the same data for their work, bottlenecks can form and the speed of accessing the data can slow. Companies have responded to this in a variety of ways, including bringing in faster computers and making copies of the data for different applications. But the former strategy has its limits and the latter introduces the kind of multi-file redundancy that we have argued against throughout this book. Also, some companies have a policy of data "ownership" in which one of several corporate functions that share some particular data has the primary claim to it and often the ability to decide who else can use it.

What all of this is leading to is simply this: Any shared corporate resource requires a dedicated department to manage it. How would a company handle its money without its finance and accounting departments? It makes little sense to have an important resource either not managed at all or managed part-time and half-heartedly by some group that has other responsibilities too. It also makes little sense to have any one of the groups competing for the shared resource also manage it—the resource manager must obviously be impartial when a dispute arises. The dedicated departments that manage the company's data are the data administration and database administration departments. And, actually, the parallel between the two corporate resources, money and data, is reflected in the parallel of having two company functions to manage each. Finance and data administration, respectively, take a more strategic or tactical-level view of each resource. Accounting and database administration, respectively, take a more operational-level view of them.

Efficiency in Job Specialization

Many of the functions involved in the management of data are highly specialized and require specific expertise. They can range from long-range data planning to working with the idiosyncrasies of a particular database management system. This argues for a full-time staff of specialists who do nothing but manage a company's data and databases.

A good example, and one on which we have spent considerable time already, is database design. To do a really good job of both logical and physical database design requires considerable education and practice. The question then becomes one of who among the information systems personnel should be responsible for designing the company's main, shared databases. The systems analysts? The application programmers? Which systems analysts or application programmers? After all, there may be several or many application development projects, each with different systems analysts and application programmers assigned, that will share the same databases. It doesn't make a lot of sense to have any of these people design the databases, for at least two reasons. One is that it is unreasonable to expect any of them to be as expert at designing databases as people who do it on a full-time basis. The other reason is that if any one application development group designs the shared databases, they will tend to optimize them for their own applications and not take into account the needs of the other applications. The solution is to have application-independent, full-time database specialists, i.e. data and database administration personnel, who are experts at database design and who will optimize the database designs for the overall good of the company.

Operational Management of Data

It is clear that at the operational level, for the day-to-day management of the company's production databases, an independent department must be responsible. The reasons for this have already been set forth above. Since the data is likely to be shared among several or many corporate functions and users, it makes sense for the data to be managed by an independent group whose loyalty is to the overall company and not to any individual function. There is also the specific example that in the shared data environment there will always be some applications or users that depend on other applications or users to collect data and/or update the tables on a regular or irregular basis. Clearly, it is prudent to have an independent data administration group keep track of who is responsible for updating which tables, and monitor whether they have kept to the expected schedule, for the benefit of everyone else who uses these tables.

Also, working with the databases at the operational level requires an in-depth knowledge of the DBMS in use, of the databases themselves, and of such specific skills and tasks as physical database design, database security, and backup and recovery. It is unreasonable to expect application programmers, systems analysts, or anyone else with their own focused duties to be experts at the techniques of data management. In short, it requires specialists.

Managing Externally Acquired Databases

In today's information systems environment, some databases are not designed by a company's own personnel but are acquired as part of purchased software packages. A prominent example of this is Enterprise Resource Planning (ERP) software like the multifunction integrated software sold by companies such as SAP and Peoplesoft. These packages consist of application modules that manage a variety of corporate functions (personnel, accounting, etc.). They typically include a central database that all the application modules share. When a company decides to go the ERP route, they are making an important commitment to a shared data resource. Once again, the only arrangement that makes sense for managing this shared resource is to have an independent group that is tasked with managing it for the overall good of the company.

Managing Data in the Decentralized Environment

With the advent in the 1980s of personal computers, local-area networks, and new, user-friendly software, many companies "decentralized" at least some of their information systems work. These technologies permitted user departments all over the company to handle some or all of their information systems needs on their own, without having to rely on the central information systems organization. There are a variety of advantages and disadvantages to this arrangement (but a book on database management is not the place to go into them). While such developments as ERP software with its centralized database concept have swung the pendulum back toward the centralized IS environment to some extent, decentralization is a fact of life to a greater or lesser degree in virtually all companies.

The question is then, in terms of the advantages of data and database administration: do we need these functions more or less in the **decentralized environment** than we do in the centralized environment? Some people might say that we don't need them. In fact, when the move towards decentralization began, one of the stated reasons was to reduce the "overhead" of the central IS department and that included database administration. Furthermore, many people are quite content to develop their own databases on their PCs using MS Access and other such PC-based DBMSs. But a very strong argument says that data and database administration are *even more important* in a decentralized environment than in a centralized one.

First of all, most large companies do not have totally decentralized IS but rather a hybrid centralized/decentralized environment. And, if nothing else, the centralized portion includes a central shared database, which certainly requires a database administration function to manage it. But, more than that, with company data present in a variety of central databases, databases associated with local-area networks, and even databases on PCs, the *coordinating role* of data administration is crucial. This coordinating role is a key element of the responsibilities of data administration, which is our next topic.

The Responsibilities of Data Administration

Since information systems are used in all aspects of a company's business, data administrators find themselves playing key roles in the corporate environment. Those who understand what data a company possesses, and how it flows both from department to department within the company and between the company and its customers, suppliers, and other external entities, are in the best position to understand how the company really functions. Data administrators often come from the ranks of systems analysts and, indeed, some companies use the term "**data analyst**" to describe them. What are the responsibilities of the data administration function? They are listed in Figure 10.2 and discussed below.

Data Coordination

With the prominent role of data in the corporate environment, its accuracy is of the utmost importance. But in the centralized/decentralized environment, with data and copies of data scattered among mainframe computers, local-area network servers, and even PCs, the possibilities of inconsistency and error increase. There is nothing more annoying than two people making important presentations in a meeting and showing different figures that should be the same. It is up to the data administrators to keep track of the organization's data including downloading schedules, updating schedules and responsibilities, and interchanging data with other companies. This is not to suggest that data administration should try to control all the databases on all the employees' PCs. That would be impossible. But total data anarchy is not desirable

> - Data coordination
> - Data planning
> - Data standards
> - Liaison to systems analysts and programmers
> - Training
> - Arbitration of disputes and usage authorization
> - Documentation and publicity
> - Data's competitive advantage

FIGURE 10.2 The responsibilities of data administration

either, and it is the job of the data administrators to maintain a reasonable amount of control over the company's data.

Data Planning

Data planning begins with the determination of what data will be needed for future company business efforts and what applications will support them. This may be limited to data generated and used internally within the company. However, today it often means coordinating with other companies in a supply chain or acquiring external customer data for use in marketing. In either case, there is the need to plan for integrating the new data with the company's existing data. A number of methodologies have been developed to aid in data planning. These methodologies take into account the business processes that the company performs as part of its normal operations and add the data needed to support them. While they generally operate at a high "strategic" level and may not get into the details of individual attributes, they do provide a broad roadmap to work from.

Related to strategic data planning is the matter of what hardware and software will be needed to support the company's information systems operations in the future. The questions involved range from such relatively straightforward matters as how many disk drives will be needed to contain the data to broader issues of how much processing power will be needed to support the overall IS environment. Another data planning issue is how metadata and the data dictionary concept (discussed later in this chapter) should be put to use. This involves what data should be stored in the data dictionary, to what uses the data dictionary should be put, who should interact with the data dictionary, and how and on what kind of schedule all of this should take place. Yet another data planning issue that occasionally faces companies is the migration of old, pre-database data and applications into the company's database environment. There is also the problem of migrating data from one DBMS to another as the company's software infrastructure changes.

Data Standards

In order to reduce errors, improve performance, and enhance the ability of one IS worker to understand the work done by another, it is important for the data administration function to set standards regarding data and its use. One example of standards is controlling the way that attribute names, table names, and other data-related names are formed. Attribute names must be meaningful and consistent. The company can't have its human resources department use Serial Number as the attribute name for employee numbers while at the same time its manufacturing department uses it for finished product serial numbers. Similarly, there is a problem if the human resources department tries to use Serial Number and Employee Number in different tables to represent the employee number. Another example of standards setting is insisting on consistency in the way the programs that access the database are written, especially in regard to the database call instructions. Care here can help to prevent database-call-related performance problems, as well as to ease maintenance by having standard, readily understood instructions.

Data standards also come into play in the IS interactions between companies in supply chains. When data is exchanged using electronic data interchange (EDI) technology, adjustments have to be made to take into account attribute structures and other differences in the information systems of the two companies involved.

Liaison to Systems Analysts and Programmers

In the role of liaison to application developers, data administrators (often called "data analysts" in this role) are responsible for providing support to the systems analysts and programmers in all matters concerning the data needed by an application. During the systems analysis phase of application development, the support may include help in determining what data is needed for the application and which of the data items needed for the application already exist in the active database.

Another aspect of such liaison activity, which is really a topic in itself, is the question of database design. Data analysts are generally involved in database design at some level, but deciding exactly what that level of involvement should be depends on a number of factors. In an IS environment in which the data administration organization is very strong and in which there is a significant amount of data sharing among different applications and different functional areas of the company, the data analysts may do all of the logical database design work themselves. Here again, they can stand as an impartial group creating the best design for the overall good of all of the users. The other choice is for the application developers to do the database design with either active consultation by the data analysts, or approval responsibility after the fact by the data analysts. In the active consultation role, the data analysts lend their expertise to the effort, as well as determining how the new data should mesh with data in the existing database, if there is to be such a merging. In the approval role, the application developers (usually the lead programmers for this activity) design the database, which is then shown to the data analysts for discussion and approval.

Training

In some companies, data administration is responsible for training all those in the company who need to understand the company's data and, in some cases, the DBMS environment. Management personnel should understand why the database approach is good for the company and for their specific individual functions. Users must understand why the shared data is secure and private. Application developers must be given substantial training in how to work in the database environment, including training in database concepts, database standards, how to write DBMS calls in their programs, possibly how to do database design, how to use the data dictionary to their advantage, and in general, what services they can expect to be provided by data and database administration.

Arbitration of Disputes and Usage Authorization

To introduce this heading, we should spend a moment on the question of **data "ownership."** Who in a company "owns" a piece of data or a database? To be technical, since data is a resource of value to the company, the data "belongs to" the company's owners or stockholders. But in practical terms, in many companies data is controlled by its user or primary user. In this case, data and database administration act as "custodians" of the data in the sense of providing security, backup, performance monitoring, and other such services. In some companies with extensive data sharing, ownership responsibility actually falls to data administration itself.

If ownership has been established and a new application requires the use of existing data, then it is the job of data administration to act as an intermediary and approach the owner of the data with the request for data sharing. This can also happen if someone in the company simply wants to query someone else's database. If there is a dispute over such data sharing, then the data administration group acts as an arbitrator between the disagreeing parties. Incidentally, the data administration group may also find itself acting as arbitrator between two database users who are sharing the same CPU and vying for better performance.

Documentation and Publicity

Using the data dictionary as its primary tool, the data management function is responsible for documenting the data environment. This **documentation** includes a description of the data and the databases, plus programs, reports, and which people have access to these items. A more complete list of such metadata items will be given later in this chapter in discussing data dictionaries.

As a related issue, the data management group should perform a publicity function, informing potential users of what data already exists in the database. Knowing what data exists might encourage employees to think about how they can use the company's data to gain competitive advantages that did not previously exist. They may discover how to automate more of their work and how to integrate their work more directly with related business processes that are already automated.

Data's Competitive Advantage

Earlier, we talked about the idea of data providing a competitive advantage for the company. Another point is that data administrators, through their knowledge of the company's data and how it flows from one company function to another, are in a unique position to understand how the company "works." This is especially true since virtually all company functions today are dependent on information systems. Combining these two concepts, a very important and very high-profile responsibility of the data administration function is to respond to questions about how the company's business procedures can be adjusted or modified to improve its operating efficiency. This can also extend to data administration taking the initiative and making suggestions for improvement on its own. This capability, which can clearly lead to decreased costs and improved profits for the company, makes data administration a particularly important company function.

The Responsibilities of Database Administration

Database administration is a technical function that is responsible for the day-to-day operations and maintenance of the DBMS environment, including such related tools as the data dictionary. This is quite analogous to the role of the systems programmers who are responsible for maintaining the mainframe operating systems. Like operating systems, DBMSs tend to include many highly product-specific features that require thorough training to handle. What are the responsibilities of the database administration function? They are listed in Figure 10.3 and explained as follows.

- DBMS performance monitoring
- DBMS troubleshooting
- DBMS usage and security monitoring
- Data dictionary operations
- DBMS data and software maintenance
- Database design

FIGURE 10.3 The responsibilities of database administration

Your Turn

10.1 The Data Administrator

There is no doubt that both the amount of data that companies hold and the importance of this data to the companies' bottom lines are continually increasing. This would seem to make data administrators more and more important within their companies. Yet data administration is often seen as a support function that is a cost to a company with no clearly quantifiable benefit.

Question:

Develop an argument in favor of dedicating more resources to data administration even if the benefits cannot be directly quantified.

DBMS Performance Monitoring

One of the key functions performed by database administration is **performance monitoring**. Using utility programs, the database administrators can gauge the performance of the running DBMS environment. This activity has a number of implications. It is important to know how fast the various applications are executing as part of assuring that response time requirements are being met. Also, this type of performance information is pertinent to future hardware and software acquisition plans. Depending on the characteristics of the DBMS and the operating system it is running under, the performance information may be used to redistribute the database application load among different CPUs or among different memory regions within a system. Finally, performance information can be used to ferret out inefficient applications or queries that may be candidates for redesign.

An additional note is that the database administrators must interface with the IS organization's systems programming staff, which maintains the mainframe operating systems. The systems programmers will also have performance and troubleshooting responsibilities that may overlap with those of the database administrators. The net of this is that it greatly facilitates matters if the two groups get along well with each other and can work together effectively as need be.

DBMS Troubleshooting

Inevitably, there will be times when a DBMS application fails during execution. The reason can range from a bug in the application code to a hardware or system software failure. The question is, "Whom do the users call when this happens?" In a strongly controlled environment, the database administrators should be the **troubleshooting** interface. The key to the troubleshooting operation is assessing what went wrong and coordinating the appropriate personnel needed to fix it. These may include server administrators, network administrators, application programmers, and the data administrators themselves.

DBMS Usage and Security Monitoring

Database administrators keep track of which applications are running in the database environment and can track who is accessing the data in the database at any moment. There are software utilities that enable them to perform these functions. Monitoring the users of the database environment is really done from several perspectives. One is the issue of security: making sure that only authorized personnel access the data. This includes instructing the system to allow new users to access the database, as ordered by data administration personnel in conjunction with the data owners. Another perspective is the need to maintain records on the amount of use by various users of the database. This can have implications for future load balancing and performance optimizing work, and may also be used in allocating system costs among the various users and applications. And a related concern is database auditing. Even assuming that only authorized users have accessed the database, accounting and error correction require that a record be kept of who has accessed and who has modified which data items. Incidentally, if the data auditing function is to be done, the tool that lets it be accomplished is a journal or log similar to the one used for backup and recovery. Depending on the nature of the auditing, this journal or log may have to record all simple data accesses, as well as all data modifications.

Data Dictionary Operations

The database administration group is responsible for the operational aspects, as opposed to the planning aspects, of the data dictionary, to be discussed shortly, and any other metadata tools. It also provides dictionary access to other personnel such as systems analysts, generates periodic data dictionary reports as required by management, and answers management's ad hoc questions about the data and the IS environment. For example, systems analysts developing a new application may want to find out if the data that they need in the new application already exists in the company's databases. IS management will want periodic reports on the company's databases, including a list of the tables and their sizes. An ad hoc query may include which people had access to certain data that leaked out of the company! We will discuss this more in the data dictionary section of this chapter below.

DBMS Data and Software Maintenance

Database administration personnel will be involved with a wide range of data and software maintenance activities, to a greater or lesser degree depending on how the IS department is organized. These activities include installing new versions of the DBMS, installing "fixes" or "patches" (corrections) to the DBMS, performing backup and recovery operations (as discussed in Chapter 11), and any other tasks related to repairing or upgrading the DBMS or the database. One particular data maintenance activity is modifying the database structures as new tables and attributes are inevitably added. This is really also an issue of database design, which we come to next.

Your Turn

10.2 The Database Administrator

Many companies have decentralized their information systems operations. This can involve different corporate divisions in one country or different divisions spread throughout several or many countries. Another circumstance in which this can happen is when a holding company owns a variety of independent companies that may or may not involve the same industry.

Question:

Consider one of these decentralized information systems environments. Are database administrators more or less important in these environments than in a centralized information systems environment? Why? Should database administration be considered a cost that can be reduced or eliminated in such an environment or a critical need that should be enhanced?

Database Design

In the mix of centralized and decentralized IS environments that exist today, there is a wide range in database administration responsibilities for database design. For shared central databases, database administration is responsible for physical database design and may also either be responsible for or be a participant in logical database design. Notice that their responsibility for physical database design is consistent with their expertise in the features (and idiosyncrasies!) of the DBMS in use and with their overall responsibility for the performance of the DBMS environment. For decentralized databases on LAN servers or even on PCs, database administrators' role in database design is often more that of consultants who are called in on request.

Data Dictionaries

Introduction

The information systems function (and within it, the data and database administration functions) is responsible for managing data as a corporate resource. Not only must the data be stored but, like any other resource, there have to be provisions for inputting more of it, outputting it (in the form of reports, query responses, data transmissions to supply chain partners, etc.), and, most certainly, processing it! To accomplish all this requires people, equipment (i.e. computers, disks, networks, and so forth) and established procedures, standards, and policies. The question before us now is, how does IS management keep track of all of this? But then, how does *any* corporate function keep track of their resources and other responsibilities? With information systems, of course! Does that mean that IS management can keep track of *its* resources and responsibilities with information systems? The apparent answer should be yes, perhaps even obviously yes. But this has been a long and at times difficult road. Do you know the old story about the shoemaker's children being the last ones to get shoes, Figure 10.4? The shoemaker was so busy making shoes for the other children of the town in order to make a living that his own children were the last ones to get shoes. And the IS function has been so busy developing and running systems to support all the other corporate functions that it was a long time before it could invest the resources to develop information systems to support itself.

Personnel Dept.   Manufacturing Dept.   Accounting Dept.   Finance Dept.   Information Systems Dept.

FIGURE 10.4 The shoemaker's children are the last ones to get shoes

What we are talking about here comes under the general term **metadata**, literally data about data. What data does an IS function need to manage itself and what kinds of tools can it employ to store and handle the data? For a long time, the term for such a metadata storage tool has been the **data dictionary**, literally a database *about* data. More recently, the term **data repository** has come into vogue. Also, the term data catalog has taken on certain specific meanings. We will discuss all of these terms and their implications in the rest of this chapter. But, since the metadata concept can be hard to grasp at first, let's begin with a simple but concrete example: part of a data dictionary.

A Simple Example of Metadata

Figure 10.5 once again shows the General Hardware Company's relational database. Recall that among the entities that General Hardware has to keep track of are salespersons and customers. Each row of the SALESPERSON table describes one entity, i.e. one salesperson. Each column of the SALESPERSON table describes one kind of attribute or feature or fact about a salesperson. Similar statements can be made for the CUSTOMER table. Why are we belaboring these points this late in the book? To contrast them with the tables of a data dictionary. We know that the SALESPERSON and CUSTOMER tables exist to help the company's sales function conduct its business. Today, we take this kind of database support of company functions, as provided by the company's information systems, almost for granted. But do all company functions have database support? Sales, personnel, accounting, finance, product development, manufacturing, and customer support certainly do. But what about information systems themselves?

Figure 10.6 shows two of the tables of a simple data dictionary, a database designed to help the IS function manage its own responsibilities. Again, we know that the sales function wants to keep track of salespersons and customers. So, what does the IS function want to keep track of? Two entities that IS must manage are the tables and attributes in the company's databases and more broadly in its IS environment. IS must have a complete list of all of the tables in the company's databases (at least in its central, shared databases), plus detailed data about the tables. It also has to track the attributes that are in the tables. Thus, Figure 10.6 shows a *TABLES table* and an *ATTRIBUTES table*. That's right, a data dictionary table listing the company's tables and a data dictionary table listing the attributes in the company's tables.

SALESPERSON

Salesperson Number	Salesperson Name	Commission Percentage	Year of Hire	Office Number

CUSTOMER

Customer Number	Customer Name	Salesperson Number	HQ City

CUSTOMER EMPLOYEE

Customer Number	Employee Number	Employee Name	Title

PRODUCT

Product Number	Product Name	Unit price

SALES

Salesperson Number	Product Number	Quantity

OFFICE

Office Number	Telephone	Size

FIGURE 10.5 The General Hardware Company relational database

In the SALESPERSON table, each row represents one of the entities: a salesperson. In the CUSTOMER table, each row represents a customer. The equivalent in the data dictionary is that each row of the TABLES table represents one of the tables in the company's database and each row of the ATTRIBUTES table represents one of attributes in the tables in the company's database. Thus, in this example, we see that each row of the TABLES table in Figure 10.6 represents one of the tables of General Hardware's database in Figure 10.5. Also, each row of the ATTRIBUTES table in Figure 10.6 represents one of the attributes in Figure 10.5.

If the sales function has decided that Salesperson Number, Salesperson Name, Commission Percentage, and Year Of Hire are attributes that it must store for each salesperson, and Customer Number, Customer Name, Salesperson Number, and HQ City are attributes that it must store for each customer, what are the attributes for tables and attributes that IS feels it must store in the data dictionary? Figure 10.6a shows that the attributes for tables are Table Name, Table Length (number of records), and Disk Number (the disk on which the table is stored). The attributes for attributes (yes, that's correct, think about it!) shown in Figure 10.6b are Attribute Name, Attribute Type, and Attribute Length (in bytes).

(a) TABLES Table

Table Name	Table Length	Disk Number
Salesperson	500	A23
Customer	6,400	A23
Customer Employee	127,000	A23
Product	83,000	A47
Sales	273,000	A47
Office	600	A47

(b) ATTRIBUTES Table

Attribute Name	Attribute Type	Attribute Length
Salesperson Number	Numeric	3
Salesperson Name	Alphabetic	20
Commission Percentage	Numeric	2
Year of Hire	Numeric	4
Customer Number	Numeric	4
Customer Name	Alphabetic	20
HQ City	Alphabetic	15

FIGURE 10.6 Two data dictionary tables

As in any database, in addition to keeping track of the basic facts about the represented entities, a data dictionary must keep track of the relationships between the entities. The data dictionary table in Figure 10.7 represents the many-to-many relationship between the tables and attributes in the data dictionary's TABLES Table and ATTRIBUTES Table. Demonstrating the nature of the many-to-many relationship between tables and attributes, first Figure 10.7 obviously shows that each table has several attributes. But also notice that the Salesperson Number attribute is associated with two tables, both the SALESPERSON and CUSTOMER tables (because it is the primary key of the SALESPERSON table and a foreign key in the CUSTOMER table).

Thus, the tables of Figures 10.6 and 10.7 contain metadata, data *about the company's data*. How is the data organized? What are the data structures called? Where is the data stored? How much data is there? These questions point to the essence of metadata. Now, let's see how it has evolved.

Table Name	Attribute Name
Salesperson	Salesperson Number
Salesperson	Salesperson Name
Salesperson	Commission Percentage
Salesperson	Year of Hire
Customer	Customer Number
Customer	Customer Name
Customer	Salesperson Number
Customer	HQ City

FIGURE 10.7 A data dictionary table representing the many-to-many relationship between the TABLES Table and the ATTRIBUTES Table

Passive and Active Data Dictionaries

Definitions and Distinctions   Commercially available data dictionaries, which date from the late 1970s, are passive in nature. Basically a **passive data dictionary** is one used just for documentation purposes. Data about the entities in the IS environment are entered into the dictionary and cross-referenced as one-to-many and many-to-many relationships. Requests for information in the forms of reports and queries about the dictionary's contents are run as needed. The passive data dictionary is simply a self-contained database used for documenting the IS environment.

In contrast, an **active data dictionary** is one that interacts with the IS environment on a real-time basis. The nature of the interaction can involve input into the data dictionary, output from it, or both. When a data dictionary is active in terms of input, an event taking place in the IS environment, such as the creation of a new database table, automatically results in new data (about this event) being input into the data dictionary. When a data dictionary is active in terms of output, responses from the dictionary are an integral part of the running of the IS environment. For example, the data dictionary may contain data about who in the company is authorized to access particular tables. If the data dictionary must be "consulted" for this data every time someone tries to access a table, then the data dictionary is considered active in the output sense.

Entities and Attributes   In the earlier example, we discussed tables and attributes as two possible data dictionary entities. Figure 10.8 shows a broader range of possibilities. This is not intended to be a complete list that fits the needs of all companies. In fact, one of the principles of the data dictionary concept is to make the data dictionary expandable and customizable to a company's particular needs.

There are two classes of attributes for data dictionary entities: those that are of a general nature and are likely to apply to any of the entities and those that are specific to particular data dictionary entities. An example of a general attribute is "Name." Most data dictionary entities must have a name or some other identifier. By far most data dictionary attributes, however, are specific to particular entities. Some examples

- Data-Related Entities
  - Databases
  - Tables
  - Attributes
  - Web Pages
- Software-Related Entities
  - Application Programs
  - Database Management Systems
  - Jobs
- Hardware-Related Entities
  - Computers
  - Disks
  - Local Area Networks
- Outputs
  - Reports
  - Queries
- People

FIGURE 10.8 Data dictionary sample entities

- Table (or file) Construction: Which attributes (or fields) appear in which tables (or files).
- Security: Which people have access to which databases or tables or files.
- Impact of Change: Which programs might be affected by changes to which tables or files. (*Note*: This has become much less of an issue due to the data independence of relational databases.)
- Physical Residence: Which tables or files are on which disks.
- Program Data Requirements: Which programs use which table or files.
- Responsibility: Which people are responsible for updating which databases or tables or files.

FIGURE 10.9 Data dictionary sample relationships

include the Value Range of a numeric attribute, the Length of a record or table row, the Home Address of a person, the Capacity of a disk, and the Language that a program is written in.

Relationships   The relationship between almost any pair of data dictionary entities can have value to IS management. Some examples of common data dictionary relationships and the entities involved are shown in Figure 10.9. With such relationships between the dictionary entities, data administration personnel can aid in new software development, data security and privacy, change management, and do a host of other IS environment tasks.

Uses and Users   Data dictionaries can be of considerable use to a variety of people in the corporate environment in general, as well as in the IS environment specifically. Clearly, the heaviest users of the data dictionary will be IS management and the data administration and database administration functions under them. The data dictionary is fundamentally the database used to store the data about the data and computer resources that these various people are charged with managing. Whether producing periodic lists of databases or tables in the IS environment or responding to ad hoc queries about which personnel had access to leaked data, the data dictionary is the information resource for IS.

Systems analysts and program designers use the data dictionary in two major ways. One is as a source of information about what entities, attributes, and so forth already exist in the IS environment that might be needed in a new application development effort underway. If the data needed for a new system already exists, then the new application may be able to use it. If there are existing database structures that the application can add on to in order to satisfy its requirements, then that might yield a large cost saving. In those and related situations, the dictionary is the repository of data to be searched. The other use of dictionaries for systems analysts and designers is as a documentation device for the new information that is generated as a result of their application development efforts. In this way, application developers have a natural vehicle for documentation and the data dictionary has a natural way of being populated with data concerning new applications.

Corporate employees in all functions and at almost all levels can benefit from the data dictionary by using it to discover the data available in the company. Exploring new ways to use the data to improve their own responsibilities will help the company as a whole. Finally, there is the benefit to corporate management. As we said earlier, it becomes increasingly important for management to understand the nature of the data in its systems, which mirrors the workings of the organization, in order to have the best grasp on how the company functions.

Relational DBMS Catalogs

An integral part of every relational DBMS is its catalog. A **relational catalog** is a highly active but limited scope data dictionary that is very closely tied to the operations of the relational DBMS. Not surprisingly, the relational catalog is itself composed of relational tables and may be queried with standard SQL commands. Typical database entity data stored in relational catalogs includes databases, tables, attributes, views, indexes, users, and disks. At the attribute level, the relational catalog will note such important facts as which attributes in the database are unique. Notice that all of these entities are very closely tied to the running of the relational DBMS. Unlike general-purpose data dictionaries, relational catalogs do not include such entities as reports and non-relational files.

The main purpose of the relational catalog is to accurately support the relational query optimizer. As we discussed earlier in the book, when a query is posed to the relational DBMS, the relational query optimizer tries to find an efficient way or "access path" to satisfy it. In order to accomplish this, the optimizer must have a source of complete and absolutely accurate data about the database. It must know what attributes are in the tables, which attributes are indexed, which attributes are unique, and whatever other data will help it to come up with an efficient solution. It finds all of this data in the relational catalog. In order to keep the relational catalog absolutely accurate, it must be highly active in data dictionary terms and must be updated in a mechanical and automated way. The system can't take the chance that a human inputting data into the relational catalog might make a mistake. So, input to the relational catalog is accomplished programmatically as changes to the database environment occur. For example, if the relational DBMS is instructed to create a new table, it does two things. It creates the new table *and* it automatically inputs data about the new table into the relational catalog. This is the only way to assure that the relational catalog will be accurate.

Another use of the relational catalog, which we already spoke about generically when discussing data dictionaries above, is to provide a "roadmap" through the database data for anyone who wants to query the data or explore new ways to use the data. The relational DBMS checks the user authorization data in the catalog before it allows a user to retrieve data he is requesting with a SELECT statement or to update, delete, or insert records in application tables.

Data Repositories

The latest realization of the metadata concept is known as the *data repository*. A data repository is, in effect, a large-scale data dictionary that includes entity types generated and needed by the latest IS technologies. One popular usage of the term data repository is associated with CASE (Computer-Aided Software Engineering) software. In the CASE environment, the data repository holds the same types of data that traditional data dictionaries hold, plus CASE-specific data such as reusable code modules. The term data repository has also been associated with object-oriented database environments in which OODBMS-specific entity types such as objects are included.

Summary

Data administration and database administration are critical information systems functions in today's information-dependent corporate environment. The data has to be managed as any corporate resource would be. Data and database administration promote the sharing of data as a corporate resource, efficiency in job specialization related to data functions, efficiency in the operational management of data, and competence in such related issues as the management of externally acquired databases and the management of data in decentralized environments.

Data administration is the corporate function that is responsible for **data coordination**, data planning, data standards, liaison to systems analysts and programmers, training, **arbitration** of disputes and usage authorization, documentation and publicity, and the promotion of data's competitive advantage. Database administration is the corporate function responsible for DBMS performance monitoring, DBMS troubleshooting, DBMS usage and **security monitoring**, data dictionary operations, DBMS data and software maintenance, and database design.

Data dictionaries are databases that store metadata or "data about data." They can be active or passive. Important implementations of the metadata concept include relational DBMS catalogs and data repositories.

Key Terms

Active data dictionary	**Data ownership**	**Documentation**	**Security monitoring**
Arbitration	**Data planning**	**Job specialization**	**Troubleshooting**
Data administration	**Data repository**	**Metadata**	**Usage and Security**
Data analyst	**Data standards**	**Passive data dictionary**	**Monitoring**
Data coordination	**Database administration**	**Performance monitoring**	
Data dictionary	**Decentralized environment**	**Relational catalog**	

Questions

1. What is data administration?

2. What is database administration?

3. What are the advantages of having data administration and database administration departments?

4. Explain and defend the following statement: Data is a corporate resource and should be managed in the same manner in which other corporate resources are managed.

5. Why is it important in terms of efficiency in job specialization to have data and database administration specialists?

6. What is the importance in terms of externally acquired databases of data and database administration?

7. Defend the following statement: Data and database administration are even more important in the decentralized IS environment than in the centralized one.

8. List and briefly explain five major responsibilities of data administration.

9. Why is it important that data administrators perform a data coordination role?

10. What kinds of planning do data administrators have to do regarding data?

11. Defend or refute the following statement: Current IS technologies and practices make having data standards more important than ever before.

12. In general, what are data administration's responsibilities to the professional and managerial employees of the company? Concentrate on training, publicity, and liaison tasks.

13. Why might data administration have to serve as the arbitrator of disputes?

14. List and briefly explain five major responsibilities of database administration.

15. Discuss database administration's role in performance monitoring and troubleshooting.

16. How do database administration's responsibilities to the data dictionary differ from data administration's?

17. Describe the role of database administration in database design and explain why that role makes sense.

18. What is metadata?

19. What is a data dictionary?

20. Explain in your own words why a data dictionary in a relational DBMS environment would have a "Tables table."

21. What is the difference between an active and a passive data dictionary?

22. List some typical data dictionary entities.

23. List some typical uses of the data dictionary.

24. How does a relational catalog differ from a general-purpose data dictionary? What is its role in the relational DBMS environment?

25. How does a data repository differ from a general-purpose data dictionary?

Exercises

1. You have just been named Director of Data Administration of General Hardware Co. General Hardware maintains a large central IS organization with several operational relational databases at its headquarters. It also has databases on several local-area network servers, some located at its headquarters and some in regional offices. Of course, there are many relational databases on individual employees' PCs, too. Certain data is sent from the central databases to the LAN databases nightly.

   You have been given a free hand to create a data administration department and supporting database administration departments for General Hardware and its IS environment. Design your data and database administration functions. Include their responsibilities and explain how they will add value to the corporation.

2. Good Reading Bookstores Database.

   a. Create a data dictionary TABLES table and an ATTRIBUTES table and enter data in them for Good Reading Bookstores database shown in Figure 7.21. Your answer should be based on the format shown in Figure 10.6. Use your judgment as to attribute type values, length values, etc.

   b. Create a relationships table for this tables and attributes data, using the format in Figure 10.7.

3. Best Airlines Mechanics Database.

   a. Create a data dictionary TABLES table and an ATTRIBUTES table and enter data in them for Best Airlines' mechanics database, shown in Exercise 8.5. Your answer should be based on the format shown in Figure 10.6. Use your judgment as to attribute type values, length values, etc.

   b. Create a relationships table for this tables and attributes data, using the format in Figure 10.7.

Minicases

1. Happy Cruise Lines.

   a. You have just been named Director of Data Administration of Happy Cruise Lines. Happy Cruise Lines maintains a central IS organization with several operational relational databases on several large servers at its headquarters. Each of its cruise ships has a medium-scale server on board with its own databases that help manage the running of the ship. Real-time transmissions are made via satellite between headquarters and the ships that keep both the headquarters and shipboard databases constantly up to date.

      You have been given a free hand to create a data administration department and supporting database administration departments for Happy Cruise Lines and its IS environment. Design your data and database administration functions. Include their responsibilities and explain how they will add value to the corporation.

   b. Create a data dictionary TABLES table and an ATTRIBUTES table and enter data in them for Happy Cruise Lines' database, shown in Minicase 5.1. Your answer should be based on the format shown in Figure 10.6. Use your judgment as to attribute type values, length values, etc.

   c. Create a relationships table for this tables and attributes data, using the format in Figure 10.7.

2. Super Baseball League.

   a. You have just been named Director of Data Administration of the Super Baseball League. The Super Baseball League maintains a substantially decentralized IS organization with the focus on the individual teams. Each team has a server at its stadium or offices near the stadium. The League has a server at its headquarters. Data collected at the team locations, such as player statistics updates and game attendance figures, is uploaded nightly to the server at league headquarters.

   You have been given a free hand to create a data administration department and supporting database administration departments for the Super Baseball League and its IS environment. Design your data and database administration functions. Include their responsibilities and explain how they will add value to the corporation.

   b. Create a data dictionary TABLES table and an ATTRIBUTES table and enter data in them for the Super Baseball League database (including the STADIUM table) shown in Minicase 5.2. Your answer should be based on the format shown in Figure 10.6. Use your judgment as to attribute type values, length values, etc.

   c. Create a relationships table for this tables and attributes data, using the format in Figure 10.7.

Database Control Issues: Security, Backup and Recovery, Concurrency

We've said that data is a corporate resource and that corporate resources must be carefully managed. Different corporate resources have different management requirements. Money must be protected from theft. Equipment must be secured against misuse. Buildings may require security guards. Data, too, is a corporate resource and has its own peculiar concerns that we have termed **database control issues**. We will discuss the three main database control issues in this chapter. The first, **data security**, involves protecting the data from theft, malicious destruction, unauthorized updating, and more. The second, **backup and recovery**, refers to having procedures in place to recreate data that has been lost for any reason. The third, **concurrency control**, refers to problems that can occur when two or more transactions or users attempt to update a piece of data simultaneously. Certainly, these very important issues require well thought out and standardized solutions. Indeed, entire books have been written about each one! Our goal in this chapter is to introduce each of these topics, discuss why they are important, explain what can go wrong, and highlight several of the main solutions for each.

OBJECTIVES

List the major data control issues handled by database management systems.
List and describe the types of data security breaches.
List and describe the types of data security measures.
Describe the concept of backup and recovery.
Describe the major backup and recovery techniques.
Explain the problem of disaster recovery.
Describe the concept of concurrency control.
Describe such concurrency control issues and measures as the lost update problem, locks and deadlock, and versioning.

Introduction

In today's world, not a week goes by without a news story involving data being compromised in some way. One week a hacker breaks into a company's computer and steals credit-card numbers. The next week someone breaks into the trunk of a parked car and steals a laptop computer that turns out to have confidential data on its hard drive. The week after that a hurricane or earthquake causes major damage to some company's computer center and a great deal of data is lost. And so on.

With industries of every kind as dependent on their data as they are today, it is critical that they protect their information systems and the data they contain as carefully as they can. This involves a wide range of technologies and actions ranging from **antivirus software** to firewalls to employee training to sophisticated backup and recovery arrangements, and beyond (all of which we will delve into in this chapter). Companies invest a great deal of money in these because breaches in computer and data security can lead to loss of profits, loss of the public's trust, and lawsuits. All of this has really become a major issue in information systems today.

Data Security

The Importance of Data Security

With data taking its place as a corporate resource and so much of today's business dependent on data and the information systems that process it, good data security is absolutely critical to every company and organization. A data security breach can dramatically affect a company's ability to continue normal functioning. But even beyond that, companies have a responsibility to protect data that often affects others beyond the company itself. Customer data, which, for example, can be financial, medical, or legal in nature, must be carefully guarded. When customers give a company personal data they expect the company to be very careful to keep it confidential. Banks must be sure that the money they hold, now in the form of data, cannot be tampered with or leaked outside of the bank. Individuals want personal information that insurance companies keep about them to remain confidential. Also, when a company has access to a trading partner's data in a supply chain arrangement, the partner company expects its data to remain secure. Governments, charged with protecting their citizens, must protect sensitive defense data from unauthorized intrusion. And the list goes on and on.

Types of Data Security Breaches

There are several different ways that data and the information systems that store and process it can be compromised.

Unauthorized Data Access   Perhaps the most basic kind of data security breach is unauthorized data access. That is, someone obtains data that they are not authorized to see. This can range from seeing, say, a single record of a database table to obtaining a copy of an entire table or even an entire database. You can imagine an evil company wanting to steal a competitor's customer list or new product plans, the government of one country wanting to get hold of another country's defense plans, or even one person simply wanting to snoop on his neighbor's bank account. Sometimes the stolen data consists of computer **passwords** or security codes so that data or property can be stolen at a later time. And a variety of different people can be involved in the data theft, including a company's own employees, a trading partner's employees, or complete outsiders. In the case of a company's own employees, the situation can be considerably more complicated than that of an outsider breaking in and stealing data. An employee might have legitimate access to some company data but might take advantage of his access to the company's information systems to steal data he is not authorized to see. Or he might remove data from the company that he *is* authorized to see (but not to remove).

Unauthorized Data or Program Modification   Another exposure is unauthorized data modification. In this situation, someone changes the value of stored data that they are not entitled to change. Imagine a bank employee increasing her own bank account balance or that of a friend or relative. Or consider an administrative employee in a university changing a student's grade (or, for that matter, the student breaking into the university computer to change his own grade!). In more sophisticated cases a person might manage to change one of a company's programs to modify data now or at a later time.

Malicious Mischief   The field of reference has to be expanded when discussing malicious mischief as a data security issue. To begin with, someone can corrupt or even erase some of a company's data. As with data theft, this can range from a single record in a table to an entire table or database. But there is even more to malicious mischief. Data can also be made unusable or unavailable by damaging the hardware on which it is stored or processed! Thus, in terms of malicious mischief, the hardware as well as the data has to be protected and this is something that we will address.

Methods of Breaching Data Security

Methods of breaching data security fall into several broad categories, Figure 11.1. Some of these require being on a company's premises while others don't.

Unauthorized Computer Access   One method of stealing data is gaining unauthorized access to a company's computer and its data. This can be accomplished in a variety of ways. One is by "hacking" or gaining access from outside the company. Some hackers are software experts who can exploit faults in a company's software. Others use stolen identification names and passwords to enter a computer looking like legitimate users. Indeed, as we suggested earlier, some data thieves actually are legitimate users: company employees who have authorized access to the company's computer system but are intent on stealing data they are authorized to see or breaking into databases for which they do not have access. In all these cases, data is "downloaded" or copied and used illicitly from then on.

Intercepting Data Communications   Intercepting data communications is the computer version of the old concept of "**wiretapping**." While data may be well protected in a company's computers, once it is transmitted outside the company it becomes subject to being stolen during transmission. Some data transmission media are more subject to interception than others. Tapping a simple "twisted-pair" telephone line or a coaxial cable takes skill but is feasible. When data is bounced off satellites it is also

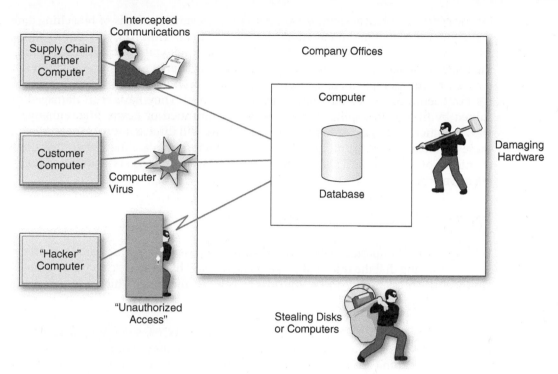

FIGURE 11.1 Data security breaches

subject to interception. On the other hand, the light pulses going fiber-optic transmission lines cannot be tapped.

Stealing Disks or Computers   Can disks or even computers (with data on their hard drives) be stolen? That would have been difficult years ago when all computers were mainframes and all disks were very large. But today, it is very possible. Flash disks and CDs have the potential to be stolen from company offices or, for example, from hotel rooms in which company employees on travel are staying. Laptop computers can be stolen, too, and many have been taken by organized teams of thieves as the laptops go through airport security stations. Even desktop computers have been stolen from company offices.

Computer Viruses   A **computer virus** is a malicious piece of software that is capable of copying itself and "spreading" from computer to computer on diskettes and through telecommunications lines. Strictly speaking, a computer virus doesn't have to cause harm, but most are designed to do just that. Computer viruses have been designed to corrupt data, to scramble system and disk directories that locate files and database tables, and to wipe out entire disks. Some are designed to copy themselves so many times that the sheer number of copies clogs computers and data communications lines. Computer viruses that travel along data communications lines are also called, "worms."

Ransomware Attacks   In ransomware attacks, hackers gain access to an information systems installation and encrypt all of the data in secondary storage, making it unusable. They will only release the encryption key to decrypt the data if a ransom is paid.

Damaging Computer Hardware   All of the previous methods of breaching data security have something in common: they're deliberate. However, this last category, damaging computer hardware, can be deliberate or accidental. Even when accidental, the issue of damaging hardware has always been considered to fall into the computer security realm. Computers and disks can and have been damaged in many ways and it's not been a matter of anything "high-tech," either. They have been damaged or ruined by fires, coffee spills, hurricanes, and disgruntled or newly fired employees with hammers or any other hard objects handy. We will discuss security measures for these problems but, in truth, no security measures for them are foolproof. That's one of the reasons that backup and recovery procedures, as discussed later in this chapter, are so very important.

Types of Data Security Measures

With the critical importance of data and all of the possible threats to data security, it is not surprising that the information systems industry has responded with an array of data security measures to protect the data and the hardware on which it is stored and processed, Figure 11.2.

Physical Security of Company Premises   In the 1950s, some progressive companies in New York and other large cities put their mainframe computers on the ground floor behind big picture windows so that everyone could see how, well, progressive they were. Those days are long gone. Today, suppose your company is located in a skyscraper it shares with other companies. Where do you put your mainframe computer (or your several LAN servers, which are often placed in the same room for

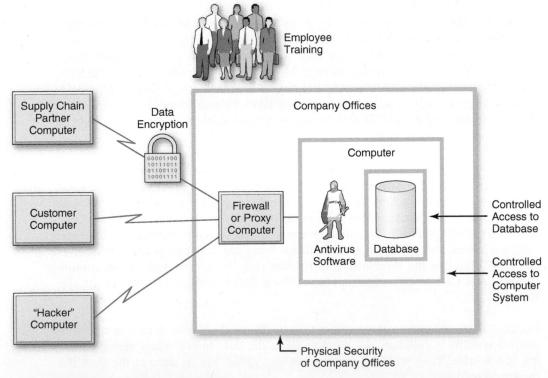

FIGURE 11.2 Data security measures

precisely the security reasons we're talking about?). Here are some rules of thumb, often learned from hard experience.

- Don't put the computer in the basement because of the possibility of floods.
- Don't put the computer on the ground floor because of the possibility of a truck driving into the building, accidentally or on purpose. (I know of a company that had its computer center in a low-rise building adjoining an interstate highway. They eventually put up concrete barriers outside of the building because they were concerned about just this possibility.)
- Don't put the computer above the eighth floor because that's as high as firetruck ladders can reach.
- Don't put the computer on the top floor of the building because it is subject to helicopter landing and attack.
- If you occupy at least three floors of the building, don't put the computer on your topmost floor because its ceiling is another company's floor, and don't put the computer on your bottommost floor because its floor is another company's ceiling.
- Whatever floor you put the computer on, keep it in an interior space away from the windows.

Another issue is personnel access to the computer room. Obviously, such access should be limited to people with a legitimate need to be in the room. Access to the room is controlled by one or a combination of:

- Something they know, such as a secret code to be punched in.
- Something they have, such as a magnetic stripe card, possibly combined with a secret code.
- Some part of them that can be measured or scanned. These **"biometric" systems** can be based on fingerprints, the dimensions and positions of facial features, retinal blood vessel patterns, or voice patterns.

There are also "electric-eye" devices that protect against a second person following right behind an authorized person into the secure room.

Believe it or not, a critical physical security issue involves the company's offices and cubicles. These contain PCs and possibly even LAN servers that contain their own data and provide access to the company's larger computers and to other PCs and servers. Such a simple procedure as locking your office door when you leave it, even for a short period of time, can be critical to data security. Logging off or going into a password-protected mode, especially when doorless cubicles are involved, is an alternative.

Of course, if data is stored in the cloud, then security of the physical premises becomes the cloud vendor's responsibility.

Controlled Access to the Computer System   What if someone has gained access to a company's offices and tries to access the computer system and its database from a PC or terminal from within? For that matter, what if someone tries to access a company's computer by dialing into it or otherwise accessing it through telecommunications lines from the outside? The first line of defense to prevent unauthorized entry to a computer system is to set up a combined ID tag/password necessary to get into the system. ID tags are often publicly known (at least within the company), but passwords must be kept secret, should be changed periodically, and should not be written down, to reduce the risk of someone else learning them. Passwords should not appear on the terminal screen when they are typed in, and the user should create them himself to reduce the chance of forgetting them. There are a variety of rules of thumb for creating passwords. They should not be too long or too short, say 6–12 characters. They should not be obvious, like a person's own name. They should not be so difficult to remember that the person herself has to write them down, since this is a security exposure in itself because someone else could see it.

Controlled Access to the Database   An additional layer of data security controls access to the data itself, once a legitimate user or an outsider has successfully gained entry to the computer system. This layer involves restricting access to specific data so that only specific people can retrieve or modify it. Some systems have such controls in the operating system or in other utility software. Basically, these controls involve a grid that lists users on one axis and data resources, such as databases or tables, on another axis, to indicate which users are authorized to retrieve or modify which data resources. Also, an additional layer of passwords associated with the various data resources can be introduced. Even after a legitimate user has given his system password to gain entry to the computer system, these additional passwords would be needed to gain access to specific data resources.

At the DBMS level, a user should not be able simply to access any data he wants to. Users have to be given explicit authorization to access data. Relational DBMSs have a very flexible and effective way of authorizing users to access data that at the same time serves as an excellent data security feature. We are referring to the combination of the logical view, or simply the "view" concept, and the SQL **GRANT** command. With this combination, users, either individually or in groups (e.g. everyone in the Accounting Department), can be restricted to accessing only certain database tables or only certain data within a database table. Furthermore, their access to this data can be restricted to read-only access or can include the ability to update data or even to insert new or delete existing rows in the table. The GRANT command is supported by several tables in the relational catalog.

How do these two features work in combination? First, using the CREATE VIEW statement, a view of a database table, consisting of a subset of the rows and/or columns, is created and named. This is done with an embedded SELECT statement! (Isn't that clever?) The desired rows and/or columns are identified just as if they were being retrieved, but instead of being retrieved they are given a view name. Then, through the GRANT command, a user or a group of users is given access to *the view*, not to the entire table. In fact, they may not even be aware that there is more to the table than their subset. They simply use the view name in a SELECT statement for data retrieval as if it were a table name.

But how is a user given the authority to access data through the use of a view (or directly using a table name?). That's where the GRANT command comes in. The general form of the GRANT command is:

```
GRANT privileges ON (view or table) TO users [WITH GRANT
OPTION].
```

Thus, the database administrator grants the ability to read, update, insert, or delete (the "privileges") on a view or a table to a person or group of people (the "users"). If the WITH GRANT OPTION is included, this person or group can in turn grant other people access to the same data.

So, to allow a person named Glenn to query the SALESPERSON table by executing SELECT commands on it, you would issue the command:

```
GRANT SELECT ON SALESPERSON TO GLENN;
```

Data Encryption So far, all of the data security techniques we've covered assume that someone is trying to "break into" the company's offices, its computer, or its DBMS. But data can be stolen in other ways, too. One is through wiretapping or otherwise intercepting some of the huge amounts of data that is transmitted today through telecommunications between a company and its trading partners or customers. Another is by stealing a disk or a laptop computer outside a company's offices, for example, in an airport. A solution to this problem is **data encryption**. When data is encrypted, it is changed, bit by bit or character by character, into a form that looks totally garbled. It can and must be reconverted, or decrypted, back to its original form to be of use. Data may be encrypted as it is sent from the company's computer out onto telecommunications lines to protect against its being stolen while in transit. Or the data may actually be stored in an encrypted form on a disk, say on a diskette or on a laptop's hard drive, to protect against data theft if the diskette or laptop is stolen while an employee is traveling. Of course, highly sensitive data can also be encrypted on a company's disks within its mainframe computer systems or servers. This adds a further level of security if someone breaks into the computer system. Why not then simply encrypt all data wherever it may be? The downside to encryption is that it takes time to decrypt the data when you want to use it and to encrypt it when you want to store it, which can become a performance issue.

Data encryption techniques can range from simple to highly complex. The simpler the scheme, the easier it is for a determined person to figure it out and "break the code." The more complex it is, the longer it takes to encrypt and decrypt the data, although this potential performance problem has been at least partially neutralized by the introduction of high-performance hardware encryption chips. Encryption generally involves a data conversion algorithm and a secret key. A very simple alphabetic encryption scheme is as follows. Number the letters of the alphabet from A to Z as 1 to 26. For each letter in the data to be encrypted, add the secret key (some number in this case) to the letter's numeric value and change the letter to the letter represented by the new number. For example, if the key is 4, an A (value 1) becomes an E (since 1+4 = 5 and E is the fifth letter of the alphabet), a B becomes an F, and so on through the alphabet. W wraps around back to the beginning of the alphabet and becomes an A, X becomes a B, and so forth. The recipients must know both the algorithm and the secret key so that they can work the algorithm in reverse and decrypt the data.

Modern encryption techniques typically encrypt data on a bit-by-bit basis using increasingly long keys and very complex algorithms. Consider the data communications case. The two major types of data encryption techniques are symmetric or **"private key"** and asymmetric or **"public key" encryption**. Private key techniques require the same long bit-by-bit key for encrypting and decrypting the data (hence the term "symmetric"). But this has an inherent problem. How do you inform the receiver of the data of the private key without *the key itself* being compromised en route? If the key itself is stolen, the intercepted data can be converted once the conversion algorithm is identified. There are only a few major conversion algorithms; the security is in the key, not in having a great many different conversion algorithms.

The key transmission problem is avoided using algorithms that employ the very clever public-key technique. Here there are two different keys: the public key, which is used for encrypting the data, and the private key, which is used for decrypting it (hence the term "asymmetric"). *The public key is* not *capable of decrypting the data.* Thus, the public key can be published for all the world to see. Anyone wanting to send data does so in complete safety by encrypting the data using the algorithm and the openly published public key. Only the legitimate receiver can decrypt the data because only the legitimate receiver has the private key that can decrypt the data with the published public key. The downside of the public-key technique is that encrypting and decrypting tend to be slower than with the private-key technique, resulting in slower application transactions when the public-key technique is used.

A particularly interesting combination of private-key and public-key encryption is used in **Secure Socket Layer (SSL) technology** on the World Wide Web. Consider a person at home who wants to buy something from an online store on the Web. Her PC and its WWW browser are the "client" and the online store's computer is the "server." Both sides want to conduct the secure transaction using private-key technology because it's faster, but they have the problem that one side must pick a private key and get it to the other side securely. Here are the basic steps in SSL:

1. The client contacts the server.
2. The server sends the client its *public key* for its public-key algorithm (you'll see why in a moment). No one cares if this public key is stolen since it's, well, public!
3. The client, using a random number generator, creates a "session key," *the key for the private key algorithm* with which the secure transaction (the actual online shopping) will be conducted once everything is set up. But, as we've described, the problem now is how the client can securely transmit the session key it generated to the server, since both must have it to use the faster private-key algorithm for the actual shopping.
4. Now, here is the really clever part of the SSL concept. The client is going to send the session key to the server, securely, *using a public-key algorithm and the server's* <u>public key</u>. The client encrypts the session key using the server's public key and transmits the encrypted session key to the server with the public key algorithm. It doesn't matter if someone intercepts this transmission, because the server is the only entity that has the decrypting private key that goes with its public key!
5. Once the session key has been securely transmitted to the server, both the client and the server have it and the secure transaction can proceed using the faster private-key algorithm.

Anti-virus Software   Companies (and individuals!) employ anti-virus software to combat computer viruses. There are two basic methods used by anti-virus software. One is based on virus "**signatures**," portions of the virus code that are considered to be unique to it. Vendors of anti-virus software have identified and continue to identify known computer viruses and maintain an ever-growing, comprehensive list of their signatures. The anti-virus software contains those signatures and on a real-time basis can check all messages and other traffic coming into the computer to see if any known viruses are trying to enter. The software can also, on request, scan disks of all types to check them for viruses. The other anti-virus method is that the software constantly monitors the computer environment to watch for requests or commands for any unusual activity, such as, for example, a command to format a disk, therefore wiping out all the data on it. The software will typically prevent the command from executing and will ask the person operating the computer whether she really wants this command to take place. Only if the operator confirms the request will it take place.

Firewalls   In today's business world, where supply chain partners communicate via computers over networks and customers communicate with companies' Web sites over the Internet, a tremendous amount of data enters and leaves a company's

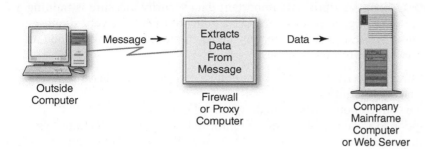

FIGURE 11.3 A firewall protecting a company's computer

computers every day over data communications lines. This, unfortunately, opens the possibility of a malicious person trying to break into a company's computers through these legitimate channels. Whether they are trying to steal, destroy, or otherwise harm the company's data, they must be stopped. Yet, these data communications channels must be kept open for legitimate business with the company's supply chain partners and customers.

One type of protection that companies use to protect against this problem is the "**firewall**." A firewall is software or a combination of hardware and software that protects a company's computer and its data against external attack via data communications lines. There are several types of firewalls. Some that are purely software-based involve checking the network address of the incoming message or components of the content of the message. An interesting firewall that is a combination of hardware and software is the "**proxy server**," shown in Figure 11.3. The idea of the proxy server is that the message coming from an outside computer does not go directly to the company's main computer, say a mainframe computer for the sake of argument. Instead, it goes to a separate computer, the proxy server or firewall computer. The proxy server has software that takes apart the incoming message, extracts only those legitimate pieces of data that are supposed to go to the company's mainframe, reformats the data in a form the company's mainframe is expecting, and finally passes on the reformatted data to the company's main computer. In this way, any extraneous parts of the incoming message, including any malicious code, never reaches the company's main computer.

Your Turn

11.1 Protecting Your Data

What about protecting your own data on your own PC? (If you don't have one, think about someone you know who does.) Think about the data you have stored on your PC's hard drive. Have you stored personal data such as your Social Security Number or your birth date? Have you written personal letters to people and stored them on your hard drive before sending them? How about your bank records? Tax records? Personal medical information?

Question:

What kinds of personal data do you have on your PC? Describe the methods you currently use to protect your PC and its data. If it's a laptop, what precautions do you take when carrying it with you outside your home or dorm? Do you think you should increase the security in and for your PC? If so, how would you go about doing it?

Training Employees   A surprisingly important data security measure is training a company's employees in good security practices, many of which are very simple and yet very important. What should the company tell its employees in terms of good data security practices? Here are a few samples:

- Log off your computer, or at least lock your office door, when you leave your office, even for just a few minutes.
- Don't write your computer password down anywhere.
- Don't respond to any unusual requests for information about the computer system (or anything else!) from anyone over the telephone. (People posing as employees of the company have phoned company personnel and said that they need their password to check out a problem in the computer system. And this trick has worked!)
- Don't leave flash disks or other storage media lying around your office.
- Don't take flash disks or other storage media out of the building.
- Don't assume that a stranger in the building is there legitimately: always check. (People have posed as telephone repairpersons to tap a company's data communications lines.)

Backup and Recovery

The Importance of Backup and Recovery

Regardless of how sophisticated information systems have become, we have to be prepared to handle a variety of events that can affect or even destroy data in a database. Trouble can come from something as simple as a legitimate user entering an incorrect data value or from something as overwhelming as a fire or some other disaster destroying an entire computer center and everything in it. Thus the results can range in consequence from a single inaccurate data value to the destruction of all the installation's databases, with many other possibilities in between. In the information systems business, we have to assume that from time to time something will go wrong with our data and we have to have the tools available to correct or reconstruct it. These operations come under the heading of backup and recovery. In this section, we will take a look at some of the basic ***backup and recovery*** techniques.

Backup Copies and Journals

The fundamental ideas in backup and recovery are fairly straightforward in concept and some have been around for a long time. They begin with two basic but very important tasks: backing up the database and maintaining a journal. First, there is backup. On a regularly scheduled basis, say once per week, a company's databases must be "backed up" or copied. The backup copy must be put in a safe place, away from the original in the computer system. (There have been cases of the copy being kept in the computer room only to have a fire destroy both the original and the copy.) There are several possibilities for storing the backup copy. For example, it may be kept in a fire-proof safe in a nearby company building. Or it may be kept in a bank vault. Often, during the next back-up cycle, the previous backup copy becomes the "grandfather copy" and is sent even farther away to a distant state or city for additional security.

The other basic backup and recovery task is maintaining a disk log or <u>journal</u> of all changes that take place in the data. This includes updates to existing records, insertion of new records, and deletion of existing records. Notice that it does *not* include the recording of simple read operations that *do not change* the stored data in any way. There are two types of database logs. One, which is variously called a "**change log**" or a "**before and after image log**," literally records the value of a piece of data just before it is changed and the value just after it is changed. So, if an employee gets a raise in salary and the salary attribute value of his personnel record is to be changed from 15.00 (dollars per hour) to 17.50, the change log identifies the record by its unique identifier (e.g. its employee number) within its table name, the original salary attribute value of 15.00, and the new salary attribute value of 17.50. The other type of log, generally called a "**transaction log**," keeps a record of the program that changed the data and all of the inputs that the program used. A very important point about both kinds of logs is that a new log is started *immediately after* the data is backed up (i.e. a backup copy of the data is made). You'll see why in a moment.

Now, how are backups and logs used in backup and recovery operations? Actually, it depends on the *reason* for the backup and recovery operation and, yes, there is more than one reason or set of circumstances that require some kind of backup and recovery.

Forward Recovery

First let's consider a calamity that destroys a disk, or an only slightly lesser calamity that destroys a database or a particular database table. The disk or the database or the table has to be recreated and the recovery procedure in this case is called "**forward recovery**" or "**roll-forward** recovery" (the word "roll" in "roll forward" comes from the earlier use of tapes to record the logs). Let's look at this by considering a lost table. To recreate the lost table, you begin by readying the last backup copy of the table that was made and readying the log with all of the changes made to the table *since* the last backup copy was made. The point is that the last backup copy is, well, a copy of the table that was lost, which is what you want, except that it doesn't include the changes to the data that were made *since* the backup copy was made. To fix this, a "recovery program" begins by reading the *first* log entry that was recorded *after* the last backup copy was made. In other words, it looks at the first change that was made to the table right after the backup copy was made. The recovery program updates the backup copy of the table with this log entry. Then, having gone back to the beginning of the log, it continues *rolling forward*, making every update to the backup copy of the table in the same order in which they were originally made to the database table itself. When this process is completed, the lost table has been rebuilt or recovered, Figure 11.4! This process can be performed with either a change log or a transaction log. Using the change log, the "after images" are applied to the backup copy of the database. Using the transaction log, the actual programs that updated the database are rerun. This tends to be a simpler but slower process.

One variation of the forward recovery process when a change log is used is based on the recognition that several changes may have been made to the same piece of data since the last backup copy of the table was made. If that's the case, then only the last of the changes to the particular piece of data, which after all shows the value of this piece of data at the time the table was destroyed, needs to be used in updating the database copy in the roll-forward operation.

If the database environment is a volatile one in which changes are made frequently and it is common for the same piece of data to be updated several times between backup operations, then the roll-forward operation as we have described it may be needlessly inefficient. Instead, it may be worthwhile to sort through the log prior to

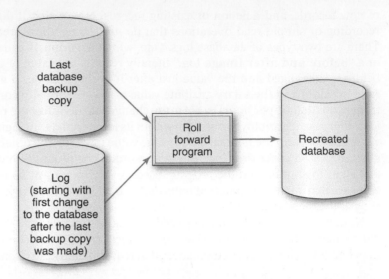

FIGURE 11.4 Forward recovery

the roll-forward operation to find the *last* change made to each piece of data that was updated since the last backup copy was made. Then only those final changes need be applied to the backup copy in the roll-forward operation.

Backward Recovery

Now let's consider a different situation. Suppose that in the midst of normal operation an error is discovered that involves a piece of recently updated data. The cause might be as simple as human error in keying in a value, or as complicated as a program ending abnormally and leaving in the database some, but not all, changes to the database that it was supposed to make. Why not just correct the incorrect data and not make a big deal out of it? Because in the interim, other programs may have read the incorrect data and made use of it, thus compounding the error in other places in the database.

So the discovered error, and in fact all other changes that were made to the database *since* the error was discovered, must be "backed out." The process is called "**backward recovery**" or "**rollback**." Essentially, the idea is to start with the database in its current state (note: backup copies of the database have nothing to do with this procedure) and with the log positioned at its *last* entry. Then a recovery program proceeds *backwards* through the log, resetting each updated data value in the database to its "before" image, until it reaches the point where the error was made. Thus the program "undoes" each transaction in the reverse order (last-in, first-out) from which it was made, Figure 11.5. Once all the data values in the tainted updates are restored to what they were before the data error occurred, the transactions that updated them must be rerun. This can be a manual process or, if a transaction log was maintained as well as a change log, a program can *roll forward* through the transaction log, automatically rerunning all of the transactions from the point at which the data error occurred.

Another note about backward recovery: some systems are capable of automatically initiating a roll-backward operation to undo the changes made to the database by a partially completed and then halted or failed transaction. This is called "**dynamic backout.**" There are situations in which it is helpful to restore the database to the

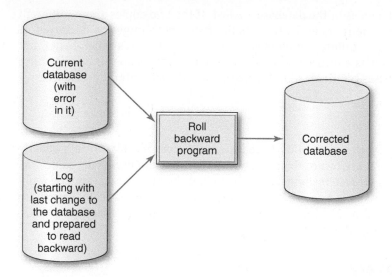

FIGURE 11.5 Backward recovery

point at which there is confidence that all changes to the database up to that point are accurate. Some systems are capable of writing a special record to the log, known as a "**checkpoint**," that specifies this kind of stable state.

Duplicate or "Mirrored" Databases

A backup and recovery technique of a very different nature is known as **duplicate** or **"mirrored" databases**. Two copies of the entire database are maintained and both are updated simultaneously, Figure 11.6. If one is destroyed, the applications that use the database can just keep on running with the duplicate database. This is a relatively expensive proposition, but allows continuous operation in the event of a disk failure, which may justify the cost for some applications. By the way, this arrangement is of no help in the case of erroneous data entry (see backward recovery above) because the erroneous data will be entered in both copies of the database!

The greater the "distance" between the two mirrored copies of the database, the greater the security. If both are on the same disk (not a good idea!) and the disk fails

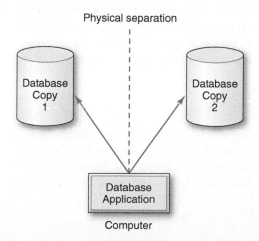

FIGURE 11.6 Mirrored databases

or is destroyed, both copies of the database are lost. If the two copies are on different disks but are in the same room and a fire hits the room, both might be destroyed. If they are on disks in two different buildings in the same city, that's much better, but a natural disaster such as a hurricane could affect both. Thus, some companies have kept duplicate databases hundreds of miles apart to avoid such natural disasters.

The Cloud

The cloud presents another possibility for backup and recovery. First of all, backup and recovery of the data becomes the cloud vendor's responsibility in the same way that data security is their responsibility. Furthermore, if the option of automatic replication of data in the cloud is exercised, the data is, in effect, automatically backed up within the cloud. If a server holding particular data goes down, the same data is available on at least two other servers.

Disaster Recovery

Speaking of natural disasters, the author lived through Hurricane Andrew in Miami, FL, in August, 1992 and learned about disaster recovery first-hand! The information systems of two major companies and a host of smaller ones were knocked out of service by this hurricane. Miami companies in buildings with major roof and window damage actually found fish that the hurricane had lifted out of the ocean and deposited in their computers (I'm not kidding!). They also discovered that when the salt water from the ocean saturated the ceiling tiles in their offices, wet flakes from the tiles fell down onto their computer equipment, ruining some of it. A company that thought that it was keeping its database backup copies in a safe place in another part of the city didn't take into account that the roof of the backup site would not stand up to a major hurricane and lost its backup copies.

Your Turn

11.2 When Disaster Strikes

Disasters can take many forms and can affect individuals as well as businesses. A disaster can take the form of a natural disaster such as a hurricane, earthquake, or tornado, but it can also take the form of fire, theft of your PC or laptop, or even a very damaging computer virus.

Question:

What would be the consequences to you if a disaster struck and you lost all your personal data? What precautions have you taken to back up your important personal data? Do you think you should take further precautions? If so, what might they be?

As its name implies, **disaster recovery** involves rebuilding an entire information system or significant parts of one after a catastrophic natural disaster such as a hurricane, tornado, earthquake, building collapse, or even a major fire. There are several approaches to prepare for such disasters. They tend to be expensive or complex or both, but with today's critical dependence on information systems, companies that want to be careful and prepared have little choice. The possibilities include:

- Maintain totally mirrored systems (not just databases) in different cities.
- Contract with a company that maintains hardware similar to yours so that yours can be up and running again quickly after a disaster. The companies providing these so-called "**hot sites**" make money by contracting their services with many companies, assuming that they will not all suffer a disaster and need the hot site at the same time.
- Maintain space with electrical connections, air conditioning, etc., into which new hardware can be moved if need be. These so-called "**cold sites**" are not nearly as practical as they once were because of the online nature and mission-critical character of today's information systems. They simply take too long to get up and running.
- Make a reciprocal arrangement with another company with hardware similar to yours to aid each other in case one suffers a disaster. Obviously, the two companies should be in different industries and must not be competitors!
- Build a computer center that is relatively disaster proof. After Hurricane Andrew, one of the large affected companies in Miami rebuilt their computer center in a building they started referring to as "the bunker."

Concurrency Control

The Importance of Concurrency Control

Generally speaking, today's application systems, and especially those running within the database environment, assume that many people using these systems will require access to the same data at the same time. Modern hardware and systems software are certainly capable of supporting such shared data access. One very common example of this capability is in airline reservations, where several different reservations clerks, as well as customers on the Web, may have simultaneous requests for seats on the same flight. Another example is an industrial or retail inventory application in which several employees on an assembly line or in an order fulfillment role simultaneously seek to update the same inventory item.

When concurrent access involves only simple retrieval of data, there is no problem. But when concurrent access requires data modification, the two or more users attempting to update the data simultaneously have a rather nasty way of interfering with each other that doesn't happen if they are merely performing data retrievals. This is certainly the case in the airline reservations and inventory examples, since selling seats on flights and using items in inventory require that the number of seats or inventory items left be revised downwards; i.e. many of the database accesses involve updates. The result can be inaccurate data stored in the database!

The Lost Update Problem

Using the airline reservations application as an example, here is what can happen with simultaneous updates, Figure 11.7. And before we begin the example, bear in mind that we are not talking about simultaneous updates only at the "microsecond" level. As you are about to see, the problem can occur when the time spans involved are in seconds or minutes. Suppose that there are 25 seats left on Acme Airlines flight #345 on March

Time	Ms. Brown	Mr. Green
1:45 PM	Reads the record Finds 25 seats left	
1:48 PM		Reads the record Finds 25 seats left
1:52 PM	Deducts 4 seats and writes updated record indicating 21 seats left	
1:56 PM		Deducts 6 seats and writes updated record indicating 19 seats left

But at this point the record should show 15 seats left!

FIGURE 11.7 The lost update problem

12. One day, at 1:45 PM, a reservations clerk, Ms. Brown, is phoned by a customer who is considering booking four seats on that particular flight. Brown retrieves the record for the flight from the database, notes that there are 25 seats available, and begins to discuss the price and other details with her customer. At 1:48 PM, another reservations clerk, Mr. Green receives a call from another customer with a larger family who is considering booking six seats on the very same flight. Green retrieves the record for the flight from the database and notes that there are 25 seats available. At 1:52 PM, Brown's customer decides to go ahead and book four seats on the flight. Brown completes the transaction and four seats are deducted from the number of seats available on the flight, updating the database record to show that there are now 21 seats available. Then, at 1:56 PM, Green's customer decides to book six seats on the flight. Green completes this transaction and six seats are deducted from the number of seats (25) that Green thought were available on the flight, leaving the database showing that 19 seats are now available.

So, the record for flight #345 on March 12 now shows that there are 19 seats available. But shouldn't it show only 15, since a total of 10 seats were sold? Yes, but the point is that neither of the clerks knew that the other was in the process of selling seats on the flight at the same time that the other was. Both Brown and Green started off knowing that there were 25 seats left. When Brown deducted four seats, for a couple of minutes the record showed that there were 21 seats left. But then when Green deducted his six, he was deducting them from the original 25 seats that he saw when he originally retrieved the record from the database, not from the 21 seats that were left after Brown's sale.

By the way, you might question the *likelihood* of two clerks going after the same record simultaneously in a large airline reservations system. Have you ever tried to book a reservation on a flight from New York to Miami for Christmas week in the week before Christmas week? The likelihood of this kind of conflict is very real in the airline reservations application and in countless other applications of every type imaginable.

Locks and Deadlock

The usual solution to this problem is to introduce what are known as software "**locks**." When a user begins an update operation on a piece of data, the DBMS locks that data. Any attempt to begin another update operation on that same piece of data will be blocked or "locked out" until the first update operation is completed and its lock on the data is released. This effectively prevents the lost-update problem. The level or "granularity" of lockout can vary. Lockout at a high level, for instance at the level of an entire table, unfortunately prevents much more than that one particular piece of data from being modified while the update operation is going on, but is a low-overhead solution since only one lock is needed for the entire table. Lockout at a lower level, the record level for instance, doesn't prevent access or updates to the rest of the table, but is a comparatively high-overhead solution because every record must have a lock that can be set.

Unfortunately, as so often happens, the introduction of this beneficial device itself causes other problems that did not previously exist. Follow the next scenario, Figure 11.8: consider an inventory situation in which clerks must find out if sufficient quantities of *each of two* parts, say nuts and bolts, are available to satisfy an order. If there are enough parts, then the clerks want to take the parts from inventory and update the quantity remaining values in the database. Each clerk can fill the order only if enough of both parts are available. Each clerk must access and lock the record for one of the two parts while accessing the record for the other part. Proceeding with this scenario, suppose two clerks, Mr. White and Ms. Black, each request a quantity of nuts and bolts. White happens to list the nuts before the bolts in his query. At 10:15 AM, he accesses and locks the record for nuts. Ms. Black happens to list the bolts before the nuts in her query. At 10:16 AM, she accesses and locks the record for bolts. Then, at 10:17 AM, White tries to access the record for bolts but finds it locked by Black. And 10:18 AM, Black tries to access the record for nuts but finds it locked by White. Both queries then wait endlessly for each other to release what they each need to proceed. This is called "**deadlock**" or "the deadly embrace." It actually bears a close relationship to the "gridlock" traffic problem that major cities worry about during rush hour.

Does the prospect of deadlock mean that locks should not be used? No, because there are two sorts of techniques for handling deadlock: deadlock prevention and deadlock detection. Outright deadlock prevention sounds desirable but turns out to be difficult. Basically, a transaction would have to lock all the data it will need, assuming it can even figure this out at the beginning of the transaction (often the value of one piece of data that a program retrieves determines what other data it needs). If the transaction finds that some of the data it will need is unavailable because another transaction has it locked, all it can do is release whatever data it has already locked and start all over again.

Time	Mr. White	Ms. Black
10:15 A.M.	Gets and locks the record for nuts	
10:16 A.M.		Gets and locks the record for bolts
10:17 A.M.	Tries to get (and lock) the record for bolts but finds it locked by Ms. Black	
10:18 A.M.		Tries to get (and lock) the record for nuts but finds it locked by Mr. White

DEADLOCK!

FIGURE 11.8 Deadlock

So the usual way to handle deadlock is to let it occur, detect it when it does, and then abort one of the deadlocked transactions, allowing the other to finish. The one that was backed out can then be run again. One way to detect deadlock is through a time-out, meaning that a query has been waiting for so long that the assumption is it must be deadlocked. Another way to detect deadlock is by maintaining a **resource usage matrix** that dynamically keeps track of which transactions or users are waiting for which pieces of data. Software can continuously monitor this matrix and determine when deadlock has occurred.

Versioning

There is another way to deal with concurrent updates, known as "**versioning**," that does not involve locks at all. Basically, each transaction is given a copy or "version" of the data it needs for an update operation, regardless of whether any other transaction is using the same data for an update operation at the same time. Each transaction records its result in its own copy of the data. Then each transaction tries to update the actual database with its result. At that point, monitoring software checks for conflicts between two or more transactions that are trying to update the same data at the same time. If it finds a conflict, it allows one of the transactions to update the database and makes the other(s) start over again. The hope is that conflicts will not occur often, allowing the applications to proceed along more efficiently without the need for locks.

Summary

There are three major technological and methodological subfields of database management that involve the protection of data: data security, backup and recovery, and concurrency control. Data security issues include types of data security breaches, methods of breaching data security, and types of data security measures, such as anti-virus software, firewalls, data encryption, and employee training, among others.

Backup and recovery includes creating backup copies of data and maintaining journals, procedures such as forward recovery, backward recovery, arrangements such as duplicate or "mirrored" databases, and the separate but related subfield of disaster recovery. Concurrency control includes issues such as the lost-update problem and deadlock and fixes that include locks and versioning.

Key Terms

Anti-virus software	**Data encryption**	**Hot site**	**Rollback**
Backup and recovery	**Data security**	**Locks**	**Roll forward**
Backward recovery	**Database control issues**	**Lost update problem**	**Secure Socket Layer (SSL)**
Before and after image log	**Deadlock**	**Mirrored database**	**technology**
Biometric systems	**Disaster recovery**	**Password**	**Signature**
Change log	**Duplicate database**	**Physical security**	**Transaction log**
Checkpoint	**Dynamic backout**	**Private key encryption**	**Versioning**
Cold site	**Firewall**	**Proxy server**	**Wiretapping**
Computer virus	**Forward recovery**	**Public key encryption**	
Concurrency control	**GRANT**	**Resource usage matrix**	

Questions

1. Explain why data security is important.

2. Compare unauthorized data access with unauthorized data modification. Which do you think is the more serious issue? Explain.

3. Name and briefly describe three methods of breaching data security. Which do you think is potentially the most serious? Explain.

4. How does the physical security of company premises affect data security?

5. How do magnetic stripe cards and fingerprints compare in terms of physical security protection?

6. Describe the rules for creating a good password.

7. Explain how the combination of views and the SQL GRANT command limits access to a relational database.

8. What is data encryption and why is it important to data security?

9. In your own words, describe how Secure Socket Layer (SSL) technology works.

10. In your own words, describe how a proxy server firewall works.

11. Explain why backup and recovery is important.

12. What is a journal or log? How is one created?

13. Describe the two different problems that forward recovery and backward recovery are designed to handle. Do mirrored databases address one of these two problems or yet a third one? Explain.

14. In your own words, describe how forward recovery works.

15. In your own words, describe how backward recovery works.

16. What is disaster recovery? Can the techniques for backup and recovery be used for disaster recovery?

17. Explain why concurrency control is important.

18. What is the lost-update problem?

19. What are locks and how are they used to prevent the lost-update problem?

20. What is deadlock and how can it occur?

Exercises

1. A large bank has a headquarters location plus several branches in each city in a particular region of the country. As transactions are conducted at each branch, they are processed online against a relational database at headquarters. You have been hired as the bank's Director of Data Security. Design a comprehensive set of data security measures to protect the bank's data.

2. The bank in Exercise 1, which it totally dependent on its relational database, must be able to keep running in the event of the failure of any one table on one disk drive, in the event of a major disaster to its headquarters computer, or in the event of any catastrophe between these two extremes. Describe the range of techniques and technologies that you would implement to enable the bank to recover from this wide range of failures.

3. The Tasty Seafood Restaurant is a large restaurant that specializes in fresh fish and seafood. Because its reputation for freshness is important to Tasty, it brings in a certain amount of each type of fish daily and, while trying to satisfy all of its customers, would rather run out of a type of fish than carry it over to the next day. After taking a table's order, a waiter enters the order into a touch-screen terminal that is connected to a computer in the kitchen. The order is sent from the touch-screen terminal to the computer only after all of it has been entered.

   At 8:00 PM there are 10 servings of salmon, 15 servings of flounder, and eight orders of trout left in the kitchen. At 8:03 PM, waiter Frank starts entering an order that includes five servings of salmon, six of flounder, and four of trout. At the same time, on another touch-screen terminal, waitress Mary starts entering an order that includes one serving of salmon, three of flounder, and two of trout. At 8:05 PM, before the other two have finished entering their orders, waitress Tina starts entering an order that includes six servings of salmon, one of flounder, and five of trout. Frank finishes entering his order at 8:06 PM, Mary finishes at 8:07 PM, and Tina finishes at 8:09 PM.

   a. What would the result of all of this be in the absence of locks?

   b. What would the result be with a locking mechanism in place?

   c. What would happen if versioning was in use?

4. Construct examples of the lost update problem, the use of locks, deadlock, and versioning for the case of a joint bank account (i.e. two people with access to the same bank account).

Minicases

1. Happy Cruise Lines is headquartered in New York and in addition has regional offices in the cruise port cities of Miami, Houston, and Los Angeles. New York has a large server and several LANs. The other three sites each have a single LAN with a smaller server. The company's four offices communicate with each other via land-based telecommunications lines. The company's ships, each of which has a server on board, communicate with the New York headquarters via satellite. Also located in New York is the company's Web site, through which passengers and travel agents can book cruises.

   a. Devise a data security strategy for Happy Cruise Lines that incorporates appropriate data security measures.

   b. Happy Cruise Line's main relational database (see Minicase 5.1), located in New York, is considered critical to the company's functioning. It must be kept up and running as consistently as possible and it must be quickly recoverable if something goes wrong. Devise backup and recovery and disaster recovery strategies for the company.

   c. A particularly popular Christmas-week cruise is booking up fast. There are only a few cabins left and the company wants to be careful to not "overbook" the cruise. With customers, travel agents, and the company's own reservations agents all accessing the database at the same time, devise a strategy that will avoid overbooking.

2. The Super Baseball League maintains a substantially decentralized IS organization with the focus on the individual teams. Each team has a server with a LAN at its stadium or offices near the stadium. The League has a server with a LAN at its Chicago headquarters. The league and each of the teams maintain a Web site at their locations. People can get general information about the league at the league's Web site; they can get information about the individual teams as well as buy game tickets through each team's Web site. Data collected at the team locations, such as player statistics updates and game attendance figures, is uploaded nightly to the server at league headquarters via telephone lines.

   a. Devise a data security strategy for the Super Baseball League, incorporating appropriate data security measures.

   b. The Super Baseball League's main relational database (see Minicase 5.2), located at its headquarters in Chicago, is for the most part a repository of data collected from the teams. The league wants to keep the headquarters database up and running, but it is more important to keep the individual team databases in their stadiums or offices up and running with as little downtime as possible. Devise backup and recovery and disaster recovery strategies for the Super Baseball League.

   c. Fans can order or buy tickets from the individual teams over the telephone, through the teams' Web sites, or in person at the teams' box offices. All of this activity takes place simultaneously. Devise a strategy that will avoid selling a particular seat for a particular game more than once.

The Data Warehouse

Traditionally, most data was created to support applications that involved current corporate operations: accounting, inventory management, personnel management, and so forth. As people began to understand to power of information systems and their use became more pervasive, other options regarding data began to develop. For example, companies began to perform sales trend analyses that required historic sales data. The idea was to predict future sales and inventory requirements based on past sales history. Applications such as this led to the realization that there is a great deal of value in historic data, and that it would be worthwhile to organize it on a very broad basis. This is the data warehouse.

OBJECTIVES

Compare the data needs of transaction processing systems with those of decision support systems.

Describe the data warehouse concept and list its main features.

Compare the enterprise data warehouse with the data mart.

Design a data warehouse.

Build a data warehouse, including the steps of data extraction, data cleaning, data transformation, and data loading.

Describe how to use a data warehouse with online analytic processing and data mining.

List the types of expertise needed to administer a data warehouse.

List the challenges in data warehousing.

Introduction

Generally, when we think about information systems, we think about what are known as operational or **"transaction processing systems" (TPS)**. These are the everyday application systems that support banking and insurance operations, manage the parts inventory on manufacturing assembly lines, keep track of airline and hotel reservations, support Web-based sales, and so on. These are the kinds of application systems that most people quickly associate with the information systems field and, indeed, these are the kinds of application systems that we have used as examples in this book. The databases that support these application systems must have several things in common, which we ordinarily take for granted. They must have up-to-the-moment current data, they must be capable of providing direct access and very rapid response, and they must be designed for sharing by large numbers of users.

But the business world has other needs of a very different nature. These needs generally involve management decision making and typically require analyzing data that has been accumulated over some period of time. They often don't even require the latest, up-to-the-second data! An example occurs in the retail store business, when management has to decide how much stock of particular items they should carry in their stores during the October–December period this year. Management is going to want to check the sales volume for those items during the same three-month period in each of the last five years. If airline management is considering adding additional flights between two cities (or dropping existing flights), they are going to want to analyze lots of accumulated data about the volume of passenger traffic in their existing flights between those two cities. If a company is considering expanding its operations into a new geographical region, management will want to study the demographics of the region's population and the amount of competition it will have from other companies, very possibly using data that it doesn't currently have but must acquire from outside sources.

In response to such management decision-making needs, there is another class of application systems, known as **"decision support systems" (DSS)**, that are specifically designed to aid managers in these tasks. The issue for us in this book about database management is: what kind of database is needed to support a DSS? In the past, files were developed to support individual applications that we would now classify as DSS applications. For example, the five-year sales trend analysis for retail stores described above has been a fairly standard application for a long time and was always supported by files developed for it alone. But, as DSS activity has mushroomed, along with the rest of information systems, having separate files for each DSS application is wasteful, expensive, and inefficient, for several reasons:

- Different DSS applications often need the same data, causing duplicate files to be created for each application. As with any set of redundant files, they are wasteful of storage space and update time, and they create the potential for data integrity problems (although, as we will see a little later, data redundancy in dealing with largely historical data is not as great a concern as it is with transactional data).

- While particular files support particular DSS applications, they tend to be inflexible and do not support closely related applications that require slightly different data.
- Individual files tied to specific DSS applications do nothing to encourage other people and groups in the company to use the company's accumulated data to gain a competitive advantage over the competition.
- Even if someone in the company is aware of existing DSS application data that they could use to their own advantage (really, to the company's advantage), getting access to it can be difficult because it is "owned" by the application for which it was created.

When we talked about the advantages of data sharing earlier in this book, the emphasis was on data in transactional systems. But the factors listed above regarding data for decision support systems, which in their own way largely parallel the arguments for shared transactional databases, inevitably led to the concept of broad-based, shared databases for decision support. These DSS databases have come to be known as "**data warehouses**." In this chapter, we will discuss the nature, design, and implementation of data warehouses. Later in the chapter we will briefly touch upon some of their key uses.

The Data Warehouse Concept

Informally, a data warehouse is a broad-based, shared database for management decision making that contains data gathered over time. Imagine that at the end of every week or month, you take all the company's sales data for that period and you append it to (add it to the end of) all of the accumulated sales data that is already in the data warehouse. Keep on doing this and eventually, you will have several years of company sales data that you can search and query and perform all sorts of calculations on.

More formally and in more detail, the classic definition of a data warehouse is that it is "a **subject oriented**, **integrated**, **non-volatile**, and **time variant** collection of data in support of management's decisions."[1] In addition, the data in the warehouse must be high quality, may be aggregated, is often denormalized, and is not necessarily absolutely current, Figure 12.1. Let's take a look at each of these data warehouse characteristics.

- The data is subject oriented
- The data is integrated
- The data is non-volatile
- The data is time variant
- The data must be high quality
- The data may be aggregated
- The data is often denormalized
- The data is not necessarily absolutely current

FIGURE 12.1 Characteristics of data warehouse data

---

[1] Inmon, W.H., *Building the Data Warehouse*, 2nd ed., John Wiley & Sons, Inc., Hoboken, NJ, 1996.

The Data Is Subject Oriented

The data in transactional databases tends to be organized according to the company's TPS applications. In a bank, this might mean the applications that handle the processing of accounts; in a manufacturing company it might include the applications that communicate with suppliers to maintain the necessary raw materials and parts on the assembly line; in an airline it might involve the applications that support the reservations process. Data warehouses are organized around "subjects," really the major entities of concern in the business environment. Thus, subjects may include sales, customers, orders, claims, accounts, employees, and other entities that are central to the particular company's business.

The Data Is Integrated

Data about each of the subjects in the data warehouse is typically collected from several of the company's transactional databases, each of which supports one or more applications having something to do with the particular subject. Some of the data, such as additional demographic data about the company's customers, may be acquired from outside sources. All of the data about a subject must be organized or "integrated" in such a way as to provide a unified overall picture of all the important details about the subject over time. Furthermore, while being integrated, the data may have to be "transformed." For example, one application's database tables may measure the company's finished products in centimeters while another may measure them in inches. One may identify countries of the world by name while another may identify them by a numeric code. One may store customer numbers as an integer field while another may store them as a character field. In all of these and in a wide variety of other such cases, the data from these disparate application databases must be transformed into common measurements, codes, data types, and so forth, as they are integrated into the data warehouse.

The Data Is Non-Volatile

Transactional data is normally updated on a regular, even frequent basis. Bank balances, raw materials inventories, airline reservations data are all updated as the balances, inventories, and number of seats remaining respectively change in the normal course of daily business. We describe this data as "volatile," subject to constant change. The data in the data warehouse is non-volatile. Once data is added to the data warehouse, it doesn't change. The sales data for October 2010 is whatever it was. It was totaled up, added to the data warehouse at the end of October 2010, and that's that. It will never change. Changing it would be like going back and rewriting history. The only way in which the data in the data warehouse is updated is when data for the latest time period, the time period just ended, is appended to the existing data.

The Data Is Time Variant

Most transactional data is, simply, "current." A bank balance, an amount of raw materials inventory, the number of seats left on a flight are all the current, up-to-the-moment figures. If someone wants to make a withdrawal from his bank account, the bank doesn't care what the balance was 10 days ago or 10 hours ago. The bank wants to know what the *current* balance is. There is no need to associate a date or time with the bank balance; in effect, the data's date and time is always *now*. (To be sure, *some* transactional data must include timestamps. A health insurance company may keep six months of claim data online and such data clearly requires timestamps.) On the other hand, data warehouse data, with its historical nature, always includes some kind of a timestamp. If we are storing sales data on a weekly or monthly basis and we have accumulated 10 years of such **historic data**, each weekly or monthly sales figure obviously must be accompanied by a timestamp indicating the week or month (and year!) that it represents.

The Data Must Be High Quality

Transactional data can actually be somewhat forgiving of at least certain kinds of errors. In the bank record example, the account balance must be accurate but if there is, say, a one-letter misspelling of the street name in the account holder's street address, that probably will not make a difference. It will not affect the account balance and the post office will probably still deliver the account statements to the right house. But what if the customer's street address is actually spelled correctly in other transactional files? Consider a section of a data warehouse in which the subject is "customer." It is crucial to establish an accurate set of customers for the data warehouse data to be of any use. But with the address misspelling in one transactional file, when the data from that file is integrated with the data from the other transactional files, there will be some difficulty in reconciling whether the two different addresses are the same and both represent one customer, or whether they actually represent two different customers. This must be investigated and a decision made on whether the records in the different files represent one customer or two different customers. It is in this sense that the data in the data warehouse must be of higher quality than the data in the transactional files.

The Data May Be Aggregated

When the data is copied and integrated from the transactional files into the data warehouse, it is often aggregated or summarized, for at least three reasons. One is that the type of data that management requires for decision making is generally summarized data. When trying to decide how much stock to order for a store for next December based on the sales data from the last five Decembers, the monthly sales figures are obviously useful but the individual daily sales figures during those last five Decembers probably don't matter much. The second reason for having **aggregated data** in the data warehouse is that the sheer volume of all of the historical detail data would often make the data warehouse unacceptably huge (they tend to be large as it is!). And the third reason is that if the detail data were stored in the data warehouse, the amount of time needed to summarize the data for management every time a query was posed would often be unacceptable. Having said all that, the decision support environment is so broad that some situations within it *do* call for detail data and, indeed, some data warehouses do contain at least some detail data.

The Data Is Often Denormalized

One of the fundamental truths about database we have already encountered is that data redundancy improves the performance of read-only queries but takes up more disk space, requires more time to update, and introduces possible data integrity problems when the data has to be updated. But in the case of the data warehouse, we have already established that the data is non-volatile. The *existing* data in the data warehouse never has to be updated. That makes the data warehouse a horse (or a database) of a different color! If the company is willing to tolerate the substantial additional space taken up by the redundant data, it can gain the advantage of the improved query performance that redundancy provides without paying the penalties of increased update time and potential data integrity problems because the existing data is historical and never has to be updated!

The Data Is Not Necessarily Absolutely Current

This is really a consequence of the kind of typical time schedule for loading new data into the data warehouse and was implied in "The Data is Time Variant" item above. Say that you load the week-just-ended sales data into the data warehouse every Friday. The following Wednesday, a manager queries the data warehouse for help in making a decision. The data in the data warehouse is not "current" in the sense that sales data from last Saturday through today, Wednesday, is not included in the data warehouse. The question is, does this matter? The answer is, probably not! For example, the manager may have been performing a five-year sales trend analysis. When you're looking at the last five years of data, including or omitting the last five days of data will probably not make a difference.

Types of Data Warehouses

Thus far, we have been using the term "data warehouse" in a generic sense. But, while there are some further variations and refinements, there are basically two kinds of data warehouses. One is called an **enterprise data warehouse** (EDW), the other is called a **data mart** (DM), Figure 12.2. They are distinguished by two factors: their size and the portion of the company that they service (which tend to go hand in hand), and the manner in which they are created and new data is appended (which are also related).

The Enterprise Data Warehouse (EDW)

The enterprise data warehouse is a large-scale data warehouse that incorporates the data of an entire company or of a major division, site, or activity of a company. Both Smith & Nephew and Hilton Hotels employ such large-scale data warehouses. Depending on its nature, the data in the EDW is drawn from a variety of the company's transactional databases as well as from externally acquired data, requiring a major data integration effort. In data warehouse terminology, a full-scale EDW is built around several different subjects. The large mass of integrated data in the EDW is designed to support a wide variety of DSS applications and to serve as a data resource with which company managers can explore new ways of using the company's data to its advantage. Many EDWs restrict the degree of denormalization because of the sheer volumes of data that large-scale denormalization would produce.

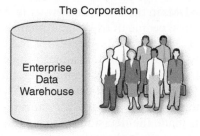

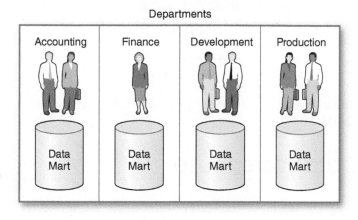

FIGURE 12.2 The enterprise data warehouse and data marts

The Data Mart (DM)

A data mart is a small-scale data warehouse that is designed to support a small part of an organization, say a department or a related group of departments. As we saw, Hilton Hotels copies data from its data warehouse into a data mart for marketing query purposes. A company will often have several DMs. DMs are based on a limited number of subjects (possibly one) and are constructed from a limited number of transactional databases. They focus on the business of a department or group of departments and thus tend to support a limited number and scope of DSS applications. Because of the DM's smaller initial size, there is more freedom to denormalize the data. Managerially, the department manager may feel that she has more control with a local DM and a greater ability to customize it to the department's needs.

Which to Choose: The EDW, the DM, or Both?

Should a company have an EDW, multiple DMs, or both? This is the kind of decision that might result from careful planning, or it might simply evolve as a matter of management style or even just happenstance. Certainly, there are companies that have very deliberately and with careful planning decided to invest in developing an EDW. There are also companies that have made a conscious decision to develop a series of DMs instead of an EDW. In other situations, there was no careful planning, at all. There have been situations in managerially decentralized companies in which individual managers decided to develop DMs in their own departments. At times, DMs have evolved from the interests of technical people in user departments.

In companies that have both an EDW and DMs, there are the questions of "Which came first?" and "Were they developed independently or derived from each other?" This can go either way. In regard to data warehousing, the term, "top-down development" implies that the EDW was created first and then later data was extracted from an EDW to create one or more DMs, initially and on an ongoing basis. Assuming that the company has made the decision to invest in an EDW, this can make a great deal of sense. For example, once the data has been scrutinized and its quality improved (see "data cleaning" below) as it was entered into the EDW, downloading portions of it to DMs retains the high quality without putting the burden for this effort on the department developing the DM. Development in the other direction is possible, too. A company that has deliberately or as a matter of circumstance developed a series of independent DMs may decide, in a "bottom-up development" fashion, to build an EDW out of the existing DMs. Clearly, this would have to involve a round of integration and transformation beyond those that took place in creating the individual DMs.

Designing a Data Warehouse

Introduction

As data warehousing has become a broad topic with many variations in use, it comes as no surprise that there are a variety of ways to design data warehouses. Two of the characteristics of data warehouses are central to any such design: the subject orientation and the historic nature of the data. That is, the data warehouse (or each major part of the data warehouse) will be built around a subject and have a temporal (time) component to it. Data warehouses are often called **multidimensional databases** because each occurrence of the subject is referenced by an occurrence of each of several **dimensions** or characteristics of the subject, one of which is time. For example, in a hospital patient tracking and billing system, the subject might be charges and dimensions might include patient, date, procedure, and doctor. When there are just two dimensions, for example, the charges for a particular patient on a particular date, they can easily be visualized on a flat piece of paper, Figure 12.3. When there are three dimensions, for example, the charges for a particular procedure performed on a particular patient on a particular date, they can be represented as a cube and still drawn on paper, Figure 12.4. When there are four (or more) dimensions, say the charges for a particular procedure ordered by a particular doctor performed on a particular patient on a particular date, it takes some imagination (although there are techniques for combining dimensions that bring the visual representation back down to two or three dimensions). There are data warehouse products on the market that have special-purpose data structures to store such multidimensional data. But there is also much interest in storing such data in relational databases. A way to store multidimensional data in a relational database structure is with a model known as the **star schema**. The name comes from the visual design in which the subject is in the middle and the dimensions radiate outward like the rays of a star. As noted earlier, Smith & Nephew employs the star schema design for its data warehouse, as does Hilton Hotels for at least part of its data warehouse environment.

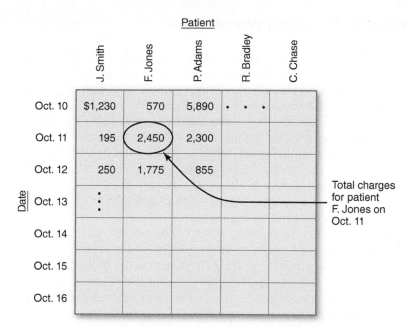

FIGURE 12.3 Hospital patient tracking and billing system data with two dimensions

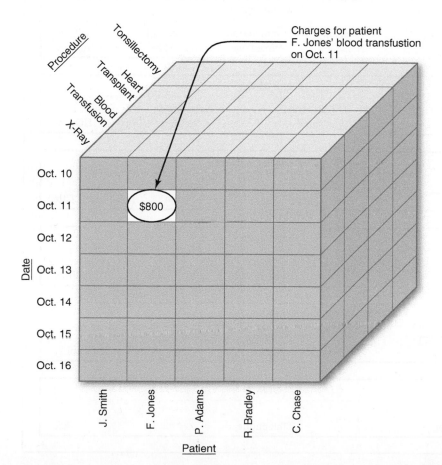

FIGURE 12.4 Hospital patient tracking and billing system data with three dimensions

General Hardware Co. Data Warehouse

Figure 12.5 repeats the General Hardware relational database and Figure 12.6 shows a star schema for the General Hardware Co., with SALE as the subject. Star schemas have a "fact table," which represents the data warehouse "subject," and several "dimension tables." In Figure 12.6, SALE is the fact table and SALESPERSON, PRODUCT, and TIME PERIOD are the dimension tables. The dimension tables will let the data in the fact table be studied from many different points of view. Notice that there is a one-to-many relationship between each dimension table entity and the fact table entity. Furthermore, the "*one* side" of the relationship is always the dimension table and the "*many* side" of the relationship is always the fact table. For a particular salesperson there are many sales records, but each sales record is associated with only one salesperson. The same is true of products and time periods.

To begin to understand this concept and see it come to life, refer back to the SALES table in Figure 12.5, in which General Hardware keeps track of how many units of each product each salesperson has sold in *the most recent* time period, say in the last week. But what if we want to record and keep track of the sales for the most recent week, and the week before that, and the week before that, and so on going back perhaps 5 or 10 years? That is a description of a data warehouse. The SALE table in the star schema

SALESPERSON				
Salesperson Number	Salesperson Name	Commission Percentage	Year of Hire	Office Number

CUSTOMER			
Customer Number	Customer Name	Salesperson Number	HQ City

CUSTOMER EMPLOYEE			
Customer Number	Employee Number	Employee Name	Title

PRODUCT		
Product Number	Product Name	Unit Price

SALES		
Salesperson Number	Product Number	Quantity

OFFICE		
Office Number	Telephone	Size

FIGURE 12.5 The General Hardware Company relational database

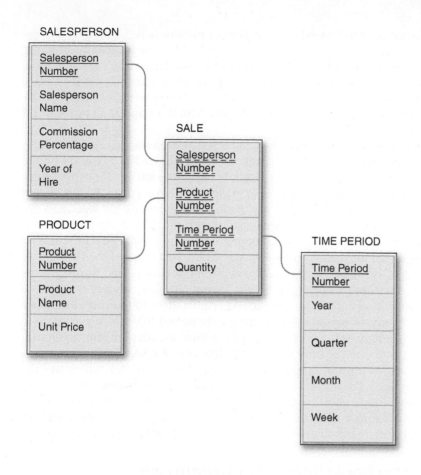

SALESPERSON

| Salesperson Number |
| Salesperson Name |
| Commission Percentage |
| Year of Hire |

SALE

| Salesperson Number |
| Product Number |
| Time Period Number |
| Quantity |

PRODUCT

| Product Number |
| Product Name |
| Unit Price |

TIME PERIOD

| Time Period Number |
| Year |
| Quarter |
| Month |
| Week |

FIGURE 12.6 General Hardware Company data warehouse star schema design

of Figure 12.6 also reflects General Hardware's sales by salesperson and product but with a new element added: time. This table records the quantity of each product that each salesperson sold in each time period stored.

The SALE table in Figure 12.6 has to have a primary key, like any relational table. As shown in the figure, its primary key is the combination of the Salesperson Number, Product Number, and Time Period Number attributes. But each of those attributes also serves as a foreign key. Each one leads to one of the dimension tables, as shown in Figure 12.6. Some historic data can be obtained from the fact table alone. Using the SALE table, alone, for example, we could find the total number of units of a particular product that a particular salesperson has sold for as long as the historical sales records have been kept, assuming we know both the product's product number and the salesperson's salesperson number. We would simply add the Quantity values in all of the SALE records for that salesperson and product. But the dimension tables provide, well, a whole new dimension! For example, focusing in on the TIME PERIOD's Year attribute and taking advantage of this table's foreign key connection to the SALE table, we could refine the search to find the total number of units of a particular product that a particular salesperson sold in a particular single year or in a particular range of years. Or, focusing on the PRODUCT table's Unit Price attribute and the TIME PERIOD table's Year attribute, we could find the total number of units of expensive (unit price greater than some amount) products that each salesperson sold in a particular year. To make this even more concrete, suppose that we want to decide which of our salespersons who currently are compensated at the 10% commission level should receive an award based on their sales of expensive products over the last three years. We could sum the quantity values of the SALE table records by grouping them based on an attribute value of 10 in the Commission Percentage attribute of the SALESPERSON table, an attribute value greater than 50 (dollars) in the Unit Price attribute of the PRODUCT table, and a Year attribute representing each of the last three years in the TIME PERIOD table. The different combinations and possibilities are almost endless.

Figure 12.7 shows some sample data for General Hardware's star schema data warehouse. The fact table, SALE, is on the left and the three dimension tables are on the right. The rows shown in the SALE table are numbered on the left just for convenience in discussion. Look at the TIME PERIOD table in Figure 12.7. First of all, it is clear from the TIME PERIOD table that a decision was made to store data by the week and not by any smaller unit, such as the day. In this case, even if the data in the transactional database is being accumulated daily, it will be aggregated into weekly data in the data warehouse. Notice that the data warehouse began in the first week of the first month of the first quarter of 1997 and that this week was given the Time Period Number value of 001. The week after that was given the Time Period Number value of 002, and so on to the latest week stored. Now, look at the SALE table. Row 10 indicates that salesperson 137 sold 59 units of product 24013 during time period 103, which according to the TIME PERIOD table was the second week of the third month of the fourth quarter of 1998 (i.e. the second week of December, 1998). Row 17 of the SALE table shows that salesperson 204 sold 44 units of product 16386 during time period 331, which was the third week of May, 2003. Overall, as you look at the SALE table from row 1 down to row 20, you can see the historic nature of the data and the steady, forward time progression as the Time Period Number attribute starts with time period 001 in the first couple of records and steadily increases to time period 331 in the last batch of records.

Good Reading Bookstores Data Warehouse

Does Good Reading Bookstores need a data warehouse? Actually, this is a very good question, the answer to which is going to demonstrate a couple of important points about data warehouses. At first glance, the answer to the question seems to be: maybe not! After all, the sales data in Good Reading's transactional database *already carries a date attribute*, as shown in the SALE table of Figure 5.16. Thus, it looks like Good Reading's transactional database is already historical! But Good Reading does need a data warehouse for two reasons. One is that, while Good Reading's transactional database performs acceptably with perhaps the last couple of months of data in it, its performance would become unacceptable if we tried to keep 10 years of data in it. The other reason is that the kinds of management decision making that require long-term historical sales data do not require daily data. Data aggregated to the week level is just fine for Good Reading's decision making purposes and storing the data on a weekly basis saves a lot of time over retrieving and adding up much more data to answer every query on data stored at the day level.

Figure 12.8 shows the Good Reading Bookstores data warehouse star schema design. The fact table is SALE and each of its records indicates how many of a particular book a particular customer bought in a particular week (here again week is the lowest-level time period) and the price that the customer paid per book. For this to make sense, there must be a company rule that the price of a book cannot change in the middle of a week, since each SALE table row has space to store only one price to

SALESPERSON

Salesperson Number	Salesperson Name	Commission Percentage	Year of Hire
137	Baker	10	1995
186	Adams	15	2001
204	Dickens	10	1998
361	Carlyle	20	2001

PRODUCT

Product Number	Product Name	Unit Price
16386	Wrench	12.95
19440	Hammer	17.50
21765	Drill	32.99
24013	Saw	26.25
26722	Pliers	11.50

TIME PERIOD

Time Period Number	Year	Quarter	Month	Week
001	1997	1	1	1
002	1997	1	1	2
003	1997	1	1	3
⋮				
101	1998	4	3	1
102	1998	4	3	2
103	1998	4	3	3
104	1998	4	3	4
⋮				
329	2003	2	2	1
330	2003	2	2	2
331	2003	2	2	3

(*continues*)

FIGURE 12.7 General Hardware Company data warehouse sample data

	SALE			
	Salesperson Number	Product Number	Time Period Number	Quantity
1	137	16386	001	57
2	137	24013	001	129
3	137	16386	002	24
4	137	24013	002	30
	⋮			
5	137	16386	102	85
6	137	24013	102	36
7	204	16386	102	111
8	204	24013	102	44
	⋮			
9	137	16386	103	47
10	137	24013	103	59
11	204	16386	103	13
12	204	24013	103	106
	⋮			
13	137	16386	331	63
14	137	24013	331	30
15	186	16386	331	25
16	186	24013	331	16
17	204	16386	331	44
18	204	24013	331	107
19	361	16386	331	18
20	361	24013	331	59

FIGURE 12.7 (Continued)
General Hardware Company
data warehouse sample data

go with the total quantity of that book purchased by that customer during that week. The design in Figure 12.8 also has a feature that makes it a **"snowflake" design**: one of the dimension tables, BOOK, leads to yet another dimension table, PUBLISHER. Consistent with the rest of the star schema, the snowflake relationship is one-to-many, "inward" toward the center of the star. A publisher publishes many books but a book is associated with only one publisher.

To help in deciding how many copies of *Moby Dick* to order for its stores in Florida during the upcoming Christmas season, Good Reading could check how many copies of *Moby Dick* were purchased in Florida during each of the last five Decembers. This query would require the Book Name attribute of the BOOK table, the State and Country attributes of the CUSTOMER table, and the Year and Month attributes of the TIME PERIOD table. To help in deciding whether to open more stores in Dallas, TX, Good

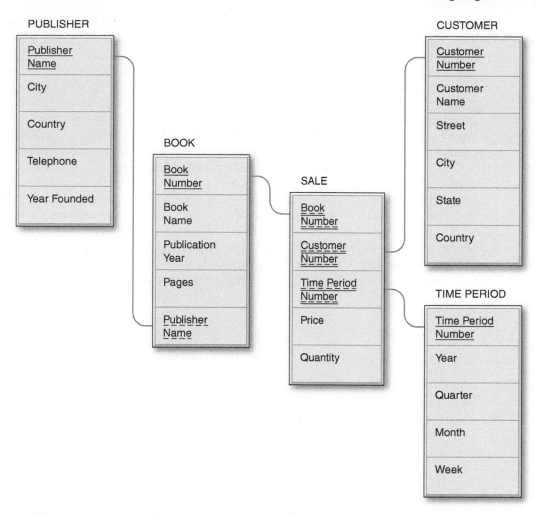

FIGURE 12.8 Good Reading Bookstores data warehouse star schema design with snowflake feature

Reading could sum the total number of all books purchased in all their existing Dallas stores during each of the last five years. The snowflake feature expands the range of query possibilities even further. Using the Country attribute of the PUBLISHER table, the State and Country attributes of the CUSTOMER table, and the Quarter and Year attributes of the TIME PERIOD table, they could find the total number of books published in Brazil that were purchased by customers in California during the second quarter of 2009.

Lucky Rent-A-Car Data Warehouse

Like Good Reading Bookstores' transactional database, Lucky Rent-A-Car's transactional database (Figure 5.18) already carries a date attribute (two, in fact) in its RENTAL table. The reasoning for creating a data warehouse for Lucky is based on the same argument that we examined for Good Reading, that its transactional database would bog down under the weight of all the data if we tried to store 10 years or more of rental history data in it. Interestingly, in the Lucky case, the data warehouse should still store the data down to the day level (resulting in a *huge* data warehouse). Why? In the rental car business, it is important to be able to check historically whether, for example, more cars were rented on Saturdays over a given time period than on Tuesdays.

Figure 12.9 shows the Lucky Rent-A-Car data warehouse star schema design. The fact table is RENTAL. In this case, as implied above, the fact table does *not* contain aggregated data. Every car rental transaction is recorded for posterity in the data warehouse. Notice that this data warehouse has a snowflake feature since the CAR dimension table is connected outwards to the MANUFACTURER table. The query possibilities in this data warehouse are very rich. Lucky could ask how many mid-size (the CAR table's Class attribute) General Motors cars were rented on July weekends in each of the last five years. To find who some of their most valuable customers are for marketing purposes, Lucky could identify the customers (and create a name and address list for them) who rented full-size cars at least three times for at least a week each time during the winter months of each of the last three years. Or, using the Manufacturer Country attribute of the MANUFACTURER table in the snowflake, they could find the amount of revenue (based on the RENTAL table's Cost attribute) that they generated by renting Japanese cars during the summer vacation period in each of the last eight years.

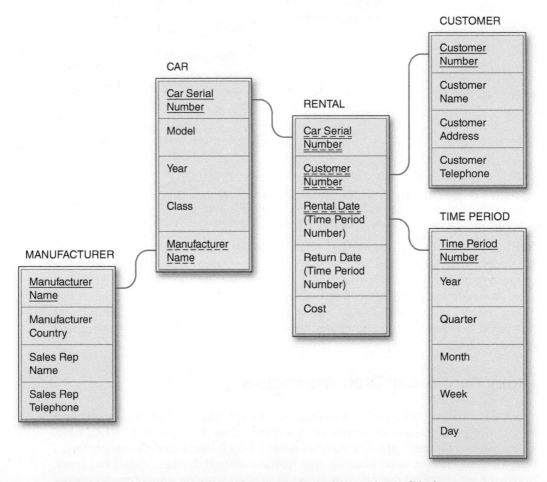

FIGURE 12.9 Lucky Rent-A-Car data warehouse star schema design with snowflake feature

Your Turn

12.1   Designing a University Data Warehouse

Universities create a great deal of data. There is data about students, data about professors, data about courses, data about administrative units such as academic department, data about the physical plant, and accounting data, just as in any business operation. Some of the data is current, such as the students enrolled in particular courses in the current semester. But it may be useful to maintain some of the data on a historical basis.

Question:

Think about what data a university might want to maintain on a historical basis. Design a data warehouse for this historical data. You may focus on students as the subject of the data warehouse or any other entity that you wish.

What About a World Music Association Data Warehouse?

Did you notice that we haven't talked about a data warehouse for the World Music Association (WMA), whose transactional database is shown in Figure 5.17? If there were to be such a data warehouse, its most likely subject would be RECORDING, as the essence of WMA's business is to keep track of different recordings made of different compositions by various orchestras. There is already a Year attribute in the RECORDING table of Figure 5.17. In this sense, the main data of the World Music Association's transactional database is already "timestamped," just like Good Reading Bookstores' and Lucky Rent-A-Car's data. We gave reasons for creating data warehouses for Good Reading and for Lucky, so what about WMA? First, the *essence* of the WMA data is historical. We might be just as interested in a recording made 50 years ago as one made last year. Second, by its nature, the amount of data in a WMA-type transactional database is much smaller than the amount of data in a Good Reading or Lucky-type transactional database. The latter two transactional databases contain daily sales records in high-volume businesses. Even on a worldwide basis, the number of recordings orchestras make is much smaller in comparison. So, the conclusion is that, since the nature of the WMA transactional database blurs with what a WMA data warehouse would look like and the amount of (historical) data in the WMA transactional database is manageable, there is no need for a WMA data warehouse.

Building a Data Warehouse

Introduction

Once the data warehouse has been designed, there are four steps in actually building it. As shown in Figure 12.10, these are:

- *Data Extraction*
- *Data Cleaning*
- *Data Transformation*
- *Data Loading*

Let's take a look at each of these steps.

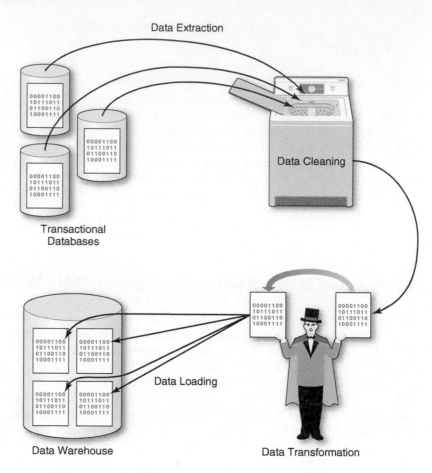

Data Extraction

Transactional Databases

Data Cleaning

Data Loading

Data Warehouse

Data Transformation

FIGURE 12.10 The four steps in building a data warehouse

Data Extraction

Data extraction is the process of copying data from the transactional databases in preparation for loading it into the data warehouse. There are several important points to remember about this. One is that it is not a one-time event. Obviously, there must be an initial extraction of data from the transactional databases when the data warehouse is first built, but after that it will be an ongoing process, performed at regular intervals, perhaps daily, weekly, or monthly, when the latest day's, week's, or month's transactional data is added to the data warehouse. Another point is that the data is likely to come from several transactional databases. Specific data (that means not necessarily all of the data) in each transactional database is copied and merged to form the data warehouse. There are pitfalls along the way that must be dealt with, such as, for example, that the employee serial number attribute may be called, "Employee Number" in one transactional database and "Serial Number" in another. Or, looking at it another way, the attribute name "Serial Number" may mean "Employee Serial Number" in one database and "Finished Goods Serial Number" in another.

Some of the data entering into this process may come from outside of the company. For example, there are companies whose business is to sell demographic data about people to companies that want to use it for marketing purposes. This process is known as **data enrichment**. Figure 12.11 shows enrichment data added to Lucky

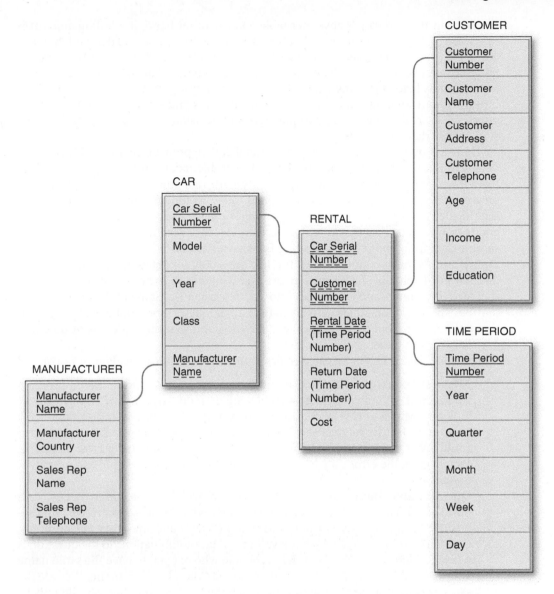

FIGURE 12.11 Lucky Rent-A-Car data warehouse design with enrichment data added to the CUSTOMER table

Rent-A-Car's data warehouse CUSTOMER dimension table from Figure 12.9. Notice that in the data enrichment process, age, income, and education data are added, presumably from some outside data source. Lucky might use this data to try to market the rental of particular kinds of cars to customers who fall into certain demographic categories. We will talk more about this later in the section on data mining.

Data Cleaning

Transactional data can contain all kinds of errors that may or may not affect the applications that use it. For example, if a customer's name is misspelled but the Post Office can correctly figure out to whom to deliver something, no one may ever bother to fix the error in the company's customer table. On the other hand, if a billing amount is much too high, the assumption is that the customer will notice it and demand that it be corrected. Data warehouses are very sensitive to data errors and as many such errors as possible must be "cleaned" (the process is also referred to as "cleansed" or "scrubbed") as the data is loaded into the data warehouse. The point is that if data errors make it into the data warehouse, they can throw off the totals and statistics generated by the queries that are designed to support management decision making, compromising the value of the data warehouse.

There are two steps to cleaning transactional data in preparation for loading it into a data warehouse. The first step is to identify the problem data and the second step is to fix it. Identifying the problem data is generally a job for a program, since having people scrutinize the large volumes of data typical today would simply take too long. Fixing the identified problems can be handled by sophisticated artificial intelligence programs or by creating exception reports for employees to scrutinize. Figure 12.12 shows sample data from two of Good Reading Bookstores' transactional database tables (see Figure 5.16). (The row numbers on the left are solely for reference purposes in this discussion.) Each table has several errors that would have to be corrected as the data is copied, integrated, and aggregated into a data warehouse. Some of the errors shown may be less likely than others actually to turn up in today's more sophisticated application environment, but as a group they make the point that there are lots of potential data hazards out there.

There are four errors or possible errors in the CUSTOMER table, Figure 12.12a:

- **Missing Data:** In row 1, the City attribute is blank. It's possible that a program could check an online "white pages" listing of Tennessee (State="TN" in row 1), look for a Mervis at 123 Oak St., and in that way discover the city and automatically insert it as the City value in row 1. But it should also be clear that this type of error could occur in data for which there is no online source of data for cross checking. In that case, the error may have to be printed in an error report for an employee to look at.
- **Questionable Data:** Rows 2 and 6, each of which has a different customer number, both involve customers named Gomez who live at 345 Main Ave., Columbus, USA. But one city is Columbus, Ohio ("OH") and the other is Columbus, Georgia ("GA"), each of which is a valid city/state combination. So the question is whether these are really two different people who happen to have the same name and street address in two different cities named Columbus, or whether they are the same person (if so, one of the state designations is wrong and there should only be one customer number).
- **Possible Misspelling:** Rows 3 and 8 have different customer numbers but are otherwise identical except for a one-letter difference in the customer name, "Taylor" vs. "Tailor." Do both rows refer to the same person? For the sake of argument, say that an online white pages is not available but a real estate listing indicating which addresses are single-family houses and which are apartment buildings is. A program could be designed to assume that if the address is a single-family house, there is a misspelling and the two records refer to the same person. On the other hand, if the address is an apartment building, they may, indeed, be two different people.
- **Impossible Data:** Row 10 has a state value of "RP." There is no such state abbreviation in the United States. This must be flagged and corrected either automatically or manually.

(a) CUSTOMER table

	Customer Number	Customer Name	Street	City	State	Country
1	02847	Mervis	123 Oak St.		TN	USA
2	03185	Gomez	345 Main Ave.	Columbus	OH	USA
3	03480	Taylor	50 Elm Rd.	San Diego	CA	USA
4	06837	Stevens	876 Leslie Ln.	Raleigh	NC	USA
5	08362	Adams	1200 Wallaby St.	Brisbane		Australia
6	12739	Gomez	345 Main Ave.	Columbus	GA	USA
7	13848	Lucas	742 Ave. Louise	Brussels		Belgium
8	15367	Taylor	50 Elm Rd.	San Diego	CA	USA
9	15933	Chang	48 Maple Ave.	Toronto	ON	Canada
10	18575	Smith	390 Martin Dr.	Columbus	RP	USA
11	21359	Sanchez	666 Ave. Bolivar	Santiago		Chile

(b) SALE table

	Book Number	Customer Number	Date	Price	Quantity
1	426478	03480	May 19, 2003	32.99	1
2	077656	18575	May 19, 2003	19.95	21
3	365905	06837	May 19, 2003	24.99	3
4	645688	21359	May 20, 2003	49.50	1
5	474640	15367	May 34, 2003	3,200.99	1
6	426478	08362	June 03, 2003	32.99	2
7	276432	03480	June 04, 2003	30.00	1
8	365905	12738	June 04, 2003	24.99	1
9	276432	06837	June 05, 2003	30.00	5
10	327467	18575	June 12, 2003	−32.99	2
11	426478	06837	June 15, 2003	32.99	1

FIGURE 12.12 Good Reading Bookstores sample data prior to data cleaning

There are also four errors or possible errors in the SALE table in Figure 12.12b. The data in this table is more numeric in nature than the CUSTOMER table data:

- **Questionable Data:** In row 2, the quantity of a particular book purchased in a single transaction is 21. This is possible, but generally unlikely. A program may be designed to decide whether to leave it alone or to report it as an exception depending on whether the type of book it is makes it more or less likely that the quantity is legitimate.

- **Impossible/Out-of-Range Data:** Row 5 indicates that a single book cost $3,200.99. This is out of the possible range for book prices and must either be corrected, if the system knows the correct price for that book (based on the book number), or reported as an exception.
- **Apparently Incorrect Data:** The Customer Number in row 8 is invalid. We don't have a customer with customer number 12738. But we do have a customer with customer number 12739 (see row 6 of the CUSTOMER table in part a of the figure). A person would have to look into this one.
- **Impossible Data:** Row 10 shows a negative price for a book, which is impossible.

Data Transformation

As the data is extracted from the transactional databases, it must go through several kinds of transformations on its way to the data warehouse:

- We have already talked about the concept of merging data from different transactional databases to form the data warehouse tables. This is indeed one of the major data transformation steps.
- In many cases, the data will be aggregated as it is being extracted from the transactional databases and prepared for the data warehouse. Daily transactional data may be summed to form weekly or monthly data as the lowest level of data storage in the data warehouse.
- Units of measure used for attributes in different transactional databases must be reconciled as they are merged into common data warehouse tables. This is especially common if one transactional database uses the metric system and another uses the English system. Miles and kilometers, pounds and kilograms, gallons and liters all have to go through a conversion process in order to wind up in a unified way in the data warehouse.
- Coding schemes used for attributes in different transactional databases must be reconciled as they are merged into common data warehouse tables. For example, states of the United States could be represented in different databases by their full names, two-letter postal abbreviations, or a numeric code from 1 to 50. Countries of the world could be represented by their full names, standard abbreviations used on vehicles, or a numeric code. Another major issue along these lines is the different ways that dates can be stored.
- Sometimes values from different attributes in transactional databases are combined into a single attribute in the data warehouse or the opposite occurs: a multipart attribute is split apart. Consider the first name and last name of employees or customers as an example of this.

Data Loading

Finally, after all of the extracting, cleaning, and transforming, the data is ready to be loaded into the data warehouse. We would only repeat here that after the initial load, a schedule for regularly updating the data warehouse must be put in place, whether it is done on a daily, weekly, monthly, or some other designated time period basis. Remember, too, that data marts that use the data warehouse as their source of data must also be scheduled for regular updates.

Using a Data Warehouse

We have said that the purpose of a data warehouse is to support management decision-making. Indeed, such "decision support" and the tools of its trade are major topics by themselves and not something we want to go into in great detail here. Still, it would be unsatisfying to leave the topic of data warehouses without considering at all how they are used. We will briefly discuss two major data warehouse usage areas: **on-line analytic processing** and **data mining**.

On-Line Analytic Processing

On-Line Analytic Processing (OLAP) is a decision support methodology based on viewing data in multiple dimensions. Actually, we alluded to this topic earlier in this chapter when we described the two-, three-, and four-dimensional scenarios for recording hospital patient tracking and billing data. There are many OLAP systems on the market today. As we said before, some employ special purpose database structures designed specifically for multidimensional OLAP-type data. Others, known as relational OLAP or "ROLAP" systems, store multidimensional data in relational databases using the star schema design that we have already covered!

How can OLAP data be used? The OLAP environment's multidimensional data is very well suited for querying and for multi-time period trend analyses, as we saw in the star schema discussion. In addition, several other data search concepts are commonly associated with OLAP:

- *Drill-Down:* This refers to going back to the database and retrieving finer levels of data detail than you have already retrieved. If you begin with monthly aggregated data, you may want to go back and look at the weekly or daily data, if the data warehouse supports it.
- *Slice:* A slice of multidimensional data is a subset of the data that focuses on a single value of one of the dimensions. Figure 12.13 is a slice of the patient data "cube" of Figure 12.4, in which a single value of the patient attribute, F. Jones, is nailed down and the data in the other dimensions is displayed.
- *Pivot or Rotation:* While helpful in terms of visualization, this is merely a matter of interchanging the data dimensions, for example, interchanging the data on the horizontal and vertical axes in a two-dimensional view.

Data Mining

As huge data warehouses are built and data is increasingly considered a true corporate resource, a natural movement toward squeezing a greater and greater competitive advantage out of the company's data has taken place. This is especially true when it comes to the data warehouse, which, after all, is intended not to support daily operations but to help management improve the company's competitive position in any way it can. Certainly, one major kind of use of the data warehouse is the highly flexible data search and retrieval capability represented by OLAP-type tools and techniques. Another major kind of use involves "data mining."

Data mining is the searching out of hidden knowledge in a company's data that can give the company a competitive advantage in its marketplace. This would be impossible

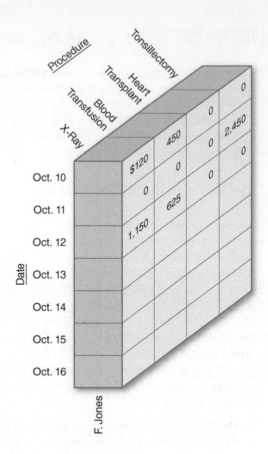

FIGURE 12.13 A "slice" of the hospital patient tracking and billing system data

for people to do manually because they would immediately be overwhelmed by the sheer amount of data in the company's data warehouse. It must be done by software. In fact, very sophisticated data mining software has been developed that uses several advanced statistical and artificial intelligence techniques such as:

- Case-based learning
- Decision trees
- Neural networks
- Genetic algorithms

These techniques will be described further in Chapter 16. But it's worth taking a quick look at a couple of the possibilities from an application or user's point of view.

One type of data mining application is known as "**market basket analysis.**" For example, consider the data collected by a supermarket as it checks out its customers by scanning the bar codes on the products they're purchasing. The company might have software study the collected "market baskets," each of which is literally the goods that a particular customer bought in one trip to the store. The software might try to discover if certain items "fall into" the same market basket more frequently than would otherwise be expected. That last phrase is important because some combinations of items in the same market basket are too obvious or common to be of any value. For example, finding eggs and milk being bought together frequently is not news. On the other hand, a piece of data mining folklore has it that one such study was done and discovered that people who bought disposable diapers also frequently bought beer (you can draw your own conclusions on why this might be the case). The company could use this to advantage by stacking some beer near the diapers in its stores so that when

	CAR/RENTAL/CUSTOMER						
	Class	Manufacture Name	Cost	Customer Number	Age	Income	Education
1	Compact	Ford	320	884730	54	58,000	B.A.
2	Luxury	Lincoln	850	528262	45	158,000	M.B.A.
3	Full-Size	General Motors	489	109565	48	62,000	B.S.
4	Sub-Compact	Toyota	159	532277	25	34,000	High School
5	Luxury	Lincoln	675	155434	42	125,000	Ph.D.
6	Compact	Chrysler	360	965578	64	47,500	High School
7	Mid-Size	Nissan	429	688632	31	43,000	M.B.A.
8	Luxury	Lincoln	925	342786	47	95,000	M.A.
9	Full-Size	General Motors	480	385633	51	72,000	B.S.
10	Compact	Toyota	230	464367	64	200,000	M.A.
11	Luxury	Jaguar	1,170	528262	45	158,000	M.B.A.
12	Sub-Compact	Nissan	89	759930	29	28,000	B.A.
13	Full-Size	Ford	335	478432	57	53,500	B.S.
14	Full-Size	Chrysler	328	207867	29	162,000	Ph.D.

FIGURE 12.14 Lucky Rent-A-Car enriched data, integrated for data mining

someone comes in to buy diapers, they might make an impulse decision to buy the beer sitting next to it, too. Another use of market basket data is part of the developing marketing discipline of "customer relationship management." If, through data mining, a supermarket determines that a particular customer who spends a lot of money in the store often buys a particular product, they might offer her discount coupons for that product as a way of rewarding her and developing "customer loyalty" so that she will keep coming back to the store.

Your Turn

12.2 Using a University Data Warehouse

Consider the university data warehouse that you designed in the Your Turn exercise earlier in this chapter.

Question:

Develop a plan for using your university data warehouse. What benefits can you think of to querying the data warehouse? What kinds of new knowledge might you discover by using data mining techniques on the data warehouse?

Another type of data mining application looks for patterns in the data. Earlier, we suggested that Lucky Rent-A-Car might buy demographic data about its customers to "enrich" the data about them in its data warehouse. Once again, consider Figure 12.11 with its enriched (Age, Income, and Education attributes added) CUSTOMER dimension table. Suppose, and this is quite realistic, that Lucky joined its RENTAL fact table with its CAR and CUSTOMER dimension tables, including only such attributes in the result as would help it identify its most valuable customers, for example those who spend a lot of money renting "luxury" class cars. Figure 12.14 shows the resulting table, with the rows numbered on the left for convenience here. The Class and Manufacturer Name attributes came from the CAR table, the Cost attribute (the revenue for a particular rental transaction) came from the RENTAL table, and the Customer Number, Age, Income, and Education attributes came from the CUSTOMER table. While it would take much more data than this to really find statistically significant data patterns, the sample data in the figure gives a rough idea of what a pattern might look like. Rows 2, 5, 8, and 11 all involve rentals of luxury-class cars with high cost (revenue to the company) figures. As you look across these rows to the customer demographics, you find "clusters" in age, income, and education. These expensive, luxury car rental transactions all involved people in their mid-40s with high income and education levels. On the other hand, rows 10 and 14 involved people who also had high income and education levels. But these people were not in their mid-40s and they did not rent luxury cars and run up as big a bill. With enough such data, Lucky might conclude that it could make more money by heavily promoting its luxury cars to customers in their mid-40s with high income and education levels. If its competitors have not thought of this, then Lucky has gained a competitive advantage by "mining" its data warehouse.

Administering a Data Warehouse

In Chapter 10, we discussed the issues of managing corporate data and databases with people called data administrators and database administrators. As a huge database, the data warehouse certainly requires a serious level of management. Further, its unique character requires a strong degree of personnel specialization in its management (some have even given the role its own name of "**data warehouse administrator**"). In fact, managing the data warehouse requires three kinds of heavily overlapping employee expertise:

- Business Expertise
  - An understanding of the company's business processes underlying an understanding of the company's transactional data and databases.
  - An understanding of the company's business goals to help in determining what data should be stored in the data warehouse for eventual OLAP and data mining purposes.
- Data Expertise
  - An understanding of the company's transactional data and databases for selection and integration into the data warehouse.
  - An understanding of the company's transactional data and databases to design and manage data cleaning and data transformation as necessary.
  - Familiarity with outside data sources for the acquisition of enrichment data.
- Technical Expertise
  - An understanding of data warehouse design principles for the initial design.
  - An understanding of OLAP and data mining techniques so that the data warehouse design will properly support these processes.
  - An understanding of the company's transactional databases in order to manage or coordinate the regularly scheduled appending of new data to the data warehouse.

- An understanding of handling very large databases in general (as the data warehouse will inevitably be) with their unique requirements for security, backup and recovery, being split across multiple disk devices, and so forth.

The other issue in administering a data warehouse is metadata; i.e. the data warehouse must have a data dictionary to go along with it. The data warehouse is a huge data resource for the company and has great potential to give the company a competitive advantage. But, for this to happen, the company's employees have to understand what data is in it! And for two reasons. One is to think about how to use the data to the company's advantage, through OLAP and data mining. The other is actually to access the data for processing with those techniques.

Challenges in Data Warehousing

Data warehousing presents a distinct set of challenges. Many companies have jumped into data warehousing with both feet, only to find that they had bitten off more than they could chew and had to back off. Often, they try again with a more gradual approach and eventually succeed. Many of the pitfalls of data warehousing have already been mentioned at one point or another in this chapter. These include the technical challenges of data cleaning and finding more "dirty" data than expected, problems associated with coordinating the regular appending of new data from the transactional databases to the data warehouse, and difficulties in managing very large databases, which, as we have said, the data warehouse will inevitably be. There is also the separate challenge of building and maintaining the data dictionary and making sure that everyone who needs it understands what's in it and has access to it.

Another major challenge of a different kind is trying to satisfy the user community. In concept, the idea is to build such a broad, general data warehouse that it will satisfy all user demands. In practice, decisions have to be made about what and how much data it is practical to incorporate in the data warehouse at a given time and at a given point in the development of the data warehouse. Unfortunately, it is almost inevitable that some users will not be satisfied in general with the data at their disposal and others will want the data warehouse data to be modified in some way to produce better or different results. And that's not a bad thing! It means that people in the company understand or are gaining an appreciation for the great potential value of the data warehouse and are impatient to have it set up the way that will help them help the company the most—even if that means that the design of the data warehouse and the data in it are perpetually moving targets.

Summary

A data warehouse is a historical database used for applications that require the analysis of data collected over a period of time. A data warehouse is a database whose data is subject oriented, integrated, non-volatile, time variant, high quality, aggregated, possibly denormalized, and not necessarily absolutely current. There are two types of data warehouses: the enterprise data warehouse and the data mart. Some companies maintain one type, some the other, and some both.

Data warehouses are multidimensional databases. They are often designed around the star schema concept. Building a data warehouse is a multi-step process that includes data extraction, data cleaning, data transformation, and data loading. There are several methodologies for using a data warehouse, including on-line analytic processing and data mining. Data warehouses have become so large and so important that it takes special skills to administer them.

Key Terms

Aggregated data	Data warehouse	Integrated data	Snowflake design
Data cleaning	administrator	Market basket analysis	Star schema
Data enrichment	Decision support system	Multidimensional	Subject oriented data
Data extraction	(DSS)	database	Time variant data
Data loading	Dimension	Non-volatile data	Transaction processing
Data mart	Drill-down	On-line analytic	system (TPS)
Data mining	Enterprise data	processing (OLAP)	
Data transformation	warehouse	Pivot or rotation	
Data warehouse	Historic data	Slice	

Questions

1. What is the difference between transactional processing systems and decision support systems?

2. Decision support applications have been around for many years, typically using captive files that belong to each individual application. What factors led to the movement from this environment toward the data warehouse?

3. What is a data warehouse? What is a data warehouse used for?

4. Explain each of the following concepts. The data in a data warehouse:

   a. Is subject oriented.

   b. Is integrated.

   c. Is non-volatile.

   d. Is time variant.

   e. Must be high quality.

   f. May be aggregated.

   g. Is often denormalized.

   h. Is not necessarily absolutely current.

5. What is the difference between an enterprise data warehouse and a data mart?

6. Under what circumstances would a company build data marts from an enterprise data warehouse? Build an enterprise data warehouse from data marts?

7. What is a multidimensional database?

8. What is a star schema? What are fact tables? What are dimension tables?

9. What is a snowflake feature in a star schema?

10. After a data warehouse is designed, what are the four steps in building it?

11. Name and describe three possible problems in transactional data that would require "data cleaning" before the data can be used in a data warehouse.

12. Name and describe three kinds of data transformations that might be necessary as transactional data is integrated and copied into a data warehouse.

13. What is online analytic processing (OLAP?) What does OLAP have to do with data warehouses?

14. What do the following OLAP terms mean?

   a. Drill-down.

   b. Slice.

   c. Pivot or rotation.

15. What is data mining? What does data mining have to do with data warehouses?

16. Describe the ideal background for an employee who is going to manage the data warehouse.

17. Describe the challenges involved in satisfying a data warehouse's user community.

Exercises

1. Video Centers of Europe, Ltd. data warehouse:

    a. Design a multidimensional database using a star schema for a data warehouse for the Video Centers of Europe, Ltd. business environment described in the diagram associated with Exercise 2.2. The subject will be "rental," which represents a particular tape or DVD being rented by a particular customer. As stated in Exercise 2.2, be sure to keep track of the rental date and the price paid. Include a snowflake feature based on the actor, movie, and tape/DVD entities.

    b. Describe three OLAP uses of this data warehouse.

    c. Describe one data mining use of this data warehouse.

2. Best Airlines, Inc., data warehouse:

    In the exercises in Chapter 8, we saw the following relational database, which Best Airlines uses to keep track of its mechanics, their skills, and their airport locations. Mechanic number, airport name, and skill number are all unique fields. Size is an airport's size in acres. Skill Category is a skill's category, such as an engine skill, wing skill, tire skill, etc. Year Qualified is the year that a mechanic first qualified in a particular skill; Proficiency Rating is the mechanic's proficiency rating in a particular skill.

MECHANIC Table				
Mechanic Number	Mechanic Name	Telephone	Salary	Airport Name

AIRPORT Table				
Airport Name	City	State	Size	Year Opened

SKILL Table		
Skill Number	Skill Name	Skill Category

QUALIFICATION Table			
Mechanic Number	Skill Number	Year Qualified	Proficiency Rating

We now add the following tables to the database that record data about airplanes and maintenance performed on them. A maintenance event is a specific maintenance activity performed on an airplane.

AIRPLANE Table			
Airplane Number	Airplane Model	Year Manufactured	Passenger Capacity

MAINTENANCE ACTIVITY Table			
Activity Number	Activity Name	Expected Duration	Required Frequency

MAINTENANCE EVENT Table			
Airplane Number	Activity Number	Date	Mechanic Number

a. Design a multidimensional database using a star schema for a data warehouse for the Best Airlines, Inc., airplane maintenance environment described by the complete seven-table relational database above. The subject will be maintenance event. Include snowflake features as appropriate.

b. Describe three OLAP uses of this data warehouse.

c. Describe one data mining use of this data warehouse.

Minicases

1. Happy Cruise Lines data warehouse:

   a. Design a multidimensional database using a star schema for a data warehouse for the Happy Cruise Lines business environment described in Minicase 2.1. The subject will be "passage," which represents a particular passenger booking on a particular cruise. As stated in Minicase 2.1, be sure to keep track of the fare that the passenger paid for the cruise and the passenger's satisfaction rating of the cruise.

   b. Describe three OLAP uses of this data warehouse.

   c. Describe one data mining use of this data warehouse.

2. Super Baseball League data warehouse:

   a. Design a multidimensional database using a star schema for a data warehouse for the Super Baseball League business environment described in Minicase 2.2. The subject will be "affiliation," which represents a particular player having played on a particular team. As stated in Minicase 2.2, be sure to keep track of the number of years that the player played on the team and the batting average he compiled on it.

   b. Describe three OLAP uses of this data warehouse.

   c. Describe one data mining use of this data warehouse.

NoSQL Database Management

As productive as relational database management has been for some 40 years at this point, it does have limitations. Relational database was not designed for "**big data**" such as video or audio clips, or for high velocity data coming from sensors or for clickstream data from the Web. Furthermore, relational database has certain design limitations. All of this has encouraged the development of new database paradigms including **key-value database**, **document database**, **column family database**, and **graph database**, which are the subjects of this chapter.

OBJECTIVES

- Recognize the limitations of relational database management.
- Explain the meaning of "big data."
- Describe the fundamental concepts of **NoSQL database** management.
- Describe key-value database, document database, column family database, and graph database.
- Explain the basis for querying NoSQL database.

Introduction

The Lead-Up to NoSQL Database Management

Relational database came on the scene in about 1980. As with any new and different technology, companies took a cautious approach to using it, especially for their critical applications. What they typically did was "try it out" on some non-critical applications to learn about it and understand its pros and cons relative to the earlier navigational (hierarchical and network) database systems that they were using, if they were using any database systems at all! It took some time, typically several years, before most companies were willing to move forward with relational database in a substantial way.

As they began working with relational database, IT personnel appreciated its straightforward tabular structure, its relative data independence, and the SQL language that came with it. Still, there were issues that caused its acceptance to be gradual. Chief among these was its performance: retrieving data, especially when the retrieval involved a join operation, could be painfully slow, compared to equivalent operations in the navigational systems which were based on direct address pointers. Plus, there were other structural issues. For example, the early relational database management systems had no referential integrity controls.

Over time, some of the drawbacks to relational database were overcome by the relational database system vendors. Data retrieval performance was progressively improved with enhancements to relational query optimizer software and with improved hardware such as increasingly faster disk drives. Referential integrity controls were introduced, as were other improvements in such areas as data security and concurrency control. It is very important to note that relational database is still an excellent choice for applications requiring straightforward, numeric and alphabetic data in a tabular format and relational database management systems are expected to be in use for a very long time to come.

But, the world is changing and information systems are changing with it. Today, we speak of "big data" with its three Vs: **volume, variety, and velocity**. Volume refers to the massive amounts of data we are increasingly dealing with and bringing into our information systems. Huge amounts of data can be collected from the Internet, from sensors on vehicles of all kinds, and from every facet of business. Variety refers to the different kinds of data that we have to deal with today. In fact, the very nature of data has advanced beyond simple tabular numeric and alphabetic data to include large blocks of text, audio clips, video clips, complex graphics and photographs, and even data representing solid objects (e.g. a vase) in the form of data designed to be fed into 3-D printers, Figure 13.1. Velocity refers to the greatly increased speed with which data enters the information systems, for example, from vehicle sensors that accumulate data while the vehicle is in motion.

It's really interesting and important that at the same time that the interest in big data has come about, there have been major changes in the hardware that stores and processes the data. Mechanical, rotating disk drives are gradually being replaced by more efficient and reliable "**solid state disks**" (SSD). This solid state memory with no moving parts has become very cheap and serves very well as secondary memory. Also, mainframe computers are being replaced in many instances by massive **server farms**: large numbers of small computers or servers, often referred to as "blades" stored in racks, Figure 13.2, that can be linked to form a huge data storage and computing resource.

But, at the same time that all of these changes are taking place, we must recognize that relational database management systems do have limitations.

Limitations of Relational Database

Relational databases were designed to accommodate numeric and alphanumeric data stored in tabular formats. This works well for traditional applications such as accounting, banking, and inventory. Relational database was never designed for

648203

Audio Clip

Video Clip

Taylor

FIGURE 13.1 A variety of data types

icon Stocker / Adobe Stock; avaicon /
Adobe Stock; Vertigo3d / Getty Images;
DenisProduction.com / Shutterstock;
Natalia Davidovich / Shutterstock

advanced data types. Another limitation is that the decisions of how to structure the
relational tables, such as which attributes must go in which tables, and where foreign
keys have to be placed, must be made in advance, when the databases are designed.
Some design changes, such as adding new columns to a table, can be made in the
future, but large-scale redesign of tables is problematic. Also, the assumption is that
every row of a table will have a value in every one of its columns. If not, then it's a
"sparse table" with a lot of wasted space.

Cybrain / Adobe Stock

FIGURE 13.2 A server farm

Advanced Database Management System Concepts

So, what features should an advanced database management system have? Certainly, it has to be able to manage big data volume, variety, and velocity, while utilizing the capabilities of server farms and solid state disks. Thus it must be able to handle every kind of data, ranging from simple, numeric tabular data to the most exotic 3-D printer data. It should be very flexible and have the ability to add fields to its structures at any time. It also should be able to have records in a file that have some fields in common but other fields that are specific to only some of its records, without creating a sparse data situation.

But, there is much more that advanced database management systems must be capable of, *in partnership with* advanced hardware options, such as large-scale server farms. We say that these systems must be scalable, meaning that they must be able to accommodate more and more data. Today, this often means adding more servers to a server farm. Also, there must be 24/7 data availability, which is typically accomplished by deliberately replicating data on different servers (generally at least three servers) in the server farm, Figure 13.3. If a server with particular data goes down, other copies of the same data can be retrieved from the other servers it was stored on. This data replication capability also, in principle, allows for the use of cheap, commodity servers which may fail more frequently than expensive ones. Again, because the data is replicated on several servers, there is less concern about a server failure.

Finally, it is desirable for these advanced database management systems to have what is known as the **ACID property**. ACID is an acronym for atomicity, consistency, isolation, and durability. The idea is that all of the actions of a transaction should be completed or none of them should be. For example, if you are taking an equal number of nuts and bolts out of inventory in one operation, reflected in a single computer transaction to update the inventory records, you would want both the record for nuts and the record for bolts to be updated. You would not want only one of the two records to be updated due to some kind of error taking place in the process. If an error did occur in the process, you would want the entire transaction to fail and be run again. Furthermore, you would not want another transaction to "see" only some of a transaction's results before all of them are completed. That's the idea of the ACID property.

FIGURE 13.3 Data replicated across servers in a server farm

Cybrain / Adobe Stock; cyberneticimages / Adobe Stock

NoSQL Database Management Systems

All of the changes in data requirements and hardware advances have led to a new class of database management systems known as NoSQL Database Management Systems. It is generally accepted that NoSQL is an acronym for "Not Only SQL," which is not really an accurate description, but that's what has developed. It is also generally accepted that there are four paradigms or frameworks under the NoSQL label:

- Key-value database
- Document database
- Column family database (also known as Big table database or Wide column database)
- Graph database

As we will see, key-value database is the most basic of the four frameworks. Document database and column family database, while structured differently, have several capabilities in common. Graph database is substantially different from the other three but has enough in common with them that it qualifies as a fourth NoSQL framework.

Key-Value Database

The Key-Value Database Concept

The simplest of the four NoSQL frameworks is the Key-Value Database. Let's start by thinking about the nature of a "key" and the nature of a "value" and how we might put the two together in a helpful way.

Whenever you search for data describing a particular entity in a relational database, you need an identifier, a unique key, to be able to find it. For example, to look for the data in a bank account you need a unique primary key account number. In a typical relational database, the keys are typically numeric, like a customer number, or in some cases they may be alphabetic, like a customer name, if customer names are unique.

Now, what if we both *generalize* and *simplify* all of this to say that the identifier that we're searching on is called the "key" and the associated data that we're retrieving is called the "value." Furthermore, the key doesn't have to be a simple numeric or alphabetic value, it can be <u>anything</u>. And, the value doesn't have to be one or more records or selected attributes of records, the value can be <u>anything</u> that can be digitized. In particular, the value can be a number, a small or large block of text or an audio clip or a video clip or a graphic or the input to a 3-D printer or, for that matter, a single numeric value or even something that looks like a record in a file. In fact, the value can be anything that can be digitized, Figure 13.4. This is the essence of a key-value database.

Let's take a closer look at the nature of the key. For comparison sake, consider the Employee Table in a relational database where Employee Number is the primary key. A particular employee number might be 483274. How do we know that 483274 is an employee number and not, say the dollar value of someone's house? We know it's an employee number because it's in the Employee Number column of the relational table! That is, the structure of the relational table tells you what the different values represent. In a key-value database, there is no structure like that. The key should be "intelligent," carrying its own meaning. Here is an example.

36287 : 648203

92482 : Taylor

Htsia65 :

Audio Clip

Osikesof :

Video Clip

7492xyz :

Uworka :

4j8a22n :

FIGURE 13.4 Examples of key-value data with the key to the left of the colon and the value to the right

icon Stocker / Adobe Stock; avaicon / Adobe Stock; Vertigo3d / Getty Images; DenisProduction.com / Shutterstock; Natalia Davidovich / Shutterstock

JHF3848 : 84720, Adams, Oak Street, 43

Grand Airlines wants to keep a historical record of the number of passengers who flew on each of its flights, every day for the last five years and it wants to do this with a key-value database. As is normal for airlines, the same flight number is used every day for a particular route, meaning for a flight that starts at a particular airport and ends at another particular airport. So, to begin, an intelligent key might consist of a combination of a flight number, say flight number 345, and a date, say 4/23/2021, so that the key is:

`345:4/23/2021`

Now, let's add a meaningful label, Passengers, meaning the number of passengers on a flight. The intelligent key now looks like

`345:4/23/2021:passengers`

Let's say that there were 87 passengers on flight 345 on 4/23/2021, which is the "value." Then, the key-value pair is

`345:4/23/2021:passengers=87`

To generalize this, we might write it as:

`flight number:date:"passengers"=value.`

This key-value pair can be stored anywhere is some data storage space (via **hashing**, as described below), independently, among many other such key-value pairs. The point is that it doesn't need to be in a structure like a relational table. Knowing that the key is a flight number followed by a date is all the "structure" that is needed to store and retrieve the data, i.e. the number of passengers on that flight.

So, what's the point of this? In addition to the ability to store any kind of data, again, a value can be any digitized string, there are other advantages. One advantage is the speed of retrieval using hashing, which was discussed earlier in this book. In relational database, retrieval is accomplished with indexes. In key-value database, hashing is used. But, since a key can be anything, including alphabetic characters, how can you hash any key? The answer is that in a computer, everything, including alphabetic characters, are boiled down internally to bits! Any string of bits can be treated as a number in the "base 2" or "binary" number system and can be hashed.

So, with key-value database, we can achieve very fast data retrieval in application situations that do not require the kind of structure provided by tables in a relational database. But, there is still more to this, which involves using server farms such as are found in the cloud. To explore this further, let's talk about Hadoop.

Hadoop

Hadoop is a data storage and retrieval system that was created by Yahoo. Hadoop is not considered to be a NoSQL database system. We include it here because certain aspects of it have a key-value orientation. Hadoop can be used to store large amounts of data for certain purposes such as data analytics applications. Also, its data storage model, **Hadoop Distributed File System (HDFS)**, can form the basis for certain NoSQL database systems such as HBase (to be mentioned later in this chapter). HDFS is based on a master/slave, also known as a name node/data node storage arrangement. To simplify this a bit (ok, to simplify this a lot), think of the data nodes as servers in a large server farm, Figure 13.5. Hadoop stores data in the data nodes. Hadoop automatically makes replicated copies of the data in a key-value format, stored on different servers, which provides backup and availability of the data in case a server goes down. Once stored, the data cannot be updated or deleted. The name node manages the data nodes and keeps track of the data in this arrangement.

Continuing the Grand Airlines example, now suppose that the company wants to store 10 years of number-of-passengers-on-a-flight data using the key-value arrangement described above:

```
flight number:date:"passengers"=value
```

The data will be stored across a set of servers, i.e. a set of data nodes, in a server farm. An interesting feature of Hadoop, known as **MapReduce**, takes advantage of this data storage arrangement to increase the efficiency of retrieving the number-of-passengers data.

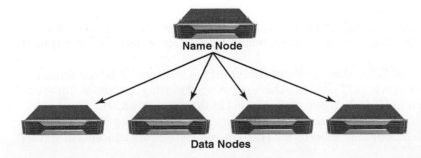

FIGURE 13.5 The Hadoop name node/data node arrangement

cyberneticimages / Adobe Stock

The idea of MapReduce is to employ a process known as **"parallel processing."** Parallel processing is the simultaneous use of many computers to solve a computing problem. Of course, every server in a server farm is a complete computer, with its own central processing unit, primary storage, and disk secondary storage (which may be rotating disks but are more likely to be solid state disks). So, it's natural to want the servers in a server farm to work on an application problem simultaneously, which would be an example of parallel processing.

Now, imagine that the 10 years of Grand Airlines number-of-passengers-on-a-flight data is spread across the servers in a server farm. One day, the president of the company wants to know the average number of passengers on Grand Airlines flights from New York to Los Angeles during the six-month period January 1, 2019 to June 30, 2019. To answer this question, a query representing the president's question is sent, simultaneously, to all of the servers that have portions of the Grand Airlines data. All of these servers simultaneously search their disks for any data that should be included in the answer to the president's question (which is an aspect of parallel processing). They send their results in to a central server that is tasked with accumulating the results from all of the servers and coming up with an answer to the question. This is the MapReduce process. The "Map" part of the process is sending the query to all of the servers and the "Reduce" part of the process is accumulating the results to come up with the answer to the question.

The Hadoop Environment

An entire software environment has developed around Hadoop to greatly increase its functionality. Here are some of the Hadoop environment tools that are available.

Hive is a Hadoop data warehousing framework that was originally developed by Facebook. It has an SQL-like language called HiveQL that allows queries to automatically take advantage of MapReduce. Hive is designed to interface with a variety of business intelligence and visualization application products.

Pig, originally developed at Yahoo, is a high-level platform, with a language called Pig Latin, which is designed for analyzing large data sets through parallel processing using MapReduce. (It was named "Pig" because it is designed to work on any kind of data, just as pigs have the reputation for eating anything!)

Flume is an application that is designed to efficiently input large amounts of data (like log data or sensor data) into Hadoop.

Oozie is a workflow scheduling system that is used to manage Hadoop jobs.

Ambari is a web-based application for administering and managing a Hadoop cluster, i.e. a group of networked servers containing Hadoop data. (An ambari is a saddle or canopied seat on an elephant in India.)

Avro is a "data serialization" application for Hadoop that takes data stored in a structured schema and converts it to a simplified stream for transfer among different hardware and software environments.

Mahout is a data mining library that implements machine learning algorithms in the Hadoop/MapReduce environment. (A mahout is a driver or trainer of an elephant in India.)

Sqoop is an application that translates data from the relational database format to Hadoop, and vice versa. As IT personnel have considered moving operations from relational database into Hadoop, Sqoop certainly makes that job a lot easier.

Spark, like Hadoop, is a broad-based data storage and processing platform. However Spark, which came later, extends the Hadoop and MapReduce concepts in several important ways. Hadoop is designed for batch processing but Spark is designed to also handle real-time data needs and process data interactively. While Hadoop is totally oriented toward storing and retrieving its data from secondary disk storage, Spark is designed to hold some of its data in main memory, greatly increasing its processing speed. Spark also has facilities to simplify and enhance its use from a programming standpoint.

YARN (Yet Another Resource Negotiator) is a resource manager that allows a wider variety of application types to take advantage of the Hadoop and MapReduce facilities and capabilities. It also permits processing types other than MapReduce to take advantage of Hadoop's HDFS data storage platform. YARN also acts as a job scheduler within the Hadoop framework.

Document Database

Consider the following classic problem in relational database. A city wants to create a relational database to keep track of its "first responder" employees. The city has three types of first responder employees: police officers, firefighters, and emergency medical technicians (EMT). As shown in Figure 13.6, the city wants to maintain certain attributes for all of its first responders. These attributes include their unique employee number, name, street (of home address), state, and age. In addition, for police officers, the city wants to keep track of their rank and years on the police force; for firefighters, their height, weight, and maximum weightlifting capability (MWC) in pounds; for EMTs, the year of their first EMT certification and their cardiopulmonary resuscitation (CPR) rating.

There are two ways to design a relational database to handle this data. One, Figure 13.7, is to create four relational tables: one for the data common to all of the first responders and one for each of the three specific types of first responders. Of course, all four of the tables would have to include the unique identifier employee number. Here's what the tables would look like with some sample data. Note that we have added a Type attribute to the Employee table with values PO for Police Officer, FF for Firefighter, and EMT for EMTs. This is to permit someone looking only at the EMPLOYEE table to know which type of first responder is represented in a row of the table.

The other way, to design a relational database to handle this data, Figure 13.8, is to put it all in one big table. Here is what that table would look like with the same sample data:

Now, here is the problem. In the four-table arrangement, if you want to find all of the data about one employee, you have to join two tables (the Employee Table and whichever of the other three tables involves that employee). If you want all of the data about all of the employees, you have to join all four tables. As we know, joins make the queries more complex and decrease the speed of data retrieval. In the one-table arrangement, we have eliminated the need for joins, but look at all of the empty space

Employee	**Police Officer**	**Firefighter**	**EMT**
Emp Num	Rank	Height	Year First Cert
Name	Years on Force	Weight	CPR Rating
Street		MWC	
State			
Age			

FIGURE 13.6 Attributes for all employees and additional attributes for selected first responders

Emp Num	Name	Street	State	Age	Type
17483	Baker	Oak	OH	35	FF
18420	Taylor	Elm	NY	24	EMT
21667	Chen	Oak	OH	41	PO
24158	Adams	Maple	TN	36	FF
26993	Roberts	Main	CA	45	EMT
28210	Kumar	Main	FL	22	FF
30623	Harris	Elm	NY	31	PO

EMPLOYEE TABLE

Emp Num	Rank	Years
21667	Sergeant	5
30623	Captain	20

POLICE OFFICER TABLE

Emp Num	Height	Weight	MWC
17483	6' 0"	180	150
24158	5' 10"	175	200
28210	6' 1"	210	170

FIREFIGHTER TABLE

Emp Num	Year Cert	CPR
18420	2010	9
26993	2021	5

EMT TABLE

FIGURE 13.7 Four relational table solution

Emp Num	Name	Street	State	Age	Type	Rank	Years	Height	Weight	MWC	Year Cert	CPR
17483	Baker	Oak	OH	35	FF			6' 0"	180	150		
18420	Taylor	Elm	NY	24	EMT						2010	9
21667	Chen	Oak	OH	41	PO	Sergeant	5					
24158	Adams	Maple	TN	36	FF			5' 10"	175	200		
26993	Roberts	Main	CA	45	EMT						2021	5
28210	Kumar	Main	FL	22	FF			6' 1"	210	170		
30623	Harris	Elm	NY	31	PO	Captain	10					

EMPLOYEE TABLE

FIGURE 13.8 Single relational table solution

there is. The rank attribute is only needed for police officers; height is only needed for firefighters; and so on. This situation is known as "sparse data" and creates other storage and performance issues. So, what is the solution to this problem? The document database framework, with products such as **MongoDB**, solves this as well as other data management problems.

The first thing to recognize about document database is that the word "document," in this context, does not mean a traditional textual document, like a newspaper article, an email, or a book, written in a natural language such as English. As we will soon find out, a document in this context serves a similar function to a record or tuple in a relational table, but with much more flexibility in its structure. It's also true that, in common with key value database, document database stores data as key-value pairs, but with a structure that key value database does not have. In fact, in document database, related attributes, like a person's name, street, and state, can be stored together, while in key value database they would be stored independently. Let's take a look at an example, Figure 13.9, continuing to use the city first responder data.

Figure 13.9 shows three "documents" (in a notational style known as JSON for JavaScript Object Notation). The first document represents the data of employee number 17483 who happens to be a firefighter. In addition to the attributes that all employees have: employee number, name, street, state, and age, it also has the attributes specific to firefighters: height, weight, and MWC. The second document, for an EMT, includes the EMT-specific attributes year of first EMT certification and cardiopulmonary resuscitation (CPR) rating. The third document, for a police officer, includes the police officer-specific attributes rank and years on the police force. Of course, if we wanted

```
{{
"Emp_Num": 17483,
"Name": "Baker",
"Street": "Oak",
"State": "OH",
"Age": 35,
"Height": "6' 0",
"Weight": 180,
"MWC": 150 },
{
"Emp_Num": 18420,
"Name": "Taylor",
"Street": "Elm",
"State": "NY",
"Age": 24,
"Year_Cert": 2010,
"CPR": 9 },
{
"Emp_Num": 21667,
"Name": "Chen",
"Street": "Oak",
"State": "OH",
"Age": 41,
"Rank": "Sergeant",
"Years": 5 }
}
```

FIGURE 13.9 Three documents in a collection

Emp Num	First Name	Middle Initial	Last Name	Street	State	Age
17483	John	L	Baker	Oak	OH	35
18420	Mary	G	Taylor	Elm	NY	24
21667	Fred	Q	Chen	Oak	OH	41
24158	Jane	A	Adams	Maple	TN	36
26993	Allen	R	Roberts	Main	CA	45
28210	John	A	Kumar	Main	FL	22
30623	Jane	G	Harris	Elm	NY	31

FIGURE 13.10 Three attributes composing the name

to model all of the original employee data, we would need seven documents, one for each employee in the example.

A set of documents is called a "collection." It should be clear that a document is functionally similar to a row in a relational table and a collection is functionally similar to a relational table. But look at the difference!! In a relational table all of the rows have the same set of attributes. This can create the kind of problem that we described using Figures 13.7 and 13.8. On the other hand, in a collection in a document database, the different documents can have some of the same attributes (employee number, name, street, state, age, in our example), but they can also have different attributes (the first document has height, weight, and MWC; the second document has year_cert and CPR; the third document has rank and years). This eliminates the kind of problem in relational database, either excessive joins or sparse data, that we described using Figures 13.7 and 13.8!! You can even add additional attributes to documents after they were initially created.

Now, let's say that instead of having a single name attribute, the relational table has three attributes that involve a person's name. This would be First Name, Middle Initial, and Last Name, as shown in Figure 13.10.

Using SQL, you can separately retrieve a person's first name or middle initial, or last name. But you can't say, "Name," and expect to retrieve a person's complete name, including their first name, middle initial, and last name. To accomplish that, you would have to separately specify all three attributes. Now, let's look at the equivalent situation in a document in document database. Figure 13.11 shows the first document (the document for employee 17483) in Figure 13.9, modified to include first name, middle initial, and last name.

```
{
"Emp_Num": 17483,
"Name": {
     "First_Name": "John",
     "Middle_Initial": "L",
     "Last_Name": "Baker"
             },
"Street": "Oak",
"State": "OH",
"Age": 35,
"Height": "6' 0^",
"Weight": 180,
"MWC": 150 },
```

FIGURE 13.11 An embedded document

In Figure 13.11, Name is known as an "embedded document." It has all of the characteristics of a document but, clearly, it is inside of the Employee document. So, another advantage of document database is that you have the choice of referring to the complete name as "Name" (the label on the embedded document in the figure) or you can refer to each of the three individual parts of the name by "First_Name," "Middle_Initial," or "Last_Name." There is no equivalent of referring to the complete name with a single attribute name, i.e. "Name" in this example, in the relational model.

Your Turn

One of the most important elements of document database is its ability to handle supertype/subtype situations without having multiple tables or a single table with many nulls as would be the case in a relational database.

Question:

Choose any industry and think about groups of personnel that have some of the same characteristics and some different characteristics. How would a document database help you efficiently store the data about such personnel?

Column Family Database

Another NoSQL paradigm is known by several different names. We will call it column family database, but it is also known by other names such as wide-column database and big table database. Simply put, column family database has many of the same characteristics as document database, but is designed to have more of a table-like feel to it, which is obvious from its various names, using words like "table" and "column."

A column family is, simply, a group of related columns. Actually, a better way to think of it is a group of related *attributes*, which are then stored as columns. If a person's first name, middle name, and last name are each considered to be separate attributes, then those three attributes taken together might be called the Name column family. Similarly, if street address, city, state, country, and postal codes are each considered to be separate attributes, then together they might be called the Address column family.

Now, let's take another look at the EMPLOYEE TABLE from Figure 13.7, repeated here as Figure 13.12.

Emp Num	Name	Street	State	Age
17483	Baker	Oak	OH	35
18420	Taylor	Elm	NY	24
21667	Chen	Oak	OH	41
24158	Adams	Maple	TN	36
26993	Roberts	Main	CA	45
28210	Kumar	Main	FL	22
30623	Harris	Elm	NY	31

EMPLOYEE TABLE

FIGURE 13.12 The Employee table

Row id	Emp Num	Name	Street	State	Age
1	17483	Baker	Oak	OH	35
2	18420	Taylor	Elm	NY	24
3	21667	Chen	Oak	OH	41
4	24158	Adams	Maple	TN	36
5	26993	Roberts	Main	CA	45
6	28210	Kumar	Main	FL	22
7	30623	Harris	Elm	NY	31

EMPLOYEE TABLE

FIGURE 13.13 The Employee table with row ids

First, we will give each row a unique sequence number or id, Figure 13.13.

Next, we'll divide the columns into column families. Let's create the Identification Column Family and assign the Emp Num and Name attributes to it. Similarly, we'll create the Location Column Family and assign the Street and State attributes to it. Finally, we'll create the Description (Desc) Column Family and assign the Age attribute to it, Figure 13.14.

As noted earlier, column family database has many of the same characteristics as document database. The way that attribute values were tagged with attribute names in document database also applies in column family database, Figure 13.15.

Notice that only the Column Family Names are above the table now; the attribute names are no longer at the tops of the columns. Also notice, very importantly, that we have returned to the concept of key-value pairs! Every value can be expressed as:

```
Row id:Column Family Name:Attribute Name:Value
```

where Row id:Column Family Name:Attribute Name is the unique key. For example:

```
3:Location:Street:Oak
```

where the key 3:Location:Street leads to the value Oak.

An advantage of this arrangement is that we can retrieve data at the attribute level or at the column family level. For example, for row id 4, we can retrieve just the Name Adams or the entire Identification column family.

```
24158, Adams.
```

	Identification		Location		Desc
Row id	Emp Num	Name	Street	State	Age
1	17483	Baker	Oak	OH	35
2	18420	Taylor	Elm	NY	24
3	21667	Chen	Oak	OH	41
4	24158	Adams	Maple	TN	36
5	26993	Roberts	Main	CA	45
6	28210	Kumar	Main	FL	22
7	30623	Harris	Elm	NY	31

FIGURE 13.14 The Employee table with column families

Row id	Identification		Location		Desc
1	Emp Num: 17483	Name: Baker	Street: Oak	State: OH	Age: 35
2	Emp Num: 18420	Name: Taylor	Street: Elm	State: NY	Age: 24
3	Emp Num: 21667	Name: Chen	Street: Oak	State: OH	Age: 41
4	Emp Num: 24158	Name: Adams	Street: Maple	State: TN	Age: 36
5	Emp Num: 26993	Name: Roberts	Street: Main	State: CA	Age: 45
6	Emp Num: 28210	Name: Kumar	Street: Main	State: FL	Age: 22
7	Emp Num: 30623	Name: Harris	Street: Elm	State: NY	Age: 31

FIGURE 13.15 The Employee table with attribute names

When we looked at document database, we saw that different documents in a collection could have different attributes. This was one of the interesting and useful features of document database. A similar capability holds for column family database! Consider, again, the attributes and values specific to police officers, firefighters, and EMTs in Figure 13.7 and how they were inserted into some of the sample documents in Figure 13.9. We can do essentially the same thing in column family database by relying on the concept of different column families being associated with different row ids, Figure 13.16.

Police Officer

Emp Num	Rank	Years
21667	Sergeant	5
30623	Captain	20

Firefighter

Emp Num	Height	Weight	MWC
17483	6′ 0″	180	150
24158	5′ 10″	175	200
28210	6′ 1″	210	170

EMT

Emp Num	Year Cert	CPR
18420	2010	9
26993	2021	5

FIGURE 13.16 Specific column families

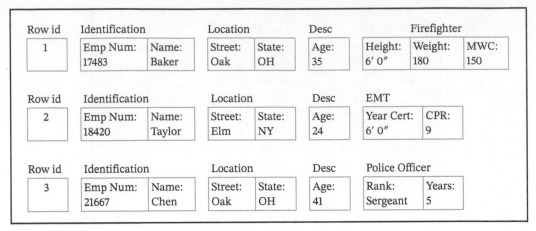

FIGURE 13.17 Three records shown as column families

FIGURE 13.18 The Identification column family with timestamps

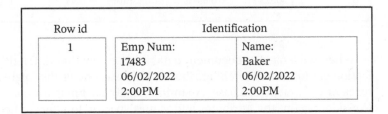

FIGURE 13.19 The Identification column family with new data inserted and timestamped

For example, we know that employee 17483, now identified by row id 1, in Figure 13.15 includes data from the Firefighter column family. In fact, the column family database equivalent of the document database example in Figure 13.9 would be Figure 13.17.

Another interesting feature of column family database is that the data is *time-stamped* when it is inserted into the database. The timestamps can be different for different attributes within the same row id. And, very interestingly, the timestamped data is saved, keeping a historical record of the data as it is updated. When the data is retrieved, the default is to return the latest data, but requests can be made to retrieve previous attribute values. This is very different from traditional data storage. Usually, when data is updated to a new value, the old value is simply lost.

For example, consider the Identification column family of Row id 1 in Figure 13.17. Let's say that both the Emp Num and Name were inserted on June 2, 2022 at 2:00PM. Then the data would look like Figure 13.18:

Then, if the employee's name changed (for whatever reason) to Jones on July 21, 2022 at 11:00AM, the column family data would look like Figure 13.19:

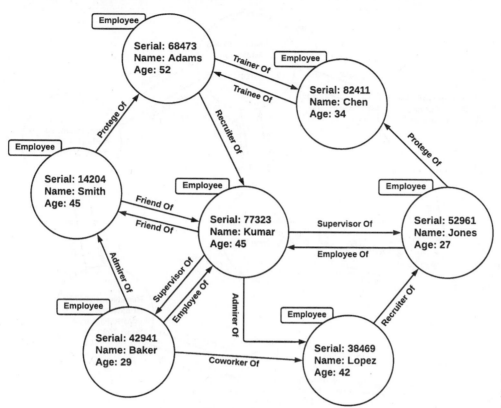

FIGURE 13.20 The Employee graph with all nodes of the same entity type

The value Jones with its timestamp is recorded and the original value Baker, with its timestamp, is also kept in the database and can be retrieved if needed.

Graph Database

The fourth and last NoSQL framework is graph database. While it is noticeably different from the other three NoSQL frameworks, it does have key-value elements that put it in the NoSQL class. Graph database is all about relationships. The relationships can be between different occurrences of the same entity type or can be between the occurrences of different entity types.

A simple example of what graph database is all about is a graph database model of how employees in a company relate to each other, Figure 13.20. Each circle or "node" of the graph represents an entity occurrence. In Figure 13.20, all of the nodes are labelled "Employee," meaning that each node is an occurrence of the Employee entity type, or, simply put, each node represents an employee. Notice that nodes can have properties, represented as key-value pairs. In this example, each employee node has three properties, employee serial number, name, and age. The lines or links connecting the nodes represent relationships between the nodes and, although not shown in this example, relationships can have properties, too. Some relationships are singular in nature: Lopez was the recruiter of Jones. Some are reciprocal: Smith and Kumar are friends of each other. Notice that the relationship links have arrowheads indicating a direction. Based on the arrowhead, we see that Smith is a protégé of Adams, not the other way around.

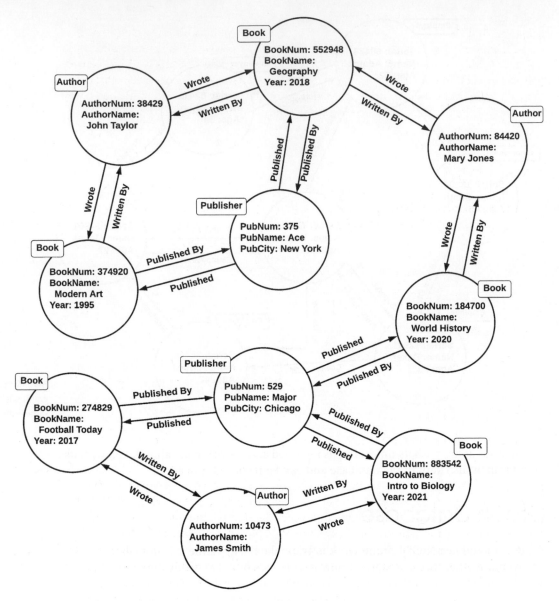

FIGURE 13.21 The Publisher graph with nodes of different entity types

Figure 13.21 is a graph in which the nodes represent different entity types: books, authors, and publishers. In fact, these entity types are taken from the Good Reading Bookstores example in Figure 2.10 in Chapter 2. But, Figure 2.10 shows an associative entity, Wrote, recognizing the many-to-many relationship between books and authors (a book can have multiple authors and an author can write or cowrite many books). Although not shown in Figure 2.10, we know that a many-to-many relationship can carry intersection data, such as, in this example, the payment that an author received for writing a book. Figure 13.21 shows that John Taylor was a coauthor of the book Geography. Since relationship links in Graph Database can have properties, the Wrote link between the John Taylor and Geography nodes can have a property called Payment and that is where the intersection data would go in this graph database!!

An interesting question is, How can we store a graph database in a computer? We can't just somehow "show" a picture of a graph to a computer and expect it to understand what it means. While it is beyond the scope of this book to go into detail on this point, we will mention, in passing, that a graph can actually be described in a few tables, very much like relations in a relational database. There can be a table of nodes, a table of links, and a table of properties, and these tables can be designed in such a way that, for example, a node can be associated with the links connected to it.

Your Turn

Graph database is especially useful for storing data about entities that have relationships with each other.

highways that connect them. Include several properties of each city and several properties of each highway.

Question:

Consider a set of cities. Construct a graph database model that shows several cities and the

Querying NoSQL Databases and the Rise of NewSQL

NoSQL Query Languages

So far in this chapter we have been looking at the structures and special features of the four NoSQL frameworks. Of course, if we store data in these frameworks, we have to be able to retrieve the data, which brings up the issue of the query languages that can be used for this purpose. And, we would expect the query languages to be designed to take advantage of the unique features of the NoSQL systems. Here are a few samples.

MongoDB is a popular document database. Suppose you have a collection of documents called "users" and you want to find all of the documents in the collection (i.e. all of the people) that have an "age" attribute with the value 27, you would write:

```
db.users.find({"age" : 27})
```

"find" is the key word in MongoDB that triggers this kind of data retrieval.

To retrieve all of the documents for users between 18 and 30 years old you would write:

```
db.users.find({"age" · {"$gte": 18, $lte" : 30}})
```

where $gte is greater than or equal to, $lte is less than or equal to, and the comma between them indicates an AND condition.

HBase is a popular column family database. The basic data retrieval command in HBase is:

```
Get(byte[] row)
```

which is based on the column family database concept of identifying rows by their row id, indicated in the command by "row."

To retrieve multiple rows from a database you would write:

```
Scan(byte[] startRow, byte[] stopRow)
```

which indicates the range of row ids that you're looking for.

And you can retrieve an entire column family with:

```
Get addFamily(byte[] family).
```

Furthermore, there is syntax in the column family database retrieval languages for taking advantage of the timestamp feature, too.

Neo4j is a common graph database and it has a data retrieval language called **Cypher**. In order to take advantage of the graph structures, Cypher has to be able to not only retrieve the data (the properties) in a node, but also must be able to traverse the graph and find nodes attached to other nodes. For example, in Figure 13.21, Cypher would have to be able to retrieve the properties in the publisher node for publisher number 375 (i.e. PubNum 375, PubName Ace, PubCity New York) but also be able to find all of the books it has published and all of the properties of those books. The syntax is fairly complicated, but it is capable of accomplishing tasks like these. The key command is MATCH.

For example, if you want to retrieve the node for publisher number 375, you would write:

```
MATCH (publisher: Publisher {PubNum: '375'}
RETURN (publisher)
```

As you read the previous passages about data retrieval in the NoSQL frameworks, it may have occurred to you that the thirty or more years in which people became skilled in SQL as a data retrieval language seem to have gotten lost in the NoSQL frameworks. You're right!! In fact, as people began experimenting with and using the NoSQL frameworks, they began seeking a solution that would allow them to use the standard SQL data retrieval language with data storage frameworks that included the advanced NoSQL features. Nature (and business) hates a vacuum and the database product vendors responded with a new class of database management systems known, informally, as NewSQL database management systems.

NewSQL

Database management systems generally classified as **NewSQL** include such products as ClustrixDB, NuoDB, MemSQL, VoltDB, and a variety of others. In the very competitive world in which these products exist, their features are a constantly moving target. They tend to be relational or tabular in structure, use SQL as their query language, and are ACID compliant.

Another common feature of NewSQL systems is that they are "in memory systems." This means that as primary memories have become progressively faster, cheaper, and larger, these systems are designed to keep entire databases or large parts of them in main memory. This allows them to run at much faster speeds, although the data must periodically be copied to secondary memory for non-volatile storage. Regarding non-volatile storage, these systems are designed for use with server farms and many have automatic data replication capabilities which promotes a high level of data availability. These systems can replicate data to multiple servers and keep track of where the copies of the data reside. If a server with one copy of a piece of data goes down, another copy of the data is available on another server. Furthermore, with the ability of server farms to add more servers for a system when needed, they also have the property of scalability.

Other features that can be found in some of these NewSQL systems include data encryption, data compression, parallel processing (in the server farms), and stored procedures. Some of them state that they can be used either "on premises" in a company's own computers or in the cloud. Some emphasize that they are designed for both transactional processing and analytical processing. Some have the capability to store data across multiple data centers.

Summary

While relational database management has many advantages and has certainly proven itself for many applications over many years, it does have several shortcomings. This fact, plus the advent of such new hardware technologies and arrangements including faster main memory, solid state disks, and server farms, has led to several new database management technologies that solve some of the problems of relational database and take advantage of the new hardware capabilities. Thus, we now have the NoSQL paradigms of key-value database, document database, column-family database, and graph database. Further, the combination of these new database paradigms plus the desire to continue to use SQL as a query language, have led to NewSQL database.

Key Terms

ACID property	**Hadoop**	**MongoDB**	**Solid state disks**
Big data	**Hadoop Distributed File**	**Neo4j**	**Spark**
Column family database	**System (HDFS)**	**NewSQL**	**Volume, variety, velocity**
Cypher	**Hashing**	**NoSQL database**	**YARN**
Document database	**Key-value database**	**Parallel processing**	
Graph database	**MapReduce**	**Server farm**	

Questions

1. What are the shortcomings of relational database management that led to NoSQL database management?

2. In general, what are the advantages of NoSQL database management?

3. What is "big data"? Explain the three "Vs" of big data.

4. What is the ACID property and why is it important?

5. What advances in hardware have enabled the transition to NoSQL database management? Why are they important?

6. Describe the concept of key-value database.

7. How do the keys and values in a key-value database differ from the equivalent concepts in a relational database?

8. What data storage and retrieval technique allows key-value database to have fast performance?

9. What is HDFS and what are its major structural constructs?

10. What is MapReduce and how does it work?

11. Describe the concept of document database.

12. What are the equivalent constructs in document database to attribute, row, and table in a relational database?

13. If documents in a document database are roughly the equivalent of rows in a relational database, what are the comparative advantages of documents?

14. How would a program processing documents have to operate differently compared to how it would have to operate if processing rows in a relational database?

15. Describe the concept of column family database. What is a column family?

16. In what ways are document databases similar to column family databases?

17. What is the timestamp property in column family database management?

18. Describe the concept of graph database.

19. What kinds of applications is graph database management good for and why?

20. Why is graph database considered a NoSQL database paradigm?

21. How can a graph database graph be described to a computer?

22. Generally speaking, what is the nature of query languages for NoSQL database management systems?

23. What is the premise for NewSQL database?

Exercises

1. You are the data administrator of a mid-sized manufacturing company. As your company begins to realize the potential of big data for product design and marketing, you realize that the limits of relational database could impede the company's progress. Make an argument for introducing one or more NoSQL databases specifically to aid product design and marketing.

2. Consider the Central Hospital entity-relationship diagram of Exercise 7.2. Focus on just the Nurse, Department, Doctor, and Degree entities and create a database schema design for a:
   a. Key-value database.
   b. Document database.
   c. Column family database.
   d. Graph database.

3. Consider the Central Hospital entity-relationship diagram of Exercise 7.2. Focus on just the Insurance Company, Claim, Patient, Operation, and Operation Type entities and create a database schema design for a:
   a. Key-value database.
   b. Document database.
   c. Column family database.
   d. Graph database.

Minicases

1. Consider the Happy Cruise Lines entity-relationship diagram of Minicase 7.1. Focus on just the Ship, Cruise, Visit, and Port entities and create a database schema design for a:
   a. Key-value database.
   b. Document database.
   c. Column family database.
   d. Graph database.

2. Consider the Super Baseball League relational database of Minicase 4.2. Create a database schema design for a:
   a. Key-value database.
   b. Document database.
   c. Column family database.
   d. Graph database.

Blockchain

With the advent of **cryptocurrencies**, its underlying foundation, **blockchain**, has become a topic of concern to the data management profession. In fact, blockchain technology is being employed in an increasingly wide range of applications well beyond financial applications. While blockchain is not, strictly speaking, "database management" as we have come to understand this term, it is nonetheless a method of storing and retrieving data and so should be understood as an option in the context of data management.

OBJECTIVES

- Explain the blockchain concept.
- Describe how cryptographic hashing is used in blockchain.
- Describe how public-key encryption is used to create digital signatures in blockchain.
- Describe additional blockchain concepts including Merkle trees, consensus, and smart contracts.

Introduction

It seems like cryptocurrencies, such as **Bitcoin** and its competitors, are in the news a lot. Cryptocurrencies represent a new form of money that is not backed by governments or gold and is not held in traditional banks. So, why should we be interested in such financial instruments in a book about data and database? The answer is that cryptocurrencies are based on an information systems concept known as "blockchain" which, in effect, is a very specialized way of storing and manipulating data. And cryptocurrencies are not the only application of blockchain. Other prominent applications of blockchain include managing electronic medical records, tracking fruits and vegetables from farm to table, managing insurance policies, and enabling voting systems, among many others.

The basic concept of blockchain is that it is a **peer-to-peer** system that is not under the control of any **central authority**. In cryptocurrencies, for example, there are no banks or governments involved. The "peers," and there can be any number of them, are individual people or companies with their computers that communicate with each other via the Internet. The data stored in the blockchain can be anything that can be digitized, including forms of money, records like medical records, and even the ownership records of digital objects such as photos or works of art, referred to as **non-fungible tokens** or NFTs. The idea, in general, is that these digital objects of value in the form of data can be owned, bought, sold, and traded between peers without the need or cost of an intermediary or "middle man." The term for this is "**disintermediation**."

But there is a reason, that we sometimes take for granted, that we have always dealt with central authorities, or intermediaries such as banks. After all, we trust them to keep track of who owns what instruments of value, such as money, and to do so in a secure manner. Without them, in a purely peer-to-peer environment, how could we be certain of who owns what items of value, whether the transfer of such items from one owner to anther is legitimate and whether or not the whole system has been hacked? There are also benefits to storing transaction history and to allowing access to the history to all who legitimately need to see it. Accomplishing all of this is where the concept of blockchain comes in.

Blockchain is a fairly complicated topic. There are public blockchains that anyone can participate in and there are private blockchains that are limited to invited participants. There are different blockchain platforms with different data structures and rules. Our goal in this chapter is not to cover every blockchain variation in detail, but rather to explain some of the basic, universal concepts that make blockchains, in general, work.

What Is a Blockchain?

Figure 14.1 shows a single **block**. Think of it simply as some data that represents a transaction with the details of that transaction. Figure 14.1 shows that Johnson bought a house on 3/5/2008 for $100,000. Figure 14.2 shows two more related transactions. Adams bought the house from Johnson on 12/15/2015 and paid $150,000 for it, creating a blockchain, literally a chain of blocks. Then, on 8/3/2022, Williams bought the house from Adams and paid $200,000 for it, extending the blockchain further.

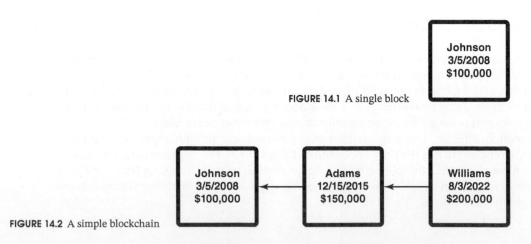

FIGURE 14.1 A single block

FIGURE 14.2 A simple blockchain

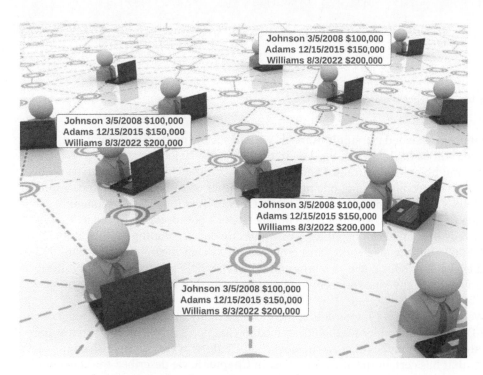

FIGURE 14.3 A copy of the ledger at every blockchain participant's node

iblist / Shutterstock

Remember that there is no central authority keeping track of these transactions. How do we know who the current owner of the house is? What if it's important to maintain a record of the sales history of the house? Part of the answer, as shown in Figure 14.3, is that everyone participating in the blockchain, that is, every node, in the network keeps its own history or **"ledger"** of all of the transactions that have taken place.

But remember, there is no central authority to maintain the security of the data in the blockchain or even to verify that the person who claims ownership of the data or who transfers ownership of the data is legitimate! How do we know that Adams really bought the house in 2015 or that she authorized the sale of the house to Williams in 2022? Without a trusted central authority to verify and keep track of all of this, anyone who has access to the blockchain, or an outside hacker, for that matter, could illegally modify the blockchain to make it reflect what they want it to.

Two technologies are used in blockchain to overcome these concerns and make the blockchain safe to use. The two technologies are **hashing** and **public-key encryption**.

Hashing

Cryptographic Hashing

We first looked at hashing in Chapter 8 on physical database design, as a method for storing and retrieving data. Recall that the basic idea in hashing is to feed some number into an algorithm that will produce another, smaller number. In Figure 8.18, we fed salesperson numbers into a hashing algorithm that produced numbers that indicated the storage slots in which to store the salespersons' records. What would this look like if we tried to hash the data in a block in a blockchain? Figure 14.4 illustrates a block

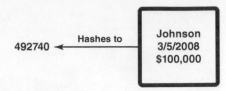

FIGURE 14.4 Hashing the data in a block to a single number

of data being hashed to a single number. We will see the use for this later when, by the way, we will be hashing both the data in the block *and its location.*

You might look at Figure 14.4 and wonder how the data in this block can be hashed. Hashing is the conversion of one number to another, as in Figure 8.18. And "Johnson 3/5/2008 $100,000" isn't exactly a number. Or is it? It is important to remember that all data in a computer, whether it is a number, text, a photo, etc., is stored in bits. Each bit, at any one time, can be either 0 or 1 and any data, including "Johnson 3/5/2008 $100,000" amounts to a (long) string of 0s and 1s. That means that any data of any kind eventually boils down to a binary number, possibly a very long binary number. So, any data of any kind in a computer can be hashed based on the binary, or base 2, number system.

We pointed out in Chapter 8 that there can be many different hashing algorithms. The Division-Remainder Method described in Chapter 8 is one of the simplest hashing algorithms. On the other hand, blockchain requires a very complex hashing algorithm that has certain specific properties. In Chapter 8, we described the concept of a collision in which two different input numbers hashed to the same output value and we described a way to handle that situation. The way we will use hashing in blockchain will not tolerate collisions. The hashing algorithm must be so complex that, for all practical purposes, collisions will not happen. Another property of a hashing algorithm used in blockchain is that it must not be possible to figure out what the input data was based on knowing the output data. In other words, you cannot go backward. You must not be able to figure out what the original data was just by knowing the output of the hashing algorithm. To accomplish all of this, blockchain uses complex hashing algorithms known as **cryptographic hashing** algorithms.

Cryptographic Hashing in the Blockchain

Figure 14.5 illustrates the use of cryptographic hashing in the blockchain. Again, Johnson bought a house on 3/5/2008 for $100,000 and sold it to Adams on 12/15/2015 for $150,000. At the time of that sale, a new block is created for Adams, as shown in the diagram. But there is more to it and here is where hashing comes in. HP1 (hash pointer 1) is a hash value that results from a combination of the data in Johnson's block and its location in the computer. As shown in the diagram, HP1 is stored in Adams' block. This creates a "chain" from Adams' block to Johnson's block. Similarly, When Williams buys the house from Adams in 2022, Adams' block and its location are hashed and the resulting hash value is stored in Williams' block as HP2. Williams still owns the house, but her block will be hashed and the hash value, HP3, will be stored in a secure location.

All of this hashing accomplishes a couple of things. First, since the hash values incorporate the locations of the blocks, it creates a chain. Starting from HP3, you can trace the entire history of the ownership of the house, all the way back to Johnson. The entire history will be stored in the ledger at every node participating in the blockchain (refer back to Figure 14.3).

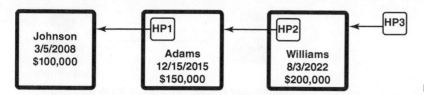

FIGURE 14.5 Blockchain with hash pointers

But there is another really interesting purpose for going to all of the trouble of hashing the data in the blocks. Let's say that for some reason a hacker goes in and changes the price that Adams paid for the house to $125,000. If you run the hashing algorithm through the data in Adams' block again, the resulting hash value will not match HP2 in Williams' block and therefore you know that the blockchain has been hacked!!! Even if the hacker is clever enough to replace HP2 in Williams' block with the new hash value, he would also have to update HP3 because that, in turn, will not match. But the concept is that HP3 is stored in a secure location that the hacker cannot reach. Thus, all of this hashing not only creates the chain, but it also provides an important layer of security.

Public-Key Encryption

Public-Key Encryption Revisited

We first looked at the subject of data encryption in the Data Security section of Chapter 11. Recall that **Private-Key Encryption** entails the use of the same key to encrypt and decrypt data. Public-Key Encryption requires a pair of companion keys: a public key and a corresponding private key. When a public key is used to encrypt data, only its companion private key can decrypt it. The public key that was used to encrypt the data *cannot decrypt it*. And, it turns out that the process also works in reverse: if the data is encrypted with the private key, only the companion public key can decrypt it.

When data is encrypted with the public key and decrypted with the private key, the concept is that since everyone has the public key, it is, after all, public, anyone can send an encrypted message to the owner of the private key who is the only one who can decrypt it, Figure 14.6.

John Smith

In public-key encryption, anyone can encrypt a message with John Smith's public key and send it knowing that John Smith, who is the only one who has the corresponding private key, is the only one who can decrypt and read it.

FIGURE 14.6 Encrypting a message with a public key in public-key encryption

John Smith

In public-key encryption, if John Smith encrypts a message with his private key and sends it to someone, they will know that it really came from him if they can decrypt it with his public key and what they get is a message that makes sense and is not garbage. His private key is his digital signature.

FIGURE 14.7 Encrypting a message with a private key in public-key encryption

But what if John Smith encrypts a message with his private key for later decryption with his corresponding public key, Figure 14.7? This is known as a "**digital signature.**" If a message supposedly sent by John Smith is received by anyone he sends the message to, and they can successfully decrypt it with his public key, they know that the message really came from him and not from an impostor. Why? Because if they could decrypt the message with his public key *and the message made sense*, they would know it really came from him. If they tried to decrypt the message with his public key and the result was incomprehensible garbage, they would know that it came from an impostor, that is from someone who did not have his private key.

In Chapter 11, we pointed out that Public-Key Encryption, with the data being encrypted with the public key, has an important use in electronic commerce. We will see in the next section of this chapter that Public-Key Encryption has important uses in blockchain with blockchain data being encrypted with the public key for certain uses and with the private key for certain other uses.

Public-Key Encryption in the Blockchain

Throughout this book, we have emphasized the need for unique keys to establish "ownership" of the related data that belongs to it. Think of a unique key in a record of a relational table as establishing "ownership" of the rest of the data in that record. The same must be true of the data in blockchain blocks. In fact, public-key encryption in blockchain is used to establish ownership of the data in the blocks. A public key/private key pair is created for every block. Figure 14.8 shows the User Account (UA) number in every block. Of course, every block has to have some identifier of the owner of the data in that block. In fact, the public key of the public key/private key pair created for that block servers as its user account number.

In Figure 14.8, UA1 is a public key that belongs to Johnson. Only Johnson possesses the corresponding private key. To verify that Johnson really owned the house (in 2008) anyone can encrypt a message with UA1 and send him a message asking for him to respond to it. If Johnson can read the message (by decrypting it with his private key, which only he possesses) then he can respond and ownership of the data in the block can be established.

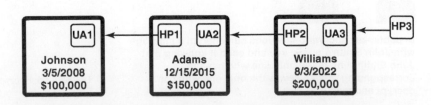

FIGURE 14.8 Blockchain showing user account numbers (UAx)

Now that we've considered verifying ownership of the data in a block, we have to consider securely transferring ownership of the data from one person to another. How can we be sure that Johnson really wanted to sell the house to Adams and on the date and at the price shown in the blockchain? We're going accomplish this by using the reverse of the public-key encryption process and begin by using the private key. Suppose that Johnson creates a message describing the transaction he wants to take place. The message says, "I want to sell the house to Adams for $150,000." First, the message is hashed into a single number to make the process more manageable. Then, the hashed result is encrypted with Johnson's private key. Next both the original message and the encrypted hash result are sent, together, to everyone participating in the blockchain, Figure 14.9.

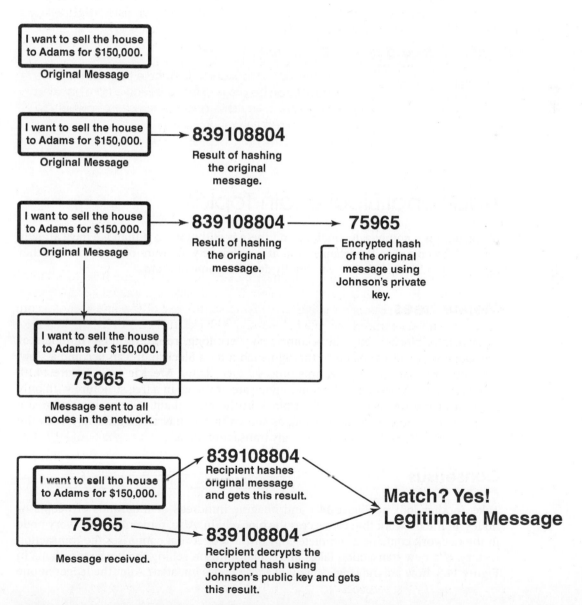

FIGURE 14.9 Starting with the private key of public-key encryption to verify a message

If someone wants to verify that the message is legitimate, that is that it really is from Johnson, here is how they would proceed. Remember that they have received both the original message and the encrypted (with Johnson's private key) hash of the message. So, first they would hash the original message. The way the cryptographic hashing algorithm works, the result of the hash will be the same result that Johnson got. Then they would decrypt the encrypted hash with Johnson's public key (which everyone has, because it's public). Then, they can compare the decrypted hash value with new hash result that they just generated. If the two hash values match, they know that the message is legitimate, Figure 14.9. If they don't match, they know that the message is a fraud.

Your Turn

Consider some authority that wants to keep track of the history of ownership of pieces of artwork. This will include buyers and sellers of the pieces of artwork and the prices paid for them.

Question:

Construct a blockchain to handle this task. Indicate how it can be assured that it is secure from hacking and how ownership and the transfer of ownership can be secure.

Additional Blockchain Topics

Blockchain is a complex technology and there is still more to it than we have already covered. To complete this chapter and at least make you aware of some of the other topics within blockchain, we will briefly describe some of them.

Merkle Trees

In principle, blockchains can become very, very long, recording huge numbers of transactions. Trying to navigate through such a long blockchain can become a slow, laborious exercise. To improve this process, there is the **Merkle tree**, Figure 14.10. Notice that in a Merkle tree the transactions are arranged in a tree structure with only the root of the tree being an actual block in the blockchain. The hash pointers are grouped, and the groups are hashed, as shown in the diagram, until they reach the root. The root itself does not contain any transaction data.

Consensus

Take another look at Figure 14.3 and imagine hundreds or thousands of people or nodes on the network that can access the blockchain. Also, remember that every node in the network contains a complete copy of the ledger that comprises the transaction history. If a new transaction takes place, like Johnson selling the house to Adams in Figure 14.8, how are the ledgers at all of those nodes updated? After the ledger at one

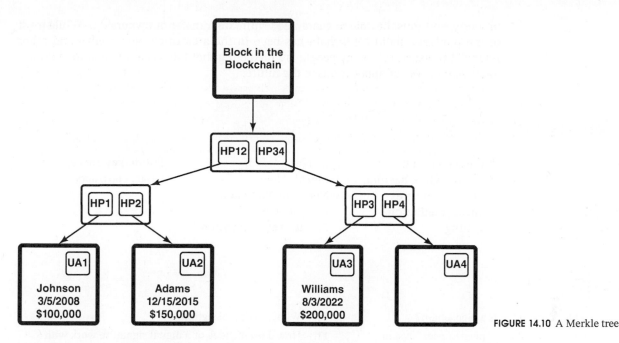

FIGURE 14.10 A Merkle tree

node is updated, messages have to be sent to update the ledgers at all of the other nodes. That can take a lot of time. What if during the time it takes to update all of the copies of the ledger, another transaction is initiated that involves the data that was just updated? Some of the copies of the ledger will reflect that last update but others will not because the message to perform the update has not reached them yet. A number of procedures to solve this problem have been developed. Going into detail on them is beyond the scope of this book. We will simply say that they involve inspecting the ledgers at all of the nodes and coming to a decision about the correct state of the transaction history based on what is found in the ledgers.

Smart Contracts

Some blockchain technologies permit the use of "**smart contracts**." In their basic form, smart contracts are executable transactions that are more flexible and have more options than the simple ownership transferring transactions that we discussed in this chapter. But, smart contracts are, in fact, computer programs written in a language that is compatible with the blockchain technology that it works with. This fact opens up a range of new possibilities of what the blockchain can accomplish and is an important feature to watch for in the future.

Summary

Blockchain is an exciting technology that has the potential to lower the costs and speed the performance of many types of business processes. Eliminating the middleman, the concept of disintermediation, is certainly desirable but not without cautions. For blockchain to be successful it must be secure, it must guarantee accurate ownership of property, and must be able to guarantee legitimate transfer of ownership. While most of the publicity about blockchain has been in the area of cryptocurrency and other financial transactions, many people are predicting that blockchain will come into use for a wide variety of applications in the future.

Key Terms

Bitcoin	Cryptocurrency	Ledger	Public-key encryption
Block	Cryptographic hashing	Merkle Tree	Smart contracts
Blockchain	Digital Signature	Non-fungible token	
Central authority	Disintermediation	Peer-to-peer	
Consensus	Hashing	Private-key encryption	

Questions

1. What is a block and what is a blockchain?
2. Why is blockchain called a "peer-to-peer" system?
3. What is disintermediation and why does this term apply to blockchain?
4. What is a ledger in blockchain? Where are the ledgers stored?
5. What is hashing and, specifically, what is cryptographic hashing?
6. How is hashing used in creating a blockchain?
7. How does hashing prevent the hacking of a blockchain?
8. What is public-key encryption?
9. How does public-key encryption normally work?
10. What is a digital signature?
11. How does the idea of a digital signature work with public-key encryption?
12. What is a digital signature used for in blockchain?
13. How and why do hashing and digital signatures work together in blockchain?
14. What is a Merkle tree in blockchain and what is it used for?
15. What is consensus in blockchain?
16. Why is consensus important in blockchain?
17. What is a smart contract?
18. What is the difference between a public blockchain and a private blockchain?

Exercises

1. The government has decided that, for safety reasons, it wants to track every automobile made from the factory to the dealership, to the first owner and then to each successive owner.
    a. Explain how this can be accomplished with a blockchain and hashing.
    b. Draw a diagram of a blockchain illustrating this.
    c. Explain how when someone wants to buy a used car that is advertised for sale, they can be sure that they are dealing with the rightful owner of the car.
2. A bank has decided to maintain its depositor accounts using a blockchain.

    a. Since there can be many transactions for each account, the bank feels that it needs to incorporate Merkle trees into the blockchain. Draw a diagram illustrating this, specifically for the bank's accounts.
    b. Explain what it would mean to the blockchain if a person with an account in this bank wants to make a withdrawal.
    c. Explain what it would mean to the blockchain if a person with an account in this bank wants to transfer money to another account in this bank.

Minicases

1. Happy Cruise Lines has decided to build a block-chain of its passenger bookings (a particular passenger traveling on a particular ship on a particular date). Its purpose is to facilitate contact tracing if any illnesses occurs during a voyage. Think about how a blockchain might be designed for this purpose and how it would operate when needed.

2. The Super Baseball League wants to create a blockchain that records which players currently and in the past have played on which teams in the league. In addition, each team in the league has a set of "minor league" teams at different levels of proficiency that serve as "farm teams" for training players to eventually play in the Super Baseball League. The blockchain must include these minor league teams. Players are frequently traded between teams at both the Super League and minor league levels. Also, players are promoted and demoted among each Super League team's farm system. Describe how all of this would operate in a blockchain environment.

Database in the Cloud

The term "the **cloud**" as used in information systems seems to be everywhere today. It's almost impossible to have a discussion about information systems anymore without the cloud being a part of it. Indeed, the concept of turning over all or part of an information systems environment to a third party that guarantees to manage it on their remote systems appears to have many advantages. But, there are also a number of cautions to take into consideration. In any case, a key aspect of the cloud is its use for data storage and retrieval, which is the subject of this chapter.

OBJECTIVES

- Explain the concept of the cloud.
- Describe cloud usage and pricing models.
- Understand the advantages of using the cloud.
- Describe the advantages and disadvantages of storing data in the cloud.
- Compare the cloud to the distributed data concept.

Introduction

When electronic computers first came on the scene in the mid-1950s, they were big, expensive, slow machines that took up a whole room and could only run one application at a time. In the 1960s, more companies and individuals wanted to use computers, but the costs of owning one were prohibitively expensive. In addition, companies that did have computers began to realize that the time that their computers were idle, for example, as they switched between applications, was a huge waste of money. The result of these problems was the development of a technology and business model known as

FIGURE 15.1 The cloud

"**timesharing**." The idea was, basically, that a company that owned a computer could rent time on it to companies or individuals that needed computer power but didn't have the resources to own one themselves. Some of the companies that provided such services were known as "service bureaus."

But remember, that we're talking about a time well before the existence of the Internet. In order to make timesharing work, companies that wanted to rent time on another company's computer had to have a "leased line" connection to it, literally a dedicated communications line that they leased from the telephone company. As the technology kept developing, another option for connecting to someone else's computer was to "dial up" a connection through the telephone system when computer access was needed. At the same time that people were dealing with these connection issues, the companies that provided the timesharing services were developing systems software that improved the ways that they could switch their computers between customers and even run multiple programs simultaneously with terms such as "multiprogramming" and "virtual machines."

Nature hates a vacuum and so do tech entrepreneurs. As early as the 1960s, we saw the advent of "minicomputers" that allowed smaller companies to own their own computer, in effect competing with timesharing services. Then in about 1980, the personal computer came on the scene, permitting individuals to have computer power on their desks. Throughout these decades, large companies built their own large computer centers. The net effect of all of these advances and innovations, plus the networking challenges of timesharing, was that the market for timesharing services effectively disappeared.

Then came the cloud, Figure 15.1.

The Cloud: What, Why, How?

New Technologies

Several advances in technology changed the picture again and renewed interest in the idea of "renting" time and resources on computers "in the cloud" maintained

FIGURE 15.2 A server farm

by companies in business to provide such services. In its simplest terms, the cloud refers to **server farms** accessible through browsers and the Internet. Public clouds are designed for anyone to lease resources on them; private clouds are proprietary and restricted. The introduction of the Internet as we know it today in about 1995 allows universal access to the cloud. The further development of personal computers and servers, and the technology that permits them to be linked together to form large-scale "server farms," Figure 15.2, allows cloud providers to offer virtually unlimited computer power. And the introduction of **"solid state disks"** (SSD), solid state secondary memory that replaces rotating disks in the servers in the server farms, makes the server farms more reliable.

From the point of view of the data itself, the use of the data and therefore the amount of the data to be stored added an additional dimension from transactional databases to informational databases such as the data warehouses that we discussed in Chapter 12. In other words, the amount of data to be stored and used increased tremendously.

Cloud Usage Models

There are several models of cloud usage but there are three that are the most common. In **Infrastructure-as-a-Service (IaaS)** customers simply rent time on the **cloud vendor's** computer system. **Platform-as-a-Service (PaaS)** is a model in which the cloud vendor provides both the hardware and software necessary for the customer to develop their applications. The term **Software-as-a-Service (SaaS)** means that customers use software applications provided by the cloud vendor. If you have ever filed your income taxes using a program provided by a vendor that is run on the vendor's computer, you have experienced SaaS.

Cloud Pricing Models

There are two main pricing models for the cloud. In the simpler of the two models, the customer specifies an amount of cloud resources (hardware, systems software, possibly application usage) that the customer wants and pays a periodic fixed fee for it.

Then, there is a more complicated variable pricing model but one that takes advantage of the flexibility and more or less unlimited resources of the cloud. In this pricing model, if on a given day or week or month you need more of the cloud's resources, the cloud management system gives it to you (and charges you more). Conversely, if in a given time period you need less of the cloud's resources, the system takes resources away from you (and charges you less). Clearly, there can be many variations on this theme, but this is the general idea. This pricing model would certainly be considered an advantage of using the cloud and there are other advantages as we go on to the next section.

Advantages of the Cloud

There are several advantages to use the cloud model and most of them are pretty obvious. To begin with, if you go with the cloud for all of your information systems work you don't have to have your own computer center. That means you don't have to dedicate space for a computer center, install computers in it, deal with such necessities as air conditioning and fire suppression systems, maintain the systems software it requires, and hire people to run it. And, you know exactly how much you're paying for information systems services: it's whatever the monthly bill from the cloud provider amounts to. Of course, all of this will vary depending on the cloud usage model you adopt, and everyone will still want their own personal computer on their desk, but overall, it still simplifies your information systems expense cost analysis.

But, if there are advantages, are there also disadvantages? Yes there potentially are, but let's consider these in the context of cloud data issues in the next section.

Data and Database in the Cloud

So far in this chapter we've set the stage for the cloud by looking at hardware, systems software, applications, and related issues. But this book is about data and database so let's turn our attention to data and database in the cloud, Figure 15.3.

FIGURE 15.3 Data in the cloud

Where Should the Data Be Stored?

Should an organization's data be stored in a database in its own computers, in its own buildings (on premises or "**on prem**" as the current terminology goes) or in a database in the cloud? This is a question that many organizations struggle with. We will look at the pros and cons in a moment, but first let's consider the possibilities. Certainly, an organization can decide to store all of its data on prem. This does not necessarily mean that it has decided not to use the cloud at all. It is possible that it can execute an application in the cloud by transferring data from its own computers to the cloud as needed for the application, Figure 15.4. Swinging the pendulum all the way to the other side, the organization can decide to store all of its data in the cloud, which most likely means that it will run all of its applications in the cloud, although it could transfer some of it to its on prem computers as needed.

Another option, which many organizations are trying, is a hybrid approach which some people refer to as the "**hybrid cloud**." In this approach, an organization decides to keep some of its data on prem and some in the cloud. For the reasons for this split and for the decisions of which data to keep in which of the two places, we have to go on to the pros and cons of storing data in the cloud.

The Pros and Cons of Storing Data in the Cloud

Data Security   Let's begin with data security, which is a huge issue today. The question comes down to: "Who do you trust more to keep your data secure?" Cloud providers can afford to hire the best data security specialists and many of them. In addition to monitoring the data security in the server farms, they can make sure that all patches to the systems software, some of which may fix security exposures that have been discovered, are installed promptly. That sounds good, but the fact remains that the data is no longer on your computers on your premises and so there may be a sense of loss of control. Also, your data is stored in the same server farm as that of other companies and so there may be a fear of other companies gaining access to your data. On the other hand, how many data security experts can your company afford to have on your own computers? And how promptly can your people install security patches on the system software? Some very large, data-oriented companies, like large banks, may be able to compete with the cloud providers in this regard, but they are the exceptions. The proof that this is a real problem is in the many reported and unreported data hacks, data thefts, ransomware attacks, and so forth, that companies have experienced in recent years. Companies struggle with the decision of which direction to go in storing their data. Some split the difference and keep some

FIGURE 15.4 Transferring data between an on prem computer and the cloud

of their data on prem and put some of it in the cloud. There is no one right answer and no "one size fits all" solution.

Data Availability   What about data availability? In today's world of Internet-based, worldwide competition, a company's data has to be available on a 24/7 basis. Do you trust your own information systems operations more in this regard than the cloud provider's systems? One deciding factor is the number of copies of the data being stored and where it is being stored. Many companies have only one immediately available set of data, with backup copies that are not immediately available stored when needed for recovery. Some companies have had their own "mirrored data storage" in which identical copies of their databases are stored on two different computers in two different locations. If one of the computers goes down, the data is available on the other one. This is expensive and requires a certain level of personnel sophistication to work. But, the fact is that the data is on the company's computers. If the data is in the cloud, for a fee, the cloud provider can arrange to have multiple copies of the data stored on different servers in its server farm. Typically, there is an odd number of copies of the data in this arrangement, most commonly three copies. This is certainly an important advantage of the cloud since any computer, including servers in the server farm, can occasionally go down. But it still means that the organization depends on either the Internet or a leased line network for the company to reach and access its data in the cloud. If the network fails, the data is not accessible.

Data Scalability   As business grows or contracts, the amount of data that a company has to store and process can also change. Here the cloud model clearly has advantages. As its business grows, a company can buy more space for its data in the cloud provider's server farm. As its business contracts, it can reduce the amount it pays the cloud provider for less space. Whether needing more storage space in the cloud or less, these changes can be made quickly. Clearly, if the company is keeping its data on prem, it is not practical or feasible to buy or sell data storage space as quickly or efficiently as it can if using the cloud.

Data Backup and Recovery   We discussed the subject of data backup and recovery in Chapter 11. At that point in this book, we assumed the data was on prem. If the data is on prem, then, simply, the cloud can be used for backup.

On the other hand, if the data is in the cloud and the replicated data model is being used with at least three copies of every data element being stored in the cloud provider's server farm, the operation of data backup is simply a byproduct of data replication. If there are three copies of every data element in the server farm, then, in a sense, it has been backed up. This, of course, assumes that the cloud is secure. A further argument is that different copies of the same data should be stored in different physical locations within the overall cloud environment.

Data and Database Administration   Chapter 10 covered the topic of database administration, which can be an expensive proposition. To run a database on prem, an organization has to pay for the database software itself plus the personnel to manage it. But, what if the organization stores its data in a database provided by the cloud provider in its server farm? In that case the cloud provider is responsible for installing and maintaining the database. The cloud provider becomes responsible for at least some aspects of performance in terms of the speed with which the data can be stored and accessed, which should be part of a service level agreement between the user organization and the cloud provider. Referring back to the terminology in Chapter 10, the user organization still needs data administration, but if the data is in the cloud, it is the cloud provider's responsibility to provide many of the services of database administration. Finally, if the cloud provider runs several different database management systems, it gives its customers, the user organizations, the opportunity to try out these different database systems for managing their data.

Your Turn

Imagine that you are the CIO of a large hospital. The data that you must store includes patient medical data, patient billing data, supplies inventory data, and employee data, among others.

1. Question: Make and defend an argument for storing the data on site, in the hospital. Then reverse it and make an argument for moving the data to the cloud.

From Distributed Database to the Cloud

Introduction to Distributed Database

Before the arrival of the cloud, there was (and still may be for some companies) the concept of distributed database. It is certainly possible for a company to concentrate all of its databases at one mainframe computer site with worldwide access to this site provided by telecommunications networks, including the Internet. While the management of such a centralized system and its databases can be controlled in a well contained manner and this can be advantageous, it has potential drawbacks as well. For example, if the single site goes down, then everyone is blocked from accessing the databases until the site comes back up again. Also, the communications costs from the many far-flung PCs and terminals to the central site can be high. One solution to such problems, and an alternative design to the centralized database concept, is known as distributed database.

The idea is that instead of having one centralized database, we are going to spread the data out among the cities on the distributed network, each of which has its own computer and data storage facilities. All this distributed data is still considered to be a single logical database. When a person or process anywhere on the distributed network queries the database, they do not have to know where on the network the data that they are seeking is located. They just issue the query, and the result is returned to them. This feature is known as "location transparency." This arrangement can quickly become rather complex and must be managed by sophisticated software known as a distributed database management system or distributed DBMS.

Distributed Database Architecture

Consider a large multinational company with major sites in Los Angeles, Memphis, New York (which is corporate headquarters), Paris, and Tokyo. Let's say that the company has a very important transactional relational database that is used actively at all

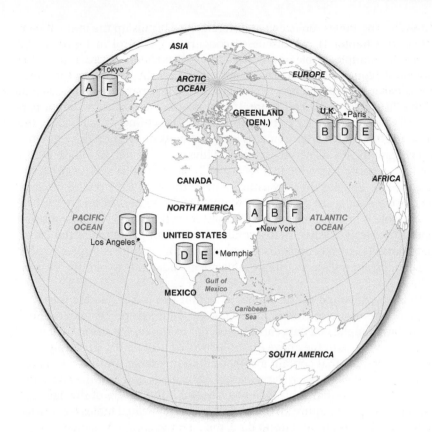

FIGURE 15.5 A distributed database

five sites. The database consists of six large tables, A, B, C, D, E, and F, and response time to queries made to the database is an important factor. There are a variety of ways of distributing the data. The most practical way is illustrated by Figure 15.5. Notice that some of the tables have been duplicated at multiple sites. There are several concepts involved in the data distribution decisions.

First, if particular tables are used at some sites more frequently than at others, it would make sense to locate the tables at the sites at which they are most frequently used. Doing this, employees at a particular site can exercise "local autonomy" over the data at their site, taking responsibility for its security, backup and recovery, and concurrency control.

Notice that in Figure 15.5 several tables have copies at more than one site on the distributed network. This has several pros and cons. One benefit of this arrangement is data availability. If a database table is stored at only one site in the distributed network and that site goes down, the data in that table is unavailable. But, with the tables replicated at multiple sites, if, for example, the site at Tokyo goes down, Table A is still available at the site in New York. Another advantage of having replicated tables is that if more than one site requires frequent access to a particular table, those sites can each have a copy of the table, speeding data access. Also having multiple copies of tables at different sites can help when tables have to be joined in a query. If the tables that have to be joined are located together at a site, the join process will be much more efficient than if data has to move across the network to accomplish a join.

Unfortunately, having tables replicated at different sites brings up the issue of concurrency control. In Chapter 11, we discussed concurrency control in terms of the problems involved in multiple people or processes trying to update a record at the same time. When we allow replicated tables to be dispersed all over the country or the world in a distributed database, the problems of concurrent update expand, too. The original possibility of the "lost update" is still there. If two people attempt to update a particular record of Table B in New York at the same time, everything we said about the problem of concurrent update earlier remains true. But now, in addition, look at what happens when geographically dispersed, replicated files are involved. In Figure 15.5, if one person updates a particular value in a record of Table B in New York at the same time that someone else updates the very same value in the very same record of Table B in Paris, clearly the results are going to be wrong. Or if one person updates a particular record of Table B in New York and then right after that a second person reads the same record of Table B in Paris, that second person is not going to get the latest, most up-to-date data. The protections discussed earlier that can be set up to handle the problem of concurrent update in a single table are not adequate to handle the new, expanded problem.

If the nature of the data and of the applications that use it can tolerate retrieved data not necessarily being up-to-the-minute accurate, then several "asynchronous" approaches to updating replicated data can be used. For example, the site at which the data was updated, New York in the above example involving Table B, can simply send a message to the other sites that contain a copy of the same table (in this case Paris) in the hope that the update will reach Paris reasonably quickly and that the computer in Paris will update that record in Table B right away. But if the nature of the data and of the applications that use it require all of the data in the replicated tables worldwide always to be consistent, accurate, and up-to-date, then a more complex "synchronous" procedure must be put in place.

The Cloud and Distributed Database

Think about everything we've said about the cloud and consider whether we still need the distributed database concept. Data in the cloud can be accessed from anywhere. Data in the cloud can be replicated by the cloud vendor with copies stored in multiple locations, making it constantly available. The cloud vendor becomes responsible for providing the access speed specified in a service level agreement and for concurrency control. The server farms that the major cloud vendors have consist of hundreds of thousands of servers spread across the globe. Thus cloud technology largely replaces the need for distributed database.

Summary

The cloud is coming into increasingly heavy use. Its substantial advantages are proving to be very popular with industry, non-profits, and government agencies across the globe. Organizations like the idea of not having to maintain their own computer centers and instead treating data and its processing as a service to be paid for like any other service. While many organizations were initially skeptical about the ability of the cloud providers to safely and efficiently handle their data, the level of trust of the cloud providers has improved dramatically as experience with them has advanced. It will be interesting to follow the progression of database in the cloud as time goes on.

Key Terms

Cloud	Data security	On prem	Software-as-a-service
Cloud vendor	Distributed database	Platform-as-a-	(SaaS)
Data availability	Hybrid cloud	service (PaaS)	Solid state disk
Data backup and recovery	Infrastructure-as-a-	Server farm	Timesharing
Data scalability	service (IaaS)		

Questions

1. What was timesharing and why wasn't it successful?
2. What advances in technology enabled the cloud?
3. Describe Infrastructure-as-a-Service.
4. Describe Platform-as-a-Service.
5. Describe Software-as-a-Service.
6. What are the two main cloud pricing models and how do they work?
7. What are the advantages of the cloud?
8. Describe the hybrid cloud model.
9. Compare and contrast the pros and cons of storing databases in the cloud.
10. Describe the concept of distributed database.
11. What are the drawbacks of distributed database?
12. Does cloud technology largely replace the need for distributed database? Explain.

Exercises

1. You are the data administration manager in a:
   a. small
   b. mid-size
   c. large

   restaurant chain that has always run its own applications on its own hardware. Your chief information officer comes to you and asks you to consider moving some or all of the company's data to the cloud. Do you recommend making the move or not? State and defend your answer to this question for each of the three different sized chains.

2. A large, multinational appliance (refrigerators, washing machines, etc.) manufacturing company has designed its information systems around the distributed database concept and has been working in that environment for several years. It is considering abandoning its distributed database and switching to a cloud-based environment. You are the company's data administration manager and you have been asked to make an assessment of this possible change. Do you think it's a good idea or a bad idea? Defend your answer.

3. Consider data security, data availability, data scalability, and backup and recovery as they relate to a large bank with global operations. Rank order them in order of importance and defend your answer.

Minicases

1. Similar to Exercise 1, above, Happy Cruise Lines been running its own, centralized data center for many years at its headquarters. This has worked reasonably well for its central, corporate operations, but connectivity to its other offices and to its cruise ships at sea has been limited and the company is dissatisfied with this arrangement. So, the company is considering changing to a cloud-based model. Explain how this might help the company in terms of its headquarters, its other offices, and its ships at sea.

2. Each team in the Super Baseball League has been collecting increasing amounts of statistical data about its own players (batting, fielding, etc.) and about the other teams in the league in order to develop advantages when playing against them. The teams want to use this data both to plan their next game against a given team and to make decisions in real time during games. Explain how the cloud can aid in this effort.

Database Applications

Data is the foundation upon which all information systems are built. In the early days of electronic data processing, the applications were primarily of an accounting nature and needed relatively straightforward accounting-type data. But, as organizations gradually discovered the competitive advantages that they could gain from cleverly using many types of data, both the nature of the data and the applications have exploded in many directions. Today, the use of enterprise resource planning (ERP), customer relationship management (CRM), and supply chain management (SCM) systems are standard practice. And the interest in data analytics and artificial intelligence applications has really taken off! The purpose of this chapter is to survey these critically important applications and the data they utilize.

OBJECTIVES

- Describe the use of data in business intelligence and data analytics.
- List and explain the various categories of data mining.
- Describe text and web mining.
- Explain how data can be used in artificial intelligence applications.
- Describe Enterprise Resource Planning (ERP).
- Customer Relationship Management (CRM).
- Supply Chain Management (SCM).

Introduction

When people think about information systems they often think first of computers, networks, and programs. But, by the time you've reached this chapter in this book, you know that none of these have any meaning without the data to be processed. The data is the corporate resource that reflects the organization's business. Without the

FIGURE 16.1 Data is used for competitive advantage in all industries

data that describes the state of the business, there would be no need for computers, networks, or programs.

In this chapter, we turn our attention from the techniques of storing and retrieving data, which have been the essence of this book, to several key technologies focused on the use of the data that are used in industries of all kinds, Figure 16.1. The first two such technologies, business intelligence, including data analytics, and artificial intelligence, are broad methodologies that are capable of producing sophisticated results in a wide variety of applications. The third technology, enterprise resource planning, is based on the concept of having a single, central data store from which all applications can access the organization's data. The last two technologies, customer relationship management and supply chain management, are major, broad-based applications that are very heavily used in industry, today.

Business Intelligence and Data Analytics

For many years, business people have been trying to design methods for using data to help them make decisions. There is a huge range in the types of decisions that can be considered. At one end of the spectrum are simple operational decisions, for example, how many of a particular part to keep in inventory this week in a manufacturing setting. At the other end of the spectrum are complex strategic decisions such as where to locate a new assembly plant. The systems that were developed for these purposes were originally known as **Decision Support Systems (DSS)**. More recently, the term Business Intelligence (BI) has replaced DSS. There are two major aspects of business intelligence. One is the activity of posing **ad hoc queries** to a database to answer specific questions that come up from time to time, which is exactly what we talked about with SQL queries in Chapter 4 of this book. The other aspect of business intelligence is what is broadly known as Data Analytics and that is the topic of this part of the chapter. A common approach to talk about data analytics is to break it down between data mining and other types of "mining."

Data Mining

Data mining refers to a variety of techniques that are designed to process data to provide organizations with a competitive edge. There are three types of data mining: descriptive analytics, predictive analytics, and prescriptive analytics.

Descriptive Analytics   Descriptive analytics refers to methods that can show the current state of the various components and operations of a company or organization. The most common way to do this is through **data visualization**. Techniques of data visualization can range from simple line graphs, bar charts, and pie charts, Figure 16.2, to complex maps with multiple overlays, Figure 16.3.

Predictive Analytics   Predictive analytics refers to methods that can predict the outcome of a business scenario based on existing data collected by the organization. There are three main categories of predictive analytics, **classification**, **clustering**, and **association**, and each of them is designed to solve a different business problem. It is important to understand that the predictions must be novel and useful. For example, in a market basket analysis (see "association" below) it is not helpful to discover that when shoppers go to a supermarket, they often buy milk and bread in the same shopping trip. That is obvious and so is not helpful.

Classification refers to examining some new data and deciding that it belongs in one of a set of existing groups. The new data can be compared to historical sets of data for which we know the outcome. A very simple but classic example is looking at the credit history and other data about a person applying for a loan. Over many years, we

FIGURE 16.2 Data visualization using graphs

Henrik5000 / Getty Images

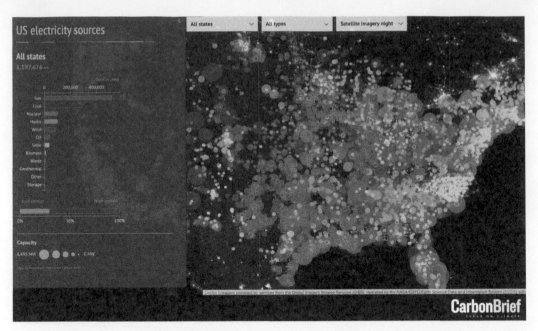

FIGURE 16.3 Data visualization using maps

Carbon brief.org

have many sets of data of people applying for loans and, for each of them, we know whether they turned out to be a good risk (paid off the loan on time) or a bad risk (defaulted on the loan). Based on this history, we can look at the new applicant's data, compare it to the data of those who have come before them, and classify them as a good risk (give them the loan) or a bad risk (deny them the loan).

One of the common techniques for classification is neural networks. The name comes from the idea that this technique is supposed to simulate the way the brain works with components that simulate neurons. A neural network has to be "trained" before it can be used, much like a person has to learn something before it is useful to him. Let's continue to use the example of loan applications. Figure 16.4 shows a simple neural network. Data is fed in on the left, then it's processed by the nodes (simulating neurons) in the middle, which then lead to one of the results on the right. The nodes in the middle have adjustable values. If a set of values associated with a known good credit risk is fed into the neural network and it correctly leads to "loan approved" on the right, then the values in the middle nodes are adjusted to strengthen such a result

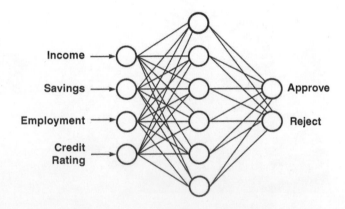

FIGURE 16.4 A neural network for loan applications

for future data sets. However, if the set of values leads to the wrong result, in this case deny the loan, then the values in the middle nodes are adjusted to try to result in loan approval for similar inputs in the future. After enough of these training sets are run through the neural network, a set of test data sets, also with known results, are run through it to see what percentage it gets correct. If the percentage is high enough, then the neural network is ready for use, otherwise it needs further training.

Clustering refers to examining many sets of data and forming them into groups with similar data characteristics. This can be very useful for marketing purposes, as an example. A classic example of clustering used for marketing is in magazine advertising. Suppose that you have a large pool of people and you know the demographics of (i.e. the personal data about) each person. Then, using clustering techniques, you divide them into groups based on similar demographics. From there, you can decide which magazines to advertise to each group, based on which magazines you think each group might be interested in. Furthermore, you decide where and how to advertise to each group, again based on their clustered characteristics.

Association refers to discovering relationships between different entities based on data history. This is another case in which data mining can be used for marketing purposes. In a classic example of association, a supermarket keeps historical data on what each person bought in a single shopping trip (also known as market basket analysis). If the historical data shows that two products were often bought in the same shopping trip, it might be advantageous to start locating the two products next to each other in the stores. That way, if a person comes into a store looking for one of the products, they might make a snap decision to buy the other one when they see it right there, next to one they came to buy.

Sometimes, prediction is also considered to be a data mining technique. For example, if a home improvement store keeps track of its customers' purchases over time (historical data!), it may notice that after several customers bought materials to build a fence, they followed-up by buying a doghouse. Then, going forward, after a customer buys materials to build a fence, the store can start marketing doghouses to them. In that sense, prediction can be considered a subcategory of association.

Prescriptive Analytics   Prescriptive analytics refers to methods that optimize or try to come as close to optimal as possible, in making business decisions. Suboptimal methods are known as heuristics (from the Greek "eureka": I have found it!). Optimization methods generally come from a field known as operations research and are beyond the scope of this book.

Text Mining and Web Mining

Since text is simply another type of data, it's not surprising that another type of analytics is text mining. A computer can process text in a variety of helpful ways. One example is known as **sentiment analysis**. By searching through a large number of customer comments that have come in by email or that have been transcribed from call center conversations, a program can look for keywords that will indicate how customers feel about a particular product. This is far more efficient and effective than if people simply try to read the comments and come to a conclusion.

There are a variety of other examples of text mining. Documents can be clustered into similar groupings based on their content. If you know what documents a user has historically been interested in, a text mining program may be able to predict what other documents she might be interested in. Sophisticated programs may be able to summarize documents. Programs may even be able to answer questions automatically by scanning relevant documents.

Web mining is essentially a variant of text mining, except that the text consists of websites and web pages. The challenge is that the material in websites is arranged in hierarchies of varying complexity.

Your Turn

Some novels are more successful than others. There are a number of factors that go into the potential success of a novel. One such factor, for example, might be its genre (mystery, humor, etc.). It is reasonable to assume that the success of the novel can be judged by its number of sales or how much money it makes.

Question:

Design a neural network to determine the potential success of a novel. Specify a set of inputs and a set of outputs.

Artificial Intelligence

As humans, we make decisions based on the knowledge that we have accumulated in our lifetimes. Whether it's a major decision such as whether to take a particular job or an almost automatic decision such as when to turn left at an intersection when we're driving, our decisions are based on our knowledge. And how did we acquire that knowledge? Ultimately, it was through data that we accumulated and processed, sometimes consciously and sometimes unconsciously. If all of this can be called "intelligence," then what is artificial intelligence?

Artificial intelligence refers to a computer performing a task that we would consider to be an act of intelligence if performed by a person. A person can add two plus two, and so can a computer, but we would ordinarily not associate this with the word intelligence. On the other hand, everyone would agree that playing chess requires a high degree of intelligence in a person and so a chess playing program could certainly be considered an example of artificial intelligence. Does a chess playing program require data? At a minimum it requires knowing where the chess pieces are on the chess board at any given point in the game and that is data! Furthermore, the history of what chess moves worked well in the past is also data.

Artificial Intelligence Applications

There are several examples of systems and applications that are considered to fall under the heading of artificial intelligence. The major ones include expert systems, natural language processing, pattern recognition, robotics, and intelligent agents.

Expert Systems   An expert system is an application that performs a task that would take an "expert" to perform if done by a person. A good example of an expert system is a program that can perform medical diagnosis. The program accepts various data, including body temperature, blood pressure, pulse, etc. as inputs and generates a diagnosis as its output. Some of these systems are designed to output several different possible diagnoses with a probability associated with each. In narrow areas of medicine, some of these systems have been shown to produce results that are quite good.

Another example of an expert system is the system that we used as an example of data mining: deciding whether to give someone a loan. This makes the point that there is considerable overlap in what today is considered artificial intelligence and what is considered data mining! Yet another example of an expert system is a program designed to figure out exactly what is wrong with a defective product coming off of an assembly line. Such a system can save money by indicating what part of the product has to be replaced rather than discarding the entire unit.

Natural Language Processing   Natural language processing (often written as NLP) is a process by which a computer can understand the real meaning of often unclear or ambiguous natural language statements and act upon them. A good and very common example of this today is processing requests typed into search engines such as Google.

Pattern Recognition   Pattern recognition tries to emulate human vision and act on it. This can include such applications as face recognition, processing a landscape for a robot to traverse, helping to control autonomous vehicles with cameras pointing ahead, and industrial applications such as automatically inspecting products coming off an assembly line.

Robotics   When most people think of robots, they think of machines that look like and act like people. While this is still largely a matter of science fiction, there are machines today that are capable of moving through an environment such as a restaurant or a hospital to deliver needed items. With a variety of sensors such as cameras, radar, and sonar, they can avoid collisions while a computer guides them to their destination. But, most robots today are stationary devices with movable arms that are designed to perform repetitive and often dangerous tasks on assembly lines, such as welding or painting cars, Figure 16.5.

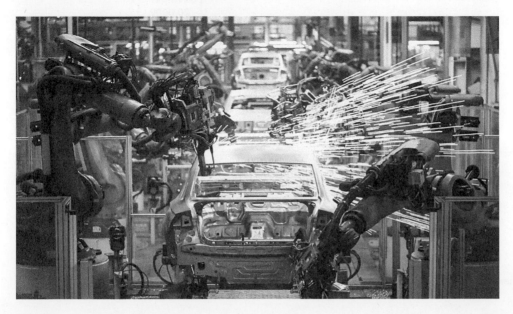

FIGURE 16.5 Stationary robots

Jenson / Shutterstock

Intelligent Agents   Intelligent agents are programs that exhibit "intelligence" by, for example, searching across the Internet for specific, targeted information in website pages.

Artificial Intelligence Techniques

A variety of techniques have been developed to make the kinds of applications listed above work. These include rule-based processors, neural networks, and genetic algorithms.

Rule-Based Processors   Rule-based processors are the underlying technology that make expert systems work. Figure 16.6 shows a hierarchy of **if-then-else rules** that drive an expert system. In this example, the expert system is another approach to whether or not to approve a loan application. General purpose expert systems, often called expert system shells, have been developed with an "inference engine" that can take any set of hierarchical if-then-else rules and process them. This means that anyone who can create a set of if-then-else rules for their application can create an expert system without having to do any programming!

Neural Networks   We have already looked at neural networks as a predictive analytics technique, but neural networks are also considered an important artificial intelligence technique in, for example, pattern recognition. Figure 16.7 shows a so-called

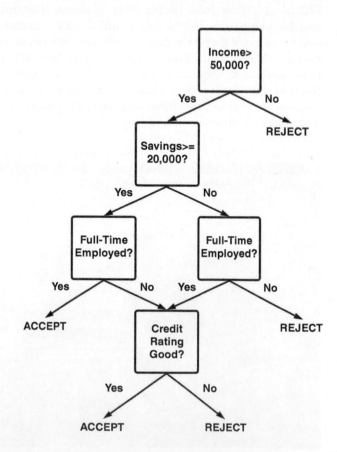

FIGURE 16.6 A hierarchy of if-then-else rules for an expert system

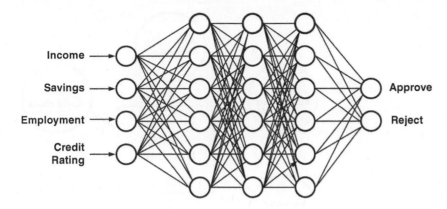

FIGURE 16.7 A deep learning neural network

"deep learning neural network" with several internal or hidden layers of neurons, designed to solve more complex machine learning problems.

Genetic Algorithms   Genetic algorithms find solutions to problems by starting with some proposed solutions and then gradually modifying and testing them. Solutions that are not helping to solve the problem are discarded while solutions that appear to be helpful are further modified to achieve even better solutions.

Enterprise Resource Planning (ERP)

Earlier in this book we considered the dangers of uncontrolled duplicate data. We talked about application developers creating new databases for each application they develop, with the result being the same data being stored in many different databases. As the data is updated, it becomes impossible to update it correctly in every database in which it is stored, even if anyone is trying to keep track of every place it is stored, which is very doubtful to begin with!

Eventually, information systems professionals and their business partners realized that if the data was stored in only one central database and every application that needed the data accessed it from that one database, then this data integrity issue could be solved. Every application would be looking at the one, accurate, set of data.

However, this arrangement comes with several cautions. Obviously, the data in the one central database must be accurate. Also, if too many transactions from too many applications try to access the one central database at the same time, it can become a performance bottleneck. Furthermore, if there is only one central source of data, then activities such as data security, concurrency control, and backup and recovery must be practiced at the highest possible level.

A system of one central database with a collection of applications utilizing it has come to be known as an enterprise resource planning (ERP) system, Figure 16.8. Historically, the first applications to use ERP systems were accounting and financial applications. But, of course, data used by the accounting and financial operations of a company is also used by other operations. For example, in a manufacturing company, the parts used in the manufacturing process may have to be ordered from supplier firms and then paid for by the company's accounting department. Thus, inventory data and accounting data have to flow among the company's various inventory control programs and accounting programs such as accounts payable. When finished goods are sold, the data has to flow among the company's various manufacturing programs and

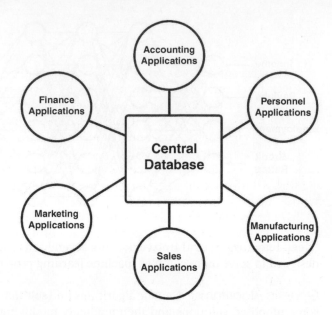

FIGURE 16.8 An Enterprise Resource Planning (ERP) system

accounting programs such as accounts receivable. And all of the accounting programs have to feed data to the company's financial accounting programs.

ERP vendors, such as SAP and Oracle, having recognized the value of data in the common, central database, being used by different parts of a company, have developed application suites that they sell as part of their ERP products on a "mix and match" basis. So, for example, you can buy an ERP system with a suite of accounting application programs. Or, you can buy an ERP system with suites of accounting, financial, and manufacturing control programs. And, you don't have to buy all of the application program suites at once. You can buy an initial set and then add more later on.

Customer Relationship Management (CRM)

Customer Relationship Management (CRM) is an umbrella term for a variety of data-intensive applications that can help organizations improve their activities and build better relationships with their customers, employees, business partners, and other constituencies. Thus, we have Customer Relationship Management (CRM) in the narrow sense, Employee Relationship Management, Partner Relationship Management, etc. (The author of this book once did a project for the US Navy entitled "Sailor Relationship Management.") The idea is to collect data about the people or companies that you want to engage with and then use the data to great effect. Such data can be collected by a company's own employees or can be purchased from companies that collect and sell individual and corporate data as a business, such as the Acxiom company. The data on individuals can include any type of contact and demographic data plus records of past purchases. The data about companies can include sales history plus personal data about the company's employees.

For example, the Kroger supermarket chain, which operates under several supermarket brand names, tracks the purchases that each of its customers makes. When checking out, a customer gives the clerk their unique Kroger bar code or enters their phone number and the system records their purchases. Then, periodically, Kroger mails the customer discount coupons for future purchases, based on what the customer has bought in the past. This "**one-to-one marketing**" keeps the customer coming back to use the discount coupons on items that Kroger knows the customer regularly buys. It is worth it to Kroger to do this to retain the customer over the long term.

Salesforce.com is a company that, among other things, allows companies to maintain data about companies with which they do business and their employees. A company's salespeople can keep track of the previous purchases its customers made and use it in future marketing efforts. It can even collect such personal data as the birthdates of its counterparts in its customer companies so that they can send them birthday greetings once a year. It's all about relationships and companies like Salesforce.com collect data that allow their customers to excel at maintaining such relationships. By the way, Salesforce.com has a major presence in the cloud as one way of making its applications highly useful.

Companies have been devising increasingly sophisticated ways of using the data that they collect about their customers. Much of what we have described above falls under the heading Operational CRM. Yet another example of this is using the collected data about a person or company to aid in customer service support when a person or company representative reaches out to, for example, a company's call center. In Analytical CRM, companies can use the data they have collected about their customers in machine learning techniques, such as data mining, to enhance their marketing efforts. CRM data can even be collected from social media and combined with the data collected by traditional means.

Finally, CRM data can be stored in an ERP system's common central database. CRM applications can form one of the optional application suites in an ERP environment. Other ERP application suites can use the CRM data and the CRM application suite can take advantage of other ERP data as needed.

Supply Chain Management (SCM)

Consider a manufacturing company such as an automobile manufacturer as a good example. Let's call it Major Motors. There are many parts that go into manufacturing a car. Major Motors may make some of the parts itself, but generally buys most of the parts that go into its cars from other, supplier, companies. These suppliers typically buy raw materials that they need to manufacture the parts from companies that deal in the raw materials. Major Motors sells its cars to dealerships, which in turn sell the cars to its customers, like you or me, Figure 16.9. Given this progression, you might think that the arrows in Figure 16.9 should only flow from left to right. That's true of the physical materials, parts, and cars. But, as you are about to learn, for all of this to work efficiently in today's world, there has to be a significant flow of data *in both directions*.

Let's focus for a moment on a supplier, let's call it General Transmissions, that makes automobile transmissions. General Transmissions wants to always have the raw materials in stock that it needs to make its transmissions, but it does not want to have more than it needs sitting in its parts inventory. That would be a waste of money since it had to pay its raw materials suppliers for the raw materials and the excess is just sitting on its shelves. It can't recover the money for the raw materials until it uses them in making transmissions that it then sells to Major Motors. On the other hand, it does not want to be a position of not having transmissions to sell to Major Motors when Major Motors needs them because it did not have enough raw materials to make them. That loss of business is also costly.

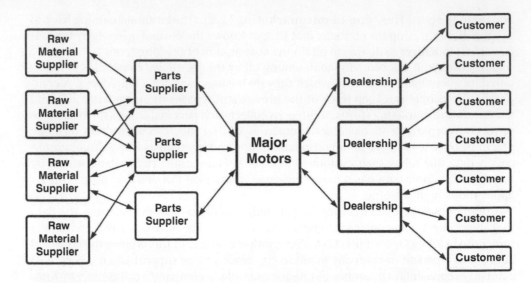

FIGURE 16.9 Major Motors' supply chain

On the retail end of the business, Major Motors sells its finished automobiles to dealers that then sell them to consumers. The situation on the retail side is similar to the situation on the supply side. Dealers want to have enough cars on their lots to sell to consumers when they want to buy cars, but they don't want to have too many unsold cars sitting on their lots for too long of a time.

To try to optimize all of this, we have the concept of supply chain management. You won't be surprised at this point to realize that this kind of optimization can only work in today's world with a heavy dose of data and information systems utilization. Major Motors' computers connect "upstream" to General Transmission's computers via the Internet. General Transmission's computers, in turn, connect to the computers of the raw materials companies that it buys from. On the other end of the business, Major Motors' computers connect "downstream" to its dealers' computers. Through this network, a dealer can order cars from Major Motors, which then sends an order for transmissions to General Transmissions, which then sends orders for raw materials to its raw material suppliers. The term "just-in-time manufacturing" is also used in this context.

Supply chain management software comes in two parts known as supply chain planning software and supply chain execution software. Based on continuously evolving experience, the planning software can forecast the amount of raw materials that General Transmissions should keep in its inventory and the number of transmissions that Major Motors should keep in its inventory. Similarly, it can help the dealers decide how many new cars to keep on its lots. The execution software manages the actual flow of goods between each of the appropriate companies. One classic problem in this arena that the software can help control is the "bullwhip effect." If customers want to buy more cars and the dealers increase their orders to Major Motors, Major Motors can overreact, sending excessive orders to General Transmissions which can overreact and send excessive orders to its raw materials suppliers. By the time this reaches the raw materials suppliers, they may think they have to produce far more of the raw materials than is necessary. This can be managed and limited by the supply chain management software.

Finally, with the complexity of how companies interact with each other, you may see the term "supply web" instead of supply chain. This can mean, for example, that General Transmissions has several raw materials suppliers for the same raw material and sources the raw material from companies in the group rather than from a single supplier.

At this point in this book, is it even necessary to say that all of supply chain management is based on the *flow of data* from one company to another? That's what supply chain management is all about. When the software sends a message from one company to another, the orders for raw materials or parts or finished goods are all in the form of data. How many of this or how much of that are needed and being ordered. Or how many or how much has actually been delivered. And, yes, supply chain management software can pass data from one company's ERP system database to another's. It's always all about data and database!!

Summary

The fact is that data forms the basis of everything that we do with information systems. Whether it is ERP, CRM, SCM, analytics, artificial intelligence, or any other information systems application, data is the fundamental corporate resource that must be processed to generate the desired results. And all of that data must be carefully managed, which makes the subject of this book, database management, a critical subject in today's world.

Key Terms

Ad hoc queries
Artificial intelligence
Association
Business intelligence
Classification
Clustering
Customer Relationship
  Management (CRM)
Data Analytics

Data mining
Data visualization
Decision Support
  Systems (DSS)
Deep learning
  neural network
Descriptive analytics
Enterprise Resource
  Planning (ERP)

Expert systems
Genetic algorithms
If-then-else rules
Neural networks
One-to-one marketing
Pattern recognition
Predictive analytics
Prescriptive analytics
Robotics

Rule-based processors
Sentiment analysis
Supply Chain
  Management (SCM)
Text mining
Web mining

Questions

1. What term replaced the term decision support systems and what are its two main components?

2. What are the three types of analytics that comprise data mining?

3. Which type of analytics uses data visualization?

4. What are the different types of predictive analytics?

5. Briefly describe association.

6. Briefly describe clustering.

7. Briefly describe classification.

8. How does a neural network work?

9. Briefly describe web mining.

10. What is an expert system and how do they use if-then-else rules?

11. How do robots make use of data?

12. What is a deep learning neural network?

13. How do genetic algorithms work?

14. What is the main database principle behind enterprise resource planning systems?

15. Describe the purpose of customer relationship management systems.

16. How do customer relationship management systems use data?

17. Describe the purpose of supply chain management systems.

18. How do supply chain management systems use data?

Exercises

1. Consider a large, national chain of retail clothing stores. Describe ways that it can use:
   a. Classification.
   b. Clustering.
   c. Association.
   d. Text mining.

2. Describe how an expert system based on neural network technology might be used for medical diagnosis.

3. Consider a large, national supermarket chain that sells toiletry items as well as food. The food comes from a variety of sources. Some of it comes directly from local farms, some from food processors that can or bottle the food, and some from meatpackers or fishermen. It also sells paper products such as tissues and paper towels. Describe a supply chain that fits this supermarket model and describe how the flow of data helps make this model more efficient.

Minicases

1. Happy Cruise Lines wants to attract passengers from a variety of different demographic categories, to make its passengers happy, and to encourage return business.

   a. How can Happy Cruise Lines use classification and clustering to enhance its advertising to attract passengers of different demographic categories?

   b. Happy Cruise Lines asks it passengers to write reviews of the cruises they have taken. How can it use text mining and web mining to determine how its passengers feel about the cruises they have taken?

   c. How can Happy Cruise Lines use customer relationship management to encourage return business?

2. The Tigers is a team in the Super Baseball League.

   a. The Tigers' management wants to predict the success of players that it is considering hiring.

   The League is willing to provide the Tigers with the history of past and present players including their characteristics (height, weight, running speed, etc.) and how successful they have been. Explain how the team can use this data to create a neural network to predict the success of players it is considering hiring and describe what the neural network would look like.

   b. How can the Tigers use classification and clustering to enhance its advertising to attract fans of different demographic categories to come to its games and even to buy season tickets?

   c. Describe some of the information systems applications that the Tigers (or a team in any sport of your choice) would need to operate and explain how they would benefit from being part of an ERP system.

INDEX

A

abstract data types, 243
access-arm mechanism, 188
accessing data, problems in, 11–12
access methods, 191–202. *See also* index
    file organizations and, 191–202
    sequential, 40–41, 191, 201
access path plan, 60
ACID property, 322
active data dictionaries, 262–263. *See also* passive data dictionaries
    attributes, 262–263
    definitions, 262
    distinctions, 262
    entities, 262–263
    relationships, 263
    uses and users, 263
ad hoc queries, 364
aggregated data, 293
aggregation, 230, 235–236
alternate key, 99
Analytical Engine, 6
AND operator, 66
anomalies data, 48
anti-virus software, 276
application characteristics, 202, 204
arbitration, 265
artificial intelligence, 368–371
    applications, 368–370
    techniques, 370–371
association, 365
associative entity, in M–M binary relationship, 21–22
asymmetric data encryption, 275
attribute, 16, 38, 96
    columns, 96
    creating uniqueness with, 23
    data normalization and, 145–146, 161
    data normalization examples, 171–175
    domain of values, 100, 128, 133
    E-R diagrams, 146–147
    inheritance of, 232, 234
    keys and, 97
    physical database design, 88, 185–221
    unique, 17
attribute names, 63, 76
ATTRIBUTES table (in data dictionary), 259–261
AVG operator, 72

B

Babbage, Charles, 7
backup, 268, 278–283
    backup copies and journals, 278–279
    importance, 278
    and recovery issues, 52
backward recovery, 280–281
balance sheet, 5
bartering, 4
base table, 61
before and after image log, 279
BETWEEN operator, 68
big data, 319
bill of materials, 24, 132, 152
binary large objects (BLOBs), 243
binary relationships, 17–23
    cardinality, 18–19
    converting entities in, 147–150
    data modeling in, 16–33
    E-R diagram, 18
    many-to-many (M–M) binary relationship, 18–23
    modality, 19–20
    one-to-many (1–M) binary relationship, 18–20
    one-to-one (1–1) binary relationship, 18–20
biometric systems, 273
bitcoin, 341

blades, 320
block, 342
blockchain, 341–351
    consensus, 348–349
    hashing, 343–345
    Merkle trees, 348
    public-key encryption, 345–348
    smart contracts, 349
block of logical records, 191
Boolean AND operator, 66
Boolean OR operator, 66–67
breaches, data security, 269–270
    methods of, 270–272
    types, 269–270
B+-tree index, 195–199
    information from, 196–197
built-in functions, 72–73
business intelligence, 364–368
    data mining, 365–367
    text mining, 367–368
    web mining, 367–368

C

calculating devices, 5–6
candidate keys, 98–99
cardinality, in binary relationships, 18–19
Cartesian product, 89, 117
cascade delete rule, 140–141
case-based learning, 312
catalogs, 89, 264, 274
cell, 97
Census, 6
central authority, 342
change log, 279
checkpoint, 281
class, 231
class diagram, 231
classification, 365
cloud, 352